Nineteenth-Century Music and the German Romantic Ideology

JOHN DAVERIO

Nineteenth-Century Music and the German Romantic Ideology

SCHIRMER BOOKS
An Imprint of Macmillan Publishing Company
NEW YORK

Maxwell Macmillan Canada
TORONTO

Maxwell Macmillan International
NEW YORK   OXFORD   SINGAPORE   SYDNEY

Copyright © 1993 by Schirmer Books
An Imprint of Macmillan Publishing Company

Schirmer Books
An Imprint of Macmillan Publishing Company
866 Third Avenue, New York, N.Y. 10022

Maxwell Macmillan Canada, Inc.
1200 Eglinton Avenue East, Suite 200
Don Mills, Ontario M3C 3N1

Macmillan Publishing Company is part of the Maxwell Communication Group of Companies.

Library of Congress Catalog Card Number: 92-42513

PRINTED IN THE UNITED STATES OF AMERICA

printing number
1   2   3   4   5   6   7   8   9   10

LIBRARY OF CONGRESS CATALOGING-IN-PUBLICATION DATA

Daverio, John.
    Nineteenth-century music and the German romantic ideology / John Daverio.
        p.   cm.
    Includes bibliographical references and index.
    ISBN 0-02-870675-7
    1. Music—Germany—19th century. I. Title. II. Title: 19th -century music and the German romantic ideology.
ML275.D38   1993
780′.943′09034—dc20   92-42513
                                                                            CIP
                                                                            MN

The paper used in this publication meets the minimum requirements of American National Standard For Information Sciences—Permanence of Paper for Printed Library Materials. ANSI Z39.48-1984. ♾™

For Elizabeth, Jim, and Teresa

Contents

Preface

This book has been a long time—perhaps too long a time—in the making. Its writing was motivated by four interrelated impulses: a firm belief in the power of history to teach us something about ourselves and our world, an abiding attachment to the music of the nineteenth century, a profound distrust of theories of musical meaning, and an equally profound conviction that music does have meaning.

It need hardly be reiterated here that the practice of history as a discipline today finds itself in a troubled and troubling state. Symptomatic of the problem are the discussions clustered about the so-called New Historicism, which for me at least too often amounts to little more than the Old Historicism in modern garb, but without the grand sweep, the comprehensive vision that still makes the reading of a Burckhardt or a Huizinga such an exciting experience. Implicit in the "new historical" approach is a reduction of artworks to documents, signifiers of cultural processes; enduring products of the imagination are hollowed out of precisely that which makes them art. By privileging the location of the artwork within a nexus of sociocultural relations, we run the risk of skirting the primary issue faced by the art historian: the fact that artworks do not lend themselves to the plot configurations of narrative history. Yet this resistance is not a given to be ignored, but rather a problem to be met—a problem that has led me to adopt the premise that the history of art discloses itself only in the interpretation of individual art products.

Among "serious" music listeners, the music of the nineteenth century is practically everyone's favorite, though many would be loath to admit it. Like the god in Friedrich Hölderlin's great hymn *Patmos,* it is "near yet hard to grasp." Proximity and distance—these are the two poles between which the question of meaning is suspended. In this connection there is at least one fact that Eduard Hanslick's protoformalist aesthetic makes abundantly clear: it is far easier to prove a negative thesis than to forward a positive account of

how music, given its discontinuous relationship with objective reality, inter-
acts with meaning. To do so requires a kind of leap over an abyss, a foray,
nolens volens, into the murky territory of musical metaphysics. What I offer,
then, is less a hard-and-fast thesis than a series of interrelated reflections on
one of the ways that the music of the nineteenth century might be said to
convey meaning. This book, that is to say, unfolds as a series of variations on
a theme: music as critique.

The present study draws in varying degrees on some of my already pub-
lished work: chapter 2 on "Schumann's 'Im Legendenton' and Friedrich
Schlegel's *Arabeske*" (*19th Century Music* 1987); chapter 3 on "Reading
Schumann by way of Jean Paul and his Contemporaries" (*College Music
Symposium* 1990); chapter 5 on "Brahms's *Magelone Romanzen* and the
Romantic Imperative" (*Journal of Musicology* 1989); and chapter 6 on
"Brünnhilde's 'Immolation Scene' and Wagner's 'Conquest of the Reprise,'"
(*Journal of Musicological Research* 1991). Still, I would hesitate to describe
these chapters as "reworkings" of the earlier articles. I will admit to having
intentionally avoided rereading my earlier studies in favor of taking a fresh
look at the ever-burgeoning files that led to them in the first place.

At the risk of making omissions, I would like to acknowledge some of the
many individuals who have supported this project. At Boston University, both
Joel Sheveloff (my former teacher and now colleague) and Jeremy Yudkin
have patiently endured my distraction during our departmental meetings of
the last several years. Mark Evan Bonds (University of North Carolina at
Chapel Hill) I thank for his astute comments on my Schumann work,
and Patrick McCreless (University of Texas at Austin) for his close reading
of the earlier Wagner study embedded in chapter 6. Karol Berger (Stanford
University) and Anna-Maria Busse Berger (University of California at Davis)
have lent me their warm support as friends and their critical insights as scholars.
My thanks also to the following scholars, all of whom have provided valuable
commentaries on my work: Hermann Danuser (Albert-Ludwigs-Universität
Freiburg), Anthony Newcomb (University of California at Berkeley), Reinhold
Brinkmann (Harvard University), Lewis Lockwood (Harvard University), and
John Crotty (West Virginia University). I owe a debt of gratitude both to the
staff of Boston University's Mugar Memorial Library, Holly Mockovak and
Richard Seymour, for responding with lightning speed to my seemingly endless requests for materials, and to the administration of Boston University, for
granting me a sabbatical leave for the 1992–93 academic year. I should also
like to mention Gerald Weale (my colleague at Boston University) and
Herbert Sprouse, who put their lovely home in the New Hampshire woods
at my disposal. Dr. Martin Bente (Henle Verlag) and Amy Guskin (European
American Music) facilitated the reprinting of several musical examples for
chapters 2 and 3. And lastly, I extend thanks to Maribeth Anderson Payne,
who saw to it that what I had been only thinking about was actually commit-
ted to paper.

A little over ten years ago, having completed a dissertation under Murray Lefkowitz on a seventeenth-century topic, and written an article or two on pre-Corellian instrumental music, I fully expected to devote the rest of my musicological career to the Italian trio sonata. Teaching assignments and the interests of graduate students with whom I have worked as dissertation advisor would lead me in another direction. Three students in particular stand out as having influenced my thinking on the music of the nineteenth century in ways great and small: James Davis (State University of New York at Fredonia), Teresa Neff, and Elizabeth Seitz. They have often spurred my imagination, sometimes tried my patience, but always garnered my respect. It is to them—as synecdochic representatives for my many students—that this book, whatever its shortcomings may be, is graciously dedicated.

Boston, Massachusetts

1 ✒

Romantic Ideas and Romantic Music

Our deficiencies themselves
are our greatest hopes.

– Friedrich Schlegel
"Über die Grenzen des Schönen" (1794)

I

This study presents a series of discrete but complementary answers to a single question: How did Romanticism manifest itself in music? As such, my work is intended as a contribution to that growing body of scholarship that seeks to chart out the relationships between music and a broader web of intellectual trends. To be sure, the question broached here has already been considered many times over. But the result, at least in many music histories, has often amounted to an affirmation of the congruence between Romanticism and its ideology—that is, a loosely knit body of preconceived ideas that just as frequently distort as promote our understanding.[1] Indeed, few cultural movements are at one with the reified idea complexes with which they eventually come to be associated; but in the case of Romanticism, the distinction between essence and ideology is more crucial still. One could say that the very act of making the distinction was central to the initial phases of the

1

movement. For preideological Romanticism—Romanticism in the strong sense of the word—was primarily self-critical and reflective, and only secondarily occupied with the diverse matters often subsumed under its banner: unremitting individuality of expression, the recovery of a chivalric past, the cultivation of the marvelous or fantastic in literature, a delight in insoluble contradictions, the mystical union of subject and object, yearning for the infinite—and on the list could go. The heady mixture of escapism and ecstasy that is still too often taken as a defining feature of the Romantic endeavor was in fact a surface phenomenon, an artful camouflage for a penetrating and carefully circumscribed societal critique that attempted to come to grips with the disquieting moments in an emerging modern world, thereby wresting from them a measure of value and hopefulness.[2] Hence the fascination with works of art as enigmatic bearers of higher meanings through their transfiguration of the "interesting," the unusual, and even the grotesque. It could be argued, therefore, that we might best locate Romanticism in music not only by turning to the most "advanced" works of the age, works that strike us because of their daring play with the various parameters of musical discourse, but also by showing how these very works engage in acts of self-criticism—a criticism, in other words, directed at their own technical presuppositions. This is my thesis *in nuce.*

The main body of this book, then, is devoted to addressing and demonstrating the mutually conditioning exchange between music and ideas: How were the crucial strands of the Romantic program realized in musical works? How can the processes that inform this music be illuminated by referring them, critically, to the ideas of Romanticism? And since Romanticism is our subject, we should properly begin with the terms *Romantic* and *Romanticism,* even if doing so requires us to tread over some familiar territory. Are these terms still useful as historico-critical designations, especially considering that already by the early nineteenth century their respective meanings had become diluted? According to a reviewer for the *Zeitung für die Elegante Welt,* writing on 20 April 1809, "The implications of the word 'romantic' grow ever more diffuse."[3] And by 1837, Robert Schumann (though clearly conscious that he was in some sense a "Romantic") must have recognized something of this conceptual hollowness in asserting that he was "sick to death of the word 'romanticist,' although I have not spoken it ten times in my life."[4]

Criticism, or at least some of its dominant strands, has followed suit. Arthur Lovejoy, in an important essay written in 1924, concluded that the plethora of connotations clustered about the terms had nearly reduced them to meaninglessness;[5] and for many subsequent critics, *Romantic* and *Romanticism* have been retained as generally understood, albeit empty, style designators. René Wellek, on the contrary, locates the essence of Romanticism precisely in the interplay between the plenitude of its diverse elements—ranging from the picturesque, exotic, historicist, and archaic to the poetic, imaginative, mythological, symbolic, unique, and expressive—and their underlying unity.[6]

In either case, however, the efficacy of the term *Romantic* and its cognates as critical categories is called into question: Romanticism, in short, can imply far too little or far too much. Music historians have troubled over this problem as well. Carl Dahlhaus wisely cautions that Romanticism (viewed as a confluence of exoticism, historicism, and folklorism) was but one of many subcurrents that ran through the nineteenth century; moreover, he suspects that as a category borrowed from the history of ideas it may lack the sharpness of focus that historical writing requires.[7]

Given the nebulous position of Romanticism as a historiographical term, is it even worth posing (or posing again) the question of its involvement with music? If we accept Maurice Blanchot's eloquent and passionate appeal to the effect that "Romanticism, as the advent of poetic consciousness, is not simply a literary school, nor even an important moment in the history of art: it opens an epoch; furthermore, it is the epoch in which all epochs are revealed,"[8] then the answer is a resounding yes. True, our project will require a leap of faith. Yet it seems to me that leaps of faith are built into the whole enterprise of writing history from the start, provided that "history" is taken to mean an ordered account of the interrelationships between and among events, and not a mere chronicle in which striking but isolated events are simply juxtaposed. I do not think it possible to make truth claims about the ties between music and Romanticism. We can, however, make historical claims whose worth may be measured against the rigor with which we sketch out the dialectic interaction of music and ideas. The path to this goal is outlined in the methodological sketch that follows.

II

By way of approaching the Romanticism-and-music question anew, I propose that we reinvigorate the term *Romantic* itself by considering it in the delimited sense in which it appears in the early writings of Friedrich Schlegel (1772–1829), that frustratingly unsystematic yet brilliant thinker whose essays and enigmatic fragments, numbering in the thousands, at once embodied and motivated the whole Romantic program. Although Schlegel, like many of his contemporaries, linked the term *romantisch* with a broad spectrum of meanings, it also figured prominently in his theory of the novel or *Roman* (developed from about 1797 to 1800) in a specific sense that is particularly important for our purposes. By analogy with the terms *epic* (*episch*), *lyric* (*lyrisch*), and *dramatic* (*dramatisch*), the adjectival forms of the substantives designating the principal genres of classical antiquity, the term *Romantic* (*romantisch*) was used to describe the *Roman*, the genre that in Schlegel's historical scheme "colors the whole of modern poetry."[9] This is certainly the sense that can be inferred from such fragments as: "Alle Werke sollen Romane, alle Prosa romantisch sein" [All works should be novels; all prose should be novelistic].[10] And although Schlegel was not the only writer of his time to employ the term in this way (examples can be found in the works of Schleiermacher, Tieck, Novalis, and even Goethe),[11] he was undoubtedly the first to apply it consistently as a genre designation. To be sure, Schlegel's notion of the *Roman,* conditioned as it was by his study of Dante's *Divina commedia,* Shakespeare's dramas, and Cervantes's *Don Quixote,* was aimed at something quite different from the extended prose narratives that we normally associate with the novel as a literary type. The kind of novel described in the *Brief über den Roman* (from his *Gespräch über die Poesie,* 1800) and elsewhere in his writings is better thought of as a poetic encyclopedia, or secular Bible, that seeks to combine, fuse, and ultimately transcend all of the traditional forms and genres.[12] In short, Schlegel's theory of Romanticism, the *Ur*-theory of the movement, was in its basic outlines a theory of the novel, or more properly, a theory of the fantastically formed and generically ambiguous artwork; and it is in this latter sense that Schlegel's theories can still be said to have implications for art criticism—and not just literary criticism—as a whole.

What does all of this have to do with music? In my view, just as Schlegel was able to assess critically the strikingly new aspects of the literature of his day and to pinpoint just those features in contemporary art that held out the greatest promise for future developments, so might we do much the same for the music of the nineteenth century. Schlegel's assertion, in the *Brief über den Roman,* that "a song can be just as romantic as a prose narrative"[13] can be read as an imperative to seek out novelizing *qualities* (not specific narratives), elements of form and genre that cut across the obvious distinctions between verbal and musical arts. As it turns out, the divinatory power of his critical prescriptions can be shown to have manifested itself in two areas: not only does his theory of Romantic poetry prefigure developments in literature that came to fruition only with the novels of Thomas Mann, Hermann Broch, and Robert Musil, but it also concords well with some of the musical phenomena that set in with full force in the 1820s and 1830s.[14]

If music critics and historians are concerned with evaluating the varying degrees of continuity or change displayed in a given series of events, then it should be made clear that the accent in this study will be placed on those musical elements of change that both mark off the 1820s and 1830s from the preceding years and stamp them with an emerging Romantic consciousness. The perspective on musical Romanticism developed here is therefore drawn somewhat differently from that suggested, for instance, in Friedrich Blume's influential *MGG* articles (published in translation as *Classic and Romantic Music*). For Blume, musical Classicism and Romanticism formed an indissoluble unity, a coherent epoch in music history extending from the mid-eighteenth to the early twentieth century, its artistic products sharing in common a canon of genres, forms, and stylistic elements.[15] Likewise, Carl Dahlhaus concurs that the early years of the nineteenth century witnessed relatively few substantial changes in compositional technique.[16] For both writers, the only really "new" genres whose addition to the canon can be attributed to the Romantics—the character piece for piano and the *Lied*—were decidedly diminutive in scope.[17] But in Dahlhaus's view, the years in and around 1814 might still represent an important historical caesura if only because of the profound alteration in intellectual outlook, registered in the writings of Wilhelm Heinrich Wackenroder, Ludwig Tieck, and E. T. A. Hoffmann, that "influenced the way music was heard for a full century."[18] Similarly, Arno Forchert defines the Romantic impulse in early nineteenth-century musical life in terms of the new way in which music was perceived; decisive for this shift in outlook was the tendency to think of instrumental music not merely as an abstract play of tones, but as the representation of some kind of emotional content.[19]

It is fair to say that these commentators take their cue primarily from those of the *Frühromantiker* whose chief interest lay in formulating an aesthetic of musical reception. The pronouncements of Tieck and Wackenroder in particular give special emphasis to the reshaping of musical experience as a quasi-mystical event, where the listener gives in to the enigmatic, wondrous, and oracular accents of pure instrumental music, an art that says most by saying nothing at all. And for Wackenroder, the musical initiate will revel in sound precisely because of the unbridgeable gap between *Gefühl*—the exalted feeling that music can inspire—and *Wissenschaft*—the mathematical laws that silently govern its creation.[20] Schlegel's, on the other hand, was first and foremost an aesthetic of production. The "New Mythology" that he envisioned in the *Rede über die Mythologie* (from the *Gespräch über die Poesie*) would take the form of the "most artful of all artworks" (*künstlichste aller Kunstwerke*); our understanding of it, in other words, must proceed from a studied consideration of the processes that went into its making.[21] A historical account of nineteenth-century music that takes as its point of departure an aesthetic of production will necessarily lead to different conclusions from those articulated in studies whose critical approach calls attention to shifting modes of reception. Our conclusions may not be any "truer," though they may serve to complement the listener-response approach that colored many nineteenth-century writings about music and that, as we have seen, has continued to resonate in more recent accounts.

Likewise, the notion of a shared Classic–Romantic canon tells only part of the story, for it can just as convincingly be shown that it is precisely in the areas of form and genre that we may locate the truly new, the quintessentially Romantic elements in the music, no less than in the literature, of the nineteenth century. More specifically, form, which in terms of the neoclassical aesthetics of the eighteenth century implies configurational wholeness, gave way to what Schlegel calls "tendency" (*Tendenz*), to intentionally fragmented or incomplete structures. At the same time, the hierarchy of discrete genres came to be displaced by a system that valued individualized *Mischgedichte*—

mixed-genre works—aimed at transcending generic boundaries altogether. And although opera, symphony, concerto and sonata, the principal genres of Viennese Classicism, continued to live on in the nineteenth century, they tended more and more to function as qualities, or "tones" (operat*ic*, symphon*ic*, and so forth) in compositions whose generic essence derived from their mixture.[22] There is hardly a monument of nineteenth-century musical art, from Schumann's *Papillons* to Mahler's *Wunderhorn* symphonies, that does not partake of these mutually dependent trends. This is not, however, to argue for the simple binary opposition of Classic and Romantic characteristics in eighteenth- and nineteenth-century art, to set a formally and generically pure Classicism against an anomalous and contradiction-bound Romanticism. Musical Classicism, too, had its ruptures and bizarreries. It is simply to assert that the "fantastic" impulse that occupied the periphery in musical Classicism (though significant, for example, in so many of C. P. E. Bach's keyboard works) took center stage in musical Romanticism, and that the formal hybrids of Classicism (such as Mozart's and Haydn's blending of sonata and rondo, or rondo and variation) continued to obey, in Schlegel's words, a "determinate law of mixture."[23]

The valorization of the fragment at the expense of the perfectly shaped whole, and of the *Mischgedicht* as opposed to the generically pure artwork, both represent decidedly nineteenth-century points of view. Together with literal readings of Schlegel's utopian prescriptions for the *Roman,* or E. T. A. Hoffmann's views on absolute music, or Wagner's theoretical restitution of the lost unity of the arts through the *Gesamtkunstwerk,* they might easily congeal into ideology, into a body of received ideas that express the special interests and prejudices of a particular social or intellectual group. But as the literary critic Jerome McGann has cautioned, it is a mistake tacitly to accept Romanticism's appraisals or representations of itself. None of the frequently contradictory concepts that the Romantics promulgated about themselves, their works, or their world—the idealization of uniqueness and creativity, the possibility of synthesizing the most disparate entities, the omnipotence of the poetic imagination, the organic quality of life and art—can be accepted at face value; rather, they must be subjected to a thoroughgoing critique.[24]

This is just the component that is missing from Leonard Meyer's recent and provocative "sketch-history" of nineteenth-century music, which purports to show how the music of the period was basically consonant with the Romantic ideology by linking the doctrines of organicism and "becoming" with parallel musical phenomena such as motivically dense but formally open-ended structures.[25] Although his study is rich in insightful observations, Meyer's embrace of the Romantic ideology frequently leads him to repeat some well-worn clichés about the nature of musical Romanticism; his assertion that "Romantic composers were better at writing small forms than large ones,"[26] for example, is predetermined by an almost exclusive focus on minutiae: Isolde's *Verklärung* from *Tristan* is the only extended passage subjected to close analysis. The lesson is obvious: pointing out the parallels between Romantic ideas and Romantic music will not suffice in itself; if criticism is to go beyond mere repetition, the dialectic between idea and artwork must be charted as well.

As McGann has argued, the status of a poetic work is directly dependent on its ability to criticize the very ideas that it seems to embody, thereby unmasking its own illusions.[27] That may well be so for literature, but how can a piece of music embody or criticize an ideological position? We cannot be so confident of music's ideological content as was a figure like Theodor Adorno. Nonetheless, let us take the opening movement of Schumann's Opus 17 Fantasie as an example. Here Schumann yokes together a fully elaborated sonata-allegro design (an emblem of the "higher" forms toward which he felt every composer should aspire) and a quasi-independent character piece, designated *Im Legendenton* (a representative of the diminutive piano pieces that flowed more easily from his pen than sonata or symphonic movements), as if to suggest that the two were capable of effecting a synthesis. Yet their uneasy juxtaposition and the unusual placement of the character piece within the design as a whole imply that such a reconciliation is indeed impossible. In other words, through purely musical means Schumann was able to explode one of the Romantics' (both literary and musical) most cherished pipe dreams: the notion that incommensurable entities would allow for a harmonious union. Schumann's work bristles with what Adorno would call "negative moments" or "alienating symptoms"—textural and formal disruptions that are intentionally composed into the piece, and which, far from signifying any failing in compositional technique, actually project a critical message. If we concur with Adorno's assertion that "modern art is more likely to oppose the spirit of its respective age than to agree with it,"[28] then Schumann's conception is eminently "modern." Yet he was at the same time obeying a dictum that Friedrich Schlegel had set down some forty years earlier: "When ALL of the constituent parts of a romantic poem have been perfectly fused, then it simply ceases to be romantic."[29]

A close attention to questions of form can therefore help us to understand the drama of ideological contradictions that is played out in the strongest products of musical Romanticism. My orientation, then, runs counter to much of the received wisdom on nineteenth-century music, which has traditionally undermined the significance of form per se in the Romantic program. (The deemphasis of formal issues goes back at least to Hegel, master systematizer and chief promulgator of an internally consistent doctrine of Romanticism, who said of the Romantic artwork that "its outer form no longer has a meaning and significance, as in classical art, in and of itself; meaning resides in the feelings ... that the outward appearance generates").[30] Meyer, for instance, suggests that Romantic composers came to devalue form as a primary compositional concern owing to a decline in audience sophistication; nineteenth-century listeners, he postulates, could no longer "respond sensitively to the subtleties of syntactic process and formal design" that characterize classical works.[31] The implication here, that Romantic designs are as often as not lacking in subtlety, is thus tied to the no less questionable assumption that nineteenth-century listeners were less competent than those of the century before.

Without calling into question the musical awareness of nineteenth-century audiences, Dahlhaus has noted that Romantic forms tend either toward the "schematic," as exemplified in the apparently simple designs of many lyric pieces for piano, or the "disintegrated," where the form of a work is conditioned by its relationship to a specific content or program. Yet in both cases, form remains an element of secondary importance, since as Dahlhaus maintains, the value of a Romantic work rested mainly on its thematic eloquence and poetic character. For Beethoven, however, structural issues often supplied the raison d'être of a work, which, according to Dahlhaus, may then be seen as a unique solution to a particular formal problem.[32] But, as I will argue, the problematizing of form, manifested in part by its transfiguration into and displacement by "tendency" (and not content), was no less an issue for the Romantics, who at once shared and intensified Beethoven's self-conscious response to the Classical canon.

Walter Benjamin's succinct claim that "the romantic theory of the artwork is the theory of its form"[33] may seem extreme at first blush, but on reflection it becomes clear that issues of form were indeed central to the Romantic undertaking—witness such complementary ideological strands as Coleridge's thoughts on organicism and Schelling's theory of the symbol, both of them varying responses to the question of how parts relate to wholes. In addition, it is precisely through these formal issues that we can begin to gauge the nature of the links between music, the other arts (literary arts in particular), and the preoccupations of the age as a whole. But my recourse to the literature and literary theory of the nineteenth century should not be taken to imply that one art form directly influenced or merged with the other— notions that count among the most prominent of Romanticism's self-*mis*representations.

Accounts of music in Romantic poetry are first and foremost verbal, not musical constructs, just as the "literarization" of nineteenth-century music through figurative titles and poetic programs is probably little more than an external means of signaling the music's claims to artistic worth in an era that prized the written word over the transient and ineffable tone as a carrier of intellectual substance. The music and literature of the nineteenth century engaged in a mutually conditioning exchange, or *Wechselwirkung* as Dahlhaus calls it,[34] that led to a number of shared musico-literary processes of an abstract, structural sort: a penchant for digressive interpolations, fragmented utterances, open-ended or circular designs, and self-reflective patternings.

That this exchange was possible in the first place stems from the fact that both musical and literary works exhibit temporal or at least quasi-temporal structures, wherein a series of discrete parts succeed one another in a fixed order. Thus we can just as well "read"—that is, interpret or reflect upon— musical works as we can "perform" literary works (it might be recalled that in the nineteenth century, novels were read aloud no less than lyric poems).[35] Moreover, the structural confluence of music and literature[36] allows us to turn to the literary-critical theory of the nineteenth century—just as, conversely, Friedrich Hölderlin's poetics was nurtured by musical concerns—for a store of cogent metaphors with which to describe the more radical qualities of nineteenth-century music.

III

A complete answer to our initial query—how did Romanticism manifest itself in music?—would amount to no less than a history of nineteenth-century music. And although my aims are considerably more circumscribed, it will still be worth pausing to reflect on some of the problems posed by historical writing, problems that are all the more acute in dealing with the nineteenth century. According to Dahlhaus, the music historian's principal challenge in- volves the search for a convincing means of reconciling the contrary demands of narrative history on the one hand, which tends to reduce individual works to exemplars of a style or trend (and whose primacy as a discursive mode in historical writing has been viewed with increasing skepticism in recent years),[37] and aesthetics, which would have us focus on individual works as if they were independent artifacts disconnectedly arrayed in an imaginary mu- seum, on the other.

Earlier in our century, Walter Benjamin's recognition of the same problem led to the radical assertion that art history (with "history" taken to mean the "extensive" and "essential" connections that define genealogical and gener- ational relationships among people) simply does not exist. In Benjamin's view, the "specific historicity" of artworks is such that it will not unfold in "art history" but rather through interpretation: "For in interpretation, inter- relations of works of art among each other appear that are atemporal and yet not without historical relevance."[38] In his magisterial history of nineteenth- century music, Dahlhaus found a way around this dilemma by tracing the evolution of the musical genres that provide the structural framework for his discussion of the intermingling of aesthetic-compositional and social- intellectual issues.[39]

I intend here to center on a limited number of compositions (thus satis- fying the aesthetic-interpretive demand), each of which embodies a particular formal problem that will be described in terms of the leading ideas of the age (in order to satisfy the demands of history); but in addition, I will try to sketch the dialectic in which music and ideas often engaged, and therefore answer a concern that our temporal remove from the nineteenth century both allows and requires—the demand of criticism. Ideas, as we will see, are not merely *reflected* in music, but are *refracted* in it as well.

The notion of music as critique is hardly new. What I do, however, hope to contribute is an incisively drawn framework aimed at marking off the bounds of this critique with a degree of systematic rigor. The elements in the frame will be based largely on the critical categories of Friedrich Schlegel, my principal spokesman for the Romantic program. But before proceeding, two questions come to mind that should be addressed now: What in fact were Schlegel's views on music? and to what extent were his ideas absorbed into nineteenth-century thought? In other words, how effective will his ideas be in providing the framework for a study of *musical* Romanticism?

Although music figured less in Schlegel's writings than in those of several of his contemporaries—Novalis, Tieck, and Wackenroder in particular—he was not insensitive to its special problems. Numerous references to music can be found scattered throughout his various collections of literary and philosophical fragments written between about 1797 and 1803. Indeed, Schlegel must be counted as one of the original proponents of the aesthetic of "absolute" music. The notion that textless, instrumental music is music in the truest sense, the view that E. T. A. Hoffmann would canonize in his 1810 review of Beethoven's Fifth Symphony, is already implicit in one of Schlegel's notebook entries of 1797: "All pure music must be philosophical and instrumental (music for thought)."[40] This idea was then elaborated into a full-blown apologia for the intellectual worth of absolute music in one of the *Athenäum* fragments (1797/98): ". . . whoever has a sense for the marvelous affinities of all the arts and sciences, will not, in any event, view the matter [attributing "ideas" to musical compositions] from the dull viewpoint of so-called naturalness, according to which music is only supposed to be a language of the feelings, but rather will not find it impossible for all pure instrumental music to show a certain tendency toward philosophy. For doesn't pure instrumental music have to create a text for itself? And aren't its themes developed, established, varied, and contrasted just like the objects of meditation in a philosophical succession of ideas?"[41]

Absent here is the ecstatic tone adopted by Tieck and Wackenroder in the essays from the *Phantasien über die Kunst, für Freunde der Kunst* (1799) that treat the same subject (the former's "Symphonien," the latter's "Das eigentümliche innere Wesen der Tonkunst . . ."). Missing too is any allusion to the mystical component that Novalis, in several of his *Allgemeine Brouillon* fragments (1798), prized so highly in "der geheimnisvolle Lehre von der Musik."[42] For Schlegel, music "has more affinity to philosophy than to poetry"; it is imbued with a "sensual logic" whose guiding principle is neither melody nor harmony, but rhythm: not rhythm on the small scale, but rhythm generated by large-scale symmetries, by "gigantic repetitions and refrains.[43]

In arguing for the aesthetic centrality of instrumental music by emphasizing the inner logic of its structures, Schlegel thus took a stance midway between Kant, who suspected that music might be "more enjoyment than culture" because of its inability to embody determinate concepts, and those of his contemporaries who valued it precisely because of that inability. If instrumental music was "pure," then opera, for Schlegel, was "universal," by which he meant hybrid, combinative, "romantisch." It brought together music and "Malerei" (scenic or spectacular display), music and drama, such that each of its moments marked the conjunction of the "present with the no-longer and not-yet"—a striking prescription left unfulfilled until Wagner's development of leitmotivic technique to its full potential. And lastly, opera's fanciful mixture of the real and the unreal, of music, poetry, dance, and spectacle, might be best justified when the composer drew his subject matter from the realm of the "marvelous," thus fashioning a musical equivalent of the "fantastischen Roman."[44]

To what extent were Schlegel's ideas known by his contemporaries, and how were they disseminated? This question is complicated by the communal philosophizing, or *Symphilosophie,* in which Schlegel and his colleagues engaged. Schlegel and Novalis, for instance, mutually refined a body of like-minded ideas that sometimes make it difficult to ascribe a particular thought to one or the other.[45] Yet scholars are in general agreement on the core of Schlegel's critical enterprise, and likewise agree that it was largely through the more coherently organized body of writings by his brother August Wilhelm that Friedrich's thoughts passed into the European intellectual mainstream.

Madame de Staël's *De l'Allemagne* (1810), the work that introduced the French public to the ideas of German Romanticism, borrowed liberally from August Wilhelm Schlegel.[46] And to cite a more specifically musical example: The outlines of Friedrich Schlegel's theory of opera were taken over and fleshed out in Lecture 4 of August Wilhelm's widely read *Vorlesungen über dramatische Kunst und Litteratur* (1808),[47] which in turn probably served as a model for E. T. A. Hoffmann's prescriptions for romantic opera in his *Der Dichter und der Komponist* (1813).[48] Even Richard Wagner turned to August Wilhelm; as Cosima Wagner noted in a diary entry for 14 August 1872: "R. is now enjoying reading A. W. Schlegel's critical essays."[49] Inasmuch as Friedrich Schlegel's ideas were recast by his brother, they were certainly well known; but there was an undeniable loss in the process of transmission. A good part of August Wilhelm's brilliance as a writer lay in his ability to popularize, that is to simplify, so that what Friedrich's program gained in clarity it lost in subtlety. The presentation of Classicism and Romanticism as antithetical movements, to cite one important example, was August Wilhelm's idea, not Friedrich's.

Some of the most telling instances of Friedrich Schlegel's "influence" on later thought do not speak to influence at all, but rather to intellectual affinity. The mixture of utopian theorizing and studied analysis in Schlegel's review of Goethe's *Wilhelm Meister,* for instance, set both the tone and standard for much of the best nineteenth-century criticism; Schlegel's method, even his observation that apparent chaos in an artwork is often a foil for the most carefully thought-out organizational plan, is basically at one with Hoffmann's approach in his review of Beethoven's Fifth Symphony, or Schumann's in his review of Berlioz's *Symphonie fantastique* (1830). Schumann's affinity with Schlegel goes even deeper. Animating and imparting unity to Schlegel's theorizing was a philosophy of history that sought to give to the unique values of individual cultural periods their due. The scheme that he developed in the fragments and essays of his Jena and Berlin years (roughly 1796 to 1800) was essentially triadic: classicism gives way to a modern condition that may not be as perfect, but that is perfectible in that it contains the seeds of a better future. Classicism, contemporary critique, and eschatology are therefore linked together in a coherent sequence.[50]

Underlying Schumann's historical consciousness is a strikingly similar point of view. As he put it in 1835, commenting on the agenda of the recently founded *Neue Zeitschrift für Musik*: "In the short time during which we have been active, a number of facts have come to light. Still, our way of thinking was fixed from the outset. Simply put, we intend: to honor the past and its works, to call attention to the ways in which new artistic creations can only be invigorated by acknowledging a source so pure; second, to oppose the tendency of the recent past to hold up mechanical virtuosity as a poor substitute for art; and finally, to prepare for and hasten the advent of a fresh and poetic future."[51] Here too, reverence for the past (the music of Bach, Haydn, Mozart, and Beethoven) is coupled with a critical attitude toward an imperfect present that nonetheless—through the agency of the *Davidsbündler* and others of like temper—offers the possibility of a poetic future. Nor is this similarity in perspective attributable to the zeitgeist: if there was a "spirit of the age," it probably remained closer to the binary oppositions of August Wilhelm Schlegel.

To summarize: Although little recognized as a figure of immediate importance for musical Romanticism, Friedrich Schlegel made significant contributions, if only indirectly, to the nineteenth-century aesthetic of instrumental music and opera. Moreover, his views on Romanticism, albeit in a popularized form, gained general currency through the efforts of his brother August Wilhelm, though telling points of contact between Schlegel's thinking and that of later critics can be discerned. If Friedrich Schlegel's ideas, in their *Urform,* were not always known, they were often enough intuited. But these observations aside, Schlegel's chief credentials as spokesman for the ideas of Romanticism lie elsewhere.

In the first place, Schlegel's efficacy for our purposes rests on his being, before all else, a *critical* thinker; the terms *Kritik* and *kritisch*—both of them possessing an almost talismanic quality in the wake of Kant's philosophy—appear more frequently than any others in the Schlegel-Novalis correspondence, the personal side of the "höherer Kritizismus" that Schlegel practiced in his essays and fragments. His was a *pre*ideological Romanticism that projected, as if by an act of prophecy, a forcefully questioning attitude toward the very ideas that would soon congeal as Romantic doctrine; hence the emphasis in his writings on irony, less as a poetic device than as a necessary mode of thought. Consider, for instance, *Athenäum* fragment 121, "An idea is a concept perfected to the point of irony, an absolute synthesis of absolute antitheses, the constantly self-engendering interchange of two conflicting thoughts,"[52] where Schlegel embraces one of the Romantics' most cherished pipe dreams, the synthesis of opposites, only to explode it, by asserting a "constantly self-engendering interchange"; the irony to which he alludes in his definition of an idea is thus built into the formulation of the definition itself. This mode of argument was not destined to last for long; by about 1810 the critical potential of Romantic criticism was, in Jochen Schulte-Sasse's words, "increasingly repressed."[53] Odd as it may appear, Schlegel's usefulness in providing us with a critical frame for our study resides in the fact that, although the whole of Romanticism was rooted in his thought, he was hardly a "representative" figure; he resisted the very program that he played such a large part in initiating.

In the second place, Schlegel's critical categories—the *Arabeske* as narrative digression, the fragment as formal "tendency," the concept of art as critique, the romantic imperative, the theory of *Universalpoesie,* the interrelated notions of organicism, allegory, and symbol, the call for a fusion of poetry and philosophy—will provide us with a starting point for a positive valuation of the "negative moments" that are part and parcel of nineteenth-century music. Schlegel's stance offers a propadeutic to that of such later figures as Adorno, who, while acknowledging a crucial distinction between eighteenth- and nineteenth-century art, sees mainly disintegration and decay in the products of the Romantic age.[54] For running alongside those elements in Schlegel's project whose logical inconsistency has been an annoyance to commentators is a clear-headed realization that fragmentation and even chaos were constitutive features of modern art that criticism could not afford to ignore. And their presence in an artwork, for Schlegel, was not a matter of negativity alone: the strongest artworks may well be those in which disruptive tendencies are the most imaginatively embodied. As Schlegel maintained in "Über das Studium der Griechischen Poesie" (1795–96), the central essay in his book on Greek and Roman culture: "[The beautiful] is so little the guiding principle of modern poetry that many of the most excellent works of recent times are actually representations of the ugly ["des Häßlichen"], so that one is forced to admit, though reluctantly, that the representation of disorder in all its abundance and despair in all its strength, as opposed to the representation of abundance and strength in complete harmony with one another, demands creative energy and artistic prudence to an equal if not higher degree."[55] Thus the positing of a relationship between modern and redemptive phases, the second and third terms of Schlegel's historical scheme, was at once a necessity and a masterstroke; for it suggests that some of the seemingly negative moments in the present offer the most promise for the future.[56] "Our deficiencies themselves," he wrote in 1794, "are also our hopes."[57] As I will try to show, this dictum might also have a place in music criticism as well.

IV

The subsequent chapters of this study focus on individual musical works or closely related groups of works, each linked with one of Schlegel's categories or a complex thereof. In that I will return to much the same mutually dependent questions—how are Romantic ideas embedded in the musical works of the nineteenth century? how can our understanding of those works be enhanced by referring them critically to the ideas of the age, indeed by interpreting them as commentaries on those ideas?—each chapter can be read as a self-sufficient entity. But, I hope, the whole will turn out to be greater than the sum of its parts. My roughly chronological arrangement of the material by composer and my attempt to treat at least one example from each of the major genres of the nineteenth century are conceits drawn from traditional historiographical practice. But the result makes no claims of being an all-inclusive history. My intent has rather been to shape a set of variations on interrelated themes.

Chapters 2 and 3 are devoted to a consideration of Schumann's search for "new forms" in his piano music of the 1830s. This may seem to place undue emphasis on a single figure, yet if there is one composer from whose output the glories and traumas of musical Romanticism radiate with equal intensity, it is certainly the composer of the *Papillons.* (Schumann's centrality for the period underlies my decision to take up Weber only later.) In chapter 2, the *Arabeske,* Schlegel's term for the narrative interpolations characteristic of modern poetry, is developed as an apt metaphor for the musical digressions that problematize many of Schumann's essays in the larger forms, principally the first and last movements of the Opus 14 *Concert sans orchestre* and the whole of the C-Major Fantasie, Opus 17. Nourished equally by the narrative techniques of Jean Paul and the musical example of Chopin (in particular the Opus 23 and Opus 38 Ballades), Schumann created a series of individualized attempts to revitalize a form that threatened, since the death of Beethoven, to give way more and more to epigonism. If Schumann's "new forms" are so difficult to evaluate according to the standards of traditional *Formenlehre,* it is largely because they set forward a critique of the very structural principles that *Formenlehre* tends to idealize. Rather than treat his recourse to the arabesque technique as a deviation within the sonata-form tradition, I will therefore view it as a product of the dialectical encounter between Schumann's aspirations toward the monumental and his proclivity for the miniature.

Chapter 3 takes as its point of departure the fundamental form of literary Romanticism, the system of fragments, and its principal musical equivalent: the Schumannian cycle of character pieces for piano. I will try to develop the idea that the fragment system—both literary and musical—is informed by a special kind of coherence, its apparent organization as disconnected utterances notwithstanding. Traditional modes of achieving "logical" coherence, whereby a thought is gradually developed in time, are often coupled with modes that ensure an "associative" coherence animated by *Witz*—a term used by Schlegel (and Jean Paul, among others) to denote a network of subcutaneous connections that may not be immediately obvious. If *Witz* is our central category, then it is further supported by a complex of others (Schumann's own notion of *Selbstvernichtung,* Jean Paul's theory of *Humor*), which together will help us to define the fanciful structural properties of the fragment collection, here represented principally by Schumann's "große abenteuerliche Geschichten," the Opus 21 *Novelletten.*

Schlegel's assertion that modern poetry should be critical through and through (just as, conversely, criticism should tend toward poetry), is the guiding leitmotif of this book. In chapter 4 it is employed to account for the troubled reception of Carl Maria von Weber's problematic masterpiece, *Euryanthe.* On one hand, Weber's "große romantische Oper" may be viewed as a critique of the utopian trend that it is supposed to prefigure: the confluence of the separate arts in the *Gesamtkunstwerk* (already subjected to a verbal critique in E. T. A. Hoffmann's allegory of romantic opera, *Der Dichter und der Komponist* [1813]). But even more telling is Weber's musical commentary on the significative powers of opera, specifically on the power of music to "symbolize." While the Romantic ideology did indeed give primacy of place to the synthesizing qualities of the symbol as opposed to the discontinuous trajectory of allegory, my analysis of the opening scene of Act III will center on the means that Weber employed to imbue his work with *both* modes of signification.

As a response to the neoclassic ideal of generic purity against which works of modern art were bound to come up short, Schlegel posited the "Romantic imperative"—the notion that the mixture and intended fusion of forms and genres in contemporary poetry was no less than a historical necessity. Chapter 5 demonstrates the centrality of this idea for nineteenth-century music by concentrating on the music of Johannes Brahms, precisely because of his refractory relationship to the intellectual currents of Romanticism. Even the period's most profound reinterpreter of the classical canon, the composer whose self-expression was mediated most thoroughly by its forms and genres, partook of the tendency to blend genres rather than to preserve them intact. This is perhaps most evident in several of the *Magelone Romanzen,* Opus 33, a work that, as a whole, creates a striking musical analogue to the literary source for its poetic texts, Tieck's *Liebesgeschichte der schönen Magelone*: by drawing on stylistic elements from *Lied* and opera, Brahms parallelled Tieck's mediation of *Märchen* and *Roman* in his *Kunstmärchen.*

But Brahms's response to the Romantic imperative manifests itself more subtly in other works. One of his favorite sonata forms in fact brings together the characteristics of a wide array of formal types: sonata allegro, concerto allegro, rondo, strophic variation. My consideration of the middle movements of the Fourth Symphony, Opus 98, accounts for this peculiarly Brahmsian procedure as a "relativizing" of formal categories analogous to the transformation of the neoclassical literary types (*Drama, Epik,* and *Lyrik*) into qualities (*dramatisch, episch, lyrisch*) in the *Roman.* The Romantic imperative, in other words, need not always project a utopian, universalizing message (as it does in the finale of Beethoven's Ninth Symphony), nor appear in the guise of a bold formal/generic experiment (as in Berlioz's ostentatious mix of symphony and opera in *Roméo et Juliette*). Brahms's corrective of the utopian position is quietly delivered but no less forceful because of it: his reconfiguration of the classical forms as qualities is tantamount to a statement that their historical moment has passed. Conversely, the interplay of tradition and innovation in one of his most unusual compositions (from the structural point of view), the slow movement of the Opus 111 String Quintet, calls into question the possibility of fashioning "new forms." As it turns out, Brahms's apparently sui generis approach to form in this movement is modeled on the strategies of an important predecessor: Robert Schumann.

The next two chapters turn to the music dramas of Richard Wagner. In Chapter 6 Schlegel's statement of the aims of *Universalpoesie* and its embodiment in the ideal *Roman,* wherein "all the parts are organized along the same lines as the resultant whole" (*Athenäum* fragment 116) is brought to bear on Wagner's *Ring* tetralogy. I will argue that *The Ring* is organized principally as a system of interrelated recapitulatory "centers of attraction" whose most telling representatives are the scenes of epic narration and the Act-finales of the various music dramas. The critical dimension of *The Ring* is therefore deeply embedded in its own structure: this is a work that is perpetually engaged in the act of self-criticism. In Wagner's hands, the solipsism that threatens Romantic consciousness at every turn is transformed into a vigorous structural principle, most impressively in Brünnhilde's monologue at the conclusion of *Götterdämmerung,* which counts as an encapsulated summation of the entire cycle. Wagner's use of the *mise en abyme,* or self-mirroring technique, can also be shown to have a dramatic/expressive function. The differing methods of musical recall employed in Siegfried's narrative (*Götterdämmerung,* Act III/ii) and Brünnhilde's closing monologue, fragmentary in the first instance and integrative in the second, make *The Ring* a massive attempt to preserve a certain quality of memory in danger of perishing at the brink of modernism.

Chapter 7 proceeds from the assumption that the Romantic artwork is marked by an almost obsessive striving for organic interconnectedness. This is the concern that animates Wagner's celebrated "art of transition," the technique that gives shape to the extended dialogue at the center of *Tristan und*

Isolde, Act II. At the same time, Schlegel's preideological stance on the organicism issue suggests that at the heart of the *Ur*-Romantic outlook was a skeptical attitude toward the realization of an ideal organic unity in the modern era. I suggest that this conflict—a variation on the dialectic play of monumentality and miniaturism in Schumann's works, or of symbolizing and allegorizing in Weber's—is also present in *Parsifal.* The organization of the work, on the one hand, marks the culmination of Wagner's technique of spinning out large-scale continuities through the "art of transition," but on the other, invites interpretation as a concatenation of musical fragments juxtaposed according to what Wagner called the principle of "rhetorical dialectics." This tension is demonstrated through a comparison of Amfortas's lament during the Act I Grail Ceremony, and Parsifal's monologue following on his attainment of "cosmic clear-sightedness" by means of Kundry's kiss in Act II. Although both are built on much the same music, Wagner thoroughly reorders the motivic material of the Act I monologue in Parsifal's Act II presentation— a procedure seemingly at odds with the musical continuity that each monologue displays when considered independently. Lastly, we will note how the *intra*textual conflict in Wagner's work became an *inter*textual concern in Gustav Mahler's early compositions (each of them individualized responses to Wagner's musico-dramatic legacy) by considering his reworking of the *Gesellen* song "Ging heut' morgens übers Feld" in the first movement of his First Symphony.

Originally subtitled "Symphonic optimism in *fin de siècle* form," Richard Strauss's tone poem *Also sprach Zarathustra* in fact speaks to concerns traceable to the beginning of the nineteenth century. In chapter 8 I suggest that Schlegel's call for the union of poetry and philosophy is paralleled by Strauss's adherence to the aesthetic demands of program music, his attempt to inform music with philosophical pretensions. The result, for Strauss, was an imposing *Mischgedicht,* but paradoxically a *Mischgedicht* largely by virtue of its absolute-musical properties. At once variation cycle, symphony, and music drama, Strauss's tone poem (like Mahler's middle-period symphonies) celebrates the combinative powers of music, but only insofar as specifically *musical* forms are concerned.

In *Athenäum* fragment 216, Schlegel singled out the French Revolution, Fichte's *Wissenschaftslehre,* and Goethe's *Wilhelm Meister* as the "greatest tendencies of the age,"[58] the chief political and cultural documents from which its history could be inferred. The works that I consider in the following pages might be said to represent some of the greatest musical tendencies of the nineteenth century. My account of their animating processes adds up to a kind of history, inasmuch as history can be read out of a period's most telling fragments.

2 ✺

Schumann's Opus 17 Fantasie and the *Arabeske*

> But even the earlier [works] will
> give you an idea of my character,
> my aspirations; yes, it is precisely
> in attempts [such as these] that
> the greatest seeds of the future lie.
>
> – Robert Schumann
> Letter to Carl Koßmaly, 5 May 1843

A Monument to Beethoven

Perhaps no one has characterized Robert Schumann's C-Major Fantasie for Piano, Opus 17, better than Charles Rosen, for whom it is "the monument that commemorates the death of the classical style."[1] The metaphor that will provide us with a means of entry into the work is Rosen's "monument," a term that likewise played no small part in the compositional history of the Fantasie. As is well known, Schumann indicated in a letter of 19 December 1836 to his prospective publisher Friedrich Kistner that "Florestan and

19

Eusebius heartily wish to do something for Beethoven's Monument, and have written something toward that end under the following title: Ruinen. Trophaeen. Palmen. / Große Sonate f. d. Pianof. / Für Beethovens Denkmal."[2] And later in the same letter, Schumann suggested that the title page feature, in gold letters on a black band also framed in gold, the rubric: "Obolum auf Beethovens Denkmal."[3] Memorials, monuments, obelisks—all of them have doubly suggestive connotations. As Schumann put it in his "Monument für Beethoven: Vier Stimmen darüber," a brief article for the 24 June 1836 issue of the *Neue Zeitschrift für Musik,* "a monument is a ruin twisted forward, just as a ruin is a monument twisted backward."[4]

Schumann's remarks on the paradoxical nature of monuments, written just as he was conceiving the work that would eventually become the Fantasie,[5] can be read in tandem with what Walter Benjamin would later describe as a "dialectical image," that is, an image "in which the Then and the Now come together in a constellation like a flash of lightning," thus creating "a force field in which the conflict between fore- and after-history plays itself out."[6] Indeed, the C-Major Fantasie will serve us well as a measure of the problems raised by the "new" music of the mid-nineteenth century precisely because it is such a striking musical equivalent of the dialectical image.

The "Then" of Schumann's dialectical sonic structure is of course provided by the figure of Beethoven. As late as October 1837, almost a year after having completed what was probably the first version of the Fantasie, Schumann was still referring to it as his "Sonate f. Beethoven."[7] Built into the piece are several more or less specific allusions to the music of his daunting predecessor, in the form of a thematic reference to the last song of *An die ferne Geliebte,* Opus 98, in the *adagio* coda of the first movement,[8] and, in the December 1836 version of the Fantasie's last movement, a quotation from the slow movement of Beethoven's Seventh Symphony.[9] Even more significant are the structural affinities, which we will consider later, between Schumann's refractory sonata forms and those of Beethoven's last period.

And as for the "Now," a good part of this discussion will be devoted to showing how it is embodied in Schumann's attempt at a fundamentally "new" form in the Fantasie's first movement. Something very odd happens here. About thirty bars into the reprise, the proceedings are brought to an unexpected halt, only to resume again, as if nothing at all had gone awry, after the nearly hundred-bar unfolding of the passage designated *Im Legendenton,* a stretch of music that sounds for all intents and purposes much like an independent miniature. The fracturing of Schumann's grandly conceived sonata design, the apparently arbitrary positioning of the *Im Legendenton* section, the ensuing sense of narrative disturbance—all of this is in line with the theory of the *Arabeske,* the first of the ideas from Friedrich Schlegel's program that I will employ as a hermeneutic tool toward the end of reading an admittedly unusual formal ploy.[10] Though it can be narrowly construed as a digression or interpolation within an otherwise straightforward narrative,[11] the *Arabeske* idea is actually far richer in implications. For Schlegel, it describes a deliberately planned moment of negativity in modern art, such that the apparent formal cleft is not necessarily a sign of technical ineptitude: it is there to make a point. In Schumann's case, the point, had it been grasped by his contemporaries, would have made for a chilling realization: the *Arabeske* element in the Fantasie asserts nothing less than the *impossibility* of writing sonatas after Beethoven.

In the course of the following discussion, we will look more closely at Schumann's yoking together of "Then" and "Now," first by considering his critical campaign for the cultivation of "new forms" and their manifestation in the first movement of the Fantasie; next by examining some of the precedents, both literary and musical, for Schumann's forms; and lastly by developing a reading of the work in its entirety as a musical critique of the possibilities for synthesis—of "Then" and "Now," character piece and "higher" forms, Beethovenian sonata and Romantic fantasy. Our observations will be guided by the complex of ideas around the *Arabeske,* which together should help to show how Schumann achieved an uneasy rapprochement between the music of the immediate past and that of a compositionally divided present.

New Forms

For Schumann the critic and observer of the contemporary musical scene in the 1830s, the historical moment for the sonata had passed. "Isolated beautiful examples of this genre might certainly appear here and there," he wrote in a survey account of 1839, "but on the whole it seems as though the form has run its life course, and this is to be sure in the order of things, for we should not repeat the same things for another century but rather be mindful of seeking out the New."[12] And what held for the sonata held for other genres as well. Schumann noted with some regret that in the six years since his journal's inception, hardly sixteen or seventeen piano concertos had come to his attention; here was another genre in danger of becoming obsolete.[13] Symphony and string quartet were faring little better, while the "brilliant period" of the variation was drawing to a close to make way for the capriccio.[14] The entire classical canon, in other words, was in a state of decay. But mingled with the wistful sense of loss was Schumann's belief that it was the composer's artistic imperative to abandon "comfortable" forms and the philistinism to which their unreflected employment might lead in favor of alternative modes of organization, hence his prescription, for example, for a three-movements-in-one, introduction-*cantabile-allegro* bravura work to replace the practically defunct piano concerto.[15] Thus Schumann's exhortations represented less a naïvely utopian program than a dialectical philosophy of history in which one set of temporally determinate genres gave way to another, so that "approving repetition" of older works (Beethovenian models in particular) was censured and their "preservation" praised.[16] "Then" and "Now" come together, though not always harmoniously, in Schumann's conception of "new forms."

This is the backdrop against which Schumann's remarks to Hermann Hirschbach, in a letter of 7 September 1838, should be considered: "You know nothing of my larger compositions, my sonatas (which have appeared under the names of Florestan and Eusebius); I believe you will see (if you haven't already in my smaller works) how plentiful and new are the forms contained therein."[17] To what "new forms" could Schumann be referring, given the outward resemblance of the sonatas to the more broadly conceived works in the classical canon? In the first movement of the F♯-Minor Sonata, Opus 11 (1833–35), one might point to the odd reversal of the instability/stability relationship that usually obtains between slow introductions and the quicker music that emanates from them. Schumann's *Introduzione* (*un poco adagio*) departs from the traditional scheme insofar as it is tonally closed and formally rounded, its *ABA* pattern and tonic-mediant-tonic tonal plan suggesting a status as independent miniature. The first twenty-two bars of the ensuing *allegro vivace,* on the other hand, given their aperiodic phrase structure, with an opening dominant pedal, motivic sequences, and buildup to an emphatic dominant at mm. 73–74, seem rather to take on the role of an introduction, a sense that is intensified when the passage at m. 75 proceeds with a variation of the previous sequential music. Form part and function are apparently at odds. A more radical interpretation might even question whether the structural layout of the opening *Introduzione* as self-contained miniature enables us to perceive it as a meaningful component of the sonata-style argument that it prefaces. Apart from its tonal link with the *allegro,* does the *Introduzione* really belong? Schumann's affirmative answer is effected only through an act of force: a fleeting reminiscence of the opening melody in F minor in the middle of the development section (mm. 268ff.).

A similar question is posed by the various versions of the first movement of the G-Minor Sonata, Opus 22, preserved in Berlin, Deutsche Staatsbibliothek, Mus. ms. autogr. Schumann 38 (1835–38?). For a time, Schumann considered following up the incisive opening theme (mm. 1–23) with an *appassionato* counterpart of markedly different character, the tetrachordal melody and straightforward rhythms of the former giving way, without the benefit of a mediating transition, to syncopated and by turns conjunct and disjunct melodic phrases over broadly expanding arpeggios. No less than the first movement of Opus 11, the first movement of Opus 22 in its early form was fitted out with *two* perfectly acceptable beginnings.[18]

The first movement of the F-Minor *Concert sans orchestre,* Opus 14 (first edition, 1836), introduces a related structural anomaly: here the orderly course of the lengthy and symmetrically conceived second group (mm. 26–59 are varied en masse in mm. 70–89) is strongly disturbed by the appearance of an *animato* interlude (mm. 62–69), which, given its temporal, melodic, and textural deviation from what immediately precedes, seems at first hardly to belong. The effect is only partially ameliorated by the interlude's motivic ties with a portion of the first group (mm. 8ff.) and by the tonal preparation for the A♭ of the exposition's close.[19] The Florestinian asides in the first movement are complemented by lyric interpolations after the manner of Eusebius in the *prestissimo possibile* finale. The *cantabile* melody (actually a soprano/bass duo) introduced in mm. 32ff. is initially contrasted with its surroundings, both gesturally (the only connective being an accompanimental reworking of the triplet figure that runs through much of the movement) and tonally (its G♭ at a tritone remove from the preceding and following C minor). But Schumann's point here is to allow for the melody's gradual assimilation: its recurrence at mm. 238ff. (again in G♭) comes in the context of a progression directed toward the dominant of F minor and the ensuing recapitulation; in mm. 363ff. its transposition to D♭ is the catalyst for the tonal shift that brings the elusive second-group music into the tonic region; and lastly, in mm. 569ff., its presentation in D♭ colors the final tonic-prolonging progression.

These examples from the *Concert sans orchestre,* like those from the Opus 11 and Opus 22 sonatas, betray a peculiarly dualistic perspective. Implicit in Schumann's notion of "new forms," that is, is a deliberate interleaving of musical materials that on first hearing seem to bear little resemblance to one another, thus producing musical designs analogous to the poetic design in works like E. T. A. Hoffmann's *Kater Murr,* where the memoirs of Murr the cat are conflated with the biography of the composer and conductor Kreisler. We will later see how this intramovement device becomes an intermovement feature of Schumann's collections of miniatures for piano.

It is tempting to read these anomalies as signs of what Charles Rosen, in a discussion of the F♯-Minor Sonata, calls "the difficulties a nineteenth-century composer had with an already-established sonata form,"[20] a latter-day echo of an important strand in Schumann reception, which, to paraphrase Franz Brendel, asserts that the composer's "subjective nature," his *Innerlichkeit,* worked against his abilities to achieve success in larger, "objective" forms such as the sonata.[21] Yet Schumann demonstrated, in cases like the opening movement of the G-Minor Piano Sonata (published version, 1839), that he was perfectly capable of fashioning an almost textbook example of formal clarity, a fact noted well within Schumann's lifetime by Carl Koßmaly in a lengthy overview of the composer's piano works.[22] Thus, the structural anomalies we have observed were in all likelihood intentionally built into the fabric of the music, so that it is not a matter, as Markus Waldura suggests in a recent study, of aiming for "value-neutral" appraisals of Schumann's sonata forms, of substituting "change" (*Wandel*) for post–Beethovenian "decay" (*Verfall*).[23] For it is precisely through a preservation of the element of *Verfall* that criticism can locate some of Schumann's most powerful and provocative statements;[24] in the instances considered thus far, for example, we can detect in Schumann's penchant for the apparently unmotivated interruption a challenge to Beethoven's forward-driving, teleological forms.

The challenge is if anything intensified in the work from this period that Schumann thought to be his "most refined,"[25] the first movement of the C-Major Fantasie, Opus 17, questions about the form of which have in turn elicited no little commentary, especially in recent years. Though most writers have been struck by the evocative *Im Legendenton* that occurs roughly at the movement's midpoint, there is some disagreement over its structural function in what is generally viewed as some variety of sonata-style form. Generally speaking, analysts are divided over viewing it as a substitute for a traditional development section,[26] or alternately as a lyric interlude within the development.[27] Both interpretations are problematic, the first because it ignores the music (mm. 82–128) between the close of the exposition and the beginning of the *Im Legendenton,* the second because it fails to account for the clear sense of return, both melodic and harmonic, at m. 97, where the opening idea recurs in the varied form it had first assumed at m. 19. Indeed, the gestures indicative of reprise are intensified in mm. 119ff., a rhythmically diminuted statement of the opening music in suitably grand form, with supporting *sforzando* C pedals and a bass line that shadows the treble melody at the lower octave. Taken together with the immense buildup in the previous fourteen measures, a much extended variant of the brief retransitional passage at mm. 95–96, a stronger set of recapitulatory signals is hardly imaginable. To be sure, the obligatory dominant preparation is lacking (both before mm. 97 and m. 119), but insofar as Schumann's opening theme is, in its initial stages, undergirded by $V^{7/9}$ harmony, a reprise can be achieved only by a powerful act of force. It should be clear, therefore, that the *Im Legendenton* (mm. 129ff.) interrupts not the extraordinarily brief development but the recapitulation that begins at m. 97. The point is further affirmed by considering the manner in which Schumann enters and quits his lyric episode: mm. 225ff., the *erstes Tempo* after the *Im Legendenton,* proceed from the point at which mm. 127–28 broke off just before it, corresponding in interrupted form to the move from m. 28 to m. 29 in the exposition. Recognition of this fact is decisive, for it confirms what Schumann has taken such extreme measures for us to hear: an apparently arbitrary disturbance in the form at just that point where a sonata-allegro movement, through parallel restatement of the events of the exposition, strives for maximal symmetry.[28] Schumann's ploy amounts to a willful denial of this kind of balanced recurrence. The structural diagram presented as Figure 2–1 is intended to highlight the asymmetrical placement of the *Im Legendenton* within the form of the movement as a whole.

These observations, along with others pertinent to the form of the movement, can be subsumed under the category that Friedrich Schlegel reserved for some of his most trenchant thoughts on the nature of romantic form: the

FIGURE 2–1
Schumann, Opus 17/i, Formal Plan

Form Part		Description		Tonality
	Exposition:			
m.1		First Group	$A^1\ A^2$	C
29			A^3	E♭
33		Transition	B (sequence)	→
41		Second Group	C^1	d
61			C^2	F
82	**Quasi-Development:**	rhetorical flourishes		D →
	Recapitulation:			
97		First Group	$A^2\ A^4$	C
129	**Parabasis**	*Im Legendenton*	$a^1\ b\ a^2\ c\ a^3$	c
225		First Group, continued	A^3	E♭
229		Transition	B (sequence)	→
233		Second Group	C^1	c
253			C^2	E♭
	Coda:			
274		on Development		C →
286		on first group	A^2	C
295		*An die ferne Geliebte* allusion		C

Arabeske. The relationship that I am proposing has nothing to do with the question of influence. That Schumann decided on a stanza from Schlegel's lyric "Die Gebüsche" as a motto for the Fantasie is (in terms of the line of argument here) an intriguing coincidence and little more. In any event, it would be almost impossible to make much of a case for direct influence. Apart from the similarities in Schumann's and Schlegel's critical perspectives pointed out in chapter 1, and the general currency of Schlegel's ideas in the wake of his early campaign for a burgeoning Romanticism, there is little evidence in Schumann's prose writings, letters, or diaries of a direct transference of ideas. (It is worth pointing out that Schumann's own *Arabeske,* Opus 18 is a delightful but slight work whose simple *ABACA* rondo form knows nothing of the asymmetry of the Schlegelian *Arabeske*). Nor is the demonstration of influence in any sense necessary.[29] The *Arabeske* is primarily useful as a critical tool; it cannot—and need not—speak for Schumann's knowledge or appreciation of Schlegel.

While the *Arabeske* figures most frequently in Schlegel's discussions of literature, it is clear from considering the 120 or so instances in which it occurs that he intended it as an all-embracing category of form. In essence, Schlegel simply borrowed a term from eighteenth-century art theory and extended its range to include a multiplicity of historical and cultural phenomena. The French Revolution, he wrote, was "the tragic arabesque of the age";[30] ontology, cosmology, and psychology were the "arabesques and grotesques of philosophy";[31] the whole of ancient mythology displayed an arabesque organization comparable to that of the "indirect" mythology of modern poetry.[32] And Schlegel's rhetorical question "Doesn't the arabesque occupy a place in painting similar to that of fantasy in music?"[33] of course ties in clearly with the parallel I am suggesting. In that the notion of the *Arabeske* was specifically geared to wrest a measure of positivity from the seemingly disturbing elements in modern culture, it should therefore find ready applicability in gauging the decidedly "new" aspects of nineteenth-century musical form.

I will proceed, then, by coordinating the first movement of Schumann's Fantasie with four components of the *Arabeske* idea: (1) the painterly *Arabeske* as a kind of design wherein *Beiwerk* (incidental construct) becomes *Hauptwerk* (constitutive event), and grotesquerie is valued for its own sake; (2) the *Arabeske* as the modern equivalent of *Parekbase* (parabasis), the quirky digressions of classical Greek comedy; (3) the *Arabeske* as a specific type of modern art whose worth, paradoxically enough, is a function of its limitations; and (4) the *Arabeske* as total and totalizing form.

Schlegel's elevation of the *Arabeske* to a central category in his poetics followed closely on a controversy in art-historical circles that occupied critics in the last decades of the eighteenth century.[34] At issue was the aesthetic value of the ornamental style, characterized by sinuous lines and fantastic shapes wherein distinctions between the animal and vegetable worlds were all but obliterated, that came to light during the fifteenth-century excavations of thriving early-Christian centers like Pompeii, and was in turn adopted by Rafael for his opulent decorations of the pillars of the Vatican loggias.[35] For Adolf Reim, secretary of the Berlin Akademie der Künste, the ornamental arabesque was "a plague on taste," a sign of artistic decadence, while classicists like Karl Philipp Moritz ("Spielarten des Geschmacks," 1793) found a way to valorize the element of imaginative free play that it embodied, so long as the decorative arabesque did not threaten to overwhelm the principal architectural or painterly work it was meant to frame.[36]

Goethe also gave a positive account of the arabesque—defined as "an arbitrary but tasteful painterly combination of the most varied objects, so disposed as to decorate the inner walls of a building"—in a brief but influential essay of 1789.[37] He was taken by the manner in which the small mythological portraits that often took central place on the walls of Pompeian houses were surrounded by symmetrically arranged stalks, flourishes, and bands, but stressed that the arabesques should serve only to emphasize the central painting and "bring it into harmony with the whole." Yet in several of the works of artist Otto Philipp Runge, a reversal sets in that would not have met with Goethe's approval: the border invades the interior; ornamental *Beiwerk* becomes essential *Hauptwerk*. This reversal is most obvious in his series of painterly arabesques titled after the times of day ("Die Tageszeiten").[38] In the ink sketch for a projected oil painting of "Morgen," for instance, the lily stalks and cherubim of the ornamental border recur as the principal content of the fanciful center; representation gives way to pure, but arbitrary, design.

Both elements—autonomy and arbitrariness of design—likewise played into Schlegel's *Arabeske*. The former dominates in fragments such as: "Landscape bereft of figures, idyllic-romantic in the grand style—arabesques represent absolute-fantastic painting," or: "The arabesque is nothing but pure pictorialism; one must be able to paint hieroglyphically without recourse to a determinate mythology."[39] The latter idea, emphasizing the grotesque turn that the arabesque style might take, obtains in one of Schlegel's most important pronouncements, *Athenäum* fragment 389. There he asserts that "if every purely arbitrary or purely random connection of form and matter is grotesque, then philosophy has its grotesques as well as poetry"; from such works "one could learn a kind of disorganization wherein confusion is properly constructed and symmetrical."[40] The arabesque/grotesque, given its play with "the infinitely arbitrary and contingent," is thus the categorical opposite of the "naïve," a point that Schlegel makes clear in several other related fragments,[41] although through the juxtaposition he intends no negative value judgment of the grotesque. On the contrary, the transformation of external ornament into internal essence and the cultivation of studied randomness were both primary features of what Schlegel described as Romantic form.

These elements resonate in Schumann's Fantasie movement as well. Here too *Beiwerk* becomes *Hauptwerk*. I am thinking principally of the relationship between the two musical designs that Schumann interleaves: on the one hand, an integrated sonata-allegro structure; on the other, the alternating pattern of the *Im Legendenton*. Although the first of the two designs *should* serve as *Hauptwerk,* Schumann's sonata allegro is oddly fractured, its forward-moving course continually deflected. The fracturing manifests itself partly in the consistently invoked tonal dualism that pervades each of its form parts (see Fig. 2–1, p. 25). Both first and second group are determined not by a single tonality but by two a minor third apart: C and E♭ in the first group, D minor and F in the second (adjusted to the tonic pair, C and E♭, in the recapitulation). And the dualism is articulated thematically as well, each tonal pair being linked with a complementary thematic repetition; the C-major music, featuring varied statements of the same idea (A^1 and A^2 in the exposition, A^2 and A^4 in the recapitulation), reproduces the pattern at yet another level.[42] A sense of arrested, or rather goalless, motion is projected by an overall design that in effect describes a spiral. The exposition, though it begins with a harmonically open idea over a V^9 pedal, proceeds to what promises to be a regular sonata-form development (mm. 82ff.), but after a mere fifteen bars this new section breaks off to allow the form to double back on itself at m. 97. The forward drive is again thwarted at the *Im Legendenton,* after which the sonata design is permitted to continue. But again, at m. 275, the form circles back for varied replays of the "sham" development and the beginning of the recapitulation.

The spiral could carry forth indefinitely if not for the appearance of the *An die ferne Geliebte* allusion; yet the song melody, in spite of its thematic preparation at various earlier points in the movement, is less a hard-won goal than an elusive point where the spiral finally dissolves. Compare this with the self-containment of the *Im Legendenton,* organized as a miniature rondo structure:

Measure	*Theme*	*Tonality*
129	a^1	V/c $\rightarrow$ c
156	b (cf. Beethoven allusion)	$\rightarrow$ V/c
173	a^2	c
181	c (cf. second group)	D$^\flat$ $\rightarrow$ V/c $\rightarrow$ V/f $\rightarrow$ f (= iv/c)
204	a^3	c
216	coda	c

Noticeably absent are the unusual tonal divigations of the surrounding sonata structure. In fact, the first conclusive cadence in the movement comes in C minor, in the eleventh bar of the *Im Legendenton.* Circularity is likewise replaced by teleology, a passionate buildup to the statement of a^3 in mm. 204ff. The design that is traditionally framed—the sonata allegro—is here made to frame a character piece of unpretentious dimensions. Incidental argument and central statement are reversed.

At the same time, Schumann's centerpiece is markedly off-center, and herein lies its connection with the grotesquerie of the painterly *Arabeske.* Its placement within the total design, as an interruption of the orderly recurrence of first-group events, is intended to create the effect of an arbitrarily positioned disturbance. Although we will see at a later point in this discussion that its location was perhaps not so randomly chosen after all, suffice it to say for now that it would be difficult at first to sense any compelling necessity in Schumann's decision to break off the first group where he did. But in so doing, he made a musical-rhetorical point that bears comparison with another aspect of Schlegel's *Arabeske* idea: the *Arabeske* as parabasis.

In his "Charakteristik der griechischen Komödie" (1803/4), Schlegel noted that the chief structural difference between Classical tragedy and comedy was the employment, in the latter genre, of *Parekbase,* that is, "a speech occurring in the middle of a play, spoken by the chorus to the audience in the name of the poet. Indeed, it was a total interruption of the work, a suspension of its orderly progress in which the chorus, in order to emphasize the suspension

of the proceedings, stepped out to the extreme edge of the proscenium."
Moreover, "this irregularity of ancient comedy was due to no lack of art or
mere unpoetic caprice . . . ; the incompatibility of parabasis with unity was
only apparent."[43]

For Schlegel, the very same rhetorical device played an important role in
works such as Cervantes's *Don Quixote,* which shared with more recent
examples of the *Roman* a tendency toward episodic structure.[44] Thus, in
Schlegel's theory of contemporary poetic genres, the *Roman* occupied a
place comparable to that of Greek comedy in the scheme of Classical types.
The link was made directly in the Cologne lectures of 1807, "Über deutsche
Sprache und Literatur,"[45] and indirectly in such fragments as "The *Roman*
tends toward parabasis," or "In the fantastic novel, the elements of parabasis
should be constant."[46] Yet as often as not, the term *Parekbase* is superseded
by *Arabeske* in Schlegel's theory of the *Roman*; witness fragments such as
"Cervantes is for the arabesque what Goethe is for the essay form."[47]
Schumann's *Im Legendenton* provides a clear musical equivalent for the rhetorical parabasis: it clearly interrupts an ongoing process, only to "speak" in
a manner that is sharply differentiated from that of the surrounding music.
Rhapsodic utterance is replaced by a pseudochorale style, long-breathed
phrases by more compact syntactic groupings, C major by its parallel minor.

The otherness of the *Im Legendenton* may even be bound up with its compositional history. The Deutsche Staatsbibliothek in Berlin has in its possession a manuscript (Mus. ms. autogr. 35 Nr. 4) containing, alongside what look
to be sketches for an unrealized Piano Sonata in E♭, a sketch for what ultimately became the *Im Legendenton*. Following immediately on a crossed out
melody-bass sketch for a C-Major scherzo come: (1) a five-measure melody
sketch, its first two measures congruent with mm. 216–17 of the *Im
Legendenton*; (2) a continuation corresponding in almost every detail to the
right-hand part of the *Im Legendenton,* mm. 174–80; and (3) a resumption
of the melody sketch, spanning mm. 181–99 of the *Im Legendenton*. Might
Schumann's lyric aside have been originally meant for another work predating the Fantasie?

This speculation aside, there is little doubt that the *Im Legendenton* represents a moment of suspension in the Fantasie movement's progress. As
Carolyn Abbate has recently argued, narrative metaphors have too often been
applied to music without recourse to the critical circumspection that is necessary to give them descriptive force. Narrativity in music, she claims, is not
an "omnipresent phenomenon" but a "rare and peculiar act" often signaled
by marked disruptions in the musical surface that suggest the aura of distance, of "once upon a time," required by all true narratives. And most important, truly narrative music must behave as though it were recounting or
reflecting upon past events.[48] The *Im Legendenton* does this and more. We
have already considered its formal disruptiveness; what remains is to remark
on the manner in which it not only recalls the past but prefigures the future
(see Ex. 2.1).

EXAMPLE 2.1

Schumann, Fantasie, Opus 17 (Reprinted by permission. Copyright © 1978 Henle Verlag.)

a. mm. 129–30 (*Im Legendenton*)

b. mm. 33–37

c. mm. 181–89 (*Im Legendenton*)

d. mm. 61–68

e. mm. 156–60 (*Im Legendenton*)

f. mm. 295–302

On the one hand, its opening theme (mm. 129ff.) draws on a motive from the preceding sonata-form retransition (mm. 33ff.), and the music of episode c (mm. 181ff.) recalls the sonata-form second group (mm. 61ff.). Only the second case can be counted as a true reminiscence. The first is more akin to the complete recasting of an ordinary experience in a dream sequence: a casual aside from the framing sonata allegro is made in an instant into the principal topic of a musical narrative. On the other hand, mm. 156ff. (like mm. 14ff., 49ff. and 69ff. in the sonata-allegro frame) point toward the Beethoven allusion at the end of the movement (mm. 295ff.), only now the casual aside is located in the *Im Legendenton,* the dreamlike reconfiguration in the movement's lyric conclusion, making it too into a parabasis-*Arabeske* of sorts.[49] And as if to affirm what is plainly audible in the music itself, Schumann titled his lyric interlude as he did; the poetic *Legende,* a genre revivified in the early nineteenth century in tandem with the general rise of a nationalistic-patriotic spirit, sought after all to evoke the past (the medieval past in particular) by idealizing it.[50]

The first movement of the Fantasie, then, "tells" the *Im Legendenton* as a bard would a ballad. Schumann noted in an 1839 review that a piano sonata might be received most enjoyably, during an evening of convivial music making, just after a few poems by Byron or Goethe;[51] in the Fantasie the recitation is built directly into the music. But divorced from its surroundings, and given its mock-pathetic tone, the *Im Legendenton* probably does not qualify as "high art," certainly not art of Goethean stature. This leads us to the third component in the complex of meanings that define the *Arabeske*: the *Arabeske* as a specific genre of modern poetry, but a genre of questionable aesthetic worth. In this sense, it ranks in Schlegel's scheme next to literary types of limited scope including the novella, idyll, and fairy tale (*Märchen*), all of them "fundamental forms" one step removed from the higher genres: epic, lyric, and drama. But the *Arabeske* was singled out for special attention because, as Schlegel maintained, it alone among the fundamental forms just mentioned qualified as a kind of contemporary *Naturpoesie,* that is, a historically time-specific type bound up with the spirit and ethos of its age. As he put it in the "Brief über den Roman": Confessions (or *Bekentnisse,* narrative accounts, often of an autobiographical nature, and often based on true events) and arabesques "count as the single romantic nature-products of the present epoch."[52] Diderot's *Jacques le fataliste* serves as Schlegel's example: "To be sure it is not high art, but only—an arabesque. But precisely for that reason it is, in my eyes, of not inconsiderable worth."[53] Diderot's *Jacques*— an arabesque given the contingencies that characterize its unfolding action, a Romantic "nature-product" in that it takes as its theme a satiric-sentimental accounting of its protagonists' amours—cannot be placed with the works of Schlegel's "great authors," figures like Ariosto, Cervantes, and Shakespeare. Nonetheless, it counts as a telling index of what art *might become.* The same holds true, in Schlegel's estimation, for two other masters of the poetic arabesque, Laurence Sterne and Jean Paul Richter. Theirs was an admittedly bizarre sensibility, a "sickly wit," but Schlegel takes this for a positive quality, for "that which has grown up in such sickly circumstances cannot of course be anything other than sickly."[54]

Some of this has an interesting bearing on Schumann's music. I intend neither to compare him to Diderot nor to imply that he was a maker of "sickly" music. Still, it will be worth considering what Schlegel was attempting to say about modern art in light of the specific example that Schumann offers. In Schlegel's view, the modern artist who was worthy of the name could not afford either to avoid or idealize the negativity of his or her historico-cultural situation, but rather should meet it head on. The volatile and confusing political shifts attendant on the French Revolution, a world literature that threatened to succumb to a stilted epigonism on the one hand and decadence on the other: neither could be willed away. On the contrary, the creative genius was challenged to embed moments of negativity into the very fabric of an artwork, and what is more, to transform them poetically.

What Schumann knew or thought of contemporary politics is beside the point; that he feared for the potential decline of musical art is beyond question. He too cultivated a kind of romantic *Naturpoesie,* a musical equivalent of the *Arabeske* as a literary type. The genre that I have in mind, the character piece for piano, is the antipode of what Schumann himself thought of as "higher" forms[55]—sonatas, symphonies, concertos, string quartets—and its representative is embedded in the Fantasie's first movement in the form of the *Im Legendenton.* Here as well is an intentional surfeit of sentimentality, an exaggeration of gestural quality that culminates in three measures of diminished-seventh harmony at mm. 154–56 and in a thunderous and passionate statement of the *Im Legendenton* theme *fortississimo* (the highest dynamic point in the movement) at m. 204. A climactic utterance of this sort seems at odds with the diminutive proportions of the interlude as a whole. Equally troubling is the mixture of unabashed sentiment projected by the theme with the aura of religiosity suggested by its initial chorale-style harmonization. There are moments, in other words, when the *Im Legendenton* tends precariously toward kitsch. It acquires aesthetic significance only when viewed as part of a broader configuration: the *Arabeske* as total form.

Schlegel argued for the valorization of the *Arabeske* as total form in the *Gespräch über die Poesie* by way of a comparison with the shape of ancient mythology, whose "motley throng" of gods produced, yet again, an arabesque. The humorous-sentimental prose pieces of Sterne and Diderot appealed to him so much because in them he detected the seeds of far grander constructs, worthy of ranking beside the infinitely rich body of literature nourished on mythological foundations. Romantic poetry was therefore to be praised for "its artfully ordered confusion, its charming symmetry of contradictions, its wonderfully unceasing alternation of enthusiasm and irony, which lives in the smallest parts of the whole," because it held out the promise of establishing an "indirect mythology" of sorts: "the organization [of romantic poetry] is the same [as that of classical mythology], and certainly the arabesque is the oldest and most original form of human fantasy."[56] Schlegel's allusions to romantic poetry were obviously aimed at the *Roman,* the contemporary literary genre most capable of actuating the fusion of fundamental forms that the quasi-mythological arabesque-as-total-form demanded.

Schumann's Fantasie movement likewise aspires to a similar totalizing effect by bringing together a wide array of fundamental forms of a specifically musical kind: sonata allegro, lyric miniature, and *Lied* (by means of the Beethoven allusion). Even an element of variation form is present in the systematic elaborations of the *Im Legendenton* refrain. This tendency toward all-inclusiveness is the obverse of the negative quality inherent in the movement's formal disruptiveness and sentimental excess. Both, as we have seen, are referable to the *Arabeske* idea. Both are of equal importance in getting at the "New" in Schumann's Fantasie.

Leaden Arabesques in the Nuremberg Style

The probable sources for Schumann's "new forms" are traceable in two areas, literary and musical. On the literary side, which we will consider first, the main impulses were perhaps furnished by his beloved Jean Paul. "I've often asked myself," runs a May 1828 entry from Schumann's diary, "where I would be if I hadn't known Jean Paul; and yet he seems to be bound up with me on at least one side, for I sensed his presence earlier; perhaps without him I would still poetize as I do, but I wouldn't shun people, as is my wont, nor dream as much. I still can't imagine what would have become of me. It's a possibility that I simply can't fathom."[57] The young Schumann's elevation of a figure who must be counted among Germany's most eccentric writers (of contemporary novelists, only Günther Grass traces his roots to Jean Paul) to the status of idol has been rehearsed often enough in the literature. It need not be belabored here.[58] What should concern us, however, is an issue that has only begun to receive scholarly attention: the points of contact between Schumann's and Jean Paul's peculiar methods of presenting and organizing their materials—not so much the *what* of their works as the *how.*[59]

Given his own psychological makeup, Schumann was naturally drawn to the apparently unresolvable conflicts engendered by Jean Paul's refraction of ideally whole personae into contrasting entities: Albano and Schoppe in *Titan,* Siebenkäs and Leibgeber in *Siebenkäs,* Vult and Walt in *Flegeljahre.*[60] And irresolvable contrast can easily spin off into infinitely continuable narratives. This was the trait Schumann had in mind when he made his famous remark about Schubert's Ninth Symphony and its "heavenly length," which seemed "like a thick four-volume novel by Jean Paul, which also seems not to end and to be sure for the best of reasons—to allow the reader to recreate it afterwards."[61] But most telling is Schumann's sensitivity to the Jean Paulian excursus, to his "knotty clauses and parentheses."[62] Schumann is almost certainly referring to Jean Paul's fondness for the parabasis technique that Schlegel ironically described as manifesting itself in "leaden arabesques in the Nuremberg style."[63] Schumann must have had something similar in mind when he wrote to Clara on 11 February 1838: "I ask that you read some of Jean Paul, above all *Flegeljahre*; at first you will have to make your way through something of a bristly poetic thicket, but then what a celestial song you will hear."[64] Cutting through the "poetic thicket" is at once a bit of necessary and in part tedious labor, and at the same time an essential part of the Jean Paul enthusiast's experience.

It is tempting to conclude, therefore, that Schumann's own taste for the musical parabasis-arabesque, as exemplified in the first movement of the Fantasie, was stimulated by his contact with Jean Paul's prose works. The point gains support from a look, not only at Jean Paul's digressions per se, but at their relationship to the narratives they interrupt and the function they fulfill as parts of a larger whole.[65] In *Die unsichtbare Loge* the principal arabesque is relegated to an appendix that relates the tale of Auenthal's merry Dominie, Maria Wuz. Yet Jean Paul's endearing tale of a naïve schoolmaster is not so far removed from the rest of the book as its terminal position would seem to indicate; Maria Wuz aspires to the same utopian ideals as the so-called "Hohe Menschen" (Gustav, Ottomar, and Dr. Fenk) in the main narrative. *Siebenkäs* includes one of Jean Paul's most celebrated arabesques, the visionary commentary in the first churchyard scene on the nature of the Godhead, where an excursus on the perils of a godless universe peopled with shattered egos clearly reflects the relationship between Siebenküs and his sinister double, Leibgeber. As in *Die unsichtbare Loge,* Jean Paul consigns the main arabesque in *Titan* to to an appendix given over to "Des Luftschiffers Gianozzo Seebuch." As in the earlier novel, the protagonist of the appended tale is imaginatively counterpointed with figures in the main narrative. The balloonist Gianozzo is no less a dreamy character than Albano, the novel's hero, though he pays for his *Schwärmerei* by meeting a tragic end.

Flegeljahre, for Schumann "a book equal to the Bible in kind,"[66] brings virtuoso examples of the technique. In fact, the novel was originally planned as an arabesque for *Titan,* its counternarrative presenting the development of a nontitanic character. The arabesques in *Flegeljahre* themselves add up to another novel in its own right humorously entitled *Hoppelpoppel* ("scrambled-egg hash"). As the literary brainchild of the protagonist twins from the main narrative, Walt and Vult, it is tied to the text from which it digresses at practically every turn; Vult, for example, learns of Walt's love for Wina by reading *Hoppelpoppel.*

In all of his major works, then, Jean Paul employs the digressive arabesque not merely to confuse his readers but to enrich his narrative. The disjunction created by an embedded or appended tale is countered by Jean Paul's efforts to forge links between arabesque and interrupted narrative. This, in turn, is the same technique that we have seen Schumann employ. The *Im Legenden-ton,* although it appears to disrupt the course of the Fantasie's first movement, is cued into its surroundings by a network of subtle motivic links pointing both backward, to the sonata-allegro music, and forward to the *An die ferne Geliebte* allusion. While the strategy makes perfectly good musical sense, it lends to the Fantasie movement a novelizing tone on a par with Jean Paul's quirky discursive style.

Another aspect of Jean Paul's narrative technique also may have served as a model for Schumann's own: his use of the device known as *mise en abyme,* or internal textual mirroring.[67] The theatrical performance in *Titan,* for instance, is less a diverting episode than a microcosm of the entire novel. Broken off when the suicidal author-director Roquairol (a character from the main narrative playing himself) actually takes his own life, it transforms the fictitious death required in the play into a horrifying reality. The element of reflexivity is further heightened in *Flegeljahre*; at Vult's suggestion, the *Doppel-Roman, Hoppelpoppel,* was almost called "Flegeljahre" (!), and was conceived when the twins stayed at the "Wirtshaus zum Wirtshaus."[68] Like the novel as a whole, the twins' embedded narrative project displays a fanciful arabesque structure, with Walt fashioning the substance and Vult the satiric digressions (on talking during concerts and the whims of the aristocracy). Schumann's *Im Legendenton* likewise qualifies as a more purely musical instance of the *mise en abyme* technique, and not only because of its position as a nexus for motivic interconnections. Its rondo structure replicates, in closed form, the circular succession of form parts in the surrounding sonata allegro; and its episodes, the first a reminiscence, the second a prefiguration, hearken to the episodic structure that the *Im Legendenton* imposes on the movement as a whole. Though impossible to prove with absolute certainty, we might still draw the likely conclusion that Schumann's youthful immersion in the works of his literary double contributed to his own profound rethinking of musical form.

On the strictly musical side, Schumann's sources are too numerous to chart in toto. By way of measuring the Fantasie's dialectical coupling of "Then" and "Now," I will therefore focus on one element, the digressive interruption technique (parabasis-arabesque), and consider its precedents in the music of Schumann's immediate past—the music, that is, of the tradition whose "higher forms," according to Schumann, were in danger of perishing—and the music of his immediate present. For an image of the past, we will look to Beethoven (though less than a decade separated his death from Schumann's work on the Fantasie, he had no doubt attained the status of *classicus auctor*); the image of the present will be provided by Chopin, Schumann's sometime friend and sometime rival. The first movement of the Fantasie can be read as a dual tribute to both composers.

Already early in Schumann's career as a composer, some critics felt that his oftentimes obscure Romanticism was a result of his having taken Beethoven's late music as a point of departure. Ignaz Moscheles put forward this view in his account of the F#-Minor Sonata, Opus 11, where he placed Schumann among that group of composers who were particularly inspired by the "mystical feeling," the "yearning for clarity and light" that characterized Beethoven's late style.[69] Schumann himself was of a similar mind. In a letter of 14 June 1839 to Eduard Krüger, he indicated that his principal compositional forebears up to that point included "almost the whole of Bach, and Beethoven for the most part in his later works . . . even in my early years, I found lyric simplicity in itself insufficient. Therefore I soon turned alternately to Beethoven and Bach."[70]

Yet surprisingly enough, Schumann the critic had comparatively little to say about Beethoven's late-period music, perhaps because it encompassed works "for whose greatness no words can be found," and for which "verbal interpretation and explanation can only run aground."[71] What we do have are brief references to the technical difficulties of works like the *Missa solemnis,*[72] an occasional allusion to the all-too-few instances where a present-day composition (e.g., Mendelssohn's Piano Sonata, Opus 6) betrays the influence of one of Beethoven's late masterpieces,[73] and rapturous praise for the late piano sonatas (the *Hammerklavier* Sonata, Opus 106, is the "einzig-großen")[74] and string quartets. The quartets, in fact, seem to have impressed Schumann most deeply; hardly anything was more "worthy of wonder" than these creations, marked as they were by "a deeply-felt formative power, a flow of ideas that soars high above all human laws."[75] And as he put it in a review of 1842, the late quartets "still conceal treasures that are hardly known to the world, and which may require years to be uncovered."[76] But as regards the specific features that make these works so noteworthy Schumann is practically silent, save for a few passing remarks, such as the aside in the C-Major Symphony review to the effect that Schubert, conscious of his "more modest powers," avoided "the grotesque forms, the daring relationships" of late Beethoven.[77]

Still, these scattered and disappointingly incomplete references can be made to form a meaningful configuration. The fascination with late Beethoven in general dating from the early 1830s, the enthusiasm for the late quartets in particular, the passing allusion to "grotesque forms"—all of this may have some bearing on Schumann's reception of Beethoven in his C-Major Fantasie.[78] We can begin with Schumann's comment on Beethoven's "grotesque forms." Of which forms, in particular, was he thinking? The forms of Beethoven's late instrumental music, with the striking exception of works like the *Große Fuge,* Opus 130, hold by and large to the principles of organization of the classical canon, yet those principles are often placed in an oddly refracted light; one might say that the later Beethoven subjected them to a thoroughgoing transformation, that he intentionally questioned them at every turn. "Muß es sein," the motto of the Finale of the F-Major Quartet, Opus 135, is in a sense invisibly inscribed over the whole of Beethoven's music, where form becomes critique.[79] The outward result was often a deliberate misshapenness, a disequilibrium in proportion geared to set in relief the convention or procedure under scrutiny.

If Schumann viewed Beethoven's grotesquerie in something like these terms, then he probably would not have failed to take note of its manifestations in one of his favorite compositions, the E♭-Major String Quartet, Opus 127. Along with the C♯-Minor Quartet, Opus 131, it appeared to Schumann, "next to some of the choruses and original works of J. S. Bach, to represent the extreme limits that human art and imagination have yet reached."[80] Most significant, though, for our purposes is a moment in the quartet's finale that can be likened to the parabasis-arabesque and hence merits closer attention. At issue is Beethoven's handling of the point of recapitulation in a movement that up to that point has proceeded with almost predictable regularity. The development arrives at four bars prolonging E♭ as dominant of the subdominant (mm. 141–44) in preparation for a statement of the opening theme in A♭; in other words, a false recapitulation, stock-in-trade of the Haydnesque sonata form, seems under way. But to call the passage a false recapitulation is to minimize the formal disruptiveness of Beethoven's repetition of the thirty-two-measure opening paragraph in its entirety, especially since the "wrong" move to A♭ is followed by ten bars of mechanically sequential, almost perfunctory transitional material (mm. 177–86) intended to right it, and yet another complete statement of the opening group in the tonic (mm. 190ff.).[81] What are we to make of the lopsided bulge that the false return and ensuing transition create in the form? Given its length, the passage occasions more than the momentary touch of humor associated with a false return; it is as if Beethoven suddenly realized, far later than he should have, that his recapitulation was spinning along in the wrong key, and then, with uncustomary nonchalance, corrected himself by means of a series of simple sequences.

The effect of Beethoven's parabasis is a serious understatement of what was often (especially during his "heroic" phase) a major point of articulation in the classical sonata form: the spot where the opening thematic material recurs in the tonic. In the Opus 127 finale, the articulative power of a firmly marked reprise is withheld by means of an unusual split: neither the false return (mm. 145ff.) nor the tonally correct return (mm. 187ff.) is convincing in every sense. The first moment is prepared "correctly," with a root position dominant-seventh chord, but a dominant of the *subdominant*; the second brings the tonic, but a tonic weakly prepared by a dominant seventh in $\frac{4}{2}$ position. The split serves to emphasize a troublesome fact that a more traditional approach to the reprise would effectively cover: the symmetry and balance that ostensibly characterize the sonata style demand only the tonic recurrence of second-group material, music that has previously appeared outside the tonic; strictly speaking, there is no compellingly logical reason for a tonic return of the first group, a gesture that in fact disturbs the equilibrium that is supposedly at the heart of the Classical style. Beethoven's parabasis exposes this paradox. The Opus 127 finale asks: "Is the fully articulated return necessary?" "Muß es sein?"

Schumann's parabasis-arabesque, the *Im Legendenton* of the Fantasie's first movement, is likewise bound up with the initial phases of the sonata-allegro recapitulation, which Schumann himself emphatically described as "the place whose treatment will ever and always remain a mark of a hard-won mastery of form."[82] Schumann too calls the gesture of reprise into question, so that from this perspective, the "arbitrary" placement of the *Im Legendenton* within the form as a whole is perhaps not so arbitrary after all.

Yet just as important are the differences between the two composers' employment of the parabasis technique. Schumann's comes just after the kind of apotheotic statement (the opening theme in mm. 119ff.) that Beethoven clearly avoids, and is all the more startling because of it: the dreamy aside purposefully negates any sense of victorious arrival that the return at m. 119 might have promised. Then too, the *Im Legendenton* fills the sonic void created by the total cessation of motion after the fermata on G_2 in m. 128, and does so with music of a widely different character from that which comes before; its meter, tempo, and phrase syntax make for maximal contrast with the surrounding sonata allegro. In Beethoven's movement, however, there is no temporal or thematic disjunction; the music continues undisturbed on its relatively easygoing course. To put it forcefully: These are the differences that separate "Then" from "Now." Even though the two works are removed in time by no more than fifteen years, they emanate from widely separated realms whose incommensurability is highlighted by the very similarities in formal strategy that we have noted. Beethoven's subtly ironic moves, his gesturally split reprise, reappear in Schumann's Fantasie movement as a fissure, a cleft filled by a parabasis-arabesque that threatens to break the form in two.

Schumann's handling of the arabesque strategy is arguably more radical than Chopin's recourse to similar devices in his first two Ballades, Opus 23 and Opus 38 respectively, works that may have occupied Schumann's thoughts while he was at work on the Fantasie. Interestingly enough, the two composers came together for a memorable meeting in Leipzig during the second week of September 1836, just a week after Schumann had recorded in his diary: "Idee zu Beitrag f. Beethoven."[83] It is possible, then, that this powerful configuration of musical personalities—Beethoven and Chopin—exercised a direct influence on Schumann's thinking during the earlier stages of the Fantasie's conception.[84] Indeed, Schumann's fall 1836 encounter with Chopin appears to have been the catalyst for a bit of *Schwärmerei* equal in intensity only to that of the summer of 1831, the period that saw the production of the famous review of Chopin's Variations on "Là ci darem la mano,"

Opus 2.[85] In a diary entry for 12 September 1836, Schumann dreamily recorded the impressions Chopin had made at Henriette Voigt's musicale: "Chopin early . . . I enjoyed the Ballade most [Chopin also played some of his etudes, mazurkas, and nocturnes]. It's very dear to me, very dear to me. . . . Bring him my Sonata [Op. 11? Op. 14?] and Etudes in return for his Ballade."[86] His report of two days later to Heinrich Dorn was more prosaic, if no less enthusiastic: "Chopin. What a joy! We spent a fine day together, which I was still celebrating yesterday. . . . I have his new Ballade, which I take to be his most ingenious if not [most] brilliant work; I even told him that it was my favorite of all his compositions. After a long and thoughtful pause, he said emphatically, 'I like it too, it's also my favorite.' Moreover, he played me a great quantity of new etudes, nocturnes, mazurkas—all incomparable."[87]

The Ballade that occasioned these outbursts of praise was undoubtedly the Second, Opus 38, a work eventually dedicated to Schumann, who wrote to Dorn of a "new Ballade," thus implying familiarity with the earlier Ballade in G Minor, Opus 23 (composed 1831–35, published 1836). This identification is further borne out by Schumann's comments on Opus 38—along with the Opus 37 Nocturnes and Opus 42 Waltz, which likewise offered up an "abundance of new forms"—in a review of 1841 that is rich in implications for our purposes: "We should yet mention the Ballade as a thoroughly noteworthy work. Chopin has already written one similarly titled composition, one of his wildest and most original works; the new one is different, ranking below the first as an artwork, but no less fantastic and spirited. The passionate episodes [*Zwischensätze*] seem to me to have been added later. I remember well that when Chopin played the Ballade here, it ended in F major; now it closes in A minor."[88]

Although the rapturous tone of the 1836 account is absent (Opus 38 now ranks below Opus 23 as an artwork), Schumann tells us something very important about the Second Ballade, and indirectly about the First. Opus 38 is cast in one of Chopin's "new forms," and presumably Opus 23—a work of equal if not greater originality, fantasy, and spirit—is as well. As Schumann indicates in the 1841 review, the "new form" in Opus 38 manifests itself partially in Chopin's recourse to the parabasis-arabesque in those "passionate episodes" that sound at first like afterthoughts, and he could not have failed to notice similar constructive devices in Opus 23.[89]

Figure 2–2 presents a schematic diagram of the form of the G-Minor Ballade, a form that it as easy to describe as it is difficult to subsume under any of the canonical types: a thematic complex made up of two ideas, a languorous waltz and a Bellinian *cantabile,* is stated twice, first in g/Eb, then a/A; following on a brief excursus (section C), the tonal elements of the first complex are repeated in reverse order (Eb/g), the whole being rounded off with a virtuoso coda.[90] The design therefore combines strophic organization (apparent in the varied restatement of the opening $A^1 B^1$ complex) with an overriding palindromic form, as clarified in Figure 2–2. At the same time, the

FIGURE 2–2
Chopin, Ballade in G minor, Opus 23, Formal Plan

	Part 1		*Part 2*			*Part 3*		
Motive:	Intro. + *A1*	B^1	A^2	B^2	C	B^3	A^3	Coda
Topos:	waltz	*cantabile*	waltz	*cantabile*	*moto perpetuo*	*cantabile*	waltz	
Key:	g	E♭	a	A	E♭	E♭	g	g
m.:	1	68	94	106	138	166	194	208

symmetry of the palindrome is countered by an unmistakable arabesque element: the motion to the climax at B^3 is arrested by the appearance of section C, acting like a kind of parenthesis.[91] Marked *scherzando,* section C is a *moto perpetuo* waltz providing maximal contrast with the more serious tone of the music around it, to which it is tied gesturally (through the waltz bass), tonally (by sharing E♭ with the succeeding B^3 climax), and motivically (cf. m. 138, right hand, in the *scherzando,* and mm. 3, 8–9, 82ff.). The structural similarities with Schumann's *Im Legendenton* should be obvious, though we would go too far in making a claim for direct modeling.

As for the Opus 38 Ballade, it actually features two parentheses (see Fig. 2–3, sections B^1 and B^2); both of them were probably present in some form as the "passionate episodes" Schumann heard in 1836. These are ostensibly the *presto con fuoco* B sections that intrude on the calm unfolding of the *siciliano* music (A^1, A^2) with which they alternate. But as the piece proceeds, it becomes clear that Chopin aims to reverse the functional relationship originally implied between sections A^1 and B^1: although the violent *presto con fuoco* material is initially perceived as parabasis-arabesque (this in spite of a fleeting allusion to the *siciliano* rhythm in mm. 63ff.), it gradually assumes the role of principal discourse. The reversal is already signaled in A^2, during which the *siciliano* twice works its way up sequentially to perorations of a magnitude more befitting the character of the *presto* (see mm. 108–15, 133–40). Section B^2 thus follows from A^2 not as interruption but as

FIGURE 2–3
Chopin, Ballade Opus 38, Formal Plan

Section:	A^1	B^1	A^2	B^2	Coda
Topos:	*siciliano*	*presto* episode	*siciliano*	*presto* episode	
Tonality:	a→g→V/A♭	F→climaxes on B♭/d	d, a	a	a
m.:	1	47	83	141	169

continuation. *Beiwerk* is transformed into *Hauptwerk,* and the transformation is all the more emphatic in the *agitato* coda, where all that remains of A^1 is a brief terminal reminiscence, and where the shift of thematic primacy from *A* to *B* is matched by a tonal shift from F to A minor.[92] While Schumann did not hear this ending in the autumn of 1836, it is likely that he did hear the piece in some form up through section B^2 (his 1841 review suggests that the "passionate episodes" were integral components of the piece in both versions; only the tonal goal was altered)—up through the point, that is, where *Beiwerk* becomes *Hauptwerk* with greater force than in the opening movement of the C-Major Fantasie.[93] Again, we cannot make a case for modeling: the exact state of Chopin's Opus 38 Ballade in September 1836, no less than Schumann's Opus 17 Fantasie in December 1836, remains a matter of conjecture. All the same, the elective affinities between the works in their final forms are unmistakable.

The same is likewise true of all the possible precedents, musical and literary, for Schumann's "new forms" that we have considered. The musical parabasis, a striking aspect of Schumann's formal strategy perhaps inspired by his youthful absorption of the works of Jean Paul, served as one possible solution to a nagging problem: how to cultivate"higher forms" in the wake of the daunting and troubling example of middle- and late-period Beethoven. By means of his employment of the parabasis-arabesque technique in the first movement of the Fantasie, Schumann was able to engage the "Now" (as represented by the *Im Legendenton*) and the "Then" (by means of the sonata-allegro design of the surrounding music) in a powerful dialectic that is largely absent in the Chopin Ballades that he prized most highly, and in which any references to the "higher forms" are at best oblique.[94] Schumann's notion of "new forms" was the more radical because it entailed preserving the past by writing its demise into the very fabric of the music.

Ruins

Up to this point, we have treated the first movement of Schumann's Fantasie as if it were an independent work. It remains to be seen, then, what kind of totality the Fantasie makes as a multimovement work, and how the dialectic between "Then" and "Now" played out in the first-movement *Arabeske* is realized at this larger level. The background for these questions may be filled in by turning to Schumann's prose writings, where we can readily perceive a complementary dialectic between a "sonata idea" and a "fantasy idea." In 1835, the year before he set to work on the "Sonate für Beethoven" that would become a "Große Phantasie," Schumann was inclined to differentiate between two distinct genres: "We are accustomed to prejudge works according to the names they bear; we make certain claims of a 'Phantasie,' others of a 'Sonata.'"[95] And although by 1839 he was making light of the distinction—

"Sonaten oder Phantasien (was liegt am Namen!)"[96]—Schumann's comment on the capriccio (a "fantasy" genre) in Herloßsohn's *Damen Conversations Lexikon* (1834–38) indicates that he held to it during the years that saw the creation of his own Sonate/Phantasie: "Strict symmetry is of course not so necessary in this genre [the capriccio] as in the great, noble genres like the sonata, etc."[97] The sonata remained for Schumann a "higher genre," a "cultivated, noble form," even if it threatened to become an endangered species in the hands of some younger composers who had reduced it to the level of a mere "specimen" or "formal study."[98]

Did Schumann the pianist-composer of the middle to late 1830s thus intend to rejuvenate the nearly moribund sonata through a fantasy idea that he never clearly defined? Or can we detect elements of the fantasy idea in his account of new methods of large-scale organization in an 1835 review of Carl Loewe's piano sonatas Opp. 33 and 41? "In my opinion," Schumann wrote, "it is the intention of sonata, concerto, and symphony composers to bring together three parts as a whole." The older generation of composers accomplished this goal through "external shape and tonality," while with younger artists the situation was somewhat different. "They were not content merely to work out an idea in a single movement, but also to conceal it in various modified forms in the other movements as well. In short, they wanted to bring in an element of historical interest . . . and since the entire age developed poetically, of dramatic interest too. Recently composers are relating movements more and more to one another, and binding them together through brief transitions." In Loewe's *Sonate brillante,* Opus 41, these "connective threads" tend more toward the "visible and perceptible," and in his *Sonate élégique,* Opus 33, toward the "spiritual."[99] Schumann's pronouncements can be reduced to a dual dialectic: the first between the "strict, symmetrical" sonata and the more freely conceived fantasy; the second between notions of a palpable as opposed to a "spiritual" totality. Let us see how these complementary conflicts are played out in the C-Major Fantasie.

We may begin by looking after the connective threads that knit the work into some kind of whole. To be sure, links between and among movements are not difficult to find. Both the second and third movements (see Fig. 2–4), for instance, restate portions of the tonal argument of the first. The E♭ that figures prominently in the first movement (as part of the first group's C/E♭ pairing in both exposition and recapitulation, and the second group's C/E♭ in the recapitulation) recurs as the main tonality of the second movement. F major functions as tonal goal in the expositions of both first movement and finale, although the route by which it is reached differs in each case: in the first movement, F results from the disposition of two minor-third pairings (C/E♭ and d/F) a step apart; in the last movement, it is established through the unfolding of a descending third chain (C–A♭–F). The first-movement third pairs are, however, echoed in the second group of the last movement, where the same motive repeats sequentially at the distance of a minor third; only in

FIGURE 2–4
A. Schumann, Opus 17/ii, Formal Plan

Major Divisions		Description		Tonality
	Part 1			
m.1		A (*aba*)	March	E$^{\flat}$
22		B	imitative/sequential	→g,c,V/E$^{\flat}$
92		A' (*a'ba''*)	March	E$^{\flat}$
	Part 2			
114		C	metric displacement	A$^{\flat}$
131		D	on B	→V/A$^{\flat}$
141		C1	variation	→V/A$^{\flat}$
	Part 3 (?)			
157		B'	imitative/sequential	→f,b$^{\flat}$,V/E$^{\flat}$
193		A (aba)	March	
214		B''	on B + Coda	

B. Schumann, Opus 17/iii, Formal Plan

Form Part		Description		Tonality
	Quasi-Exposition:			
m.1		First group	A + B (chorale +	C
30			continuation)	A$^{\flat}$/F
33		Second group	C	
68		Closing	D	F
	Quasi-return:			
72		First-group fragment	B	F
87		Second group	C	D$^{\flat}$/B$^{\flat}$,C
119		Closing	D	C
122	**Coda**		on A + C	C

the last movement, ascending gives way to descending motion (the A$^{\flat}$/F of the quasi-exposition recurs as D$^{\flat}$/B$^{\flat}$ in the quasi-return). In addition, all three movements share similar large-scale formal preoccupations.

Linda Roesner has noted that the first and last movements both exhibit "parallel" structures;[100] but the second movement also deserves mention, just as "parallelism" is better replaced by the idea of circularity. The second movement, a scherzo substitute in a sense, traces a tripartite march–trio–march form in which are embedded yet further three-part constructs: in Part 1 (see Fig. 2–4a) the march proper (section *A*, an *aba* form unto itself) alternates with a contrasting middle section (*B*) built around imitative parries on a dotted motive implied already at the end of the march (mm. 18ff.); the "trio," Part 2, is also tripartite, its opening section (*C*), like the opening of Part 1, a self-contained *aba'* unit, and its central section (*D*), a variant of the preceding with asides on the dotted motive from Part 1. But the "trio" is not so nicely rounded off; instead it passes without a break into music from Part 1 (*B'*). We do not experience this moment as a clearly articulated return (hence the question mark in my diagram), for Schumann begins not with the march theme but with material from the imitative/sequential central section of Part 1 (cf. mm. 157 and 54). The form, in other words, spirals back on itself, and as if to firm the point, does so yet again. The movement might well have ended on the downbeat of m. 214, with the last statement of the march (*A*), but instead proceeds with the opening portion of *B*. The spiral is broken only with the strong E♭ cadence at mm. 231–32 and the subsequent virtuoso coda.

The third movement is similarly shaped. Here too we arrive at a spot just after the completion of a major structural division (the quasi-exposition, mm. 1–71) where the form doubles back into the middle of a previous section: the music of mm. 72ff. recalls, at the lower fifth, the second component of the opening theme group. The point at which the doubling back occurs is functionally ambiguous, and purposefully so. At once a melodic digression from what precedes it, a tonal continuation of the same (F major is both the tonal goal of the quasi-exposition and the point of departure for the quasi-return), and a reprise of the improvisational opening idea, it lends to the music a sense of infinite progress. And as in the second movement, the spiral winds down only in the coda, a by turns dreamy and passionate reflection on the arpeggios from the first group and the main melodic idea of the second. Circles, spirals, the infinitely continuable that is brought to a halt at the last moment—all of these qualities figure in the sonata-allegro design of the first movement too.

Tonal and formal connections are therefore undeniably present among the movements of the Fantasie. Nevertheless, they are largely abstract, decidedly less palpable than the kinds of ties that would lend the work a measure of teleology or "historical interest," to borrow Schumann's phrase, and thereby transform its three parts into a unified whole. Conspicuously absent in the Fantasie are the obvious motivic links among movements that characterize the sonatas Opus 11 and Opus 14.[101] Indeed, Schumann has gone out of his way to eschew links of this order. As is well known, the earlier version of the last movement of the Fantasie transmitted in the *Stichvorlage* for the 1839 printing closed with an almost literal restatement of the last fifteen measures of the first movement.[102] In the end, Schumann must have decided that recalling the Beethoven allusion would have created too definitive a gesture of closure;[103] better to leave the listener with the impression that there is "more to come," to allow the musical "reader" the opportunity of finishing off the story after his or her own fashion.[104] Given its recurrent tonal and formal arguments, the Fantasie may be viewed as a totality of sorts, but a curiously incomplete one at that.

Nor does the affective sequence of movements—impassioned but fractured sonata allegro, march, evocative-rhapsodic *cantabile*—neatly add up to a harmonious whole. Schumann's progeny are only slightly better behaved than those that Chopin yoked together and (as Schumann tells it in his often-cited review) somewhat presumptuously called a sonata.[105] Schumann's comments on Chopin's B♭-Minor Sonata, Opus 35, can be read as a projection of views that he held about his own earlier endeavors to revitalize the "higher" forms. Particularly in the Fantasie, Schumann seems to register his dissatisfaction both with the wholeness of the older sonata idea (especially its prescribed movement sequence and outwardly imposed formal symmetries) and the wholeness of a newer fantasy idea that strives for totalizing effects through motivic interconnections. The totality of the Fantasie (like that of Chopin's Opus 35) cannot be completely subsumed under either. It is not the totality of the beautifully shaped whole that the Fantasie exemplifies, but rather the fullness (Schlegel called it "unendliche Fülle") of the *Arabeske*.

The Fantasie as a whole, then, is a musical critique of the very idea of unity, both as it manifested itself in the instrumental music of the classical tradition and as it *might* manifest itself in the synthesizing totality that served as the basis for many a romantic pipe dream. Schumann's words are worth repeating again in this context: "In my opinion, it is the intention of sonata, concerto, and symphony composers to bring together three parts as a whole." The Fantasie is a powerful reminder that, in light of the historical situation of the "higher forms" in the 1830s, such grand attempts at synthesis were questionable endeavors. The strong composer, like Schumann, asserts the impossibility in his musical works themselves. The first movement of the Fantasie, for instance, plays on the contrast between sonata and character piece, the two genres that also represent the poles around which Schumann's early creative efforts clustered. In spite of the subtle tonal and thematic ties that bring the *Im Legendenton* in touch with its surroundings, its unusual placement within the framing sonata-allegro design asserts the irreconcilability of "higher" and "fundamental" genres. And both elements—motivic connectedness and formal juxtaposition—are necessary to make the point. The three movements of the Fantasie share a number of concerns, but in the final analysis they remain three obstreperously distinct children, perhaps not as wild as those of Chopin's Opus 35, but every bit as independent.

I have reserved for last a consideration of the issue in which all these interrelated conflicts—between sonata idea and fantasy idea, palpable and "spiritual" links, harmonious totality and arabesque fullness—are reflected: the peculiar history of the name of the work. Few compositions have been titled as variously as Schumann's Fantasie:

1. *Sonate für Beethoven* (December 1836, *TB* 2, p. 30; October 1837, *TB* 2, p. 42)
2. *Ruinen. Trophaeen. Palmen. Große Sonate f. d. Pianof. für Beethovens Denkmal. Obolum auf Beethovens Denkmal* (19 December 1836, Erler, *Schumann's Leben,* vol.1, p. 101)
3. *Ruinen. Trophäen* [a shortened reference to item 2] (31 January 1837, *Briefe und Gedichte aus dem Album Robert und Clara Schumann,* p. 262)
4. *Phantasieen f. Pfte. / Phantasieen / Phantasien* (4 February 1838, Erler, *Schumann's Leben,* vol. 1, p. 139; 13 February 1838, announcement in *NZfM* 8 [1838]: 52; 20 March 1838, *TB* 2, p. 52)
5. *Phantasie in drei Sätzen* (19 March 1838, *BrKG* 1, p. 126)
6. *Dichtungen* (31 March 1838, *TB* 2, p. 476)
7. *Phantasien: Ruine, Siegesbogen u. Sternbild, Dichtungen* (13 April 1838; *BrKG* 1, p. 145)
8. *Ruines: Fantasie pour le Pianoforte,* Op. 16a (post-July 1838, Erler, *Schumann's Leben,* vol. 1, p. 101)
9. *Dichtungen: Ruinen, Siegesbogen, Sternbild,* Op. 16 (crossed out in National Széchenyi Library, Budapest, Ms. Mus. 37, dated 19 December 1838)
10. *Fantasie,* Op. 17 (Budapest Ms, as cited above)
11. *Phantasie* (20 December 1838, *TB* 2,pp. 475–76; 26 January 1839, *BrKG* 2, p. 369; 22 April 1839, *BrKG* 2, p. 495; 28 May 1839, Erler, *Schumann's Leben,* vol. 1, p. 203; 9 June 1839, *BrKG* 2, p. 562)
12. *Große Phantasie* (15 March 1839, Erler, *Schumann's Leben,* vol. 1, pp. 193–99)

The shift from "Sonate" to "Phantasie" (which in turn alternated with "Dichtungen") came sometime between October 1837 and February 1838, and perhaps indicates a shift from sonata to fantasy idea. At about the same time, we see Schumann undecided over whether he had composed a single "Phantasie," or a set of three "Phantasieen" or "Dichtungen." Yet one term survived the switch from sonata to fantasy, remaining constant as Schumann juggled with overall titles and movement titles like "Dichtungen," "Siegesbogen," and "Sternbild": indeed, "Ruine" or "Ruinen" may have been linked with the work just up to the completion of the final version. Its frequency of occurrence confirms the notion that Schumann was commemorating the death of Beethovenian classicism, or more properly attempting to redeem it through the "ruin," which is after all a synonym for the dialectical image we considered at the beginning of this chapter: the monument.

3 ✦

Schumann's Systems of Musical Fragments and *Witz*

> Dear Robert, I beg of you—
> finally bring something to completion.
>
> > – Robert Schumann
> > Diary entry for 19 June 1831

Schumann and the Incomprehensibility Topos

The central *etwas langsamer* section of "In der Nacht," the fifth of Schumann's Opus 12 *Phantasiestücke,* brings a series of measures that must be counted among the strangest in the composer's output. In the first (see Ex. 3.1), the F-major tonic harmony is embellished by $G^\sharp$, a lower appoggiatura to the third degree; similarly, $C^\sharp$ is introduced in the following measure as appoggiatura to the root of the submediant harmony. While none of this is out of the ordinary, the third measure presents a harmonic configuration that clearly *is,* for here, as the harmony describes dominant-tonic motion in the supertonic region, the $C^\sharp$ of the previous bar is simply retained, rubbing ungratefully against the $C\natural$ in the melody. And it remains lodged in the tex-

EXAMPLE 3.1
Schumann, *Phantasiestücke,* Opus 12, "In Der Nacht," mm. 69–76   (Reprinted by permission. Copyright © 1978 Henle Verlag.)

ture, like an obsessively repeated wrong note, for yet another two measures, coloring the V/ii harmony in the fourth bar just as its enrichment of the subdominant harmony in the fifth helps mask the caesura between the two opening four-bar phrases. Only in the sixth bar does C♯ resolve upward to D, though harmonic complications return in the next measure with F♯ working against G in the melody and F in the bass, thus functioning much as C♯ had in the first phrase.

We might well imagine that passages of this sort elicited the reproach of incomprehensibility that runs like a nagging leitmotif through the earlier critical accounts of Schumann's works. For Carl Koßmaly, writing in 1844, much the whole of Schumann's output during the 1830s, given the composer's persistent striving for originality of expression, was marred by moments of "completely unpleasant bizzarrerie," "excess," and "confusion" (*Verworrenheit*), the latter surfacing more often than any other term of censure.[1] Even an advocate like Franz Brendel had to admit that Schumann's ultrasubjectivity frequently led to downright "turbid patches" and "muddled spots," especially in the early piano music.[2] Performers too were puzzled; some, like the young Clara Wieck, were actually members of Schumann's private circle. As late as 1838, after almost a decade of contact with Schumann and his music, Clara saw fit to praise the G-Minor Piano Sonata, Opus 22, precisely because it *wasn't* "so very incomprehensible."[3] And Schumann himself acknowledged, at about the same time, that yes, "many of my compositions are so difficult to understand, because they draw on such disparate interests."[4] Although the last two quotes address varying issues—inherent musical complexities and quasi-programmatic references, respectively—both attest to the enigmatic essence of Schumann's music.

Apparently much of the puzzlement was elicited in particular by the early collections of miniatures, among them the *Papillons,* Opus 2 (witness Schumann's friend Christoph Sörgel, writing in May of 1832: "We still don't understand it"),[5] the *Davidsbündlertänze,* Opus 6 (on which Louis Spohr decided to withhold judgment until having heard the composer's own rendition),[6] *Carnaval,* Opus 9 (a failure with audiences into the 1850s in spite of Liszt's efforts),[7] *Kreisleriana,* Opus 16 (which Liszt shied away from programming because the public might find it "too difficult to digest"),[8] and the *Nachtstücke,* Opus 23 (whose fanciful succession of pieces amounted to little more, for Koßmaly, than "fortuitous caprice").[9] Of course, Schumann will not have been the first composer whose achievements were little appreciated or understood. The music of Beethoven's last period comes to mind as a repertory more "deserving" of its early, and bewildered reception, while Schumann's musical language, at least on the surface, strikes us as relatively tame and well behaved. Idiosyncratic harmonic gestures, like those in the *Phantasiestücke,* are admittedly few; only the close of the *alternativo* to No. 5 of the Opus 4 Intermezzi offers a roughly comparable example. Why then were Schumann's miniatures greeted with such perplexity? Was the charge of incomprehensibility a mere quirk of reception history, or did it touch on an element that attaches to the aesthetic substance of the works?

A review of the pertinent documents reveals that incomprehension was in large part a function of Schumann's approach to the miniature form itself; his designs were not just limited in scope, they were perceived as being oddly incomplete. For the *Allgemeine musikalischer Zeitschrift*'s anonymous reviewer of Opera 1, 2, 3, and 5, the "jean-paulisierende" *Papillons* lacked a printed text, an explanatory program that alone would provide a definite meaning for the listener.[10] A decade later, Brendel would argue that an unspoken but decipherable "poetic thought" actually served as the "connective thread" for the *Papillons,* an equivalent of the purely musical modes of coherence in earlier repertories.[11] Many astute commentators, however, were troubled by the unfinished quality of the musical material itself. The *Davidsbündlertänze,* in Koßmaly's estimation, were "dashed off more in the manner of sketches than of fully elaborated character pieces";[12] Gottfried Weber's telling description of *Papillons* as "Gedankenspänen," literally "thought splinters," strikes a similar chord.[13] In 1839 we find Clara making a special request for a "completely coherent [*zusammenhängendes*] composition" that is neither too long nor too short.[14]

The quandary is aptly represented by the sixth through eighth pieces of *Carnaval,* where a continual play with beginnings and endings makes it virtually impossible for the listener without access to a score to locate the divisions between the three miniatures. The first ("Florestan") begins in G minor (obliquely suggested through *sforzando* diminished-seventh chords on F$^\sharp$), though it veers regularly to B♭. But in its last bars it swings back to the diminished harmony that set off the spiraling alternation between a tentative G minor and a more firmly established B♭ in the first place. Resolution for the cliff-hanging dissonance at the end of "Florestan" comes with the opening three measures of the following piece ("Coquette"), a *closing* gesture in B♭ (see Ex. 3.2). The recurrence of the same figure throughout the diminutive "Replique" thus creates the impression that the last piece in the triptych is a continuation and completion of its predecessor. But surprisingly enough, the ending of "Replique" is curiously skewed in terms of the tonal expectations set up in "Florestan" and "Coquette," for the previous emphasis on B♭ gives way, in a final and unexpected twist, to G minor. Thus, it is equally misleading to speak of either one piece or three. Considering the incompleteness of each item in the grouping, the long-range motion toward and abruptly away from B♭, and the lack of overall melodic rounding, we are more justified in thinking of an entity fragmented as a whole *and* in its parts.[15]

Indeed, I intend to explore here the implications of the assertion that Schumann's collections of miniatures were met with charges of incomprehensibility largely because of their fragmented form. For what was originally meant as a reproach, and might signal for us an imperfect mode of perception, can be turned to positive ends. Incomprehensibility is, after all, the flip side of delphic prophecy. Schumann's pieces may be said to pose an enigma, though not of a specifically hermeneutic sort, for the puzzle resides not in the Clara themes, anagrams, and Jean-Paulian allusions, but rather in the discontinuous mode of utterance itself. The notion of the fragment, like the incomprehensibility topos, is also tinged with pejorative connotations. Schumann's own aphoristic imperative—"Don't underestimate the worth of little pieces"[16]—was seemingly contravened by a string of exhortations directed at younger composers (including Joseph Kessler, Stephen Heller, Frédéric Chopin, and Robert Franz), whose success in the small forms threatened to keep them from fashioning works of larger dimensions.[17] Yet this ambivalence can be easily accounted for as a veiled self-critique: commentators such as Ludwig Rellstab had, in their turn, found "nur Aphoristisches" in much of Schumann's music, a charge that certainly rankled the young composer.[18]

EXAMPLE 3.2
Schumann, *Carnaval,* "Coquette," mm. 1–3

Reference to fragments, in other words, need not call up a negative value judgment, nor any value judgment at all for that matter.[19] Music criticism need only accept the simple fact that the fragment, as constructive mode and artistic phenomenon, was fundamental to the whole Romantic worldview. The radically broken lives of so many of the early Romantics—Novalis, Hölderlin, Kleist, Byron, Keats, Shelley—found poetic expression in the broken lives of their fictional characters (Goethe's Werther, Byron's Manfred) and in the all-pervasive imagery of the ruin in their lyrics (e.g., Novalis's "Aus Kloster in Ruinen," or Wordsworth's "Tintern Abbey"). For Friedrich Schlegel, in a re-markable series of statements prefiguring more recent thought, the fragment was simply a given of modern experience, a manner of shaping and perceiving that affected literary prose (novellas = fragmentary novels),[20] poetry (lyric poems = "Romantic fragments"),[21] philosophy (the whole of ancient philosophy = a fragment of a larger project),[22] contemporary thinkers (witness Lessing's fragmentary genius),[23] scholarship (biography = a historical fragment),[24] journalism (the essay = an "intentional" fragment),[25] politics (the French Revolution = an epoch-defining fragment),[26] and even geography (Germany = an amalgam of territorial fragments).[27] The central insight here translates for the calculating artist into a clearsighted realization that the fragment cannot be overcome, though it must be confronted, creatively deployed: "Fantastic poetry, sentimental poetry . . . can only be presented in fragmentary form; romantic fragment-form."[28] This was no less the case for Schumann the crafter of enigmatic miniatures than it was for Schlegel the unsystematic system-builder or Hoffmann the teller of fractured tales.

Attempts to neutralize the "incomprehensible" moments in Schumann's miniatures by way of analytical sophistry will therefore miss the point. If our sketchy account of this repertory's reception carries a lesson, it takes the form of an admonition for criticism to confront elements of radicality, even madness, head-on as constitutive aesthetic qualities of Schumann's oeuvre.[29] And if, as we have seen, the radicality in Schumann's approach to the classical forms emerges in his penchant for the interrupted utterance, then in the collections of miniature it is a function of the continual abrogation of a series of utterances. Our task is not to reconfigure fragment clusters as discrete wholes, but to investigate the principles that differentiate, for example, the *Davidsbündlertänze* or *Kreisleriana* from discrete wholes on the one hand and chaotic jumbles on the other. Some preliminary but important work along these lines has already been undertaken. Patrick McCreless's account of the Eichendorff *Liederkreis,* Opus 39; Jonathan Dunsby's application of a provisional "multi-piece" theory to Brahms's Opus 116 Fantasien; Peter Kaminsky's recent studies of modes of coherence in Schumann's miniature collections—all of these address the problem of dealing with a musical form/genre type for which there is no accepted theoretical grammar, no morphology.[30] I will proceed from the assumption that the "heterogeneous totality" (as exemplified by Schumann's miniatures), unlike the "harmonious unity," in fact allows for neither morphology nor grammar. We can, however, at least propose a typology for a particular body of musical fragments, and map out the categories that animate it as a "system" of sorts.

The "system of fragments" was one of Friedrich Schlegel's favorite conceits (like so many of them, an oxymoron); and it is from him, with some assistance from Jean Paul, E. T. A. Hoffmann, Novalis, and Schumann himself, that I take my primary cue. Implicit in Schlegel's outlook on the fragment is a sense for the multivalence of the total forms that fragment clusters may create. To cite a particularly clear example: the memoir or "confession" as "fragment system" may be built up from a series of epistolary exchanges, each of which projects the dialogue (a chain or "garland" of fragments) onto a larger scale.[31] If the motion from dialogue, to letters, and finally to memoir constitutes the processive form of a given fragment system, then the operations of *Witz,* the faculty that allows the creative mind to fashion subtle interrelationships and the imaginative beholder to perceive them, ensure the system's inner coherence: "the system of chemical fragments," as Schlegel put it, "is at once an apotheosis of *Witz.*"[32]

Whether or not Schumann directly knew of Schlegel's theory of the fragment is difficult to ascertain; a stronger case could probably be made for his acquaintance with the aesthetics of Novalis, Hoffmann, and of course Jean Paul.[33] At the same time, it is hardly necessary to document an absolute connection, inasmuch as Schumann's "translation" of a poetic theory into musical terms is not at issue. Schlegel has the advantage of supplying us with a readymade theory of the fragment that is both free of value judgments and topically neutral. It neither embraces nor rejects the fragment form, which might surface in politics (or music) as distinctively as in literature. Schlegel aims instead to describe the phenomenon as the confluence of a multivalent form and a "witty" content. In that the Schlegelian "system of fragments" is, in short, a fundamentally critical concept, it offers us with a useful framework for examining Schumann's specifically musical embodiment of the same principle.

Schumann and the System of Musical Fragments: Precedents and Typology

Schumann was surrounded by fragments, or more exactly, he had highly developed ears and eyes for picking them out of his cultural environment. From Chopin and Carl Maria von Weber he learned that the virtuoso variation set and the potpourri of dances, contemporary genres whose aesthetic worth was in inverse proportion to the degree of their cultivation, could be artistically enlivened through a judicious application of the fragment principle. It is probably no accident that Schumann's favorite among Chopin's Opus 2 "Là ci darem la mano" Variations was the fifth,[34] an *adagio minore* in which the syntax of Mozart's symmetrically recast tune is significantly altered. The original four phrases of the melody are answered by three in the variation, and only the second of these makes clear reference to the original theme. In addition, closure in B♭ minor (the local tonic) is replaced by motion to a dominant pedal. But by casting his *minore* as a variation-fragment, Chopin binds it more intimately to the bravura finale that ensues; what would have been a mere link in a static variation chain is transformed into a dynamic introduction to the closing *alla polacca*. In Weber's *Aufforderung zum Tanz,* the fragment acts as a signal that what began as a waltz medley will conclude with weightier formal pretensions. Following on the third dance (in F minor) and a brief transition come motivically elaborated references to the first. Our sense that a kind of sonata form is under way increases with the reprise of the opening waltz, terminally expanded, in the tonic D♭. And finally, fragmentary allusions to the introductory gestures convert the would-be sonata allegro into an arch form. Neither Chopin's nor Weber's example was lost on the Schumann of the 1830s,[35] who drew on a whole arsenal of devices directed at transforming variation chain and dance medley into high art by means of the fragment form.

On the literary side, Schumann's fascination with the fragment is equally in evidence—witness the numerous diary notes on Novalis and Hoffmann, and the actual form of the entries themselves. In the *Hottentottiana* (diary entries from May 1828 to June 1830), in essence a series of autobiographical musings cum aphoristic treatise on musical poetics, Schumann displayed his penchant for a literary genre whose chief early-Romantic representatives include Novalis's *Logologische Fragmente* (1798) and Friedrich Schlegel's *Ideen* (1800). And his "Grobes und Feines," a collection of twelve aphorisms published in the first volume of the *Neue Zeitschrift* (1834) culminates in "Das Aphoristische," a panegyric to an undervalued form:

> Why, lofty philistines, do you so grandly turn up your noses at the aphoristic? By God, is the world flat? Doesn't it have mountain pastures, streams, and people of all kinds? And is life a system? Isn't it patched together from single and half-torn leaves scrawled over with childish ideas, overturned tombstone inscriptions, and the white centaury herbs of destiny? I maintain the latter. To be sure, it might not be without interest to sketch out the very image of life in art, just as Platner and Jacobi have similarly done in entire philosophical systems.[36]

But the most intense period of musico-poetic cross-fertilization had already come a few years before: Schumann's immersion in the writings of Hoffmann and his plans to undertake a "poetical biography" of the writer and composer in the summer of 1831 coincided precisely with the last stages of his work on *Papillons,*[37] where music and literature come together less in the Jean-Paulian allusions—their aesthetic status still a matter of debate—than in the form that the work takes as Schumann's first system of musical fragments.

As Harald Eggebrecht has pointed out, Schumann's piano works of the 1830s know "keinen stets abrufbaren Formenkanon"[38] ["no consistently fixed formal canon"]. Still, it might be useful to posit for the collections of miniatures a rough typology, whose simplicity will have the advantage of allowing us to place Schumann's varied approaches to the fragment form into some kind of context. In his letters and diaries, Schumann held to a basic distinction between "kleine Stücke" built on the *Papillons* model[39] and "größere Stücke" worthy of taking a place beside his sonatas and the Opus 17 Fantasie. The former might be likened to collections such as Schlegel's *Ideen,* elliptical utterances seldom longer than a sentence or two, where meaning emerges less from the individual (and usually cryptic statement) than from the cumulative effect of the fragment cluster.

When Schumann noted in a diary entry of 9 June 1832 that the *Papillons* contained "something critical but certainly nothing artful,"[40] he did not, I think, intend to discount the artistic worth of the composition that had occupied him at various points over a three-year period. The sublimated artfulness of the isolated musical fragment, he seems to imply, is subordinate to the "critical" interaction of the fragments as a totality. Schumann's "größere Stücke," on the other hand, are comparable to the philosophico-critical mini-disquisitions that comprise Schlegel's *Athenäum Fragmente.* They give the lie to the notion that every fragment is necessarily a miniature. And while the relationship between part and whole that I have suggested for the "kleinere Stücke" would appear, in works like *Kreisleriana,* Opus 16, or the *Novelletten,* Opus 21, to be precisely reversed, we will see that the emphasis still rests on the heterogeneous totality: Schumann's compositional problem here devolved on the fashioning of a coherent large-scale grouping out of apparently self-sufficient entities. It would be a mistake to think of one type of grouping as "higher" than the other. Throughout the 1830s, Schumann's work on "kleine" and "größere Stücke" both alternated (*Phantasiestücke, Kinderszenen*) and overlapped (*Davidsbündlertänze, Phantasiestücke*). Our types therefore represent parallel streams, differing solutions to the problem of shaping a musical system of fragments.

All of Schumann's collections drew to some extent on the principle he called *Aufhebung* (annulment) or *Selbstvernichtung* (self-annihilation). Originally employed to described the rapid-fire alternation of moods that made the *Papillons* so difficult for its early audiences to fathom,[41] the *Selbstvernichtung* principle applies with particular force to the other sets of "kleine Stücke" too—*Carnaval,* the *Davidsbündlertänze, Kinderszenen*— where each successive piece seems to cancel out the effect of its immediate predecessor. I will have more to say about this idea in the following section; for now it suffices to note that *Selbstvernichtung* goes hand in hand with the system "fragmented as a whole and in its parts"—Schlegel's diasporactive imperative, which is realized in Schumann's "kleine Stücke" and characterizes them as a distinct group.[42]

Take, for example, the *Davidsbünlertänze*. Well over half the pieces in the set are cast in some variant of the ternary pattern that would become paradigmatic for the nineteenth-century character piece. Yet as often as not, key elements of the *ABA* design are treated so oddly that the conventional ternary idea itself is called into question. The third piece falls into three sections: an opening "strike-up-the-dance" phrase moving from G to the dominant of B minor, a central *schneller* in D, and a return to the initiatory music. Ostensibly it adds up to a little *ABA* form in G major, pure and simple. Yet the unusual proportions of the sections—eight, sixty, and twenty-six measures respectively—serve as a clue that Schumann has in fact turned the form of its head, or better yet, inside out. The opening phrase is hardly a complete form part; on the contrary it is a mere fragment of the return, which appends an eighteen-bar conclusion to the original idea. In any event, the main business of the piece is not localized in the G-major framing sections, but rather in the extended D-major *schneller*; what looks to be the *Beiwerk* in an *ABA* scheme is more properly heard as *Hauptwerk* flanked by fragments. And the fragmented part is at the same time projected onto a fragmented whole; the reversal of function observable in No. 3 likewise informs the entire set of dances, where closure via melodic recurrence is effected not in the first and last but in the second and punultimate (seventeenth) pieces. As in the diminutive No. 3, the principal key of the set is neither announced at the outset (in the opening G-major dance) nor firmed at the end (in the C-major waltz added by Eusebius "Ganz zum Überfluß"); B minor is withheld until No. 2, then magically dissolved after No. 17. The mirroring of whole in part, the fragmentation on the large and small scale, the peculiar light in which the ABA form is placed—all this converts a lighthearted string of dances into an ironizing commentary on the dance as vehicle for higher art forms.

Schumann set great store by his "größere Stücke"; more than once he alluded with pride to the *Phantasiestücke, Kreisleriana,* and *Novelletten* as ranking among his best compositions of the 1830s.[43] The *Humoreske,* Opus 20 (or "großen Humoreske," as Schumann called it in an 11 March 1839 letter to Clara),[44] belongs here as well, though technically speaking it is not a set of pieces at all; as a single-movement work with numerous inner divisions, it makes for a more extended counterpart to another piece conceived at about the same time, the *Blumenstück,* Opus 19.[45] And finally, we can round out the list with the Intermezzi, Opus 4, or "längere Papillons" as Schumann called them,[46] the first of the miniature collections that upon closer inspection turn out to be not so miniature after all.

What all these works share is a surface preoccupation with strategies intended to generate longer-breathed structures. Fully half of the eight *Phantasiestücke,* for example, feature sonata-form recapitulation traits (without thereby being "in" sonata form), which Schumann eschews in most of his other collections. In two cases, "Grillen" and "In der Nacht," this involves the recurrence of earlier episodic material at the lower fifth; the tonal motion is reversed in "Aufschwung," in deference perhaps to its title. Sonata-principle implications are strongest in the penultimate piece, "Traumes Wirren," where the tonally unstable march music of mm. 17ff. reappears near the end of the work in a clear tonic context.

The extensiveness of the component parts of the *Phantasiestücke* is matched by Schumann's attempt at an extended whole in the Intermezzi. Here the element of connection is provided by the attaccas that outwardly link the central four pieces of the set of six, thus highlighting the fifth and third tonal relationships (E minor–A minor–C/A minor–D minor) that further bind them together. Indeed, the C-major vamp that sets off No. 4 grows directly out of the closing cadence of the previous piece. The attaccas are in turn mirrored by the more subtle *Verknüpfung* devices employed within several of the pieces (Nos. 1, 3, and 6) to link principal material and contrasting *alternativo*. Wittiest in this regard is No. 6: the two cadential progressions that preface the opening gesture of its *alternativo* reappear in reverse order at the conclusion of the same; the harmonic sleight-of-hand that allows for easy passage from B minor to the central D major ($V^7 \rightarrow$ i in B minor, then $V^7 \rightarrow$ I in D) is therefore transformed at a stroke into an equally economical move back to B minor ($V^7 \rightarrow$ I in D, $V^7 \rightarrow$ i in B).

But these strategies of large-scale connection notwithstanding, the point of departure for Schumann's "größere Stücke" still remains the phenomenon of the fragment, whether explicitly, as in the kaleidoscopic array of musical ideas that in the Humoreske are elaborated to form a total structure of sonata-like dimensions, or implicitly, as in the *Novelletten,* where the large dimensions of the individual pieces belie a marked predilection for the medley, the chain of dance fragments. To be sure, the latter collection, Schumann's largest, poses a difficult analytical-critical problem: How can we square the apparent self-sufficiency of the individual pieces with Schumann's insistent claims for their large-scale cohesion? How can we interpret them, in other words, as a system of musical fragments? We will return to these issues at the conclusion of this chapter.

Schumann and the System of Musical Fragments: Categories

Cutting across Schumann's collections of miniatures, regardless of their inner elaboration or outward scope, is a series of principles and properties that stamp them as musical fragments in the first place. The five categories considered below, although not exhaustive, will nonetheless provide us with a point of entry into the workings of the musical fragment system. Proceeding from lower- and to higher-level categories, from those that touch mainly on the quality of individual fragments to those governing the shape of whole systems, we will begin with the quotation (both literal and figurative), moving on to Schumann's interleaving or *Kater Murr* technique, as I will call it, his employment of *Selbstvernichtung* as an ordering principle, and his musical refiguring of Jean-Paulian *Humor* as an agent of motivic and tonal dualism; finally, we will investigate the role of Schlegel's *Witz* as an agent of large-scale coherence.

Quotation

Quotations are fragments of the thought complexes from which they have been forcibly torn, and although Schumann was not the first artist to translate the technique into musical terms, few nineteenth-century composers explored the possibilities of the allusive reference as thoroughly as he.[47] Schumann's self-quotations describe a path that meanders from one collection to the next: the third piece from the *Davidsbündlertänze* brings a phrase from "Promenade" in *Carnaval,* whose "Florestan" alludes to the first of the *Papillons* dances. In the first movement of the *Faschingsschwank aus Wien,* Opus 26, he raises the art of quotation to the second power, as it were, by quoting a quote, the "Großvatertanz" that figures in the *Papillons* finale. More subtle is the transformation of the opening rhythmic gesture of "Von fremden Ländern und Menschen," the first of the *Kinderszenen,* into the grim funeral-march motive that dominates the initiatory and, in somewhat varied form, concluding pieces of the *Nachtstücke,* Opus 23 (see Ex. 3.3).

Schumann's web of allusions ensures for the collections an obliquely literary and specifically Jean-Paulian dimension; one thinks of Dr. Fenk, who wanders from *Die unsichtbare Loge* to *Hesperus* and "authors" a part of the "Komischer Anhang" to *Titan* (as do Viktor, the hero of *Hesperus,* and Siebenkäs, the protagonist of the novel of the same name). Then too, the allusive network provides for a historicizing dimension—particularly when Schumann quotes from popular tunes (the "Marseillaise" in *Faschingsschwank aus Wien*) or refers to works of other composers (Schubert's "Gretchen am Spinnrade," D. 118, in No. 2 of the Intermezzi)—by situating the "quoting" work in a definite present removed in time from the text it cites. In addition, the quotation technique goes hand in hand with the notion of the fragment as isolated image or frozen "Seelenzustand": as Schumann put it, "and then I will prettily arrange the little things, of which I have so many, and call them 'kleine Blumenstücke,'" much as one would name pictures."[48] Schumann's quotations, like the miniatures as a whole, display an imagistic, snapshot-like quality, especially in cases where they stand out from rather than blend in with their environment.

Consider, for example, the *Papillons* quotation in "Florestan," the sixth *Carnaval* piece. The tempo shifts from *passionato* to *adagio,* the character from that of frenzied exhortation to genial waltz, the tonality from G minor to B♭ major. The musical events are thus calibrated to allow the quotation to be perceived as such. Even the listener without access to a score—where Schumann "signs" the second appearance of the quote "(Papillon?)"—or unaware of the specific reference, will probably not fail to get the point. There

EXAMPLE 3.3, a–c
a. Schumann, *Kinderszenen,* No. 1, mm. 1–4. (Schumann, *Kinderszenen,* Op. 15,
edited by Goebels, Vienna Urtext Edition. © 1973 by Wiener Urtext Edition,
Musikverlag, Ges.m.b.H. & Co., K. G. Wien. All Rights Reserved. Used by
permission of European American Music Distributors Corporation, sole U.S. and
Canadian agent for Wiener Urtext Editions.)

b. Schumann, *Nachtstücke,* No. 1, mm. 1–4

c. Schumann, *Nachtstücke,* No. 4, mm. 2–5

are other instances where Schumann signs a musical phrase, thereby marking it as a quotation, when in fact, no earlier source is actually being quoted: the "Innere Stimme" in the *Humoreske,* the "Stimme aus der Ferne" in the eighth and last of the *Novelletten,* even the "Sphinxes" in *Carnaval,* are all cases in point. It is only a step from here to the realization that the totality of Schumann's musical fragment systems are perhaps constituted as chains of quotations. The carefully sculpted gesture, the startling harmonic turn, the form that is barely allowed to fill itself out, the rapidly shifting textures: these features speak for the notion that Schumann quotes even when, according to the strict definition of the term, he is not quoting at all.[49]

Kater Murr Principle

Viewed as a web of either clearly identifiable or obliquely suggestive quotations, the system of musical fragments may be described as a literary-historical montage of sorts. The literary component of the equation is accented by the second of our categories, the technique of interleaving. No doubt Schumann derived more from E. T. A. Hoffmann than the titles of his *Phantasiestücke, Kreisleriana* (with its attendant mood shifts *à la* Johannes Kreisler), and *Nachtstücke.* Among the "neue Welten" that would have opened up for him in a novel like *Kater Murr,* for instance, is an organizational mode based entirely on the principle of incompletion.[50] As announced in its full title, *Lebensansichten des Katers Murr nebst fragmentarischen Biographie des Kapellmeisters Johannes Kreisler in zufälligen Makulaturblättern,* Hoffmann's work presents itself as the conflation of two manuscripts: an autobiography of Murr the cat and a biography of Johannes Kreisler, the torn pages from which, as Hoffmann's fictive editor explains, Murr has used for "backing and blotting" in his own confessional account. A more thorough celebration of the fragment, at all levels, is difficult to imagine: in that a third and final volume, though promised in the narrative, never materialized, the novel as a whole remains a fragment; and Kreisler's "original" biography was itself composed of a series of fragments, whose incompleteness was further emphasized when Murr disassembled the manuscript to make blotting paper for his own.

But most important for our immediate concerns is the novel's peculiar rhythm and its articulation through an interleaving technique accented by Hoffmann's beginning many of the Kreisler sections in midsentence and ending them with an ellipsis. Something similar obtains in the eleventh of the *Papillons,* though here the *Kater Murr* principle is directed at ends different from Hoffmann's. For Schumann the narrative ploy becomes a means of creating a sonic illusion. His little piece divides into three parts: an opening polonaise in ternary form, a *più lento* trio, also ternary, and an abbreviated reprise of the polonaise, thus yielding the following letter scheme:

$$A^1 :\|B\ A^2 \mid c^1 \|:d\ c^2 :\| B\ A^2$$

Most notable is the manner in which the abbreviation is accomplished. After the G-major trio, Schumann does not return, as one might expect, to the beginning of the D-major polonaise music, but rather to its central episode, which moves from the dominant of D through the minor subdominant, the flat submediant, and finally on to the tonic. The real point of the shortened return, then, resides not so much in its function as return per se, as in the disjunctive effect created by the cleft between G major (at the end of c^2) and the dominant of D (at the return of B). We are meant to imagine that polonaise and trio each proceed in their own physical space, and that the subsequent fragmenting of the opening unit (BA^2) aims to represent our apprehension of music *already in progress.* A^1 is unheard but not really omitted; it has been stated, though in a location from which we cannot hear it, during the G-major trio.[51] In the second of the Intermezzi, also a ternary-form piece (A^1BA^2), the return is amplified, but in a manner whose peculiarities may again be read as signals of spatial dislocation. A^2 begins with a fragment of A^1, its concluding sixteen bars, and ends with another A^1 fragment, this time its *opening* sixteen bars. The amplified return is thus more aptly described as a fragment of several repeated playings of A^1, renditions that have been proceeding during the central B section, but from a different location in space.

As might be expected, some of the most subtle instances of the *Kater Murr* principle come in the Hoffmann-inspired *Kreisleriana.* In Nos. 5 and 7 we can indeed begin to speak of an interleaving of fragmented form parts that emphasizes narrative fluency (or trickery, as the case may be) over spatial effects. Both are ternary pieces with returns bringing only the last two members of an initial *aba* unit. The middle section (B) of No. 5 is organized as a miniature rondo with three refrain statements and two episodes, such that the first portion of the concluding *ba* unit sounds not like a return but like another episode in the alternating rondo pattern. Only with the appearance of *a* is it absolutely clear that Schumann's earlier move involved a midsentence beginning. With No. 7 we come full circle: the fragmented return is not perceived as a fragment at all. The central part of this C-minor piece, though a fugato, takes on a diminutive ternary design whose last segment works up to a climactic dominant pedal, the point of the flurried activity being an emphatic restatement of the opening unit's *b* music in the tonic, whereas earlier it had appeared in the minor dominant. The fragmented quality of the utterance is downplayed in favor of a dynamic gesture of reprise. In each of these *Kreisleriana* pieces Schumann therefore proceeds from one "manuscript" to fragments of another, without our realizing that an act of interleaving has even been performed.

Selbstvernichtung

When extended beyond the individual piece, the interleaving of musical fragments may lead to an effect that disconcerted so many of Schumann's early listeners. "It appeared to me that the *Papillons* didn't go over well with the assembled guests," Schumann wrote in his diary in reference to Clara's performance at one of Friedrich Wieck's soirées, "for they exchanged strange looks and seemed unable to grasp the rapid alternation [of pieces]."[52] Shortly thereafter he would describe this kaleidoscopic quality as a "Sich-selbst-vernichten" that caused special problems to the first-time listener, who "still has the previous page in his head when the player has already finished the next."[53] By flitting quickly from one affect to another, each successive *Papillon* effectively cancels out its predecessor.

But it is not only through the continual fluctuation of musical moods that Schumann introduces an element of "self-negation" into his collections of miniatures. Tonal issues are equally significant. The *Papillons* may be described as being, at some level, "in D," the key of the introductory, opening, and closing pieces; placed more or less at the work's midpoint is the D-minor No. 6; likewise, most of the other pieces relate to D, and to each other, by third or fifth. Nos. 2 and 10, however, seem to stand disturbingly apart from what would otherwise be a logical scheme. In what sense does the opening E♭-major flourish of No. 2 proceed from the D major of No. 1? How should we explain the C major of No. 10 vis-à-vis the B♭-minor close of the preceding piece and the D-major start of the following?

Though an interpretation of C as passing tonality may suffice in the abstract, it minimizes the jarring effect that the tonal sequence makes in actual performance. Nor should we attempt to explain away the tonal oddities of the *Papillons* through an appeal to its long and complex compositional history. Schumann knew very well how to fashion a logical and coherent tonal plan—when he wanted to.[54] The D/E♭ and B♭/C/D tonal disjunctions are better viewed as intentionally calculated moves in an overall strategy governed by the principle of *Selbstvernichtung,* where a given tonality may neither prolong its predecessor nor prepare for its successor but instead negate the implications of the former while its own implications are then negated by the latter. We are, after all (to quote Roland Barthes), in the realm of the perpetual intermezzo: "what interrupts is in its turn interrupted, and this begins all over again."[55] Barthes was certainly correct in asserting that Schumann's fondness for the interruptive gesture can make for "a rather dizzying notion when it extends to all of music,"[56] yet it can at the same time function as part of a perfectly sensible scheme.

In the *Davidsbündlertänze,* for instance, the insistent *Selbstvernichtung* of the *Papillons* recedes in favor of a more subtle alternating process whose workings can be demonstrated by again focusing on tonal matters. The keys of the nine dances of Book 1:

1	2	3	4	5	6	7	8	9
G	b	G	b	D	d	g	c	C

describe an open-ended path for which it is difficult to posit a tonal center. Indeed, the point of the series would seem to lie precisely in its calling into question the idea of a single tonal center. Does the succession prolong G? aspire to D? or to C?

The three possibilities can be synthesized if we recognize in the tonal pattern a variant of the *Selbstvernichtung* principle whereby the primacy of G is gradually undermined. Initially prolonged by its upper third, G is next displaced by D (Nos. 5 and 6); briefly reestablished, but as the weaker G minor; and finally neutralized by the turn toward C (at once a new tonic and the subdominant of G). Any sense of G as tonic is subsequently obliterated by the tonal cleft between the functionally ambiguous C-major close of Book 1 and the D-minor opening of Book 2. The undermining of G in the first half of the collection is then complemented by the steady rise of B (minor) in the second, its primacy clinched in the penultimate piece (No. 17) through the recall of the music of No. 2, as before, in B minor. But this too is soon denied, or rather magically transformed, by the opening sonority of No. 18, the last piece; a dominant seventh built on G, over a C pedal, it points backward as German sixth in B, and forward as dominant of the concluding C-major waltz.[57] Paradoxically then, *Selbstvernichtung* need not be viewed as a negative, destructive category. On the contrary, it may represent the obverse of a traditional concept of tonality that rejects centricity in favor of multiplicity. And for Schumann, tonal multiplicity often figures as a component of the pervasive dualism that more properly belongs under our next category.

Humor

The connotations of its English cognate aside, Schumann took his *Humor* very seriously. In the context of a report on his most recent compositions (the *Kinderszenen, Kreisleriana,* Fantasie, *Arabeske, Blumenstück,* and *Humoreske*) to Simonin de Sire, Schumann paused for an excursus on those characteristics that made his compositions quintessentially German and consequently so difficult for foreigners (especially Frenchmen) to understand. Among the most prominent was the notion of *Humor,* that "felicitous blend of geniality and wit" whose "deep-rootedness in the German nationality" was not to be conveyed by any corresponding term in the French language: "Also the word 'Humoreske' will be incomprehensible to the French." The almost immediate reference to Jean Paul—"Do you know our great writer, Jean Paul? I've learned more counterpoint from him than from any music teacher"—is highly suggestive.[58] In that Jean Paul's aesthetics gave primacy of place to *Humor* (in contradistinction to the aesthetic of the Beautiful proclaimed by eighteenth-century writers), it is likely that Schumann's own thinking on the concept, along with the element of *Humor* in his music already noted by such nineteenth-century commentators as Moscheles and Brendel,[59] is traceable to the writings of his favorite author.

Jean Paul's *Vorschule der Ästhetik* (1804/1813) devotes much attention to the comic modes—satire, irony, wit, and even the ridiculous—that earlier critics had either undervalued or ignored. The centerpiece of the volume arguably comes in a whole series of chapters on *Humor* that together artic-ulate a theory presented in language whose verbal somersaults themselves draw on the comic modes that Jean Paul scrutinizes at other points in the treatise. In spite of the purposeful linguistic convolutions, the broad outlines of his thinking on *Humor* remain clear enough. For Jean Paul, *Humor,* or the "Romantic comic," results from the contrast of incommensurable entities. By applying finitude to the infinite, the humorous poet produces contrasts at every turn, both within the situations and images portrayed, and through their varied and colorful grouping. Jean Paul also speaks of an "annihilating" ("vernichtende") *Humor* (at once a feature of Haydn's music and Laurence Sterne's prose, and a likely source for Schumann's "Sich-selbst-vernichten") that "delights even in contradictions and impossibilities" and takes pleasure in "the emptiest conclusions."[60] But the principal activity of the humorist will involve setting the "small" against the "infinite" world (Jean Paul's own ten-dency to couple "Hohe Menschen" and simple-hearted village folk comes to mind), so that "a kind of laughter results containing both pain and great-ness."[61]

The complex of ideas that converge in Jean Paul's theory of *Humor*—infi-nite contrast, implausible contradictions, trivial conclusions, higher versus lower worlds—finds ready analogues in Schumann's miniature collections. The pulsations of an eminently serious *Humor* animate the system of musical fragments from smallest detail to overarching whole. At the simplest level, there is the contrast between elegiac "Eusebius" pieces and more exuberant "Florestan" pieces, initialled "E.," "F.," or "F. u. E." in the first edition of the *Davidsbündlertänze.* A similar affective alternation serves to establish a co-gent sequence in the *Phantasiestücke,*[62] where character contrast is further intensified by a complementary dualism in the tonal realm. While the first Book of the collection centers on D♭:

1	2	3	4
D♭	f	D♭	b♭/D♭

the balance is tipped toward F in the second:

5	6	7	8
f	C	F	F

Schumann accomplishes this through a subtle but compelling shift of em-phasis: in Book 1, D♭ primacy is colored by the F-minor tonality of the second piece, "Aufschwung"; the tables are turned in Book 2 given the role of D♭ as subsidiary key in the two closing F-major pieces, "Traumes Wirren" and "Ende vom Lied."

Yet another and more far-reaching form of contrast obtains in works that play on stylistic duality. Schumann's answer to Jean Paul's infinite contrast of otherworldly sages and country parsons takes the form of a continual interpenetration of high and low styles. The sublime and the trivial rub shoulders (sometimes uneasily) in Schumann's musical fragment systems, each deriving meaning from its relationship to the other. Although it makes for a paradoxical aesthetic claim, we will not do justice to Schumann's peculiar brand of musical poetry unless proper recognition is given to the sustenance that it draws from the trivial. Nietzsche's contemptuous allusion to Schumann's taste as "basically a *small* taste (namely, a dangerous propensity, doubly dangerous among Germans, for quiet lyricism and sottishness of feeling),"[63] should not be dismissed out of hand; it touches on a very real element (which needn't be judged so harshly as Nietzsche would like) in the music.

Schumann addressed the problem, if obliquely, in one of his most telling statements on the musically poetic:

> Therefore I take satisfaction in so few [contemporary] compositions, because technical shortcomings aside, they dawdle with musical feelings of the lowest type through commonplace [sonorities] and lyric exclamations; the highest that can be achieved here doesn't even come up to the starting point of my musical world. The former [contemporary music] may be a flower, but the latter [Schumann's own] is an evermore spiritual poem; the former is a sprout of unrefined Nature, the latter a product of poetic consciousness."[64]

Schumann's eloquent account of the conflict between nature and art translates a long-standing debate into musical terms. For the composer, nature appears in the guise of the "lower" genres, the commonplace harmonic turn, the unabashedly lyric gesture, although Schumann's rejection of those features was not as complete as the quotation might lead us to believe. For earlier on in the same letter, Schumann locates the difficulty of his own music in his desire to absorb all the varied and unusual phenomena that the age had to offer. And in his critical writings, Schumann showed a marked willingness to embrace one type of musical *Naturpoesie* in particular: the dance, the genre "where art is sensuously allied with common life."[65] The musical artist cannot afford to ignore any of the currents that surround him, not even the most frankly popularizing, but "must also know all his contemporaries from the first to the last; that includes, for instance, [Johann] Strauss [Sr.], who is in his own way the most representative of his time."[66] The goal is not to circumvent nature, for which a "lower" genre like the waltz may stand in as a fitting musical representative, but to transfigure it; after all, "the best fugue will always be that which the public takes for a Strauss waltz."[67] We might even infer that in Schumann's eyes, contemporary music could aspire to the poetic *only* insofar as it took the trivial and the commonplace as points of departure for the purpose of ennobling them.

This dialectic of triviality and sublimity is arguably the message of the miniature collections, given their rootedness in the dance, and their "humorous" play on high and low styles. The social dance character of several of the

Papillons, signaled by the rollicking vamps that play a part in Nos. 6, 8, and 10, is counterbalanced by an appeal to contrapuntal devices: canon in No. 3 (supposedly a representation of the "Giant Boot" from *Flegeljahre*), or the combination of the "Großvatertanz" and opening waltz in No. 12. Contrapuntal artifice, again in the form of canonic parries, likewise figures in the central *schneller* of the third of the *Davidsbündlertänze.* ("It is quite incredible," Schumann wrote to Clara in the spring of 1838, "how markedly my invention tends toward the canonic, and how I discover the answering voice only later, often in inversion or concealed rhythms.")[68] Rhythmic or metric irregularities may likewise enliven what would otherwise have been a gesturally straight-forward dance idea. In No. 1 of the *Davidsbündlertänze,* a simple waltz bass supports a melody whose persistent metric displacements and cross accents culminate in a passage (mm. 42ff.) where the sense of triple time is all but obliterated. The middle section of "Grillen," the fourth of the *Phantasie-stücke,* combines metric displacement (its opening bars shift the previous $\frac{3}{4}$ meter one beat "to the left"), hemiola patterns both complete (mm. 62–65) and incomplete (mm. 66–67), and unnotated but implicit mixed meters ($\frac{4}{4} + \frac{3}{2} + \frac{3}{4} + \frac{4}{2}$), all of which contrast sharply with the regular triple-time accentuation of the preceding music (see Ex. 3.4).

Lastly, the play of high and low styles may manifest itself through Schumann's coupling of unpretentious melodic material with formal ideas of some complexity. Opus 19 proclaims its artlessness by means of a fanciful title—*Blumenstück*—whose "nature" connotations are obvious. The simplicity of melodic design and transparency of texture alike seem directly in line with the kind of studied naïveté that Schumann so beautifully projected in the *Kinderszenen.* Yet the form of Schumann's little piece is far from naïve: it is a kind of free-wheeling double theme and variations, the second theme (in A♭) deriving both motivic substance and texture from the first (in D♭). Yet the inattentive listener is not apt to notice that, following the deft and inob-trusive introduction of a new episodic idea about midway through the piece, the first theme never reappears, its function as principal melody and even its D♭ tonality having been taken over by the second theme.

Perhaps the most significant manifestations of the principle of humorous duality, however, are to be noted in Schumann's handling of tonality. We have already seen how the play on D♭ versus F colors the whole of the *Phanta-siestücke.* Variants of the same approach are a vital presence in most of the other collections, extending from isolated details to the tonal shape of the whole. Schumann's fondness for tonally dualistic forms, that is, for what are apparently fragments of fully rounded tonal entities, already emerges in the *Papillons,* several of which (Nos. 2, 4, and 7) begin in one key only to end in another.[69] No. 9, like Nos. 4 and 7, plays on the close relationship between relative major and minor, subtly demonstrating that dualism may surface just as strongly in a piece that at first glance seems to prolong a single tonality. Even though No. 9 begins and ends in B♭ minor, it is difficult to maintain that

EXAMPLE 3.4

Schumann, *Phantasiestücke,* "Grillen," mm. 61–80.   (Reprinted by permission.
Copyright © 1978 Henle Verlag.)

the piece is "in" that key. Its form can be described as an inverse bar—abb′—
which is to say that *a* functions as an introductory flourish, moving from B♭
minor to its dominant, and that *b* marks the beginning of the real business of
the piece. Yet *b* and *b′* together behave much like a binary unit in the relative
major, the first half proceeding from D♭ to its dominant, the second returning
to D♭ just before the piquant turn that brings a B♭ minor close. Ostensibly a
closed form in B♭ minor, the little piece is in fact built as introduction cum
tonal fragment.

The C-major opening and close of No. 4 of the Intermezzi are equally deceptive: the real substance of the piece is contained in the A-minor song
melody (based on the 1828 *Lied* "Hirtenknabe"), and not in the C-major
vamps with which it alternates.[70] In some cases, then, dualism may figure as
a directionally motivated tonality proceeding toward an alternate goal; in oth-

ers, its presence may be muted by apparently closed forms. There is also a further possibility. The twelfth of the *Davidsbündlertänze* (marked *mit Humor*) opens in B minor only to move just as decisively to E. Although Schumann's single-sharp key signature strengthens the case for interpreting the harmonic motion of the diminutive piece as v → i(I) in E, the firm articulation of B minor at the outset, with a cadentially rounded four-bar phrase, argues for i → iv(IV) in B. Which is it? Neither and both, if we concede that the tonal message of the piece takes the form of a virtually insoluble question.

Tonal dualism may also extend beyond the limits of the isolated musical fragment. Indeed, Schumann discovered relatively early in his career that this variety of musical *Humor* might act as a forceful means of binding together and articulating larger fragment clusters. Each of the concluding three pieces of the *Kinderszenen*—"Fürchtenmachen" (No. 11), "Kind im Einschlummern" (No. 12), and "Der Dichter Spricht" (No. 13)—emphasizes one side or the other of a G/E tonal pair. No. 11 states the argument through a refrain phrase whose chromatic inner voices at first suggest E minor, but that ultimately cadences in G. The balance tips toward E in No. 12, with G functioning as mediator between its major and minor forms, only to revert to G in No. 13, where E priority is recalled only by two held diminished-seventh chords on D♯ (which may, in any case, proceed just as logically to G as to E). In that the opening piece of the set, the G-major "Von fremden Ländern und Menschen" turns on the same contrast, its second half headed off by a phrase colored by the relative minor, G/E duality can be said to provide a tonal frame for the entire collection.

One of Schumann's favorites among the miniature collections of the 1830s, *Kreisleriana* plays almost entirely on the contrast between the elements in a g/B♭ tonal pair deployed in a kind of chain pattern, the subsidiary tonality in one piece being taken up as the principal tonality in its successor:

1	2	3	4	5	6	7	8
d(B♭)	B♭(g)	g(B♭)	B♭ → V/g	g(B♭/D♭) → [V/g]	B♭	c(g) → E♭	g(B♭)

While adjacent pieces may embody sharply differing affects, the tonal plan mainly proceeds as a single sweep, the only exceptional moment coming with the break between No. 6 in B♭ and No. 7 in c/E♭, a lower-fifth variant of the "tonic" pair. Additional variants figure within the other pieces as well: witness the coupling of B♭, from the tonic pair, with D♭ in No. 5, or the d/F, a/C pairs in the penultimate episode of No. 7. The sense of continuity is further enhanced by the half cadence on the dominant of G minor that not only connects Nos. 4 and 5 but also bridges the gap at the composition's precise midpoint (Schumann's elimination of the V/g fermata at the close of No. 5 in the first edition was perhaps motivated by a desire to enhance the symmetry). The thoroughness with which tonal pairing is employed both within and between pieces therefore serves as a fitting analogue for the humorous duality that made E. T. A. Hoffmann's Kapellmeister Kreisler such a compelling fictional character for Schumann.

With the *Humoreske* the coloristic possibilities of tonal dualism in general, and the g/B♭ pair in particular, were exploited with even more intensity. As indicated in Figure 3–1, the tonal palette is limited almost entirely to the "Kreisleriana" keys of G minor and B♭. (Melodic and textural connections between the works are also worth noting: the second Intermezzo of *Kreisleriana* No. 2, for instance, invites comparison with the "third movement" *sehr lebhaft* of the *Humoreske*.) The elliptical opening harmony of the *Humoreske* already presages and encapsulates the tonal dialectic of what is to come: as a D-B♭-F♯ augmented triad, it may resolve with equal ease to G minor (through its dominant) or B♭.

Although the work appears to unfold as an extended array of shortwinded utterances, Schumann shows an equal concern for imbuing the whole with a

FIGURE 3–1
Schumann, *Humoreske,* Opus 20 Formal Plan

[Movement]	Inner Division	Comment	Tonality
Introduction	einfach (A)	ternary form: a-b-a'	B♭–G♭–B♭
	sehr rasch und leicht		B♭
	noch rascher	horn calls + bell topos	g–B♭–g
	erstes Tempo	on sehr rasch	B♭
	wie im Anfang	on A	B♭
[1. Allegro]	hastig + nach und nach schneller	"Innere Stimme" + free fantasy (bell topos) + chorale (on A)	g→B♭→d→ B♭→V/g
	wie vorher	on hastig	g→B♭
[2. Andante]	einfach und zart		g→B♭→g
	Intermezzo (bell topos)		B♭
	(einfach . . .)	on einfach . . .	g
[3. Intermezzo]	innig	rondo form: a-b-a-c-a	B♭→g→B♭
	sehr lebhaft	bravura, "Kreisler" close	g→B♭
[4. Introduction + Finale]	mit einigem Pomp	fanfares	E♭→A♭→V/B♭
	zum Beschluß (+ allegro close)	recitative topos; binary form: a-a'	B♭→E♭→B♭

measure of coherence; the *Humoreske* is a mosaic, but a mosaic artfully conceived. Thus, the recurrence of the opening *einfach* music at *wie im Anfang,* framing a return of the *sehr rasch und leicht* passage at *erstes Tempo,* articulates an introduction that gives way to a similarly rounded "first movement" (*hastig*). Melodic rounding also sets off the second movement (beginning at *einfach und zart*) from the more virtuosically oriented third, while the gesturally (and tonally) idiosyncratic *mit einigem Pomp* acts as prelude to the finale (*zum Beschluß*), whose hearkening back to the principal material of the second movement adds yet another cohesive element.

But most important for our purposes is the persistence with which the components of the tonic pair are maintained as harmonic points of reference: in an introduction centered on B♭ but colored by its relative minor, an open-ended first movement that gives added emphasis to the minor-key half of the pair, a second movement that reverses the relative weight between B♭ and G minor established at the outset, a third movement again centered on B♭, and a finale where G minor is at last vanquished in favor of B♭. As paradoxical as it sounds, it may well have been the *Humor* in the *Humoreske,* as projected by an obstinately dualistic tonal plan, that occasioned Schumann's valuation of the work as his most melancholy composition.[71]

Witz

Schumann noted in his diary that Jean Paul's art was constituted by a "threefold spirit—feeling [*Gemüth*], humor [*Humor*], wit [*Witz*]—much like a turkey has three kinds of meat; one explains the other, and they are just as clearly related as the various turkey meats."[72] The first term, *Gemüth,* was one of Schumann's personal favorites; the latter two are among the most significant categories in nineteenth-century aesthetics. We have already seen how *Humor,* the centerpiece of Jean Paul's poetics, played into the organization of Schumann's musical fragment systems. It remains for us to examine the role of *Witz,* likewise a notion treated in Jean Paul's *Vorschule,* but more importantly a decisive element in Friedrich Schlegel's program.

That Schumann was aware of the attention that the early Romantics gave to *Witz,* the ability to discern remote similarities, is beyond question.[73] And his acquaintance with the peculiarly Schlegelian variety is probably affirmed by a remark on the "deeply combinatorial, poetic, and humorous" qualities of contemporary music;[74] for Schlegel too, *Witz* was a "tiefcombinatorisch" property.[75] But what makes Schlegel an apt spokesman is less his possible influence on Schumann than the method he adduced for dealing with a problem that is closely related to our present concerns: How is the critic to deal with a work or body of works whose form is undeniably fragmentary, but in whose construction we nonetheless sense a measure of intuitive logic? The answer was provided by a theory that fastened on a peripheral aspect of eighteenth-century aesthetics (where *Witz* was treated merely as a counterpart to its opposite, *Scharfsinn* or "acumen," the ability to form judgments by differentiating apparently similar objects) for the purpose of addressing a pressing issue in modern art.

Insofar as Schlegel recognized *Witz* as the power that allows us to posit connections between markedly contrasting entities, his thinking was in line with that of Jean Paul and Novalis.[76] A devoted student of Kant's philosophy, Schlegel associated *Witz* with the "understanding," much as "sense" and "judgment" (or acumen) came under the respective headings of "imagination" and "reason."[77] As a cognitive faculty, *Witz* proceeds with rapid-fire velocity; it is, as Schlegel put it in a fragment somewhat at odds with his Kantian formulation, "the appearance, the outward lightning bolt of the imagination, hence its divinity and its similarity to mysticism."[78] Taken in this sense, *Witz* serves as a category of perception: the "chemical" reaction, as Schlegel often called it, that *Witz* sets in motion involves our immediate transformation of a seemingly random juxtaposition of antithetical terms into a meaningful configuration.[79]

The "lightning bolt" metaphor serves as a reminder that perceived syntheses are by their very nature ephemeral.[80] Yet for Schlegel, more so than for most of his contemporaries, *Witz* was just as much a productive quality as it was a receptive faculty. As a formal property residing in an object, it was "the appearance of absolute antithesis,"[81] and thus supplied, in Schlegel's estimation, the constructive basis for entities as diverse as modern philosophy, with its "eternal uniting and separating"; the poetry of Dante, Boccaccio, and Shakespeare; the Bible; allegorical genres; and given the "chemistry" of its revolutions and commercial enterprises, the entire modern age.[82] Schlegel needed only take these observations one step further to arrive at the conclusion that *Witz* was a quintessential property of that characteristically modern phenomenon, the system of fragments.[83]

Schlegel's assertion that fragments and fragments alone represented the "actual" products of *Witz*[84] therefore harbors both a historico-philosophical and an aesthetic claim: the harmoniously rounded products of bygone ages admit to a kind of logic that is simply not a possibility for the modern artwork, where logic gives way to contingencies, the "fantastic constructions and experiments" of combinatory *Witz*.[85] And Schlegel amply demonstrated that these reflections allowed for practical application in his critique of Lessing, the variegated content of whose oeuvre would not easily hold up under the scrutiny of a neoclassic conception of unity. Schlegel argued, however, that Lessing's fragmentary output might not represent an "offensive monstrosity"; on the contrary, he detected an "intentional formlessness" whose fragmentation was "not only excusable but also laudable and purposeful." In Schlegel's estimation, "there should be a place for artworks that aim to stimulate and not to represent, artworks in which universality [extremely varied content] is the most decisive factor."[86] This statement should not be taken as a mere dithyramb to the fragment. What counts is that we first recognize a product as art and, insofar as "absolute formlessness is not possible for an artist," open ourselves to the alternate possibility that the normative modes of ensuring cohesiveness have been displaced by other means: the "audacious combinative spirit," the "chemical blending and mixing" of *Witz*.[87]

Schlegelian *Witz* therefore valorizes the system of fragments by positing an alternative mode of development for the ideas that constitute it. "Logical" unfolding is not to be expected of a body of utterances that is by nature both aphoristic and enigmatic;[88] the hidden connections, the allusive links, the network of relationships that the "witty" artist produces and the "witty" receptor of the text descries now count for everything.[89]

These reflections have an important bearing on Schumann's miniature collections, works whose constructive logic is frequently located not in the step-by-step evolution of a musical idea (in traditional developmental techniques, that is) but in more elusive unifying methods comparable to those that Schlegel intuited in Lessing's output. This is not to say that conventional modes of integration are entirely lacking, or that every relationship requires the unriddling powers of *Witz* in order to be understood. On the contrary, Schumann employed absolutely straightforward means of establishing long-range connections in several often-cited cases: the recurrence of the opening waltz (and at the same tonal level) in the *Papillons* finale, or the recall of the B-minor No. 2 (again in the same key) in the penultimate piece of the *Davidsbündlertänze,* both instances of what Peter Kaminsky calls motivic cross-reference.[90] But these easily perceptible bonds are complemented, in Schumann's arsenal of unifying devices, by a body of recondite, camouflaged, "witty" connectives operating at formal, motivic, tonal and melodic levels. Nos. 7, 8, and 9 of the *Papillons,* for instance, stand out as a subgroup by virtue of their reliance on the same unusual pattern, a vamp phrase followed by a small binary unit; in none of these pieces is the apparent beginning the actual beginning. The *lettres dansantes* in *Carnaval* likewise furnish a layer of subcutaneous motivic links for the entire set. "Der Dichter spricht" rounds out the *Kinderszenen* not through clear-cut melodic recall but by means of an allusion to the ambiguous G/e harmonic topos already announced in the first piece of the set. And although the *Kreisleriana* pieces are rounded off by a melodic return, it is effected by an abstract gesture, not a tangible theme: the five-octave descent from g^3 to G_2 in No. 8 answers to the five-octave ascent from D_1 to d^4 in No. 1.

Just as the palpable cross-reference finds its counterpart in the "witty" link, so too does the principle of variation, a tried-and-true means of ensuring harmonic and tonal cohesion, bear comparison with what I will call the "witty" summation. In his explication of the variation idea in a review that takes many contemporary composers to task for the "wretchedness" and "banality" of their contributions to the genre, Schumann noted that "even variations should form a whole whose focal point is the theme (which one may therefore sometimes place at the middle or the end of the piece)."[91] Although examples from the early nineteenth-century repertory fitting the specifications of Schumann's parenthetical observation do not readily come to mind, it is possible to detect in his own miniature collections a radical rethinking of the variation idea. The result is, to be sure, a far cry from the traditional theme-and-variations form (Rudolph Réti's reading of the *Kinderszenen* as such is fundamentally wrongheaded),[92] for "theme" gives way to a loose network of musical topoi whose exposition may or may not be localized in a single piece, and "variation" to the "witty" reworking of these ideas. Theme-and-variation form is thus reconfigured as Schlegelian fragment system.

In Schumann's systems of musical fragments, centers of topical density, "witty" summations, function both as theme and variation, thereby dissolving the syntactic requirements of the traditional form. The concluding three pieces of *Papillons* warrant description as topical centers of this sort. Although the C major of No. 10 may be at odds with the set's principal D tonality, the piece couples oblique references to many of its predecessors (in particular the vamp of No. 6 and the "vamp + main dance" form of Nos. 7–9) with a clear allusion to the motive of the *Introduzione.* No. 11 brings a whole series of "witty" references to earlier pieces, including the D tonality of the *Introduzione,* No. 1 and No. 6, the polonaise topos of No. 5, the vamp openings of Nos. 7–9, and the horn calls of No. 4—all of which nicely prepare for the return of the first waltz in the finale.

Cumulative allusions to earlier topoi also occupy a terminal position in the Intermezzi. The last piece, No. 6, hearkens to a whole array of previously introduced ideas: its "humorous" coupling of B minor and D points to similar tonal pairings in Nos. 2 (e/G), 4 (C/a), and 5 (d/F); echoes of No. 2 come with the gesturally incisive opening theme presented in octaves (the rhythmic displacement in the second piece answered by hemiola in the last), the "call to arms" on a long-held F♯ that prefaces and concludes the central *alternativo* (cf. the rhetorical E and G articulating the respective first and second halves of No. 2's *A* section), and the central episode's persistently rising thirds (an allusion to the melodic thirds of "Mein Ruh' ist hin" in No. 2). In addition, the punning transition into and out of the *alternativo* points back to similar ploys in Nos. 1 and 3, whose circle-of-fifths progressions (e.g., at mm. 7–9 in No. 3) figure in the last piece as well (see, e.g., mm. 20–22, 24–26).

In the *Davidsbündlertänze,* on the other hand, the opening piece serves as topical repository: its coupling of trivial waltz bass and either enriching metric techniques (displacement, cross-accents) or hints of contrapuntal artifice, its construction as a series of fragmented variations, its play on the duality of relative major and minor, even the mysteriously held B of its fourth and fifth bars (excised in the 1850/51 edition)—each will be taken up, in one form or another, in the subsequent pieces of the set.

We know from both his letters and his critical writings that Schumann was much taken with the paradoxical notion of writing a set of variations *without* a theme.[93] He came close to realizing this unusual goal in the works that we have briefly considered, miniature collections in which the variation idea is effectively stood on its head, systems of musical fragments wherein the gradual and logical evolution of ideas recedes in favor of an associative web. To be sure, the web is woven from "themes," but the principal theme is no longer a discrete rhythmic-tonal-harmonic entity; it is a cluster of topoi that may at times be presented and elaborated consecutively, and at times not. Development—taken to mean purposive temporal unfolding—is displaced by *Witz.*

"Zusammenhängende abenteuerliche Geschichten"

"A fragment, like a miniature work of art, has to be entirely isolated from the outside world and complete in itself like a porcupine"[94]—so runs Friedrich Schlegel's odd claim, in *Athenäum* fragment 206, about a form whose nature we tend to think of as expressing the very essence of incompletion. Yet degrees of completeness may vary; what at first impresses us as a fully rounded entity may divulge its full meaning only when considered as a part of a total system of fragments. This is often true of Schumann's "größere Stücke," and particularly of his *Novelletten,* Opus 21, the work that will, by way of bringing together the threads of our previous discussion, occupy us here.

Conceived "mit großer Lust"[95] in the main between January and April of 1838, the *Novelletten* are among the most high-spirited of Schumann's "Clara" pieces. "My bride," he wrote to her in June 1839, "in the *Novelletten* you appear in all possible attitudes and postures and irresistible guises";[96] and, while at work on them earlier in the year before: "I compose only in major; the minor is too old-fashioned."[97] Well into the 1840s, when Schumann tended to see his piano compositions from the previous decade as youthful caprices of less aesthetic significance than the chamber and orchestral projects that then engaged him, he still ranked the *Novelletten* among his best achievements.[98] Indeed, the collection offers ample evidence of an artful handling of all the categories that stamp it as a system of musical fragments: the quotation, the *Kater Murr* principle, *Selbstvernichtung, Humor,* and *Witz.*

While the *Novelletten* include no quotations in the literal sense, there is an important idea that is, as it were, placed within quotation marks: the "Stimme aus der Ferne," alluded to earlier, that binds the first part of the extended eighth piece with its *Fortsetzung und Schluß.* And other ideas, though not accorded special superscriptions, also create a similar impression, for in the *Novelletten* the potpourri principle (adumbrated in Schumann's description of the work as "jocular tales, *Egmont*-stories, family scenes with fathers, a wedding, in short, only the most amiable things")[99] reigns supreme. This is especially pronounced in two of the pieces, Nos. 6 and 8, for all intents and purposes medleys (strings of popular dance-tune quotations) pure and simple—yet on reflection, perhaps not so simple. In No. 6 the complications involve the gradually diminished claims and ultimate elimination of the initial idea, the growth of the second dance theme into quite another, and a central development featuring third chains and long-range sequence. The medley turns out to be an evolving structure, a kind of developmentally enriched rondo whose first episode, by the end of the piece, is perceived as the refrain.[100] If in this piece one rondo *theme* is displaced by an alternate idea, then in No. 8, the last and largest piece in the set, an entire *form* is displaced by another. Its first half unfolds as a fragmented rondo (again, the initial "refrain" disappears) whose second episode (trio 2) brings the "Stimme aus der Ferne," at once serving as transition to the quasi-palindromic *Fortsetzung und Schluß* and as allusive reference within it. In both cases, then, seemingly innocuous dance melodies, quotations in gestural profile if not in name, act as a foil for sportive but subtly crafted forms.

Schumann's letter to Clara of 11 February 1838, written when his creative powers were most intensely focused on the *Novelletten,* is worth citing in this connection: "For four weeks I've done practically nothing but compose . . . [musical ideas] flowed toward me, and I continually sang along—for the most part my efforts have paid off. I'm playing with forms." [101] The "play" in the second of the *Novelletten* turns on the interleaving, or *Kater Murr,* principle. Essentially patterned as a three-part design, the return in this D-major piece is fragmented in a manner that we have encountered before: its first sixteen measures, the *A* of an *ABA'* form, are curiously absent. Thus the final D-major segment of the middle section (also an *ABA'*) fulfills two functions, providing melodic closure for a central episode that had commenced in A major, and a sense of tonal return that under normal circumstances would have arrived with a reprise of the opening music in the tonic.

Schumann had employed much the same mediating device in Nos. 5 and 7 of *Kreisleriana,* with which the *Novelletten* share a number of tonal strategies. Here too we encounter a harmonic palette strongly colored by dualistic or "humorous" tonal fluctuations: witness the D/b and Bb/Db pairings in No. 3 (with D priority localized in the outer sections and B minor in the central Intermezzo), the extension of the tonal pairing idea to form minor-third chains in the quasi-development of No. 6, and the F–Db–A major-third chain that spreads over the whole of No. 1. Given the overlap in their respective dates of composition, it is little wonder that the *Novelletten* and *Kreisleriana* should take up related concerns.[102]

In terms of ethos, No. 2 and the first half of No. 8 of the former collection might easily stand beside the more agitated pieces in the latter. Yet telling differences in Schumann's approach to tonal matters set the works apart from one another. While the persistent adherence to a single dominating tonal pair (g/Bb) in the *Kreisleriana* is offset by the varying emphasis that alternate pieces give to the members of the pair, more than half of the *Novelletten* center on the same tonality. D is asserted in five of the pieces (Nos. 2, 3, 4, 5, and the *Fortsetzung und Schluß* of No. 8)[103] with a relentlessness that borders on obsession, a feeling intensified by the contiguity of the first four D-major pieces and their culmination in a raucous rondo-polonaise (No. 5) that brings no fewer than five statements of its refrain theme: an obsessive tonal idea is thus linked with an obsessively extended form.

The "D-ishness" of the set is further highlighted by a limited reliance on the tonal *Selbstvernichtung* technique. Only the E-major No. 7 and the F#-minor opening of No. 8 are separated by a harmonic cleft, which is probably intended to set the last piece into relief. The kaleidoscopic shifts in *Papillons,* the abrupt contrasts in *Kreisleriana*—neither seems to figure in the tonal world of the *Novelletten,* whose insistent hammering away at the tonic pitch D is perhaps geared to remind us that rapid-fire alternation and obsessive repetition are both aspects of the same phenomenon, a phenomenon that Roland Barthes alluded to in a comment that might strike us as extreme, but actually fits the situation in the *Novelletten* quite well: "for many Schumannian pieces, the tonal range has the value of a single sound which keeps vibrating until it maddens us."[104]

Each of the categories considered thus far—the figurative quotation, the *Kater Murr* principle, *Selbstvernichtung,* humorous duality (or its complement, obsessional centricity)—may illuminate a particular feature of Schumann's most extended system of musical fragments. They may even have led us into the murky waters of hermeneutics, and to the provisional conclusion that the *Novelletten,* on the surface lighthearted and gay, actually harbor an element of madness. But to what extent are we dealing with a single system? Twice Schumann referred merely to "vier Hefte" (each comprising two pieces), suggesting that the set was more a loose assemblage than an integrated whole.[105] Yet his compelling remarks on the cohesiveness of the work as a whole cannot be ignored. Writing to Joseph Fischof in April 1838, Schumann dubbed the *Novelletten* "zusammenhängende abenteuerliche Geschichten" ("cohesive, quixotic tales"), and a little over a year later (in the same letter to Hirschbach that refers to "vier Hefte") he repeated the point by way of a similar descriptive phrase: the *Novelletten,* Schumann insisted, were "innig zusammenhängend."[106]

The argument for cohesion is further strengthened by his comments to Clara regarding the performance of individual pieces of the set; in this connection, Schumann was "totally against [an isolated rendition of] the *Novellette* in A [No. 6]—it works only in the context of the entire cycle; likewise, the *Novellette* in E [No. 7] goes by too quickly [to be performed alone]. . . . With the second piece in D you would certainly create the best effect; it has a beginning and ending, spins itself out nicely, so that the listeners will be able to follow its course, and even maintains a good melodic flow in its trio."[107]

Schumann makes a number of thought-provoking observations: the set, he tells us, is a "cycle" (a term that rarely crops up in his accounts of the miniature collections), whose component parts manifest varying degrees of completeness. Interestingly enough, in Schumann's view neither No. 6 nor No. 7 is as complete as No. 2, even though both are tonally closed, and No. 7 traces a nicely rounded three-part form. They are fragments—No. 6 presumably because of its lack of melodic closure—that take on meaning as a consequence of their placement within a system. The more complete No. 2, as the first in a series of four D-major pieces, is at the same time the "first" piece in the system proper, with No. 1, an F-major march, serving as introduction, Nos. 6 and 7, potpourri and waltz, as tonally digressive fragments, and No. 8 as finale. And that Schumann should have described the *Novelletten* in April 1838 as "*zusammenhängende* Geschichte" sheds some light on the system's special brand of coherence; inasmuch as the pieces were definitively ordered some four months later,[108] the "cohesive tales" of the April reference could not have derived their connective sense from a logically unfolding, order-determinate pattern, but rather from a web of "witty" associations. We can, in other words, infer from the documentary evidence what the music will confirm for us momentarily, namely, that the *Novelletten* do indeed constitute a single system whose inner coherence is ensured by the workings of *Witz.*

The principal "theme" of the *Novelletten,* the "idea" that allows us to perceive the work as a heterogeneous if not harmonious totality, is best thought of as a configuration of musical topoi. This is not a matter of equating meaning with topical content (the first piece, for instance, is concerned with the musical elaboration of a marchlike figure, not with the march per se); "meanings" emanate from the witty relationships between motivic particles that can, for the sake of convenience, be named after their musico-rhetorical equivalents. Two such figures, both of them practically as old as tonal-harmonic music itself, count as the most prominent elements in the substrate of chromaticism that colors the pieces of the set from first to last. Though latent in the sequential continuation of the opening piece's four-bar refrain, each of the figures is accorded a clear exposition only with No. 2—another reason to view it as the true beginning of the set. Its quasi-Kreislerian opening gesture, which surrounds F$\sharp$ with half steps from above and below like the *circulatio* of musical oratory (Ex. 3.5a), is answered by the chromatically filled-in descending tetrachord (or lament figure; Ex. 3.5b) that furnishes the remainder of the A section with its principal melodic substance. (To be sure, chromaticism is the decisive feature in a piece numbering among Schumann's most harmonically daring: witness the eight measures of pure octatonicism just before the opening gesture's return [Ex. 3.5c], and the whole-tone tonal plan: D–e–F$\sharp$–A$\flat$–b$\flat$.)

Circulatio and lament together serve as the chief elements of a motivic web spun ever more densely as the set continues. In the Intermezzo of No. 3, the first figure of the pair even recurs at its original D-major pitch level, and though confined to an inner voice, retains its function as initiatory motto (Ex. 3.5e). Indeed, the *circulatio* pattern, or slight variants thereof, is associated with motto ideas throughout, including the polonaise-refrain of No. 5

EXAMPLE 3.5, a–v
Schumann, *Novelletten*
a. No. 2, mm. 1–3; *circulatio*

b. No. 2, mm. 5–8, 17–20; lament figure

c. No. 2, mm. 83–90

d. No. 3, mm. 42–49

e. No. 3, Intermezzo, mm. 1–3

f. No. 4, mm. 1–3 (bass)

EXAMPLE 3.5, a–v (*continued*)

g. No. 4, mm. 25–33

h. No. 5, motto

i. No. 5, mm. 33–35

j. No. 5, mm. 65–66

k. No. 5, mm. 104–8

l. No. 6, mm. 17–21, 25–32, 69–71, 285–97 (coda)

m. No. 7, mm. 8–16, 50–64

EXAMPLE 3.5, a–v (*continued*)
  n. No. 8, mm. 1–3

  o. No. 8, trio 1, mm. 49–51

  p. No. 8, mm. 290–305

q. No. 8, mm. 320–24

r. No. 8, mm. 365–81

EXAMPLE 3.5, a–v (*continued*)

s. No. 8, mm. 389–401

t. No. 8, mm. 413–17

u. No. 8, mm. 157ff.

v. No. 8, appearances of "Stimme aus der Ferne"
mm. 193–227

mm. 228–35 (*Fortsetzung*)

mm. 446–69 (*Fortsetzung und Schluß*)

(Ex. 3.5f) and the dotted motive of No. 8's trio 1 (Ex. 3.5o). While this figure remains relatively fixed in shape and limited in function, its counterpart does not; the transformations of the lament pattern are more far-reaching, wittier. In No. 4, for instance, interlocking statements of the figure in inversion create a bass line for the main waltz melody (Ex.3.5f), as does a pentachordal variant of the descending *Urform* in No. 7, another waltz (Ex. 3.5m). (Note also, in No. 4, the appearance of the inverted tetrachord in an inner voice as part of the hemiola that sets the first strong D-major cadence into relief; a segment of the descending form in the bass, likewise holding to the hemiola pattern, then effects a modulation to C; Ex. 3.5g.)

No. 6 elaborates both tetrachord and pentachord (the former in inversion), and introduces a further element of contrast between diatonicism and chromaticism (Ex. 3.5l). The F-major idea at m. 17, a chromatically enriched descending pentachord, points in two directions: it is at once the source for the rising chromatic tetrachord of mm. 25–32 and the descending diatonic tetrachord of mm. 69–71, which in turn generates, on reappearing in the coda, a fully chromatic descent through the octave from $c^{\#1}$ to $c^{\#}$. The piece comes full circle from chromatic to diatonic and back again. And finally, No. 5 presents the lament figure in yet another guise, here as chromatic countermelody or cantus firmus, first in the B♭-major episode at m. 33, next in the retransition to the refrain at mm.65ff. (and in subsequent retransitions as well), and then in the D major episode at mm. 104–8 (Ex. 3.5i–k).

All of these elements—*circulatio* and lament, tetrachord and pentachord, inversion and *Urform,* diatonicism versus chromaticism, melodic extension versus contrapuntal combination—are in turn represented in the sprawling No. 8. Extending for some 561 measures, it makes a fitting conclusion for the set in light of the sheer cumulative force of its "witty" references, if not its ability neatly to resolve the issues previously raised. Here Schumann yokes together two of his unruliest progeny, the first a driving "Kreisler" piece, its harmonic vehemence summed up in the four juxtaposed diminished-seventh chords of mm. 1–2 (an allusion, perhaps, to a similar progression in the far jollier No. 3; cf. Exs. 3.5d and n), the second an unrelenting, quasi-arch-form series of waltzes, whose diatonic surface is continually charged by incursions from inverted forms of the lament figure and variants thereof. Some of these are metrically displaced in inner and upper voices (mm. 290ff.; Ex. 3.5p), others in the bass (mm. 320ff., 365ff.; Ex. 3.5q–r). An inversion of the main melody of the central D-minor dance (a chain of *circulatio* patterns) in turn calls forth the lament motive in its chromatically descending shape (cf. mm. 389ff. and 397ff.; Ex. 3.5s), the *Urform* thus supplying structural tones for melody and cadential bass alike (mm. 413ff.; Ex. 3.5t).

To the diatonic/chromatic dialectic Schumann adds another of equal force. The "Kreisler" music that dominates the first half of No. 8 is disposed as a succession of pseudofugal entries (although genuinely supportive contrapuntal voices are lacking, a *stretto* passage appears in mm. 25–28); it is, in other words, interpretable as a cipher for learned counterpoint. The second half, in contrast, presents a sequence of homophonic dance forms artfully arranged. In short, the piece is about the purging of chromatic via diatonic elements, and the giving way of contrapuntal to homophonic textures.

The mediator in both disputes is musically configured as the "Stimme aus der Ferne," whose appearance is the central event of the last of the *Novelletten.* Localized in three spots—at the dissolving close of the first half of the piece, the interstice between the two halves, and a bit past the midpoint of the second half (see Ex. 3.5v)—it neatly embodies the conflicts alluded to above: the diatonicism of the "Stimme" itself is offset by the chromaticism of the accompanying voice; in addition, its character as finely spun-out melody is amplified by the contrapuntal wedge formation of which the "Stimme" proper is but a part. The "Stimme aus der Ferne" and its amplifying voices can also be heard as a nexus of witty allusions to the chief topoi of the whole set. Prepared by a diatonic form of the tetrachord descending from D to A_1 (mm. 157–72; Ex.3.5u), the "Stimme" melody traces two gracefully descending arches—pentachords from f♯ to B and b to e—before arriving at d through a cadential *circulatio* figure. The *circulatio,* chromatically embellished, also serves as inner voice for the first presentation of the melody (mm. 193ff.; Ex. 3.5v), just as alternately truncated and extended forms of the lament figure in inversion furnish bass-line undergirding and, insofar as they complete the wedge formation, contrapuntal density as well. The melody that Schumann places in quotation marks is clearly more than a manifestation of the lyric excess that occasioned Nietzsche's scorn; as a prime example of productive *Witz,* the "Stimme aus der Ferne" is among the most striking of the passages that allow us to understand the *Novelletten* as "zusammenhängende abenteuerliche Geschichten."

Schumann the Allegorizer

"I hear it said: Schumann wrote so many short pieces *because he didn't know how to develop.* A repressive criticism: what you *refuse* to do is what you *can't* do."[109] Yet the corrective to Roland Barthes's charge, in much of the more recent analytical literature on Schumann, remains repressive to the extent that it sees in his miniatures of the 1830s the quest for a "Ganzheit" that eluded his grasp, or seeks to show that Schumann very well *did* know how to develop, or searches for increasingly sensitive modes of large-scale organization from the "fragmented" *Papillons* to the "cohesive" *Davidsbündlertänze,* or looks to a discontinuous method of composition by way of apologizing for the discontinuities of the result.[110] The corrective that I would argue for attempts to accept the fragment (though not to celebrate it) as an intentionally cultivated mode that should not be explained away. For implicit in the progressive side of Schumann's philosophy of history, a scheme that reserved places of veneration for past masters, was his recognition that the moment for the "untroubled whole" (whether or not it indeed existed in the music of Bach, Mozart, and Beethoven) could not be expected to come in an increasingly fragmented present.[111] Schumann's solution to the problem generated by his own historical consciousness—the problem of *emulating* his predecessors without *imitating* them—led him to criticize the "untroubled whole," not to seek it out; to poeticize the fragment, not to overcome it.

The most obviously beneficial aspect of Schumann's critique of the ideology of the whole is the new approach to musical "reading" it engenders. The composer of the *Papillons* and the *Novelletten* set out to disturb his listeners, whose horizon of expectation is continually challenged by the nervous leaps from one affect to another that constitute the principal rhythm-in-the-large of the musical fragment system. Jolted out of a state of complacency, the listener becomes a producer by wittily linking together what may be noncontiguous utterances, thus creating fragment complexes, associative chains of discontinuous musical ideas. The possibilities for grouping are many and varied, so that in a sense Schumann's fragment systems submit to a fixed order only in performance. The listener attuned to their witty structure will, however, produce ever new configurations, thereby continuing the process of experimental reordering of sketches and drafts that antedated Schumann's completion of *Papillons, Carnaval,* the *Phantasiestücke,* the *Kinderszenen,* and the *Novelletten.*[112] In these works, compositional history dovetails with receptive mode. But in all of the miniature collections, Schumann demands that we "read" music in new ways, thus reminding us that although his texts are *constructed,* none are fixed *constructs.*

Schumann might be said to have possessed a highly developed allegorical intuition, though it was not so in the crude sense of the determinate meanings toward which his fanciful titles, inscriptions, mottos, and ciphers seem to point. Schumann's feeling for allegory is closer to that defined by Walter

Benjamin in his study of the German *Trauerspiel,* its structure built up from objects that "stare out" from the whole as if "incomplete and imperfect," its "beauty as a symbol" evaporating "when the light of divine learning falls upon it." What Benjamin said of seventeenth-century tragic drama is no less true of Schumann's miniatures: "The false appearance of totality is extinguished."[113] And if Benjamin could hail Jean Paul, his "children's nurseries" and "haunted rooms" comparable to the "magicians' dens" and "alchemists' laboratories" of the Baroque, as "the greatest allegorist of German literature,"[114] might we not make a parallel claim for Schumann, whose allusion to "Totentänze" (Op. 6) and "Familienscene" (Op. 21) are mere verbal signifiers for the more profoundly allegorical—because fragmented—structure of the music itself?

True, the fixation on allegory is most pronounced in Schumann's piano music of the 1830s, yet a penchant for the fragment never left him (the *Lieder* and *Lieder* cycles are ample proof of this), not even in the outwardly tamer confrontations with classical models in his symphonic works of the next decade. We need think only of the finale of the Second Symphony, Opus 61, its first theme displaced by another by the end of the movement[115] (shades of the *Novelletten*), the truncated recapitulation of the Fourth Symphony's first movement (cf. *Kreisleriana*), or the fanciful play of motives in the third movement of the *Rhenish* Symphony (cf. *Papillons*). Each instance sounds the same note of caution that Friedrich Schlegel uttered in *Kritische Fragmente* no. 103: "many an artistic product whose coherence is never doubted is not a complete work (and this the artist himself knows quite well), but only a fragment, or one or more fragments, a mass, a plan. But so powerful is humanity's urge for unity that the creator himself will often complete something that in fact does not admit to absolute integration or completion."[116]

4 ✒

Euryanthe and the Artwork as Critique

> Only when applied to the inner world,
> when a philosophy criticizes its own spirit
> and creates its own letter on the whetstone
> and with the file of polemics, only then
> can it lead to logical correctness.
>
> – Friedrich Schlegel
> *Athenäum Fragmente,* no. 399

A Challenge for the Historian of Reception

In outlining the methodological premises for his *Arcades Project,* Walter Benjamin claimed that he would "make use of nothing of value." The material most suited for his historical account of the nineteenth century, as filtered through the Parisian Arcades, was to consist of "rags and tatters, detritus." "And these I will not inventory, but rather allow them to come into their own in the only possible manner: by using them."[1] It would probably be unjust to consign Carl Maria von Weber's *Euryanthe,* the *große romantische Oper* that occupied him in the wake of his resounding triumph with *Der Freischütz,* to the "rags and tatters" of history. Still, there is no denying that Weber's chivalric opera, if not a deeply flawed *Meisterwerk,* is at least a highly problematic one.

The unqualified praise that Schumann lavished on the work clearly places him in the minority: "We haven't raved like this for a long time. The music is far too little known or appreciated. Yet it was [Weber's] very life-blood, the noblest that he ever created. To be sure, it cost him a piece of his life, but through it he has become immortal. A chain of sparkling jewels from beginning to end."[2] Not even those critics who sympathized with Weber's high-minded hopes and desires—to compose a work whose intellectual pretensions would place it beyond the popularizing success of *Freischütz*—were as unstinting in their praise. In the eyes of many, *Euryanthe* is to be reckoned with less for what it is than for what it promises to be, that is, to quote Franz Liszt, "a wonderful divination of the future form of the drama."[3] This "future form" is of course the Wagnerian music drama, a point explicitly made by commentators as different in their aesthetic orientation as Eduard Hanslick and Hugo Wolf, and repeated, in various forms, by writers well into our own century.[4] It is ironic, however, that *Euryanthe* should have been salvaged historically, if not aesthetically, as precursor to a genre whose creator found that the work was not music-dramatic enough. In his penetrating critique of Weber's work in *Oper und Drama,* Wagner claimed that Weber's plans misfired because he still held to a compositional approach that favored "Absolute Melody"—in this context, self-sufficient, fully rounded musical forms—even in places where the text or dramatic situation clearly demanded otherwise.[5]

Nor is this the most striking contradiction that we run up against in considering the reception of Weber's *Euryanthe.* Even Helmina von Chézy's libretto, almost universally blamed for the opera's ultimate failure to hold a place in the repertory, has had its defenders. No less a Weberophile than Hans Pfitzner questioned whether the *Euryanthe* text was as miserable as opinion would have it. And while not all the verses may have been "pearls of operatic poetry" (Pfitzner's description of the arias and romances for the principals), it must be admitted that Chézy was a more gifted poet than her detractors have maintained. In addition, Pfitzner rightly observed that when all is said and done, Weber's music and Chézy's text are almost inseparable; one is hardly imaginable without the other.[6]

Even more to the point is the contradiction between another of the more prominent strands of *Euryanthe* criticism and Weber's stated aims as a composer of dramatic music. As Michael Tusa has noted in his excellent study of the opera, many of Weber's contemporaries were puzzled by what they perceived as a lack of self-sufficiency in the music itself.[7] Indeed, a persistent leitmotif in the negative accounts of the work is the reproach that Weber overly emphasized the part, the striking detail, at the expense of the whole. Franz Grillparzer, Weber's sharpest-tongued critic, heard only "disjointed thoughts, held together merely by the text and without inner musical consequence."[8] This critical theme was subjected to any number of variations: from the "isolated exclamations and chords" that troubled an anonymous reviewer for the *Allgemeine musikalische Zeitung*; to A. B. Marx's complaint that Weber "self-consciously directed his whole being toward the dramatic expression of the whole in each separate moment"; or the lack of "inner development of the melodic segments, one out of the other" that Amadeus Wendt pointed out in his lengthy analysis of the work.[9]

Wagner's reference to a "lacquered declamatory mosaic" comes out of the same critical tradition,[10] as do numerous more recent diagnoses of *Euryanthe*'s ills. According to Carl Dahlhaus, for instance, *Euryanthe* must be counted as a "failed magnum opus" in part because Weber allowed the continuities of traditional operatic forms "to crumble into 'musical instants.'"[11] And this point of view has been bolstered by Tusa's study of Weber's compositional process, which reveals a composer less concerned with purely musical modes of elaboration and extension than with highlighting individual details as sharply as possible.[12]

Yet how are we to square these reproaches with Weber's own thoughts and intentions vis-à-vis dramatic composition, so eloquently expressed in his major statement on the nature of opera, the 1817 review of E. T. A. Hoffmann's *Undine?* At least as a critic, Weber evinced a great sensitivity to the interrelationship of part and whole in opera, where each isolated effect is dependent for its meaning on "presentation and arrangement," and where each detail should relate organically to the totality of which it is but a part.[13]

The music of *Euryanthe* is worthy of close study if only to determine whether Weber's intentions and his compositional results were in fact so much at odds. And although it can no longer be said, as Wagner did in *Oper und Drama,* that "criticism has never dealt with *Euryanthe* in the measure that its instructive content deserves," Weber's *große romantische Oper* remains an underanalyzed work.[14] To my knowledge, none of the more extended scenes has been the object of close scrutiny. By way of addressing this gap in the critical literature, we will focus, in the closing section of this chapter, solely on the opening scene complex of Act III. But my chief aim here is to develop the notion that while *Euryanthe* is deeply bound up with the ideology of early nineteenth-century opera—an ideology to which Weber himself contributed much—it casts the ideas of Romanticism in a penetratingly critical light.

Friedrich Schlegel was so much taken by Goethe's *Wilhelm Meister* because for him, it was "one of those books that judges itself, thus relieving the critic of his duties. Indeed, it not only judges itself, it is a representation of itself."[15] *Euryanthe* can also be shown to embody a critique of the aesthetic presuppositions that went into its making. On the surface, Weber's opera can be seen as a tentative manifestation of the *Gesamtkunstwerk* idea, but more specifically, it is characterized by a daring play on the significative capabilities of dramatic music. If most of the early Romantic thinkers tended to give primacy of place to *symbolizing* relationships, where the part is continuous with the whole, and where signifier and signified are at one with each other, then it is arguable that Weber, in addition to recognizing music's symbolic potential, likewise imbued his work with a markedly *allegorical* dimension, whereby signifying elements are removed from their referants by an unbridgable gulf. Here, in the interplay of apparently incompatile signifying modes, lies the "problem" articulated in the troubled reception history of Weber's *große romantische Oper.*

Euryanthe and the *Gesamtkunstwerk* Idea

"Euryanthe must be something completely new—it must stand alone on its peak. Heap difficulty upon difficulty; try to think up poetic meters that will drive one to distraction!"[16] Thus runs Weber's enthusiastic charge to his librettist. But where can we localize the "newness" that Weber so desperately sought after, and that, in all likelihood, added to the consternation of his critics? Michael Tusa has argued persuasively that the uniqueness of *Euryanthe* is a function of Weber's bold experimenting with issues related to genre. On the one hand, the constant presence of the orchestra in *Euryanthe* betrays the influence of French grand opera ("große Oper"); on the other, the chivalric milieu and supernatural elements in the plot, together with the use of strophic *Lieder* and *Romanzen,* point to the German Romantic opera tradition; the result, a "große romantische Oper," was nourished on operatic practices that had previously been kept separate.[17] Still, it is difficult to measure Weber's originality of conception in generic terms alone. The genres that he purportedly set out to fuse were themselves hybrids, each of them the result of a confluence of diverse national traditions: the chief proponent of grand opera before Weber, Johann Nepomuk Poissl, was after all a German composer well acquainted with the riches of Viennese instrumental music; and Romantic opera, given the influx of elements from the *opéra comique* in works like Weber's own *Freischütz,* was hardly a purely German affair. In the early nineteenth century, the German lyric stage was perhaps the single place where generic hybrids were not only tolerated but actually expected. *Euryanthe* is therefore absolutely in line with a body of works where stylistic heterogeneity is the rule, not the exception. Its uniqueness for the early nineteenth century, in other words, must lie beyond the attempted fusion of genres.

At the same time, it is tempting to interpret *Euryanthe* as a realization of the utopian claims for German opera that Weber set out in his critical writings. "Of course when I speak of opera," he maintained in his *Undine* review, "I am speaking of the German ideal, namely, a self-sufficient work of art in which every feature and every contribution by the related arts are molded together in a certain way and dissolve to form a new world."[18] This is, of course, nothing less than a prefiguration of what Wagner, in *Das Kunstwerk der Zukunft* (1849) would proclaim as the doctrine of the *Gesamtkunstwerk,* whereby the late eighteenth-century notion of the *combined* arts (as presented in the neo-Aristotelian accounts of figures like Charles Batteux and Jean-Jacques Rousseau) was displaced by a call for their *fusion*; in the *Gesamtkunstwerk,* the various arts do not merely exist side by side—they are rather, to borrow Hegel's multifaceted term, *aufgehoben,* subsumed in the *Kunstwerk* itself.[19]

That Weber intended to actualize something along these lines in *Euryanthe* seems to be confirmed by his own utterances. As he noted in a letter of 20 December 1824, by way of expressing his disapproval of a projected concert performance of his opera by the Akademischer Musikverein of the University of Breslau: "*Euryanthe* is a purely dramatic essay, building its hopes only on the united collaboration of all the sister arts, and surely ineffective if robbed of their assistance."[20] But even by the early 1820s, during the period, that is, that saw the creation of *Euryanthe,* the idea of the *Gesamtkunstwerk* was hardly new. Friedrich Schelling, a philosopher with whom Weber was on close terms, had already suggested in his 1801/4 lectures on the philosophy of art that the "perfect composition of all the arts," the restoration of the wondrous totality of ancient drama, could come about only through the unification of poetry and music in song, and of poetry and painting in dance.[21] And in his highly influential *Vorlesungen* of 1808/9, August Wilhelm Schlegel would come forth with an account of opera that closely approximates the *Gesamtkunstwerk* ideal.[22] In addition, it would be difficult to gauge just how thoroughly Weber subscribed to the totalizing aspects of the idea. That is to say, there is a good chance that the *Gesamtkunstwerk* represented, for Weber, an ideology that he felt compelled to repeat.

Grillparzer may well have overstated his case in deriding Weber as a "theory man" and hence an "anti-artist": "criticism will be the end of him."[23] But the harsh denunciation contains a grain of truth. Stated in less shrill terms, it suggests that we should exercise caution in differentiating those aspects of Weber's pronouncements that serve heuristic as opposed to purely critical ends. As an ideologue (and as self-proclaimed judge and teacher for the German public in matters of operatic taste), Weber was content to toss off, almost in the manner of an obligatory aside within the course of his *Undine* critique, the doctrine of the united arts. As a satirist, he had no qualms about caricaturing, in the riotous *Agnes Bernauer: A Romantic-Patriotic Music Drama* episode in *Tonkünstlers Leben,* some of the very elements of *Schauerromantik* that he would later incorporate in his own *Freischütz* and *Euryanthe.* But as a serious critic, he was more than willing to admit that the union and dissolution of the various arts in the *Gesamtkunstwerk* just as often as not amounted to an intense struggle among and between them.

In his exchange on the nature of text setting with the poet and playwright Adolf Müllner, for instance, Weber began by commenting that one of the composer's principal problems stemmed from the poetic conflict between speech accent, or stress, and prosodic quantity, noting further that this dichotomy is often intensified by music, which possesses a precisely fixed rhythmic system of its own. Indeed, he was forced to concede to Müllner's principal point: that the sense of a poem can be radically altered when set to music.[24] The uneasy relationship of music, poetic accent, and meaning that often obtains when the arts of word and tone come together in practice therefore stands in sharp contrast to their theoretical blending in the *Gesamtkunstwerk*. So too does Weber's demand to Chézy, quoted at the beginning of this section, for unusual poetic meters and irregular rhyme schemes.

Let us consider a specific example from the opening scene of the last act of *Euryanthe,* beginning at the spot where Adolar, convinced of Euryanthe's faithlessness and determined to put her to death, pauses to reflect on happier days. The dialogue begins as follows:

ADOLAR
Wie liebt' ich dich!
Du warst mein höchstes Gut.

EURYANTHE
O Stille deines Zornes Glut!
Mein Herz ist rein wie meine Taten.

ADOLAR
Der höchsten Liebe sprachst du Hohn!
So gräßlich ward noch nie die Treu verraten;
Empfange nun der Untat Lohn!

Chézy heeded Weber's charge well: here we have a single unrhymed line (actually, it is answered by Euryanthe's "O höre mich!" some seven verses later, just after the second of Adolar's speeches), followed by six lines of varying lengths arranged in an aabcbc rhyme scheme, which is in any event obscured inasmuch as it cuts across the exchanges of the principals. The prevailing poetic meter, however, is iambic, and Chézy uses it to articulate an important dramatic idea. Adolar is just as distraught over the fact that a love that once was can be no more as he is over Euryanthe's alleged indiscretion, hence, "Wie *liebt'* ich dich!" (How I *loved* you), "Du *warst* mein höchstes Gut." (You *were* my dearest possession), or in his second speech, the similar emphases on "sprachst" and "ward."

Weber softens Adolar's fixation on the past, or rather replaces it with an obsessional focus on Euryanthe (see Ex. 4.1). The metrical placement of "Du" on the first beat of a measure, thus initiating a lyric phrase that is then more emphatically restated at a higher pitch level, is clearly at odds with both the meter and the meaning of the poem. Although it would be a mistake to speak of a willful distortion, there is little doubt that Weber's music produces a subtle put powerful shift of meaning. Likewise, the music all but obliterates what is already a precariously elaborated rhyme scheme toward the end of setting the characters' varying affective stances into relief. The rhyme between

EXAMPLE 4.1

Weber, *Euryanthe,* Act III/i, mm. 97–115   (Excerpts from Weber's *Euryanthe* reprinted by permission, Gregg Publishing, © 1969.)

EXAMPLE 4.1 (*continued*)

"Gut" and "Glut" is weakened by the interpolated repetition of the opening verse, which consequently places the rhyming term in the center as opposed to the end of a syntactic melodic unit. The rhyme between "verraten," which comes at the end of an almost frantic outburst, and "Taten," which closes Euryanthe's lyric phrase, is likewise suspended, as is the parallelism between "Hohn" (part of a recitative-like cadential phrase) and "Lohn" (the highpoint of a declamatory utterance).

In the first part of this example, then, textual and musical meaning come into conflict, while in the second, poetic rhyme and musico-dramatic meaning are played against each other. In both cases, though, the principal point holds: there is no harmonious blend of text and music here. What obtains is rather a kind of "musical prose" wherein the continuities of the *Gesamtkunstwerk* ideal give way to a discontinuous, allegorical relationship between and among music, poetry, and meaning. And the critical background for this relationship is to be found not in the utopian theorizing of Weber or his philosophical predecessors, but in the tale of poetry and music unfolded in E. T. A. Hoffmann's dialogue on operatic composition, *Der Dichter und der Komponist*. Ferdinand, the worldly poet, and his friend Ludwig, the introspective musician, the two interlocutors in the dialogue, have been separated for some time, come together to debate the contrary demands of their respective arts, but ultimately part without having reached an agreement. It requires only a slight effort of the imagination to see through the story, more precisely the "allegory," and uncover the meaning toward which it points. Ferdinand and Ludwig are ciphers for poetry and music, two arts that may have been at one during some Golden Age in the distant past, and that may, for brief periods, interact in the present, but that ultimately will have to assert their independence. This, it seems to me, is the line of argument that Weber translates into tones. The radicality of his *Euryanthe* resides not in the manner through which the arts of poetry and tone are fused, but rather in the assertiveness with which their mutual boundaries are proclaimed.

Euryanthe in the Wilderness

The flip side of Grillparzer's harsh dismissal of Weber's music is provided by his cool-headed account of the nature of musical signification, which in turn takes us to the heart of the *Euryanthe* problem. According to Grillparzer, his stance rooted in the formalist outlook of Kant's *Kritik der Urteilskraft,* Weber belongs to that class of composers who confound the differences between poetry and music, words and tones. He erred in *Freischütz,* the poet asserts, and even more seriously in *Euryanthe* (we might presume), by treating musical figures as if they were arbitrary signs for determinate objects and ideas, at the same time seeming to forget that music is a thing unto itself, an autonomous art form that develops according to its own laws.[25] But the argument is hardly air-tight. It in fact entails a notable discrepancy: Grillparzer's unequivocal statement of music's lack of signifying potential as a self-referential art form—"Music has no words, i.e., arbitrary signs, that first acquire meaning through that which is signified"—is immediately followed by a subtle but telling reversal—"A musical tone is not only capable of being a sign but also a thing."[26] Weber, I would like to argue, held firmly to the latter point of view, and attempted to realize it as never before. In *Euryanthe* music is treated as a "sign" for something that it is not (as a kind of "prose," but without the pejoritave connotations that Grillparzer lent to the term), *and* as a "thing" with its own rights to autonomous existence. Weber strove, in other words, for a kind of music that would "signify" in as potent a manner as possible.

Stated in terms of the ideas of Romanticism, Weber aimed at creating music that was at once symbolic (self-referential) and allegorical (designative), music that not only endeavored to match a poetic text and dramatic situation as closely as it could, but also made autonomous claims for itself qua music. The various contradictory strands of *Euryanthe* criticism can thus be seen to complement one another. The critics who faulted Weber for the fussiness of his declamation and his overly studied focus on the depiction of details attended only to the allegorical dimension of his work. Those who attempted to salvage *Euryanthe* historically by viewing it as a precursor of the Wagnerian music drama gave more weight to the totalizing, symbolizing qualities of the proto-*Gesamtkunstwerk.* Yet Weber's aims were in fact more complicated than either position, taken alone, will allow.

Moreover, the particular configuration of symbolic and allegorical qualities that we will trace in the *Euryanthe* score departs significantly from their relative position in the dominant ideology of Romanticism, which gave primacy of place to symbolic at the expense of allegorical relationships. As Tzvetan Todorov has shown, the whole of the Romantic doctrine can be interpreted as a semiotic theory that opposed synthetic or symbolic modes with disjunct or allegorical ones. By aligning themselves with the symbol and disavowing the potency of allegory as a vehicle for modern poetic expression, the Romantics were able to clear out a space for their own achievements as thinkers and artists. For Goethe, who introduced the opposition, the simultaneous presence of the general *and* the particular in the symbol (whose existence in and of itself counts for more than its role as signifier) accords with the very nature of poetry, while allegory is described as a mere means of seeking access to the general *through* the particular. The symbol is therefore intransitive (self-referential) and synthetic (capable of fusing contraries); insofar as it can be employed to point beyond itself, it also belong to the class of motivated or natural signs. Allegory, on the other hand, is transitive, its poetic force exhausted as soon as its referent has been determined; and as an unmotivated or arbitrary sign, it signifies directly, much like a hieroglyph. If the symbol affords a means of expressing the inexpressible, then allegory answers to this infinity of meaning with a fixed term whose expressive power is used up at the very moment when its meaning has been uncovered. And although subject to some slight variations, the general outlines of this Goethean opposition were retained in the writings of a whole generation of thinkers: Schelling, Herder, Friedrich Ast, and Friedrich Creuzer among them.[27]

The views of one commentator, however, stand apart from those of his contemporaries with special prominence. Friedrich Schlegel's thoughts on the symbol-versus-allegory question differ in a number of important details from what can safely be thought of as the mainstream. It is worth pausing to reflect on some of these differences, first as a reminder that the dominant position is neither the only nor the "truest" position, and second so that Schlegel's poetic critique may be taken to serve as the background for Weber's more specifically musical critique of the significative modes.

Like most early nineteenth-century writers, Schlegel defined symbolism as a synecdochic relationship, where the part is subsumed within the whole, and allegory as a metonymic mode in which the relation between signifier and signified is discontinuous. "Der Witz ist die Kraft der Allegorie": this fragment calls attention to the contrasts that may obtain between two signifying terms, contrasts that can only be mediated by the lightning flash of *Witz.*[28] Symbolically related terms, on the other hand, are harmoniously bound together. "In feminine beauty," he states in another fragment, "there is more harmony and symbolism; the masculine variety displays more allegory, enthusiasm, and energy."[29] Yet it was precisely this enthusiasm and energy that placed allegory, in Schlegel's eyes, at the very center of modern poetry.[30] Not only was it at the heart of such genres as the *Märchen* and the "fantastic" *Roman*,[31] but it was also, no less than the "philosophical concept," the "foundational mythology" of poetry itself.[32] As he put it in one particularly dithyrambic fragment: "Allegory marks the conjunction of philosophy, poetry, and historical philology. . . . Allegory is an artful, mystic, philosophical, progressive myth; it is a mystical artwork."[33] What many of his contemporaries attributed to the symbol—features such as the interpenetration of signified and signifier, or the expression of the inexpressible—Schlegel reserved for allegory.[34] Nor did this merely amount to the substitution of one term for another: as we have seen, allegory and symbol remained discontinuous and continuous relationships respectively in Schlegel's poetics; the allegorical mode was prized because of and not in spite of the oppositional relationship of signifier and signified. And as Manfred Frank has observed, Schlegel realized that "absolute unity" was a philosophical chimera. All that we can hope for is the allegorical intimation of unity that only art provides. The unknowable cannot be adequately represented, nor should the poet attempt to do so; the only available path lies in *hinting at it* through allegory.[35]

Schlegel the divinatory aesthetician thus viewed allegory as a means of gaining access to the infinite. But more important for our present discussion, Schlegel the critic recognized in allegory a corrective to the utopian doctrine of the symbol. The central truth of his critical theory resides in his recognition that the significative process is marked by a cleft between the terms involved. Similarly, we will see that operatic signification, as practiced by Weber in *Euryanthe,* is also marked by tears and ruptures. But they do not come about, as many of the opera's earliest detractors thought, from Weber's single-minded focus on the painting of individual details and nothing more. They mark the points where symbolizing and allegorizing modes come into direct conflict.

It will be necessary, then, to view the technical innovations that Weber employed in his *große romantische Oper* (and which he outlined in his prose writings) from two angles. The move toward the elimination of closed operatic numbers, a feature already detectable in the cantata *Kampf und Sieg*[36] and likewise evident in portions of *Euryanthe,* Act III, is "allegorical" to the extent that it will enable as naturalistic a depiction of rapidly proceeding events as music will allow. The continuous flow of the music thus matches the continuous flow of the stage action without our being able to say that one directly calls forth the other. But inasmuch as through-composition may help to facilitate the kind of unity that the alternation of concerted numbers with recitative or spoken dialogue automatically rules out, it evinces a "symbolizing" dimension as well.

In his description of the precompositional tonal planning of *Kampf und Sieg,* Weber equated musical tonalities with emotional moods.[37] Although there is no direct proof that his work on *Euryanthe* was preceded by a tonal

sketch of this sort, there is no denying that specific tonalities are often coupled with specific ideas, affects, or groups of characters.[38] In accordance with
the late eighteenth- and early nineteenth-century conventions summarized,
for example, in Christian Schubart's *Ideen zu einer Ästhetik der Tonkunst*
(1806), Weber often settled on a key for its tonally significative potential.
Hence flat keys are often employed in *Euryanthe* as tonal allegories for the
hero and heroine, and sharp keys for both the villains and the more evil or
sinister elements in the plot. The principal tonality of the opera, E♭, thus
stands for divine or virtuous elements; C major is the key of Euryanthe's love;
E major and minor are associated with the wicked Eglantine; D major is a
chivalric tonality.

Yet the theory of tonal allegory will get us only so far with the actuality of
Weber's music, for some of the tonalities encountered in *Euryanthe* appear
to have little or no extramusical significance at all. The pairing of A major
and A minor in the duets, Nos. 7 and 15, and in the *Lied mit Chor,* No. 21,
may, as Tusa suggests, have something to do with the contrast of fidelity and
faithlessness, or of downfall and renewal.[39] But in No. 7, A minor can just as
easily be taken as a token of Eglantine's duplicity; and whereas the characters
complement one another in No. 7, they stand opposed in No. 15. Likewise, B
major, is put to striking use in three instances: (1) Euryanthe's chromatically
charged vision of Adolar's deceased sister Emma, associated in its various
occurrences with the evocative sound of *divisi* strings, *con sordino*; (2) the
gripping duet for the "evil pair," Eglantine and Lysiart, in Act II (No. 11), often
cited as a model for Wagner's Ortrud-Telramund music in *Lohengrin*; and (3)
Euryanthe's declamatory arioso, "Schirmende Engelschaar," sung in the
opening scene of Act III as Adolar goes off to do battle with the dragon. It is
hard to imagine that Weber was trying to make a point about the connection
between these disparate elements in the drama by placing them in the same
key. The connotations of G major—the key of the opening choral tableau, the
middle portion of Lysiart's *Arie* No. 10, and Euryanthe's plaintive *Cavatine*
No. 17—are equally diverse. Yet the tonal allegory idea is not so much wrongheaded as incomplete. What it leaves out of account is Weber's "symbolizing,"
that is, self-referential use of keys for purely musical reasons. And most interesting, as we will see in considering the Euryanthe-Adolar dialogue of Act III,
are those cases where Weber's attempt at a key plan that is at once coherent
in itself *and* designative results in dynamic tonal ruptures.

The associative use of melodies, motives, gestures, and even textures is also
dual-natured. It hinges first of all on recurrence, one of the most obvious
means, as Weber pointed out in his brief piece on his incidental music to the
play *Preciosa,* of binding together a musico-dramatic work as an organic
whole.[40] In *Euryanthe,* therefore, the recall of extended melodic blocks—
Adolar's "Ich bau' auf Gott," (originally part of the overture's first-theme
complex), or the lovers' "Hin nimm die Seele mein"—acts as an agent of
continuity in a work of admittedly large proportions.

But in order to ensure that this internal, "symbolizing" relationship would register in the first place, Weber fashioned a whole array of distinctive musical ideas for the purpose of characterizing individual details as precisely as possible. Among the simplest of these allegorizing figures are mere gestures, such as the "vehement" appoggiatura or sigh (a musical emblem of grief or evil depending on its placement in the music for the principals or the villains), the sudden VII°⁷ "outburst" (an apt representation of shock in tones), or the rhythmically chiseled octave leap (a sign for regal ceremony in the Act II and III finales). Textures may serve similar ends: witness Weber's frequent use of continuously throbbing eighths in the strings (and less often in the winds) to represent inner agitation, or of *forte* string *tremolando* to serve as a backdrop for formalized utterances such as oaths (Adolar's "Vermessener! frohlocke nicht! in the *Terzett mit Chor,* No. 4) or pleas (Euryanthe's "Der du die Unschuld kennst" in the Act II finale). The consistency with which a bit of serpentine figuration (little more than a horizontal embellishment of a diminished-seventh chord) is linked with Eglantine in her initial exchange with Euryanthe (*Dritte Scene,* Nos. 6, 7, and 8) makes it into a leitmotif of sorts. Tonal and timbral features are combined in figures that merit description as *Klangfarben,* such as the unsupported parallel thirds, either in the upper strings or the winds, that go hand in hand with the desolation shared by the wrongly accused Euryanthe and the restive spirit of Adolar's sister. And to be sure, Weber saves his most unusual *Klangfarbe* for Emma: the conjunction of muted violins and wandering tonality in the music associated with her ghost.

The "dramatic truth" that guided Weber's hand thus embraced two realms, one geared toward minute depiction, the other toward large-scale coherence. There is of course little reason to assume that the two cannot work in tandem. They often do. But at the same time, *continual* accord is less a practical than an ideological possibility. It belongs to the Romantic doctrine of the symbol, but not to the practice of a dynamically oriented composer of stage music for whom continuous harmony, even if it were attainable, was anathema. The most fascinating portions of Weber's *große romantische Oper,* and likewise the most "dramatically true," are thus to be found where the allegorical and symbolic dimensions are somewhat at odds.

This interaction is especially telling in the opening scene complex of Act III, where Adolar, convinced that Euryanthe has betrayed his trust, leads her into the wilderness to meet her death. Amadeus Wendt devoted considerable attention to this scene in his critique of the opera for the *Allgemeine musikalische Zeitung,* singling it out as a particularly fine demonstration of Weber's powers of musical *Karakteristik.*[41] Coupled with Weber's characterization of individual details, moreover, is an incredible sense for the integration of those details into a whole—a whole, however, that must have struck Weber's audience as unusual indeed, and that retains its singularity to this day.

In structural terms, the Euryanthe–Adolar dialogue is perhaps the most remarkable in the entire opera—which, contrary to the claims of many commentators, is essentially a number opera. Even its larger scene complexes (the Euryanthe–Eglantine dialogue in Act I, or Lysiart's accusation at the close of Act II) tend to be build up from self-sufficient musico-dramatic units that are tonally closed and melodically rounded off. On the basis of these criteria, Weber's number divisions here (15 and 16) count for little. The *Recitativ und Duett,* No. 15, is composed of an extended orchestral introduction in D minor, a tonally wandering recitative, a duet in A, and a brief monologue—actually, a series of modulatory outbursts—for Euryanthe. The *Scene,* No. 16 (untitled in Weber's autograph),[42] begins with what Wendt called a "Rhapsodie" for Euryanthe,[43] in B, a few final words for the principals, and an orchestral postlude closing in E♭. Consider as well that the conclusion of No. 15 (Euryanthe's monologue, followed by a rhythmically driving orchestral transition) acts as a preface to No. 16, and it is obvious that neither number alone makes much sense as a syntactically complete musical unit. The dramatic action is likewise strangely skewed against the number division: too much happens in No. 15 and too little in No. 16.

To be sure, the scene comprises several smaller units, but these are not at one with the designated numbers. The "number," in other words, gives way at the larger level to the scene, and at the local level to subdivisions not unlike the poetic-musical periods that Wagner described in *Oper und Drama.* As indicated in Figure 4–1, the scene divides into seven smaller sections (labeled A–G), each of which can be linked with a definite stage in the action. The orchestral introduction (*A*) depicts the arrival of Euryanthe and Adolar in the wilderness, Sections *B, C,* and *D* are given over to statements of their contrasting positions (Euryanthe insisting on her innocence, Adolar just as firmly proclaiming her guilt), and a few moments of agitated commentary on the same. In section *E,* Euryanthe reacts violently to the suddenly approaching serpent, which Adolar duly vanquishes during the heroine's ensuing "Rhapsodie" (*F*). And finally, in section G, the victorious Adolar mercifully abandons his former beloved rather than putting her to death. Furthermore, the moment of *perepeteia,* occasioned by the appearance of the monster, justifies a division of the scene into two large parts, the first comprising sections *A–D,* the second, sections *E–G.*

Although the action may strike us as silly (the episode with the giant snake has caused even devotees of the opera to wince), Weber approached it with the utmost seriousness. The scene became, for him, a paradigm for the opera composer's fundamental challenge. As he put it in the *Undine* review:

> The very nature and inner constitution of opera—as a whole containing other wholes—has this essential drawback, which only a few heroes of the art have managed to surmount. Every musical number has its own proper architecture, which makes it an independent and organic unity; yet this should be absorbed in any study of the work as a whole. Ensembles, in par-

FIGURE 4–1

Weber, *Euryanthe,* Act III, scene i; Overview

Section	Tempo	Mm.	Tonality	Action
Part 1				
A. Orchestral Introduction [No. 15]	*adagio non lento* (= 66)	1–36	d→E♭→d	Adolar and Euryanthe arrive at the ravine
B. Recitative	[*adagio*] *con moto* + *a tempo* (= 66) *allegro* (= 160)	37–66	d→B→c →V/A	Euryanthe insists on her fidelity
C. Arioso dialogue	*moderato* (= 88) *più moto* (= 138)	97–107 108–40	A→c♯–b–a →V/a	Adolar stands firm in his resolve to put Euryanthe to death
D. Duet: "Du klagst mich an"	*agitato* (= 96)	140–90	a–e–a–c–a	Reflection on the above
Part 2				
E. Dramatic monologue: "Entsetzen" (Eur.)	*non tanto allegro* (= 88) *presto* (= 116)	191–210	[c]–[d]→e♭ E♭→B	Euryanthe warns Adolar of the approaching serpent; Adolar rushes off to do battle
F. *Rhapsodie*: "Schirmende Engelschaar" (Eur.) [No. 16]	*molto appassionato* (= 152)	220–82	B–(D)–B	Euryanthe summons a host of guardian angels to protect Adolar, then rejoices in his victory
G. Recitative and Orchestral Close	— *poco ritenuto* (= 132) *adagio vivace* (= 160)	283–85 286–98 299–302 303–29	B→ E♭	Adolar, unable to kill Euryanthe, abandons her instead

ticular, can and should show a number of different aspects simultaneously, a Janus-like image, whose different faces are visible at a single glance.[44]

Friedrich Schlegel's laconic statement of the same dilemma is worth quoting as well: "Also in poetry every whole may well be a part, and every part actually a whole."[45] But how was the artist to assure this interdependence of detail and total design? In *Euryanthe,* Weber's solution hinged on his fashioning an associative web of musical elements, each in itself an "allegory" for the situation immediately at hand; but taken in their entirety, the elements comprise a powerful means of ensuring the coherence of the whole. True enough, the web is not all-embracing: not every segment of the *große romantische Oper* is a reflection in miniature of the drama in its totality. It can be argued, however, that the opening scene of Act III embodies the "Januslike image" that Weber prescribed as an ideal for the operatic ensemble. Like the Wolf's Glen scene in *Freischütz,* it is the dark center of the opera (both figuratively and literally: both scenes play by moonlight), a nexus for the development of gestures, motives, and *Klangfarben* that figure throughout the work.

If the confrontation of Adolar and Euryanthe in the wilderness is a microcosmic presentation of the darker, supernatural side of the drama of which it forms a part, then its opening segment (section *A*) acts in many ways as an encapsulated center for the musical issues that inform the ensuing scene. For here, as in much of the dialogue that follows, the point-by-point, "allegorical," correspondence between music and scenic display leads to a prose-like construction that is likewise coherent in a strictly musical sense (see Ex. 4.2). The opening duo-recitative for the violins is already shot through with signifying references to emotional states and pantomimed action: the thinly textured opening phrase not only concords with the barrenness of the physical landscape but also, through the parallel thirds of mm. 4, 5, 7, 12, and 13, points to the heroine's desolation. The serpentine violin figuration provides an apt musical backdrop for Adolar's descent to the ravine, its tortuous chromaticism a further signal of the principals' consternation. The confluence of diminished-seventh chord and sigh at m. 8 (and more persistently in mm. 19–21) contributes further to this generalized portrayal of grief, while the throbbing eighths in the winds (mm. 15–18) add an element of agitation as well.

Harmonic details are also employed to highlight specific turns in the action: Adolar pauses to ponder his situation just as the music turns decisively from D minor to E♭ (mm. 15–18); Euryanthe's actual appearance on the scene (m. 24) is articulated by the appearance of the D-minor $^6_4$ that clearly brings the music back into the tonic region after several measures of harmonic instability. Texture and gesture also set the heroine's entrance into relief: Euryanthe nervously observes the surroundings to the plaintive tones of a solo horn melody made up principally of a series of sigh figures.

EXAMPLE 4.2

Weber, *Euryanthe,* Act III/i, orchestral introduction   (Excerpts from Weber's
Euryanthe reprinted by permission, Gregg Publishing, © 1969.)

EXAMPLE 4.2 (*continued*)

But Weber's tone-poem-in-miniature also makes good sense as music in and of itself. The first phrase of the violin recitative (mm. 1–8) acts as antecedent (moving from i to V/V) to a parallel statement initiated at m. 10 and proceeding from dominant harmony. As it turns out, though, the consequent recitative phrase gives way to what begins as a full-blown melody articulated by thicker orchestral texture (the winding figure in the violins now transported into the bass) and tonic harmony (m. 15). The phrase syntax is thus richly ambiguous, but eminently logical nonetheless; what begins as a conventional antecedent-consequent disposition is reinterpreted, as the music proceeds, to function as an introduction. Yet the untroubled progress of the D-minor melody is soon arrested by a stunning turn to E♭ and by several measures of harmonically divigatory music (mm. 17–23) that in turn lead to the D-minor cadential melody in the horn (mm. 24–36). Once again, in other words, a supposedly initiatory melody must be viewed retrospectively as a preface for things to come.

The musical sense of Weber's procedure is clearly discernible; a tried and true periodic syntax is employed as a point of departure for a logically evolving structure. The allegorical tone poem turns out to have a symbolic, self-referential consistency of its own. Still, the two worlds do not entirely mesh. The most notable cleft comes with the abrupt move to E♭ at m. 15, a harmonic jolt made all the more striking by a *subito* shift from *piano* to *forte* dynamic. But even this is valorized by future events; the E♭ harmony, though an isolated detail at this point, will return more prominently at the end of section *E,* and yet again as the tonal goal of the entire scene.

Section *B* is devoted to the first stages of the dialogue between Adolar and Euryanthe. Strictly speaking, this is a dialogue in name only, for the characters, each entrapped in separate worlds, speak more to themselves than to each other. Their comments reverberate, if at all, in a void. To underscore the notion that the dialogue is actually a series of simultaneously proceeding inner monologues, Weber relies heavily on the principle of contrast. Euryanthe's words are supported by the wispiest of string textures, Adolar's by the darker *Klangfarbe* provided by *divisi* violas and bassoons in parallel thirds (for his annunciation of Euryanthe's death at mm. 58ff.; see Ex. 4.3) or by agitated *tremolando* figures for the full complement of strings. Tonally, Euryanthe begins in the d/B sphere, to which Adolar responds in a remote C minor. These contrasts, however, should be considered in conjunction with the links between this music and what has gone before, both in the scene and in the opera. The opening portion of Euryanthe's first speech recalls the violins' parallel thirds from section A, just as her closing lines ("Ein lindernd Wort") call up the texture of Emma's "ghost" music, and its characteristic B tonality, in the orchestra (a texture that surfaces again after Adolar's speech, for the setting of Euryanthe's "Ich bin mir Liebe nur bewußt!"). The apparently new melody at Adolar's annunciation of death (mm. 58ff.) turns out, on closer inspection, to be a gestural relative of the D-minor melody from the

EXAMPLE 4.3

Weber, *Euryanthe,* Act III/i, mm. 53–80; Adolar's annunciation of Euryanthe's death   (Excerpts from Weber's *Euryanthe* reprinted by permission, Gregg Publishing, © 1969.)

235
XXIV
a tempo
XXV
XXVI
XXVII
XXVIII
XXIX
XXX
XXXI
XXXII
XXXIII
XXXIV
pp
cre - - scen - - do poco a poco
Wort! Es we - cke mei - ne Stimme dein schlummerndes Ge - wis - sen! du sollst in mei - nem Grimme Er - barmen nicht ver - missen; be - reu'!
f
pp

orchestral introduction, its parallel-third texture hearkening at the same time to Euryanthe's previous monologue. And his second, more vehement declaration ("Vernimm mein letztes Wort!") brings with it the throbbing eighths from section A. Even the obvious tears in the musical proceedings are Janus-faced.

The most telling of these clefts between extramusical allegory and self-referential symbolism comes just after Euryanthe's first speech. Her closing line is matched to B-major and E-minor harmonies, but given the fluidity of the tonal discourse at this point, they might imply I to iv in the former tonality, or V to i in the latter (see mm. 54–56 in Ex. 4.3). Following on a fermata, the first violins alone sustain a single B, which moves without transition into the full C-minor harmony of Adolar's annunciation of death. Wendt's commentary on this apparently allegorizing portayal of the contrast between Euryanthe's plea and Adolar's grim pronouncement hints at an interpretation addressing the self-referential aspects of the spot: "The move from the sustained B into a C-minor chord shows how well Weber knew to choose his tonalities; for the horror of the situation must be deeply felt."[46] Isolated tonal events (the single B, the C minor chord) are surely significant, but what counts just as much is the abstract relationship between them, in this case, a half-step shift echoing the passage from D minor to E♭ in section A. Furthermore, the B/C tonal allegory is reconfigured as a unifying device at the end of Adolar's monologue, where the very same gesture (the B now part of a diminished seventh harmony) recurs to round off the speech. The same musical idea therefore contributes to the allegorical depiction of contrary emotional states and to the inner cohesion of a purely musical construct.

We have already considered the discrepancies between musical and poetic meaning, poetic rhyme and musical syntax, in section *C,* where Adolar's fleeting remembrance of happier times occasions a move toward more frankly lyric utterances. But with Adolar's resolve to silence Euryanthe's "siren-song" forever, lyricism is displaced by rhetorically charged declamation. Weber signals the affective break by introducing a driving dactylic figure in the strings (see m. 109ff. in Ex. 4.4), an idea whose significance extends beyond its ability to register Adolar's abrupt affective reversal: this seemingly scrappy idea provides the motivic substance in the orchestra for the entire closing portion of the section, and will return again, in the last measures of section D, as Euryanthe spots the giant snake.

Of greater moment for the unfolding dialectic of the scene is the role of section *C* as mediator between its neighbors. Tonally, it is more closely bound up with the A-minor "Du klagst mich an" that follows. To be sure, the A major articulated at the beginning of section *C* holds for less than a dozen measures; but the subsequent C#-minor music (at Adolar's "Der höchsten Liebe") proceeds with inexorable logic, by means of sequence, to B minor, and back again to A in its minor-mode form (each stage of the sequence is further articulated by the dactylic string motive). On the other hand, the third rela-

EXAMPLE 4.4

Weber, *Euryanthe,* Act III/i, mm. 107–40   (Excerpts from Weber's *Euryanthe* reprinted by permission, Gregg Publishing, © 1969.)

EXAMPLE 4.4 (*continued*)

tionship between the C and A music of sections *B* and *C* respectively is minimized by the tonal instability of the Adolar–Euryanthe exchange at the end of section *B* (a passage Wendt criticized for its overly rapid modulations.)[47] But syntactically, section *C* relates more directly to the music that comes before. The lyric setting of "Wie liebt' ich dich" may presage the symmetry of phrasing that predominates in "Du klagst mich an," but this syntactic regularity is shortlived. It soon gives way to the textural shifts and naturalistic declamation that figured earlier in the scene. Poised between accompanied recitative and concerted number, the Janus-faced section *C* occupies the space between no longer and not yet.

Section *D* brings the scene's most conventional music. Ushered in by the stock recitative cadence at the conclusion of section *C,* it follows the course of a typically reflective set piece. Two complete statements of the text (along with frequent internal text repetitions) are needed to fill out a straightforward binary form, the first half moving from tonic (A minor) to major dominant (converted during the last moments to a diminished- then dominant-seventh harmony), the second half providing a varied replay of much the same music in the tonic (see Ex. 4.5 for the music of the first half). Although the dialectic between part and whole that we have been tracing in earlier sections is largely absent here, the self-sufficiency of the section *D* music is to an extent counterbalanced by the lyric idea (itself a variant of the section's *Hauptmotiv)* introduced at m. 151 ("Mein Leben war in Dir allein"), an echo of the orchestral phrase at m. 86 and of Euryanthe's "Ein lindernd Wort," both from section *B.*

The emphatic A-minor close of the "duet" (and with it, the close of Part I) is marked by the frantic return, in the orchestra, of the dactylic figure from section *C,* and leads directly to the central event of the scene: Euryanthe's horror at the sight of the approaching serpent, and her selfless realization of the threat that it poses to Adolar's life. The heroine's benumbed shock is portrayed, at one level, by one of the most hackneyed devices that music has at its disposal for such situations: the *Hammerschlag* diminished-seventh chord (see Ex. 4.6). But here Weber intensifies the gesture to good effect: the E♭ of the chord is sustained *fortissimo* by horns, trumpets, and bass trombone (the latter two instruments introduced for the first time), so that a dissonant tritone relationship with the preceding A-minor duet is further brought into play. The musical fabric of Euryanthe's ensuing declamatory arioso, "Entsetzen," is likewise saturated with all three diminished-seventh harmonies.

At the same time, the shock effects should be weighed against their reference to similar gestures from earlier on in the scene. The opening *Hammerschlag* recalls similar strategically placed occurrences of the diminished-seventh chord: it is the first chordal sonority that we hear in the scene after the initial, tonality-defining D-minor triad; it occurs, and at the same pitch level as in section *E,* at the climax of Adolar's last speech in section *B*; Adolar's "empfange nun der Unthat Lohn!" from section *C* culminates in

EXAMPLE 4.5

Weber, *Euryanthe,* Act III/i, "Du klagst mich an"   (Excerpts from Weber's *Euryanthe* reprinted by permission, Gregg Publishing, © 1969.)

EXAMPLE 4.6

Weber, *Euryanthe,* Act III/i, Euryanthe's "Entsetzen" monologue   (Excerpts from
Weber's *Euryanthe* reprinted by permission, Gregg Publishing, © 1969.)

the VII°⁷ on E♯; and lastly, the central orchestral interlude of section *D* arpeggiates the VII°⁷ on G♯ in the winds. The diminished-seventh harmonies of Euryanthe's "Entsetzen" monologue likewise imply a series of sequentially disposed tonalities—C, D, and E♭—that mirror the C♯-B-A series that led into section *D*. The effect of the tonal shocks, in other words, is ameliorated by their place in an internal, self-referential network. It is also worth pointing out that the string figure from the *presto* transition to Euryanthe's "Schirmende Engelschaar" reverses the pattern of the dactylic motive familiar from Sections C and D.

Section *F*—Euryanthe's prayer for divine protection, and her exultation over Adolar's triumph—is set in high relief by another jarring shift in the tonal course; and while the move here from E♭ to B may not be as sudden as the earlier juxtaposition of A to E♭, it is nonetheless effected in a singularly compelling manner, by means of a chromatic descent in bassoons, bass trombone, and lower strings from E♭ to B♭, and then a fitful ascent from G♭ to its enharmonic equivalent, F♯, now treated as the dominant of B. According to Wendt, Euryanthe's monologue "completely transcends the usual forms of recitative and aria; it is a stirring rhapsody, characterized by splendid declamatory writing." Even today, the music of "Schirmende Engelschaar" stands out as the most "advanced" in the *Euryanthe* score; though he never said as much, Wagner is certain to have studied it carefully. As Tusa has pointed out, the section can be viewed as a bar form consisting of two roughly parallel *Stollen* ("Schirmende Engelschaar ..." and "Schäumend in Kampfes Wuth ..."), a parenthetical phrase ("Wie sie dichter ihn umzingelt!") and an *Abgesang* ("Nein! mein Held ringt sich auf").[48] It might also be thought of as a kind of evolving form, much like the orchestral introduction to the scene: the two *Stollen* likewise relate as antecedent (moving from tonic to dominant) and consequent, although the answering phrase is reinterpreted as preface to the jubilant *Abgesang*.

Either way, there can be little doubt that the most noteworthy music occurs within the first half (the two *Stollen*) of the *Rhapsodie* (see Ex. 4.7). Presumably with an eye toward "dramatic truth," Weber has piled one syntactic irregularity atop another. His treatment of the text (itself an irregular mix of dactylic and trochaic metres) for the first vocal phrase:

> Schirmende Engelschaar,
> Wachend allimmerdar
> In tiefster Nächte Schooß
> Über der Menschen Loos,
> Blicke herab!

is geared toward making its maximum effect on the final verse, hence the headlong rush toward "Blicke herab!": the 2 + 2 grouping for the first and second verses is compressed into a 1½ + 1½ pattern for the third and fourth, only to expand again to a two-measure setting for the climactic verse. Set against the vocal line is a syncopated motive in the lower strings whose oddly disposed beat groupings—5 + 4 + 3 + 5 + 4—all but obliterate a firm sense for the barline accent. The measure groupings are somewhat regularized in the setting of the next text segment (to form a 2 + 2 + 2 + 2 pattern), but an element of unrest is still preserved in the lower-string motive, whose four-beat units are now consistently shifted one beat "to the right." These are, of course, allegorizing ploys, intended to highlight either the rhetorical quality of the text or (through the syncopations in cellos and basses, and *tremolo* in the upper strings) the emotional distress of the heroine. Still, the whole is assured its own internal coherence by way of a tightly wrought form (either bar or amplified period) and a motive elaborated with all the persistence of a Wagnerian leitmotif.

The sequence of textures in section *G*, vocal recitative and orchestral postlude, precisely mirrors that of sections *A* and *B*, thus serving to round off the scene. Likewise, its tonal move from B to E♭ reverses the direction from E♭ to B in sections *E* and *F*. And just as the orchestral introduction acts as a repository for some of the scene's principal musical ideas, so does the postlude refer back to many of the same. The forceful dotted motive (metrically displaced by one beat) that sets in just after Adolar's final cadence recalls similar

EXAMPLE 4.7

Weber, *Euryanthe,* Act III/i, Euryanthe's "Schirmende Engelschaar" (Excerpts from Weber's *Euryanthe* reprinted by permission, Gregg Publishing, © 1969.)

EXAMPLE 4.7 (*continued*)

gestures in sections *E* and *F*; also, the wind chords of mm. 305–8 and 311–14 look back to the similarly spaced chords that mark the transition from section *B* to section *C*. Like the orchestral introduction, the closing portion of section *G* is a miniature tone poem, an allegorical portrayal of the stage action— Adolar's flight from the helpless Euryanthe. But here too there is a notable element of self-referentiality, a bit of musical symbolism facilitated by the nature of the poetic text itself. Adolar's pause for a last backward glance at Euryanthe parallels his moments of immobile brooding at the very beginning of the scene (see Ex. 4.8). It will be recalled that Weber had linked the earlier action with a sudden move from the prevailing D minor to E♭. Much the same happens here: by way of suggesting Adolar's hurried departure, the music builds to a *fortissimo* climax on D°7, subsequently resolving to E♭. The fleeting glance comes with a *subito* shift to *piano,* a neighbor-note figure in parallel thirds, and an isolated sigh in bassoon and cellos. Once again, tone painting and internal reference are complementary.

Amadeus Wendt, to whom I have referred several times, was no doubt one of the more astute of *Euryanthe*'s early critics. Yet it should be clear by now that his description of the opening scene of Act III as a fascinating essay in musical *Karakteristik,* though not incorrect, was incomplete. The scene does have more than its share of startling, even shocking effects, but I have tried to emphasize the need, in most cases, to interpret these clefts from two points

EXAMPLE 4.8

Weber, *Euryanthe,* Act III/i, conclusion   (Excerpts from Weber's *Euryanthe* reprinted by permission, Gregg Publishing, © 1969.)

of view. Their depictive, allegorical dimension will perhaps strike us most forcefully on first hearing; but this immediately disruptive aspect is frequently the obverse of a self-referential, more purely musical scheme. And as our observations on sections *A* and *B* in particular have made clear, the clefts tend to appear at those points where the allegorical and symbolic realms do not come into harmonious accord.

As Weber noted in his *Undine* review, maintaining the proper balance of part and whole is almost as problematic in operatic analysis as it is in operatic composition: "any detailed technical examination of structure and so forth entails a minute dissection in which the work as a whole simply dissolves."[49] Mine hardly purports to be an exhaustive account; still, given our focus on the nature of individual sections within the scene, it might be well to consider more closely the precise sense in which the scene of Euryanthe's abandonment in the wilderness adds up to a meaningful whole.

Enough has been said about the scene's internal motivic structure and about the relationship between its gestural content and the rest of the opera. Weber's associative web may not be as tightly woven as that in a Wagnerian music drama; nor is it really fair to compare the two. What matters is that the notion of the associative network was a reality for Weber, and that he elaborated it in his own terms. Granted that our scene coheres as a melodic entity, both in itself and in terms of the *große romantische Oper* of which it is a part, how well does it hold together in terms of other musical elements?

Weber's clearest means of suggesting a gradual *Steigerung* involves his employment of gradually quickening tempi (see Fig. 4–1). These can be calculated quite precisely, for Weber left a series of metronome markings for the entire opera in conjunction with a request from Aloys Präger, who planned to mount a production of *Euryanthe* at the Leipzig Städtisches Theater in May 1824. Although Weber asked that his markings be kept private, there is no reason to doubt their authenticity.[50] The temporal plan of the opening scene of Act III proceeds in three main stages: from the *adagio* of section *A* and most of section *B,* through the *moderato* of the section *C* opening, and finally to the more agitated tempi of sections *D* through *G.* Weber's tendency, especially in Part 2, to lunge forward and then retreat before increasing the tempo yet again, is in perfect keeping with Euryanthe's passionate utterances. Tempi are therefore treated as allegories for the principals' intensifying emotions at the same time that they figure in a musically logical scheme.

The temporal *Steigerung* works together with a *Bogen*-form textural disposition: pure instrumental sonority (section *A*) gives way to a thin-textured accompanied recitative (section *B*), then to arioso (section *C*), concerted duet (section *D*), and richly supported declamation (sections *E* and *F*), before dissolving back into recitative and pure orchestral sound (section *G*). Not surprisingly, the highpoint of the textural arch coincides exactly with the temporal curve, both converging on Euryanthe's rhetorically charged monologues "Entsetzen!" and "Schirmende Engelschaar." Textures, no less than tempi, are not only coordinated with the affective course of the scene but also deployed as part of a musically sensible pattern.

The tonal disposition of the scene is unusual by any standard. It would be misguided to maintain that the scene is "in" any one of the various keys through which it seems nervously to pass. One rather senses that each tonal area is intended to mark off a discrete segment of the action, and that each tonal shift is geared to project, in music, the affective shifts in the emotional lives of the characters. Tonality, in other words, would appear to be more a function of allegorizing portrayal than of purely musical elaboration. But a closer look (and listen) reveals that the tonal scheme is not as discontinuous as it might seem at first. Part 1, though tonally open, is governed by a perfectly conventional move from minor tonic to minor dominant (mediated by the major dominant at "Wie liebt' ich dich!"). Part 2 circles around E♭, prolonged by its lower third, B, at Euryanthe's "Schirmende Engelschaar." The only real cleft, the only point where tonal allegory and tonal symbolism are in direct conflict, comes with the A–E♭ tritone "hinge" separating Part 1 from Part 2. On the one hand, this is a frankly allegorizing ploy, a blatant means of underscoring Euryanthe's terror at the sight of the serpent. But on the other hand, it may be viewed as an aspect of the self-referential dimension of the scene. In the first place, it is no accident that Euryanthe's "Entsetzen" monologue (and with it, the turn to E♭) coincides precisely with the peak of the temporal and textural curves. Second, the tonal "hinge" is mediated by the implied C minor at the beginning of the monologue, which divides the tritone into two minor thirds, the motion to the upper third of the pair realized through a sequential passage through an implied D.

The tonal plan reveals its Janus face in yet another and subtler sense. In one of the earliest surviving manuscripts of the *Euryanthe* libretto, a two-act draft in Chézy's hand, the equivalent of what would eventually become the first scene of Act III was to include an aria for Euryanthe during which the spirit of Adolar's dead sister (then called "Mathilde") made an appearance.[51] As Tusa has observed, the idea of introducing a supernatural being connected with a dark family secret comes straight out of the contemporary *Schicksalstragödien* by Adolf Müllner and others, which would have been well known to Weber and his librettist.[72] Although critics have found Emma's (or Mathilde's) troubled ghost just as questionable as the giant serpent, Weber and Chézy obviously felt that they had found a suitable substitute for an element in *Euryanthe*'s literary source—Gerbert de Montreuil's thirteenth-century *Roman de la violette*—that would have never cleared the Viennese censor: the violet-shaped mole on Euryanthe's breast. Questionable or not, Weber and Chézy stuck by their wandering spirit. To drive the point home, Weber planned at various stages of his work on the opera to bring the spirit on stage, not only, as mentioned above, at the beginning of Act III (originally Act II), but also during the overture's *Pantomimische Prolog Szene* and at Emma-Mathilde's pantomimed reunion with her husband, Udo, near the end of the work.[53] Although he ultimately decided against these stage appearances, Weber did make Emma's spirit a real presence by calling up its characteristically evocative music at several points throughout the opera: in the development section of the overture; during Euryanthe's narration of Adolar's secret to Eglantine (the Vision episode) in the third scene of Act I; as the central event in Eglantine's hallucinatory monologue just before the Act III finale; and immediately preceding the jubilant chorus that concludes the opera.

The idea that I wish to put forward here is that Weber also managed to suggest Emma's presence in the opening scene of Act III, if not, as he had first planned, through an actual appearance, then through a property of the music itself. And to be sure, the property that I have in mind reaches beyond the allusions to the "spirit music" textures in sections *A* and *B* to encompass the music for the scene as a whole. Let us first consider Emma's evocative music itself. When it appears in the overture, the Act I Vision, and Eglantine's Act III "mad scene," it is associated with a highly chromaticized B tonality. In fact, the ostensible B minor/major wanders so far afield that we might more justifiably speak of a tonal complex that takes B as its point of departure. Example 4.9 gives the *Urform* of the passage from the overture (in the Act I/iii Vision, the same music is temporally expanded to accommodate Euryanthe's text; Eglantine's mad scene presents only the first four bars in slightly varied form). The passage divides into three segments of roughly equal length, the first two of which (mm. 1–6, 6–11) are elided to form a single long phrase, and the last of which (mm. 12–15) corresponds to the first, making for an overall *ABA* pattern.

Although there are no strong inner cadences, the principal points of tonal articulation are nonetheless clear: the B minor/major of the opening measure and a half, the E$\flat$ at which the meandering first phrase finally arrives (via a D^{o7}), and the B major at the return of segment *A*. The music thus prolongs B through a motion to its upper third and back, underscoring the major-third relationship with particular force in mm. 11–12, where the return to B is effected through an enharmonic common tone (E$\flat$/D$\sharp$ as I of E$\flat$ minor and III of B major). Within the first long phrase, Weber's tonal dodges obfuscate more than they clarify: the aimless wandering of Emma's restive spirit is nicely depicted through a series of harmonic moves that either resolve deceptively or imply a tonality rather than assert it. The V^7/F$\sharp$ in m. 3 proceeds to D instead, which is immediately reinterpreted as IV of a weakly established A minor (m. 6). Just as B gives way to D, its upper third, so too does A proceed to C (m. 9), its reconfiguration as V$^4_2$/F deflected to yield E$\flat$, the upper third of C. The larger motion from B to E$\flat$ is thus accomplished by a series of sequentially related minor-third pairings, the second in fact a double pair (A/C, C/E$\flat$). True to its role as a musical representation of a continually searching spirit, the passage remains tonally open, poised on an equivocal dominant of the main tonality, B. (Only after all of the plot complications have been

EXAMPLE 4.9
Weber, *Euryanthe*, Ouverture, *Pantomimische Prolog Szene* (Excerpts from Weber's *Euryanthe* reprinted by permission, Gregg Publishing, © 1969.)

sorted out at the end of the opera is this music granted closure, and in a C major purged of all chromatic elements—a lone F♯ excepted.)

The relationship between the ghost music in the overture (or the Vision) and the design of the Euryanthe–Adolar dialogue is as obvious as it is compositionally daring: the principal tonal goals of the extended scene at the beginning of Act III are precisely those of the earlier fifteen-measure "tone poem." (There is an obvious parallel here with the Wolf's Glen scene from *Freischütz*; its principal tonalities—F♯, A, C, and E♭—are precisely those of the diminished-seventh chord that figures throughout the opera as a musical representation of evil.) Emma's music is "symbolized" in the scene with Euryanthe and Adolar in the wilderness in that its tonal elements are taken over intact, but radically reordered. The B–E♭–B configuration of the spirit music is reversed to form an E♭–B–E♭ pattern in Part 2 of the scene from Act III. The components of what were previously B/D and A/C third pairs are realigned in Part 1 to create a suitable backdrop for Adolar's annunciation of Euryanthe's death (B/C), and a fifth-related tonal frame for the entire first portion of the scene (D/A). While the scene's understated references to the texture of the spirit music are, I think, intended to be perceived, these tonal reorderings are not. The textural references signify directly; they operate in an allegorizing sphere where musical gesture points toward textual meaning. The tonal references are of a different order. They point inward, toward a network of purely internal, tonally abstract relationships. In any case, Weber had his way. The ghost of Adolar's departed sister figures in the Act III dialogue, both allegorically and symbolically.

In sum, the balance between melodic part and melodic whole that we observed in our consideration of the individual sections of the Euryanthe/ Adolar dialogue is complemented by a similarly logical handling of the temporal, textural, and tonal dimensions of the scene. Weber's essay in musical characterization is also an essay in musical logic, the allegorizing of the former matched by the symbolizing of the latter. But it is not perfect. There is no getting around the fact that the A-minor "duet" at the center of the scene, "Du klagst mich an," falls flat.[54] The sudden halt in the action to allow the characters fitfully to ponder their respective situations, the abrupt shift to regular phrase syntax, the frequent word and text-phrase repetitions, the vocal duet texture—all of them the stock-in-trade of number opera—seem oddly out of place in a scene where operatic conventions are for the most part abrogated. One might argue that a sudden shift of this sort is hardly to be faulted, given that the scene is saturated with disruptive effects. But there is a difference. Most of the clefts we have observed mark the interface between contrary signifying realms. Here the dialectic is absent: Weber simply composed a more or less conventional duet passage because the "rules" of operatic composition demanded it. And yet the passage is instructive. It serves as a reminder that Weber's scene can be read in two ways, as a critique of the Romantic doctrine of the symbol, and as a critique of the very conventions that the scene embodies.

5

Brahms and the Romantic Imperative

"All the classical poetic genres are now ridiculous in their rigid purity"

An unescapable consequence of Friedrich Schlegel's sweeping dismissal of the Classical genres as vehicles for modern poetic expression, a charge leveled mainly at the epigonism that he and his contemporaries found so distasteful, would look to be, on first blush, a utopian theory of genre. The poets of literature's long-gone Golden Age might have unreflectingly taken up and operated within the confines of a set of generic limitations inscribed by tradition; the modern poet, however, could not. Modern artists were compelled to follow what Schlegel called the "romantic imperative," the impulse that "demanded the mixture of all poetic types."[1] By troping on Kant's categorical imperative, Schlegel made clear his belief that no choice on the part of the artist was involved; following the dictates of the Romantic imperative was both a professional and a moral obligation. The process would culminate in the *Roman,* at once the single contemporary genre worthy of comparison with the epic of classical antiquity, and the ideally combinative artwork toward which the modern poet should aspire.

According to Schlegel's overview of the contemporary literary scene, poets had produced novels classifiable as either fantastic, sentimental, philosophical, or psychological, but "in actuality there is only One *Roman.*" The "absolute" *Roman* would thus bring together, in a marvelous unity, all the disparate tendencies and types that had previously been kept separate.[2] The notion of generic mixture, a peripheral element in earlier literature, therefore takes center stage in modern poetry by means of the *Roman* as real and ideal form. And this literary form was in turn destined to lend its name to an entire cultural enterprise: hovering behind Schlegel's use of the term *Romantic* is a meaning translated best as "novelizing" or "generically mixed."[3]

It is arguable that the first clear realization of the ideals articulated in Schlegel's genre theory came first in music and not in literature. The novels of Jean Paul, E. T. A. Hoffmann, Novalis, Brentano, Hölderlin, and Schlegel himself may point the way to a poetic future, but they do not thoroughly inhabit it. Yet little effort of the imagination is required to hear in the finale of Beethoven's Ninth Symphony—or even in the *Eroica* finale—a musical embodiment of the Romantic imperative's call to overcome the strictures of generic boundaries. At the most basic level, the Ninth Symphony finale presents a series of variations on the *An die Freude* theme. In this respect, it answers to a classicizing aesthetic of the symphony whereby the weightiest formal arguments are reserved for opening movements, countered in the *lieto fine* by less pretentious designs, most frequently variations or rondos. The unassuming variation finale of Haydn's Symphony No. 31, the "Horn Signal," is in this sense a precursor of Beethoven's grander utterances in the Choral Symphony. But Beethoven's variations group themselves into quasi-movements whose sequence suggests the plan of an entire symphonic work. Following on a lengthy orchestral introduction and the baritone recitative, the first "movement" is given over to solo and choral presentations of the *Freude* theme; the $\frac{6}{8}$ tenor solo ("Froh, wie seine Sonnen fliegen") and orchestral fugato stand in for the traditional scherzo; "Seid umschlungen Millionen" heads off a slow movement; and its combination with the *Freude* theme up through the concluding *stretto* comprises the finale proper. The tonal plan of this compressed symphony—D→B♭→modulatory middle section→G major/minor→D—presents an affirmation-digression-return pattern comparable to that of the sonata allegro, the form whose development section is evoked in the modulatory orchestra fugato. Yet another of the instrumental genres, the concerto, is suggested by the layout of the movement's opening phases. In that the material of the orchestral introduction, a series of instrumental recitatives prefacing the *Freude* theme, is immediately restated by baritone solo and chorus, we hear it as a ritornello of sorts.

These allusions to the chief genres of instrumental music are likewise complemented by features associated with vocal genres. The presence of vocal soloists and chorus, the sectionalized treatment of the text—both traits call up the cantata. The baritone's initial exhortation to set aside the serious strains of the orchestra in favor of the more joyful accents of song could well be given to the narrator in an oratorio. Hints of opera are abundant: motives of reminiscence, a stock-in-trade of French Revolutionary opera and *opéra comique,* come with the orchestra's references to music from earlier movements in the opening introduction. The use of janissary instruments, the triangle, cymbal, and bass drum that first appear in the second-"movement" tenor solo, derives from the *Singspiel* tradition: witness Mozart's *Entführung aus dem Serail* or Weber's *Abu Hassan.* The joyous close of Beethoven's own *Fidelio* parallels the vocal-instrumental *stretto* in the symphonic finale. Lastly, the secular dimension fuses with the sacred in Beethoven's decision to present, as his principal material, a hymnlike tune; the balance here between secular and sacred topoi is precisely the reverse of that in the *Missa solemnis,* particularly its Gloria and Credo, each a multimovement "symphony" compressed into a continuous design.

In sum, Beethoven realized his desire to send out a universalizing message directed at the "ganzen Welt," in compositional-technical terms, by fashioning his finale as a compendium of purely musical forms and genres. In one of the *Lyceum* fragments Schlegel noted: "Many of the very best novels are compendia, encyclopedias of the whole spiritual life of a brilliant individual. Works having this quality . . . thereby take on a novelistic hue."[4] Beethoven goes Schlegel one better; the novelizing tone of the Ninth Symphony finale results not only from the ultrasubjectivity of its composer but from his encapsulation of an entire epoch's forms and genres in the space of a thirty-minute musical movement.[5]

There is no little irony in the fact that a highly individual conception such as this (the closest relative in Beethoven's own oeuvre, apart from the *Eroica* finale, is the *Große Fuge*) should have led to the establishment of a musical genre, the symphonic cantata; for as paradoxical as it sounds, here we are faced with a genre (its chief representatives including Mendelssohn's Symphony No. 2, the *Lobgesang,* Berlioz's *Roméo et Juliette,* Liszt's *Faust* Symphony, and the finale of Mahler's Eighth Symphony) that consists entirely of exceptional works.[6] It then becomes the task of the critic, who sets out less to classify than to clarify, to determine which genre traditions the composer attempted to mediate, thereby enabling an appropriate reception for a work that might at first strike the listener as an odd jumble of conflicting elements.

Berlioz's oxymoronic designation for his *Roméo et Juliette,* a "dramatic symphony," embodies *in nuce* the paradox of the atypical genre. How can the reflective genre par excellence, the symphony, be brought into line with an essentially dialogic form whose principal aim is the unfolding of a specific action? Interestingly enough, Berlioz's most compelling solutions to this problem come not in the texted portions of the work, but in those that take advantage to the fullest degree of the undeniable contradiction inherent in the idea of absolute music, namely, that as wordless discourse it "speaks" most eloquently when it doesn't speak at all. Neither Romeo nor Juliet utter a single word in song. This is due, as Berlioz explains in his *Avant-propos,* to the very sublimity of their passion; its depiction required such sensitive handling by the composer "that he had to give his imagination a latitude that the positive sense of the sung words would not have given him, resorting instead to instrumental language, which is richer, more varied, less precise, and by its very indefiniteness incomparably more powerful in such a case."[7]

The first movement of the *Deuxiéme partie,* subtitled *Roméo seul– Tristesse–Bruits lointains de concert et de bal–Grande fête chez Capulet,* divides into two broad sections: a slow introduction depicting the solitary Romeo's sadness, and an *allegro* whose boisterous accents contrastingly point to the merrymaking at the Capulets' grand ball. But it would be a mistake to hear in this pattern an evocation of the introduction-*allegro* pattern characteristic of the symphonic *allegro* and nothing more. *Roméo seul* is represented through an instrumental recitative; historically, it thus stands midway between the cello-contrabass recitatives of Beethoven's Ninth Symphony finale (the work that Berlioz takes as his point of departure), and the languorous opening of *Tristan* (the melodic similarities between the *Tristan* idea and the Romeo music confirm the notion that Wagner in turn took Berlioz's composition as one of his starting points). *Tristesse* takes the form of two lyric paragraphs separated by a brief *allegro* interlude, the latter a prefiguration of the upcoming *Grand fête* music, and hence an apt portrayal of *Bruits lointains.* The vocal quality of the material is matched with appropriately lyric forms: the first *cantilena* is cast as a simple *ABA'* pattern wherein each segment of the design is articulated by a series of thirds up from the tonic (F–A♭–C); distant sounds of the festivities (on timpani and tambourine) punctuate the second *cantilena,* a single, long-breathed oboe melody in the dominant (C). The tonic is immediately reestablished (and never again really challenged) in the closing *allegro,* the musical depiction of the *Grande fête* that brings the whole complex to a close.

Again, the form is more easily referable to vocal than instrumental traditions. Two roughly parallel strophes culminate in a third, featuring an impressive "Réunion des deux thèmes, du larghetto [the second *cantilena*] et de l'allegro." (This is of course the stuff of grand opera. Berlioz makes use of the same musico-spatial device in the great Carnival scene from *Benvenuto Cellini*; Balducci, Teresa, and Ascanio/Cellini each enter with sharply differentiated material that, miraculously, works perfectly well when all the parts are combined.) Another contrapuntal tour de force initiates the coda: a fugato over a descending ostinato whose chromaticism can be traced back to the opening violin recitative. The vocal qualities that govern the individual parts obviously affect the shape of the whole, which is designed as a virtuoso *Scena ed aria* with recitative (*Roméo seul*), two-part *cavatina* (*Tristesse*) and *cabaletta* (*Grande fête*). Berlioz's movement thus "speaks" largely through its form. The fusion of genres, operatic and symphonic, is achieved by giving over to the orchestra a form that until the mid-nineteenth century had been the exclusive property of the star singer.

In the symphonic cantata or the dramatic symphony we can therefore justifiably speak of a genre whose exemplary compositions present highly individual and unrepeatable responses to the problem at hand; Berlioz's precise mode of blending opera and symphony in the *Roméo seul* movement was, so far as I know, without a direct precedent and was not subsequently imitated.[8] The odd notion of a genre made up of exceptional compositions in turn points to one of the central dialectics of nineteenth-century poetics: the most original artists of the age may have sought to dissolve the boundaries between genres whose rigid purity was viewed as artificial and outmoded; but the listener must still have a clear idea of the work's generic underpinnings in order fully to assess its originality. Genre was truly given over to a Hegelian *Aufhebung,* at once affirmed and suspended. Thus, it is not surprising that the desire to overcome the strictures of genre discernible in many of the period's artworks was coupled with an intense genre consciousness in contemporary criticism. According to Schlegel, many paths could lead to a "boring genre," and "the shortest route is when a work itself is unsure of its proper genre."[9]

J. Becker, who reviewed Mendelssohn's *Erste Walpurgisnacht* for the *Neue Zeitschrift für Musik,* did not claim that the composition was "unsure of its genre"; still, he raised a question that would surface time and again in nineteenth-century criticism. The problem lay in the work's resistance to generic classification. Although it partook of some of the features associated with the oratorio and cantata, the *Erste Walpurgisnacht* could not be subsumed under either designation: its secular subject matter would have been out of place in an oratorio, just as its epic qualities outweighed the moments of lyric reflection constitutive for the cantata as a genre.[10] Berlioz registered similar qualms about his own work. He insisted that *Roméo et Juliette* was "neither a concert opera nor a cantata, but a choral symphony." If Romeo and Juliet's declaration of mutual love are given to the orchestra and not the singers, the reasons, Berlioz argues, are many and easy to understand: "First, and this alone would be sufficient, [the work] is a symphony and not an opera."[11] Berlioz's reasoning is ultimately not very convincing: Friar Laurence's words, for example, are indeed sung. The quotation speaks less to the composer's denial of the generic dichotomy written into the fabric of the music than to the critic's obsession with the idea of genre.

The dialectic of genre—as critical category and artistic reality—is an omnipresent force in nineteenth-century music. But it would be too facile to argue for the centrality of the Romantic imperative by looking to the works of Berlioz or Liszt, the self-proclaimed radicals of the age. For this reason, the following discussion will try to show how even the supposed upholder and preserver of the Classical canon of forms and genres, Johannes Brahms, answered to its call. We will consider three sets of examples, each geared to demonstrate—and in turn be illuminated by—the differing facets of an idea whose subtlety is hardly captured in catchphrases such as "fusion of genres" or "combinative artwork." Our first set manifests the Romantic imperative in a fairly straightforward manner, while in the other examples its presence may not be as readily apparent. A look at the totality of Schlegel's major statements on the nature of genre in modern poetry will likewise reveal a critical dimension without which the utopian side of his Romantic imperative is little more than a fanciful pipe dream, a tiresome cliché, a bit of ideology. His writings will provide the critical pendant to the musical realization of the critique in Brahms's compositions.

In Schlegel's poetics, Romantic prose and critical prose both brought together the same styles—philosophical, logical, historical, systematic, analytic, synthetic—but with a crucial distinction: "the former [prose style] is mixed, the latter fused."[12] The Romantic poet effects a chemical reaction whereby the constituent properties of his elemental building materials, the fundamental genres, are transformed into a radically new product and not merely juxtaposed in an artistically inept hodgepodge. For Schlegel, the *Romanze* emanates from the conjunction of idyll and arabesque, the *Fantasie* from elegy and fairy tale.[13] On the musical side, we have just seen a manifestation of this idealizing aspect of the Romantic imperative in Berlioz's *Roméo,* where operatic aria and symphonic movement coalesce in an individual and convincing manner. Brahms, too, attempted something similar in one of his most problematic works, his settings of the interpolated lyrics from Ludwig Tieck's *Liebesgeschichte der schönen Magelone und des Grafen Peter von Provence.*

The *Magelone Romanzen,* Opus 33, were a product of the composer's youthful fling with the *Ur*-Romanticism of E. T. A. Hoffmann and Eichendorff. As such, they have evinced mixed reactions from critics bound to the image of a classicizing Brahms. The status of the work as a cycle—as opposed to a collection—remains to be settled,[14] but more important for our purposes is the discomfort that so many commentators have felt with the distance separating many of these songs from the ideal-typical Brahms *Lied.* Spitta's designation of the *Magelone* settings as "symphonische Gesänge" was value-neutral;[15] more recent writers have responded less favorably to the breadth of conception in songs variously described as "ungainly," "blatantly episodic," "undisciplined," "sprawling," and "loosely constructed" after the manner of opera arias.[16] Various reasons have been adduced to account for Brahms's singular blending of lyric and operatic elements. The tradition of interpreting the *Romanzen* as biographical documents is traceable to Max Kalbeck, who justified the extravagance of Brahms's approach by using it as evidence of the young composer's identification with the hero of Tieck's tale.[17] But usually the high degree of contrast in several of the songs, and the frequent shifts of meter, tempo, material, and texture, have been viewed as a threat to the unity of tone taken as a hallmark of the *Lied.*[18]

The sticking point, in other words, is the question of genre; and Brahms's experiment has been none too approvingly received. Eric Sams puts it most emphatically. The *Magelone* songs, he says, present "insoluble formal and stylistic contradictions"; as a whole they must "be counted as failures in the attempted genre."[19] Yet it seems hardly fair to rule out, a priori, the possibility of bringing together two genres—*Lied* and aria—whose incompatibility may turn out to be an issue for the purist alone. Brahms's *Romanzen,* in any event, are bound to come up short when measured against a classicizing aesthetic of genre that they do not share. Rather than translate Brahms's recourse to the Romantic imperative into a negative value judgment, let us then attempt to analyze it.

More so than any of his other songs, Brahms's *Magelone Romanzen* aptly reflect the changing position of the *Lied* in later nineteenth-century concert life. Once the exclusive property of enthusiasts and devotees, the *Lied* was gradually making its way into the concert hall; Brahms himself participated in this shift as a performer. Among the catalysts for his setting of the *Magelone* lyrics was a series of performances undertaken in the spring of 1861 with the baritone Julius Stockhausen, featuring Beethoven's *An die ferne Geliebte,* Schubert's *Die schöne Müllerin,* and Schumann's *Dichterliebe.*[20] Indeed, Stockhausen was one of a very few singers who devoted himself to the cultivation of the *Lied* in both private and public spheres. His 1856 performance of Schubert's *Müllerin* cycle in its entirety was greeted as something of a novelty by the Viennese press. "As far as we know," wrote Hanslick, "the idea is new."[21] Hence, Brahms's incorporation of dramatic elements into his *Magelone Romanzen* may be viewed as a musical pendant to changing trends in the history of performing practice. The dual presence of the *Lied* in the private salon and the public concert hall is reconfigured as a dialectic between lyric reflection and dramatic exuberance in Brahms's settings.

In addition, the character of the *Magelone* settings reveals that Brahms's sympathy with the mixed-genre status of Tieck's story may have been greater than he was willing to admit.[22] The Magelone tale, in Tieck's retelling, is a *Kunstmärchen,* that is, a *Mischgattung* that, in Schlegel's hierarchy of contemporary genres, results from the conjunction of fantasy and criticism, poetry and prose.[23] The *Wundersame Liebesgeschichte* thus plays on the mixture of naïve, once-upon-a-time narrative (a latter-day evocation of the style of its twelfth-century Provençal model, the Magelone poem of Bernard de Trèviers) and poetic, reflective prose. Furthermore, its alternation of prose narrative and lyric poems—a common enough feature of many early nineteenth-century novels, including Goethe's *Wilhelm Meister,* Novalis's *Heinrich von Ofterdingen,* Hoffmann's *Kater Murr,* and Tieck's own *Franz Sternbalds Wanderungen*[24]—situates it midway between fundamental forms, such as the *Volksmärchen* and the isolated lyric, and the ideally combinative *Roman.*

Brahms aimed for a remarkably similar *Mischgattung.* Here it is important to recognize that the critical tradition that hears in the *Magelone Romanzen* ungainly operatic arias with piano accompaniment has passed down an inadequate representation of the musical facts. Relatively few of the songs (Nos. 3, 6, 8, and 15) are referable to the design of the grand aria, and even in these cases, the decisive issue is not Brahms's abrogation of the *Lied* aesthetic but rather his *mediation* of aria and *Lied,* an experiment made possible in the first place by the reflective character that both genres share. The dialectic between fundamental form (*Lied*) and combinative artwork (opera) played out in the *Magelone Romanzen* is thus comparable to the tension between fairy-tale tone and novelizing form in Tieck's *Kunstmärchen.* In this sense, Brahms's work can be interpreted as a musical reaction to the generic mixture in his literary source. True, Brahms does not (and could not) create a precise musical equivalent for Tieck's tale.[25] The dialectic between fundamental form and *Roman,* which manifests itself in the *Kunstmärchen* largely, but not exclusively, through the alternation of narrative and reflective lyric, is localized in Brahms's settings of individual poems.

"Wie soll ich die Freude," the sixth of the *Magelone* lyrics that Brahms set to music, centers on the poetic conceit neatly encapsulated in the title that Tieck affixed to it in the *Gesamtausgabe* of his poems: "Anticipation." Count Peter, nervously awaiting the longed-for meeting with Magelone set for later in the day, reaches for his lute and "sings" the lyric both to quell his passions and to give vent to his thoughts on Time, the force that separates him from an immediate union with his beloved. As the lyric should take its cue from a single idea, from which others radiate like the spokes of a wheel, so Peter's musings circle about the notion of Time, its uneven passage reflected in the irregular construction of the poem, none of whose six strophes are identical in meter, rhyme scheme, or number of lines.[26] Temporal images thus predominate: the uncontrollable pounding of the enamored hero's heart that threatens to rend his soul in two (strophe 1), the all-too-short-lived hours of love (strophe 2), the by turns ponderous tread and feather-light steps of time (strophe 3), the steady beating of a faithful heart (strophe 4—a variant of the contrasting idea in strophe 1), and the torrential rush of the "Tiefer Strom der Zeit" (strophes 5 and 6).

Peter, in other words, is caught in a temporal predicament; he finds himself uneasily poised between a time of anticipation that seems to proceed with leaden steps and a time of fulfillment whose joys will pass far too quickly. Time is thus pictured as a fickle goddess: through her, all things perish, even love (a variant of this notion, first introduced in strophe 2, comes with the dying echoes of the lute tone in strophe 4); she is mutable, forever changing today into yesterday (strophe 5). But Peter's solution to his temporal dilemma comes with the realization that precisely in Time's uneven pace ("lustig bald, dann still") resides the continuity that is required to help him through this period of nervous expectancy. The initial conflict between his delicate soul and his violently beating heart is resolved, in strophe 6, by "bringing love and life together" in the "stream of Time." Tieck does not take his leave without introducing an ironic twist: he reminds us that the stream of Time ends in Death. The final goal of Peter's journey is not the ecstasy of love, but the peace of the grave.

Tieck's focus on a central idea, his thematization of Time and its irregular passage, his employment of a series of interrelated images, and Peter's reflection on the same—all of this is in perfect accord with the demands of lyric poetry. All the same, several aspects of the poem push it beyond the relatively limited confines of the lyric genre. Peter's sudden resolve to give himself over to the torrential flow of Time, signaled in strophe 6 by his exclamatory "Nein, der Strom wird immer breiter," is more in the spirit of a dramatic rather than a lyric monologue. Likewise the emotional journey that the poem describes, from uncontainable joy (strophe 1) through calming introspection (strophes 4 and 5) to exuberant resolution, makes for an affective range extending past the bounds of lyric contemplation. It will be evident, even by reading the poem apart from the narrative in which it is embedded, that the "lyric I," in this case, is a romance hero poised for action.

Tieck's infusion of dramatic elements into a basically lyric frame called forth from Brahms an extended *Romanze* that strikes an analogous balance between aria and *Lied*. The poem's progress from extroverted joy to inner calm and back again is reflected in the song's division into three broad parts—settings of strophes 1–3, 4–5, and 6, respectively—each articulating the transformation of outer into inner world and the reverse. For Brahms, at least in this song, the generic signifier of the outer world is the opera aria, its gestures most obviously invoked in the *vivace, ma non troppo* setting of the last four lines of the poem. As if to drive home with unmistakable clarity the poem's final conceit—Peter's decision to embrace the world of action—Brahms brings these closing lines twice, the second time resorting to extravagant repetitions of the concluding rhymed couplet: "Fröhlichen Ruderschlags fahr' ich hinab, / Bring Liebe und Leben zugleich an das Grab." The heroic tone, the frequent repetitions of phrases and entire lines, the closing series of cadential extensions—all of these features propel the *Romanze* from the lyric into the dramatic realm.

In contrast, Peter's moments of quiet self-contemplation, like his passage into an inner world of lyric calm in strophes 4 and 5 of the poem, are linked with a musical setting at one with the *Lied* tradition. Brahms sets off the shift by means of a simple but effective tonal contrast: the A major of the first part of the song gives way to a dreamy F♯ major for the second. The "wundersame Ton" that Tieck singled out as a constitutive feature of the *Märchen*[27] is neatly projected, in Brahms's parallel settings of the two strophes, by a whole range of evocative musical topoi: the sigh figures of the piano's brief transition between Parts 1 and 2 of the song, which are then taken up in the "inner world" settings; the chromatic descent over a tonic pedal at "Wie Lautenton vorüberhallt" and "Wandelst bald aus Morgen Heut"; the mesmerizing triplet ostinato at the close of each strophe.

Yet the two realms, lyric and dramatic, are not merely juxtaposed; the subtlety of Brahms's approach derives from the manner in which they are mediated, both at local and global levels. Take, for example, the move into the dreamy central section. The contrast between *allegro* "outer world" music and *poco sostenuto* "inner world" music is softened by the sigh figures of the transition: although they will underpin the subsequent "Schlage, sehnsüchtige Gewalt," they point backward as well, to the descending melodic third of the piano's countermelody at the end of Part 1. Likewise, the F♯ major of Part 2 is foreshadowed by the F♯ minor of the Part 1 (strophe 3) close. The slow–fast succession of Parts 2 and 3 may recall the tempo disposition of the virtuoso aria, but it is at the same time enfolded within a larger fast–slow–fast sequence, producing a ternary shape that points to a quintessentially songlike pattern. The *Romanze* therefore is neither *Lied* nor aria, but in a sense turns on the transformation of one into the other. Part 1 displays a clearly strophic design; in that the material of the piano's preludes to each vocal entrance is subjected to variation in the ensuing strophe, the three-strophe layout is actually doubled. Part 2 presents two practically identical strophes. Only in Part 3 does the decisive shift to operatic posturing take place. But even here, properties of the *Lied* commingle with aria-like gestures. Part 3 begins with music drawn from Part 1, whose motives also surface in the concluding *stretto.* The thematic recall, that is, suggests an overall *ABA* design for the *Romanze* that not only works in tandem with the three-part temporal disposition but more significantly, seems to bring the opera aria back into line with the formal requirements of the *Lied.*

These observations should cause us to view with some circumspection Brahms's insistence on the gulf separating his *Magelone Romanzen* from Tieck's *Kunstmärchen.*[28] His later remarks reported by Kalbeck—"Aren't they after all a kind of theatre?"[29]—are probably closer to the mark. And the theatre that Brahms alluded to may well have been close to the one described by Tieck in his *Phantasus,* in the *Rahmengespräch* following on the *Wundersame Liebesgeschichte der schönen Magelone*:

> Thus, without a doubt we must allow for a type of poetry that even the best theater could not use, one that rather constructs a stage for the imagination within the imagination; it seeks out works that are at once lyric, epic, and dramatic, thereby attaining a scope denied even to the *Roman*; indeed, these works display a certain boldness that would not be suitable in any other dramatic work. This stage of the imagination opens a great new area for romantic poetry, and the Magelone tale along with many other old and charming stories might well venture to appear on it.[30]

The "stage of the imagination" is the ideal *locus* for works that follow the dictates of the Romantic imperative, the impulse that manifests itself in distinct but complementary fashions in Tieck's *Kunstmärchen* and Brahms's song cycle alike.

"One might just as well say that there are *infinitely many* poetic genres, or that there is only *one* progressive genre"

As we have seen, the multiplicity of generic indicators summoned together in the finale of Beethoven's Ninth Symphony can be interpreted as a musical manifestation of Schlegel's Romantic imperative. But Beethoven's project is even more closely bound up with Schiller's thoughts on the nature of modern poetry. In his great essay on naïve and sentimental poetry, Schiller held out a degree of hope for healing the split that torments contemporary humanity; the discrepancy between subject and object, between Self and Other may be reconciled "in the spiritual harmony of a completely fulfilled education."[31] The literary form that gave expression to the process of healing was the idyll. Schiller's program recommended this genre to the artist so that he or she might "display that pastoral innocence even in creatures of civilization and under all the conditions of the most active and vigorous life, of expansive thought, of the subtlest art, the highest social refinement, which, in a word, leads man who cannot now go back to Arcady forward to Elysium."[32] The reconciliation of the opposition between actuality and ideal, no less than the intimate union of naïve and sentimental poetry in the idyll, is clearly at one with the affirmative, universalizing message of Beethoven's symphonic finale.[33]

By way of contrast, a number of Schlegel's utterances on genre should be read as a critique, or at least a corrective, of the utopian doctrine he seemed to promulgate in the Romantic imperative. The call for generic fusion is contravened in a notebook fragment whose importance in Schlegel's thought system is emphasized by the fact that he underlined every word: "When ALL the constituent parts of a romantic poem are fused ("verschmolzen"), then it simply ceases to be romantic."[34] The utopian aspect of Schlegel's theory of genre is but one part of a more refined scheme, a scheme that recognizes the historicity of genres by associating them with specific points in time. His conflation of poetics and *Geschichtsphilosophie* yielded a triadic pattern whereby tragic drama was accorded primacy of place for the Greeks, satire for the Romans, and the novel or *Roman* for the moderns.[35] This is not merely to say that the *Roman,* for instance, is the most "important" of the modern poetic genres. It dominates in the sense that it determines the character of other genres; it allows them to assume their own distinctive "tones." Hence the force of Schlegel's assertion that the novel "colors" (*tingiert*) the whole of modern poetry.[36] There is no utopian posturing here, only the studied calm of the historian of art who recognizes that all postclassical poetry, if it is worthy of the name, will partake to some extent of the generic multiplicity that characterizes the novel. Not only is the Romantic imperative thus a call to action, a promise for the future, but it also speaks to a condition already realized in the present. The critic need only analyze its workings, preferably in cases where they are most artfully concealed.

Brahms was just such a master of concealment. His works afford us many examples of this "quieter," but no less instructive side of the Romantic imperative. The sustained lyricism and reflective character of the slow movement of the Fourth Symphony, Opus 98, would seem on first hearing to place it beyond the bounds of a principle whose presence we have traced thus far in works notable for their gestures of affirmative union. Nonetheless, the movement answers to the Romantic imperative. From the point of view of traditional *Formenlehre*, Brahms's slow-movement design is curiously ambiguous.

The presentation of two distinct thematic groups, the first in the tonic (E) but strongly colored by the flat submediant (see mm. 1–3), the second initiated by an antecedent-consequent phrase in the dominant (mm. 41–50), strongly suggests the layout of a sonata-form exposition. Yet these ideas unfold with a leisureliness that knows little of sonata-form dynamism. The first group partitions itself off as a little ternary unit, a self-contained *ABA'* pattern with two phrases on the opening motto idea modulating from tonic to mediant, a contrasting segment developed out of the same material, and a varied reprise of the opening two phrases firmly anchored in the tonic. The immediately following music (mm. 30ff.) helps to effect the transition to the dominant, but in terms of the architecture of the total form represents a kind of thematic extravagance unusual for the motivically parsimonious Brahms; though a logical outgrowth of what comes before (it takes up the rising-third gesture of the opening motto), this richly scored idea is destined never to return in the same form. In addition, the turn to the dominant for the second group is immediately negated by a retransition to the tonic and a partial reprise of the first group (mm. 64ff.). A closely argued sonata form, that is, gives way in a stroke to the easygoing alternation of a rondo, the pattern also suggested by the terminal references to the music of the first group (mm. 103ff.).

The lyricism of the main thematic ideas is thus complemented by a suitably lyric form: the movement divides into three "song strophes" of unequal length, each initiated by the opening idea in the tonic. The sequence of events in strophe 2, however, is clearly modeled on that of strophe 1. The elaborative expansion at mm. 74ff., far from being a "displaced" sonata-form development, simply takes up the correspondingly situated music from strophe 1 (mm. 15ff.). Taken together with the parallel statement of the second-group idea in the tonic (mm. 88ff.), this imparts to the movement the nature of a binary form.

These relationships are summarized in Figure 5–1. The tabular presentation firms our sense for the multiple implications of the form: the thematic-tonal layout of strophe 1, like the developmental expansion in strophe 2 and its reprise of the second group in the tonic, point toward the sonata allegro; the threefold statement of the opening idea suggests a rondo pattern; parallelisms between strophes 1 and 2 are in line with binary procedure; and the

FIGURE 5–1
Brahms, Opus 98/ii, Formal Plan

Description		Tonality	Description		Tonality
	Strophe 1			Strophe 2	
	first group:			first group:	
m.1	a(motto)	E			
5	a¹	E	64	a¹	E
9	a²	E→g♯	68	a²	E→g♯
13	on a	E→	72	on a + elaboration	E (G, E♭)→ V/b
22	a¹	E			
26	on a²	E→			
30	b	E→V/B			
36	c	V/B→	84	c	b→e→
	second group:			second group:	
41	d (on c; periodic)	B	88	on d	E
50	e (on d)				
55	retransition (on e)	B→			
				Strophe 3	
			103	on a	(IV/E)
			107	on a²	→V/E→
			113	on a (motto)	E

overall articulation of the movement into three broad sections calls to mind the strophic song.

To be sure, this is but one of many movements from Brahms's orchestral and chamber works that play on a similar set of ambiguities.[37] The diverse ways in which this peculiarly Brahmsian *Mischform* has been described—as an anomalous sonata allegro with the first group omitted from the reprise,[38] as sonata form with displaced development or conflated response,[39] or as an amplified binary construct[40]—need not compel us to decide in favor of one or the other; to do so would be tantamount to reducing the form to a mere formula. On the contrary, the varying outlooks on Brahms's favorite *Mischform* confirm the essential point of our brief look at the Fourth Symphony's slow movement: the multivalence of the structure.

Likewise, there are precedents for Brahms's procedures in the *Misch-formen* of Viennese classicism, particularly in Haydn's, Mozart's, and Beethoven's fondness for blending traits of sonata form and rondo. But on the whole, these examples observe what Schlegel would have called a "fixed law of mixture."[41] Brahms's patterns do not. The equipoise of the form parts in the Classical mixture of sonata and rondo, just like the complementarity of the two designs, means that a recognition of the diverse formal signals is constitutive for an adequate reception of the composition. The listener must also attend to the subtleties of Brahms's designs, but here one set of formal principles seems effectively to neutralize the other.

The closest that we can come to a direct precursor for the Brahmsian form comes with a large body of Mozart movements frequently described as sonata rondos with one refrain statement omitted (*AB'ACB''A*).[42] But here too there is a decisive difference. Mozart's peculiar mediation of sonata and rondo most often issues from his attempt to give greater weight to the finale of a concerto or concertante chamber work.[43] Brahms's *Mischform,* as we will see, was aimed at different ends.

These observations can be placed within the framework of a theory of genre transformation that draws on one of Schlegel's most telling fragments: "Manner, tendency, and tone are constitutive for romantic poetry. Classical genres, on the other hand, [are determined by] form, content, and style."[44] The beautifully shaped whole of classical art gives way to the suggestive "tendency," to the fragment. A clearly delimited content is reconfigured, by the Romantics, as a mood, a mobile "tone."[45] The interdependence of the Classical categories is such that the confluence of form and content will yield a generalized style, a body of characteristics that future generations of artists can take up and mold as they see fit. Tendency and tone, however, function less as elements of a commonly held language than as components of an individual and unrepeatable "manner." If we agree that in a musical work, the content-tone pair will manifest itself through harmonic-melodic character and vocal or instrumental setting, then it might be further added that the categories of form, content, and style will determine a ritualistic-social "event," while tendency, tone, and manner more properly belong in the province of the autonomous artwork.

Strictly speaking, Brahms's symphonic slow movement adheres to no specific "form"; it brings together shards of other forms, "tendencies" culled from the Classical heritage that the composer so revered. What remains of the content of the original forms is a vague but unmistakable tone: the serious tone of the sonata allegro, for instance, in the developmental episode in strophe 2; hence the retrospective quality of this music, the sense that Brahms is recalling a distant and no longer identifiable source. Gone too is a classicizing interdependence of form and content. For A. B. Marx, the sectional form of the sonata rondo goes hand in hand with a characteristically light-hearted tone,[46] a prescription borne out by any number of actual compositions from the late eighteenth and early nineteenth centuries. For Brahms, the categories are permitted to go their separate ways. His "rondo" is decidedly lacking in *buffa* qualities; the sonata rondo, as formal tendency, is shadowed by a pervasively lyric tone.[47]

Mozart's recourse to similar formal strategies in several of his instrumental finales ties in directly with the exigencies of a specific family of genres—the concerto and its relatives. Brahms's *Mischform* cuts across generic boundaries. What serves him here for the slow movement of a symphony serves just as well in an orchestral serenade (the Opus 11 finale), two piano quartets (the first and last movements of Opus 25, the finale of Opus 26), a string quartet (the finale of Opus 51, No. 1), a violin concerto (the Opus 77 finale), an independent orchestral work (the *Tragic* Overture, Opus 81), or a diminutive piano piece (the Opus 116, No. 1, Capriccio). The Mozartian *Mischform,* that is, demonstrates the mutual dependence of genre and function; Brahms's employment of apparently related structuring techniques answers to the requirements of the autonomous artwork alone.

Brahms's autonomous artwork is nonetheless a symphony, and I would like to argue that he put the Romantic imperative to good use—not only in the slow movement, but throughout the work—as a means of addressing a particularly pressing concern: how to write symphonies at all in the wake of Beethoven's inspiring but daunting example. A remarkable aspect of the Fourth Symphony is the fact that *all* of its movements partake of the formal "tendencies" we have noted in the *andante moderato.* That the uniformity of approach to patterning does not immediately strike the listener speaks to the independence of "tendency" and "tone" throughout the work.

The character of the boisterous third movement, *allegro giocoso,* is far removed from that of the second, yet Brahms shapes the course of events in his scherzo substitute much as he had in the *andante.* Each of its three "strophes" begins with the same idea either firmly in the tonic (strophes 1 and 2) or tending strongly toward it (strophe 3). The tonic (C major) reiterations coupled with a theme of exuberant character are therefore in keeping with the form and tone of a rondo. The tonic-to-dominant motion within the first strophe and its presentation of two contrasting ideas (their common motivic source notwithstanding) lend to the movement a sonata-like dimension. As in the slow movement, the first group takes the shape of a tripartite construct, its central member here given over to a tutti fanfare in the flat mediant (E♭). Also like the *andante* are the parallelism between strophes 1 and 2, and the lengthy developmental episode (mm. 113–98) within the reprise of the first group that enlivens what would otherwise have been a largely symmetrical return. The elaborative expansion, itself based on the opening phrases of the movement, unfolds in two stages: first a series of motivic parries involving double counterpoint and melodic inversion (a consequence of the opening gesture's presentation of the *Hauptmotiv* and its free inversion as a combinative unit), the second a *poco meno presto* transformation of the first group's central fanfare. The contrapuntal gambits of the first stage, along with its tonal move from A minor to C♯ minor, thus strike a sonata-like tone, whereas the relaxed variant of the fanfare in bassoons and horns adopts the quieter tone that we might expect of a scherzo movement's trio. We can thus observe the same configuration of "tendencies" found earlier on in the *andante moderato* (only the contrapuntal element is new); but in the *allegro giocoso* each is linked with a markedly different tone. Lyricism is displaced by comedy (or the closest to it that Brahms comes) as the dominant ethos.

Even the variations of the passacaglia finale take an overall shape much like that of the *Mischform* of the middle movements.[48] The thirty-two statements of the passacaglia theme group themselves into two "strophes," the second heralded by a return to E minor after several intervening E-major variations, and the prominent placement of the melodic ostinato in the upper winds (mm. 129ff.). The even more emphatic treatment of the passacaglia melody at the outset of the *più allegro* coda marks off a third strophe. The minor-major modal contrast in the variations of strophe 1 substitutes for the tonic-dominant polarity that we would expect in a sonata-allegro movement, just as the tonally divagatory variations of strophe 2 (mm. 137–92)—relatives of the similarly located elaborative expansions of movements 2 and 3—hearken to sonata-form developmental procedures. On the surface, then, the movement appears to take the form of a mere variation chain; a closer examination reveals that it actually embodies a complex of formal "tendencies"—strophic *Lied,* rondo, sonata allegro. If the formal underpinnings of Brahms's finale remain concealed on a casual listening, it is because their characteristic tones have been supplanted; sonata-, rondo-, and songlike tendencies are brought to bear on a quasi-liturgical chorale tone.

Only the first movement stands somewhat apart from the others, thus doing double duty as introductory and initiatory utterance. Of the various "tendencies" encountered here, sonata form clearly dominates. Nonetheless, it will be useful to reaffirm a point that other commentators have made about this movement: though sonata-like in outward design, it derives much from Brahms's proclivity for song-form structures.[49] Sonata-form teleology, represented by the move from the E-minor tonic to first minor and then major dominant in the exposition, is countered by an insistence on the tonic at both the beginning and the midpoint of the development, traditionally the most wayward spot in the form. In that the exposition, development, and recapitulation all proceed from the tonic (and with the same music), we can once again discern a three-strophe pattern behind the ostensible sonata form. Likewise, the large-scale strophes are mirrored at the local level by varied restatements of the principal ideas of both first and second groups. Sonata-form and *Lied*-derived tendencies rub shoulders in a movement whose embodiment of the Romantic imperative is no less evident than that of its successors.

We are now in a position to appreciate the singularity of Brahms's approach and to measure its distance from Classical models. The various forms—sonata allegro, variation, three-part song, and rondo—that are traditionally associated with individual movements of a symphony are simultaneously projected onto *each* of the movements of Brahms's work. It has been frequently pointed out that the Fourth Symphony as a whole is unified by the prominence of melodic third chains in both the first movement and the finale. Yet the mutually reflective forms of the various movements provide just as powerful a unifying element. The Romantic imperative thus emerges here in a paradoxical guise: the principle that on the one hand generates absolutely individualized creations may in cases like this actually contribute to the overall unity of an artwork. Moreover, it enabled Brahms to develop a means of establishing large-scale coherence that would set him apart from his revered predecessors. Mutual reflectivity of forms, and the "tendency"/"tone" disjunction within them, belong more to Brahms's arsenal of compositional techniques than to the musical language of the composer of the *Eroica* Symphony.

Gustav Jenner's pithy assertion—"Brahms hat die Sonata wieder lebendig gemacht" ["Brahms brought the sonata to life again"][50]—is one of the earlier variants on a persistent leitmotif of Brahms criticism: the composer's revival of the classical forms. On reflection, though, it will be difficult for us to retain much of the sense of what has certainly become a tired cliché. For in point of fact, the canonical forms resurface in Brahms's music as something essentially different from what they once were.

Schlegel's poetics can once again help us to make the point. In one of the *Kritische Fragmente* he complained that there were already many theories of *genres,* but as yet no concept of *genre:* "Perhaps we will have to make do with a single theory of genres."[51] And on another occasion he noted that the usual classifications were no more than "dead pedantry" when it came to modern poetry and its fluctuation between "divisibility and union."[52] Schlegel's conviction that there was either one contemporary poetic genre or infinitely many[53] was neither a sign of utopian wishfulness nor a call for the abrogation of the genre idea altogether. The single poetic genre that he had in mind was the *Roman,* within which the Classical types had been relativized, transformed as qualities. Substantives—*Epik, Lyrik, Drama*—give way to adjectival forms—*episch, lyrisch, dramatisch*—in the fragments where he describes this process: "There is an epic ("epische"), lyric ("lyrische"), dramatic ("dramatische") *form* that exists apart from the spirit of the older poetic genres that go by these names, but of a determinate and eternal difference"; or. "Even among novels ("Romanen") there is a lyric-epic-dramatic genre."[54]

There may, in other words, be but one reigning modern genre (the *Roman*), but in each of its individual manifestations the artist will have brought together the qualities of the older types (epic, lyric, drama) in a distinctive and unrepeatable way. Schlegel's combinatorial system of modern genre(s) thus accomplishes two goals at once: it resolves the contradiction between "division and union" that appears to make contemporary poetry resistant to the notion of genre, and it allows the critic to gauge the distance between old and new, "then" and "now," by pointing to the transformation of the older forms into qualities, "tendencies," "tones."

This is precisely the kind of transformation that Brahms effects. His Opus 98 is to be sure a "symphony," but it is also something else. More properly, it is a musical *Roman,* a symphonic work that retains from the older genre an outward division into four movements but that relativizes the Classical forms within each of its movements: the sonata recurs as the sonata-*like,* the rondo as the rondo-*like,* and so forth. The Fourth Symphony merits description as a musical *Roman* in another sense as well. Its generic and formal dominants (to borrow a term from Hans Robert Jauss) derive equally from both instrumental and vocal realms: the four-movement symphony is arguably a sequence of extended *Lieder ohne Worte.* Though not a single word is sung, Brahms's covert blend of song and symphony is as decisive as Beethoven's overt blend in the paean to joy that closes his Ninth Symphony. Beethoven's response to the Romantic imperative is directed at a world audience; Brahms's more introspective reaction, on the other hand, speaks to the "lonely crowd."

"Up to now, modern poetry has seen no new genres, yet every classical work creates its own genre"

For the artistic follower of the Romantic imperative, the creative goal is the radically individualized *unica,* not the mere imitation of a type or norm. The demand to transcend genre therefore goes hand in hand with an aesthetic that prizes the characteristic (the idiosyncratic or exceptional) over the beautiful (the nobly simple or exemplary). Much of Brahms's music, then, presents us with a paradox. His works disclose the force of the Romantic imperative, but at the same time take their cue from the structural principles of the forms and genres of Classicism, structural principles, that is, that belong in the domain of the beautiful. Among the quotations, aphorisms, and snippets of verse that the young composer copied into his *Schatzkästlein des jungen Kreislers* is the following excerpt from J. P. Eckermann's *Beiträge zur Poesie:*

> Form is that which has been cultivated by the thousand-year-old efforts of the most cultivated masters, whose followers we cannot too quickly make our own. One would have to harbor the most foolishly deluded and badly misunderstood notions of originality to think that each artist fumbled and

groped about to discover something that already existed in a greater degree of perfection.[55]

Most critics would probably agree that the mature composer held to this dictum just as firmly.

But in at least one of his instrumental compositions, a movement even more remote from the Classical canon than the *Mischformen* of the Fourth Symphony, Brahms appears to have set out to fashion an essay in the characteristic. The *adagio* of the G-Major String Quintet, Opus. 111—the work Brahms thought of as his *opus ultimum* until coming under the spell of Richard Mühlfeld's clarinet playing in the spring of 1891[56]—stubbornly resists formal classification. As a freely unfolding series of reinterpretations of the same melody, it seems to partake more of the formal principles associated with, for example, the *Vorspiel* to Wagner's *Lohengrin,* than with those of the time-honored forms beloved of Brahms. Its structural singularity, noted early on by Joachim—he dubbed it "das tiefe, originell geformte Adagio"[57]—perhaps had something to do with the relative lack of comprehension with which it was met at its first performances. Reporting on the Berlin performance of 10 December 1890, Joachim noted that while the "Intermezzo" (the *un poco allegretto* third movement) had to be repeated, "the Adagio, to my amazement, was least understood, yet it is probably my favorite movement."[58] The diversity of opinion encountered in subsequent accounts of the movement's form—as theme and free variations (i.e., what Brahms would have called "fantasy" variations), three-part song form, modified strophic design, or idiosyncratic sonata allegro[59]—serves as an indication that the *adagio* continues to mystify.

Just as in the Fourth Symphony, we can point to a relativizing of the formal categories of Classicism; but here the process of transformation is decidedly more emphatic. The symphonic *Mischformen* occupy a place within a fairly large group of movements sharing the same structural ambiguities. The Quintet *adagio,* on the other hand, has comparatively few relatives in Brahms's oeuvre, possibly the slow movements of the first two piano sonatas (Opera 1 and 2) or the Opus 9 Schumann Variations. It is curiously suspended between two formal paradigms, the variation cycle and the sonata allegro, forms that it calls up only to deny.

Let us begin by considering the movement's relationship to the variation idea. Outwardly, there can be little doubt as to the appropriateness of the paradigm. The movement is partitioned into five sections or "strophes," the last four of which amplify the material of the first (see Fig. 5–2). Yet there are a number of features that set the *adagio* apart from Brahms's usual approach to the art of variation writing. In the first place, the theme itself (given as Ex. 5 1) is unusually complex. It is cast as an *ABA'* unit whose symmetry is offset by a progressive diminution in phrase lengths (8 + 4 + 2 measures) such that *A'* brings a compressed statement of the viola's initially long-breathed

FIGURE 5–2

Brahms, Opus 111/2, Formal Plan

	Viola Melody-A				B	A'
Strophe 1 theme antecedent	Head Motif: a^1	a^2/a^3 (Dotted Motive)	a^4 (Sequence)/ a^3	Close: (a^5)	Sighs + x	Viola melody, compressed $(a^1 + a^5)$
	(d) mm.1–2	3–4	5–6	A 7–8	→V/a 9–12	→V/a 12–14
Strophe 2 consequent	a^1	a^3/a^2			$b + x$	$a^1 + x$
	d 15–16	→V/d 17–24			→V/d 25–28	→Aug. VI(g) 28–32
Strophe 3 consequent Dev't	a^1	a^2/a^3	a^4/a^3	$a^5 +$ dev't on a^5		x
	(g) 33–34	35–36	37–38	→D,g,d→ 39–50		V/d 51
Strophe 4 Apotheosis	a^1+a^3/a^2	a^2/a^3	a^4/a^3		b'	extension/ viola cadenza
	D 52–55	d 56–57	58–61		61–66	→V/d 66–68
Strophe 5 Recap	a^1	a^2	a^4			a^1
	d 69–70	71–72	→D 73–76			D 77–80

"gypsy" tune. As indicated in Figure 5–2, *A'* comprises a^1 plus a variant of the cadential a^5. The opening eight measures (*A*) likewise reveal a web of connections: both a^2 and a^4 are supported by a dotted figure in the bass (a^3), which proceeds imitatively with a^4; a^5, the closing segment of the melody, is initiated by the same rising-third gesture that set off a^4. *A* is further bound to *B* by another rising-third motive: the second viola line of m. 1, labeled *x* in Example 5.1, recurs at the end of *B* (m. 12), so that an ostensibly opening figure functions just as well as a close.

Equally distant from Brahms's usual practice (and from the techniques of the Classical variation canon as a whole) are the syntactic divergences of strophes 2–5 from their model. Strophe 2 lacks the entire closing portion of *A*; strophe 3 makes do without *B* and *A'* in their entirety; and the last two strophes fail to bring *A'* and *B* respectively. But in each case (the last strophe excepted), Brahms balances the omissions through rhapsodic developmental expansions, elaborated with increasing intensity as we move through the form, so that the climactic strophe 4 is practically all developmental. In ret-

EXAMPLE 5.1

Brahms, Opus 111/ii, mm. 1–16

(*continued*)

EXAMPLE 5.1 (*continued*)

rospect, then, the theme is more accurately defined as a thematic configuration from which subsequent strophes freely draw. Brahms's procedure even exceeds the bounds of what he would call the "fantasy" variation in letters to Schubring and Elisabeth von Herzogenberg, a type associated with some of Schumann's works (the *Symphonische Etüden,* Opus 13) and with the variations of lesser composers such as Henri Herz and Heinrich von Herzogenberg.[60] The Brahmsian fantasy-variation idea, as Elaine Sisman has pointed out, relates principally to the melodic dimension; composers of this type of work may retain the basic motives of the given theme from variation to variation, but will at the same time subject their model to far-reaching alterations of phrase structure, meter, and tempo.[61] The syntactic alterations in the Quintet *adagio,* however, involve more than the melody alone. As we will see, freedom of harmonic treatment is just as much at issue.

   The variation (or fantasy-variation) cycle is for the most part a static form, each of its elements arrayed like quasi-independent links in a chain. Yet in the Quintet "variations" the tonal open-endedness of each strophe creates the impression of a single sweep from beginning to end. In addition, the logical working out of a motivic process outweighs the architectural symmetries usually expected of a variation work. Here each strophe is functionally bound to that which follows. Strophe 1, moving from D minor to A minor, and strophe 2, remaining within the orbit of the tonic until its last measures, relate as antecedent and consequent. The first phrase of strophe 3 (mm. 33–40) likewise stands in a consequent relationship to the corresponding phrase of strophe 1, so that in essence the entire first half of the movement hinges on a periodic structure. Strophe 3 then leads, by way of motive *x,* to the apotheotic D major of strophe 4, whose concluding viola cadenza serves as *Eingang* to the final strophe. The movement thus assumes a single, clearly directed shape that moves from an initial periodic statement (strophes 1 and 2), through an intensifying phase (strophe 3), onward to an apotheosis (strophe 4), and finally a serene close (strophe 5). The rhetorical path traced in the Quintet *adagio* may also be interpreted in light of the formal and melodic problems of the complex opening strophe: the "solution" entails the steady reshaping of this strophe into the syntactically regular pattern (8 mm. + 4 mm. close) it assumes at the conclusion of the movement (strophe 5). Brahms's theme thus follows a teleological course, generating a form that stands in direct opposition to the general stasis of the variation cycle.

   Yet the most serious challenge to the variation idea involves Brahms's treatment of the theme's head motif, which recurs more or less intact at the beginning of each strophe. The element of variation seems limited to the transposition of a^1 to G minor for strophe 3, and then to D major (along with slight melodic and harmonic readjustments) for strophe 4. But while the actual sound material of the head motif is not varied much from one strophe to the next, its harmonic implications, depending on the tonal contexts in which the motif is placed, are significantly altered. In fact, its first four presentations embody a measure of harmonic ambiguity that is not resolved until strophe 5. In strophe 1, a^1 is supported by a simple alternation of tonic and dominant harmonies in D minor. But mm. 3–4 set off for the minor dominant with enough force to allow the Bb⁶chord of m. 6 to be heard as a neapolitan in A minor. In retrospect, the D-minor tonic has been undermined from the outset, by the melodic G♯ of m. 1, and the C–B half step of m. 2; likewise, the melody of mm. 1–4 draws from the so-called gypsy minor scale on A, not on D. And when the head motif recurs, rhythmically transformed as A′ (m. 13), but at the same pitch level as at the opening, we hear it clearly in A minor. Even the bass that supports the head motif on its first presentation (D–A–D–A) is not as clear a harmonic signifier for D minor as one might think. Timbrally disembodied, given the pizzicato indication, and harmonically undercut in mm. 1–2 by the B♮ and G♯ in the second viola, which cross below the cello's D, the tonal force of the bass line is clearly weakened. The harmonies of the opening measures, in other words, can be read as i → V in D minor, though a plagal iv → I reading in A provides an alternate possibility.

The relative weight of these readings is reversed in strophe 2. Coming directly on the heels of the firm A minor at the close of strophe 1, the statement of a^1 in mm. 15–16 belongs to the minor dominant tonal region, in spite of its near identity with the music of mm. 1–2. The G minor/D minor ambiguity of strophe 3 (with emphasis on the first element in the pair) then parallels the D minor/A minor dichotomy of strophe 1. Clearly, there is nothing ambiguous about the initiatory D-major progression of strophe 4, but the resolution of the minor-key ambiguities of strophes 1–3 is reserved for strophe 5 (see Ex. 5.2). Whereas previously we have had single presentations of the head motif, each allowing for two harmonic interpretations, here we have two head-motif statements, each unequivocally linked with one harmonic reading. The dominant prolongation that prepares strophe 5 allows for a i → V reading in mm. 69–70, while mm. 77–78 (where the head motif is transposed down a fifth) articulate a iv → I progression in D. The steady reshaping of the opening melodic unit thus proceeds in tandem with another of the movement's processive concerns: the gradual unriddling of a harmonic enigma. Again, the teleological impulse is at odds with the stasis of the variation idea.

The *adagio*'s high seriousness of tone derives in part from its invocation of sonata-form rhetoric and procedures, but here, too, Brahms places the canonical form in a curious light. It is of course possible to hear strophes 1 and 2 as a repeated exposition, and strophes 3, 4, and 5 as development, recapitulation, and coda respectively.[62] But strophe 2 moves toward the tonic, not away from it as an exposition should; only the concluding twelve measures of strophe 3 are truly developmental; and even though m. 51 functions as a retransition to the D-major "recapitulation" at the beginning of strophe 4 (m. 52), its gestural power is undercut by the more extensively prolonged A pedal of mm. 62–68, which ushers in the D-minor "recapitulation" at m.

EXAMPLE 5.2

Brahms, Opus 111/ii, mm. 69–80

69. Sonata-form traits are wrenched from their usual placement in a pre-scribed scheme, and literally scattered throughout the movement: each of the three central strophes incorporates both developmental elaboration and gestures of reprise.

Hence, the Quintet *adagio* is first and foremost an individualized solution to a melodic and harmonic problem. Brahms extracts from both of the dominant structural paradigms—variation cycle and sonata allegro—those elements that will enable him both to articulate and resolve the self-generated dilemma. The result, in terms of structure, is that Brahms comes close to fashioning one of those "new forms" that Schumann had crusaded for earlier in the century. And in terms of genre, the result is a movement taking its place in a work that strives to be considerably more than a String Quintet. We should recall that the Quintet was, if only briefly, an *opus ultimum*. On 11 December 1890 Brahms wrote to Simrock: "With this slip of paper [the close of the first movement in piano four-hand arrangement] you may bid farewell to my composing, for it is high time to stop."[63]

As such, it is little wonder that Brahms conceived the work as a compendium, a summarizing *Kunstbuch,* in short, as yet another embodiment of the Romantic imperative. The opening of the first movement, with the cellist straining vigorously to let his tune be heard through the tumultuous wash of accompanying *forte* sextuplets in the upper strings, adopts a concerto tone.[64] Concertante allusions likewise figure in the last movement: the similarities between a segment of the first group (mm. 17ff.) and an idea from the finale of the B♭-Major Piano Concerto, Opus 83 (mm. 105ff.), were strong enough for Elisabeth von Herzogenberg to have pointed them out.[65] The languid theme of the slow movement "variations" can in turn be traced to a symphonic source: the third movement, *poco Allegretto,* of the Third Symphony, Opus 90, is built around essentially the same melody, but in diatonic form.

Allusions to the "higher" genres likewise interact with gestures drawn from the popular sphere, in particular the waltz topoi that determine the melodic substance of the first and third movements, and the gypsy topoi of the slow movement, *un poco allegretto,* and finale.[66] But throughout there is a marked dissociation of structural conceit and affective surface, of "tendency" and "tone." The gypsy waltz flavor of the third movement, for instance, is enriched through a remarkable display of contrapuntal devices: bits of canonic imitation infuse practically every bar of the principal waltz section (in particular, mm. 14–24, 25–32) culminating in a reprise of the principal subject in inversion (mm. 43ff.). In addition, the G-major middle section explores the possibilities for invertible counterpoint inherent in its opening duos for violas and violins (the coda, mm. 170ff., even brings the duos in melodic inversion).

The "individually formed" slow movement, just like the embodiment of the Romantic imperative in a work with all-inclusive generic implications, represents only one side of the Brahmsian dialectic of form and genre. For as it turns out, the form of the *adagio* is not so "new" after all. Brahms appears to have taken his cue from Schumann, the *adagio molto* of whose Third Quartet, Opus 41, No. 3, may even have served as a model. Schumann's Quartet movement, like Brahms's *adagio,* is based on a complex thematic configuration elaborated in three successive strophes. Admittedly, Schumann's opening forty-four-measure "strophe" is more extended than Brahms's: it consists of a complete periodic unit (A) followed by a series of texturally contrasting phrases (B) that, in addition to modulating far afield from the D-major tonic, already begin to develop the A material. But as in Brahms's Quintet movement, subsequent strophes omit significant portions of the opening configuration. Strophe 2, fundamentally a transposition of the first strophe down a fifth from D to G, shortens both segments *A* and *B,* the second of which is further condensed in strophe 3. Both movements therefore pose fundamentally similar problems. Schumann, like Brahms, presents an opening unit whose tonal and melodic vagaries are eventually filtered away, until we are left, in the final strophe, with a syntactically regular construct—a periodic phrase followed by a brief close, both firmly anchored in D major.[67] Schumann's quasi-hymnic tone is a far cry from Brahms's evocation of the slow *czardas,* but the structural affinities between the movements are unmistakable.[68]

On the whole, Brahms's compendium of forms and genres in the Opus 111 Quintet is singularly retrospective. His slow movement *Hommage à Schumann* is one of a sequence of musically emulative essays. The first movement evokes the sonata allegro cum variations design that distinguishes, for example, the opening *allegro molto moderato* of Schubert's G-Major String Quartet, D. 887.[69] Brahms infuses his movement with variation-cycle procedures from the start: the first group (mm. 1–15) and transition (mm. 16–25) of the exposition relate as theme and variation, while the second group (mm. 26–46) and close (mm. 46–56) are cast as a triple variation set; the extended coda brings further variations on the close (mm. 148–56), the second group (mm. 157–73), and the first group (mm. 173–81), producing a retrograde variation of the entire exposition. The third movement, at once waltz and contrapuntal tour de force, calls up the Minuet of Mozart's A-Major String Quartet, K. 464, which, as Schoenberg delighted in pointing out, conceals a wealth of artifice (the combination of motives with their inversions, invertible counterpoint, brief canonic forays) beneath its apparently *galant* surface.[70] The finale's harmonically deceptive principal theme in turn recalls Beethoven's use of a similarly conceived rondo tune for the finale of his E-Minor Quartet, Opus 59, No. 2. The Quintet theme remains firmly in B minor for some nine measures before swerving unceremoniously to the real tonic, G (mm. 9–13). Brahms's iii → I progression therefore reconfigures the VI → i move that spices Beethoven's theme. To be sure, nearly every one of Brahms's mature compositions discloses a dense network of allusions. What is noteworthy in the Opus 111 Quintet is their systematic disposition. Schubert, Schumann, Mozart, and Beethoven—the dominating figures in Brahms's pantheon of musical masters—are each emulated in turn. The musical *Roman* unfolds as commemorative *opus ultimum.*

Thus, despite the singularity of the *adagio,* and despite the encyclopedic, "novelizing" qualities of the Quintet as a whole, Brahms confirms Schlegel's pronouncement —"Up to now, modern poetry has seen no new genres"[71]— almost a century after the fact. This is an odd remark, especially considering that it comes from the framer of the Romantic imperative. It means, however, that the decisive element in modern art is not its individuality pure and simple. The true follower of the Romantic imperative *cannot* in fact be an absolute individual. The crucial element in the artwork that is worthy of the name resides in its dialectical embodiment of "Then" and "Now." The message of Brahms's Opus 111 Quintet is therefore at one with that of Schumann's C-Major Fantasie. The upholder of tradition and the crusader for new forms were not so far apart after all.

6 ❧

Wagner's *Ring* and *Universalpoesie*

Reflection constitutes the actual
form of thought. Its counterpole is
objective thought or productive
fantasy. Hence Art is not human but divine.

– Friedrich Schlegel
Philosophische Fragmente, Erste Epoche III,
no. 643

Friedrich Schlegel's Romantic Manifesto
and Wagnerian Music Drama

If it were necessary to reconstruct a theory of the nineteenth century's outlook on art from a single text, that text would certainly be Schlegel's *Athenäum* fragment 116, his encapsulated summary of the *Ur*-Romantic program
in its entirety. It begins as follows:

> Romantic poetry is a universal-progressive poetry. Its destiny is not merely
> to reunite all the separated genres of poetry, and to put poetry in touch with
> philosophy and rhetoric. It aims to and should at once mix and fuse poetry
> and prose, originality and criticism, artful and natural poetry; and make po-

155

etry lively and sociable, and life and society poetic; poetize wit and fill and
saturate the forms of art with genuinely instructive content of all sorts, and
enliven them with the pulsations of humor. It embraces everything that is
only poetic, from the greatest systems of art—themselves containing yet further systems—to the sigh or the kiss that the poetizing child breathes out in
artless song. It can so lose itself in what it represents that one might believe
its be-all and end-all was the characterization of all kinds of poetic individuals; and yet there is no other form better suited to expressing the author's
spirit completely; so that many artists who only intended to write a novel
wound up, quite accidentally, representing themselves. It alone, like the
epic, can become a mirror of the whole surrounding world, an image of
the age.

Here, then, is a restatement, and a decidedly poetic one at that, of many of
the ideas that we considered in the previous chapter under the rubric of the
Romantic imperative, the idealizing command to blend together the disparate
genres of poetry. But the quotation tells only half the story. It deals with the
universal content of the "new" poetry before moving on to an account of its
progressive form:

And more than any other poetic type, it can hover midway between the representation and the represener, free of all real and ideal interest, on the
wings of poetic reflection, ever raising this reflection to a higher power, as if
multiplying it in an endless series of mirrors. It is capable of the highest and
most versatile development, not only from within outwards but also from
without inwards; for the organization of its parts is similar to that of the productive whole, thereby opening up the prospect for a boundlessly developing classicism. Romantic poetry is among the arts what wit is in philosophy,
and what society, intimacy, friendship, and love are in life. The other poetic
types have been perfected and can now be fully analysed. The romantic type
is still in the process of becoming; indeed, this is its actual essence: that it
should be ever becoming and never completed. It cannot be exhausted by
any theory, and only a divinatory criticism would dare attempt to characterize its ideal. It alone is infinite, just as it alone is free; and it recognizes as its
first law that the free will of the poet will suffer no other law. Romantic poetry is the only poetic type that is more than a type, for in a sense all poetry
is or should be romantic.[1]

The *anaphora* of Schlegel's quasi-hieratic peroration ("It alone is infinite . . .
it alone is free") should not blind us to his keen awareness of the chief danger
facing the poetically inclined individual: total withdrawal into the self. Nor is
Schlegel's account of universal-progressive poetry to be taken as a paean to
unbridled subjectivity. The *poem* may "lose itself in what it represents," but
the *author* cannot, for self-abandonment means inactivity; it stands opposed
to the cool and calculated labor required to construct the poem in the first
place.

A careful reading of Schlegel's text will reveal that this in fact is what universal-progressive poetry is all about: the ordered construction of the poem. The first half of the fragment, the account of the universal side of the new poetry, indicates that the author's task is to represent the idea of art in the artwork itself.[2] This representation is accomplished not through a chaotic jumble, an aimless piling of one form atop another. Already in his third sentence, Schlegel begins to suggest a directed sequence for the author's activities. He proceeds from *Kunstpoesie* (that is, poetry in the strict sense), to criticism, to *Naturpoesie,* and finally to life and society. The process describes an ever-widening spiral, the shape that should likewise inform the artwork itself. Schlegel says as much in the next sentence, where the spiral contracts only to reach the same goal: the artwork is an all-embracing system, a system enfolding other systems that finally converge on the artless song, the sigh, the kiss, on life. The poem "loses itself," but it does so in accordance with a directionally fixed scheme.

At the precise midpoint of the fragment comes the assertion that the new poetry promises to become "a mirror of the whole surrounding world." (That Schlegel first introduces the word *mirror* at this spot is no accident: the remainder of the fragment will mirror what has gone before. Schlegel puts his theory into practice by constructing the fragment as a miniature representation of the artwork it describes.) How does Romantic poetry mirror the world? Schlegel's turn to a discussion of the "progressive" side of the artwork makes explicit what was implicit in the spiral patterns of the first part of his definition: Romantic poetry mirrors the world by mirroring itself. Again we have a clearly directed process, moving from the "whole surrounding world" to the artistic individual (the "representer"), each enfolding the other through the agency of the artwork (which hovers "midway between representation and representer") like the systems within systems from earlier on in the fragment. The terminal point, the locus in which the spiral is embedded, is the artwork. Without it, all the talk about world and artistic individual collapses into self-indulgent rhapsodizing. The hyperreflectivity that threatens to paralyze the artist can be put to productive use by inscribing it into the structure of the poem, organized such that all of its constituent parts proceed along the same lines as the whole that encloses them. A tall order indeed.

Schlegel's fragment has been cited often enough as a dithyramb to growth, progress, incompletion, "becoming." Yet it is easy to overlook his vision of a "boundlessly developing *classicism*" as the goal toward which universal-progressive poetry pointed. And Classicism, for Schlegel, meant not only the poetry of antiquity, but its organization en masse: "All the poems of the ancients embrace one another, until a whole is formed from ever greater masses and members; everything interpenetrates, and everywhere there is one and the same spirit, only expressed differently. And thus it is no empty assertion that ancient poetry was a single, indivisible, perfect poem. Why shouldn't that which once was come into being again? Of course, in another way. And why not in a more beautiful and greater way?"[3]

The system made up by the whole of ancient poetry would therefore devolve on the single work conceived according to the principles of universal-progressive poetry. The systems within systems of the universal-progressive poem correspond precisely to the *whole body* of Classical poetry, with its division into types and subtypes. "Classicism" survives (and is surpassed) in the modern artwork, therefore, through its self-mirroring structure. Again, a tall order. The accent on poetic structure in the second half of *Athenäum* fragment 116 likewise serves as a corrective to the artist's potential loss of self hinted at in the first half. Pure reflection is a danger; reflection productively embodied becomes the goal. Universal-progressive poetry, far from embracing a cult of subjectivity, rather casts it in a critical light.

My aim here is to show how Richard Wagner participated in this critique of subjectivity by placing the principle of reflection at the constructive center of *The Ring*. Schlegel's structural prescription for universal-progressive poetry, as we will see, makes for a remarkable parallel with Wagner's compositional practice. Wagner hardly took up our *Athenäum* fragment as a recipe for music drama. Questions of influence, in any case, are beside the point. Schlegel's account can, however, provide us with a useful springboard for interpreting the musical structure and textual thematic of *The Ring*.[4]

Inasmuch as *The Ring* embodies the aims of universal-progressive poetry, it is a musical novel of sorts. This is not, in itself, a new claim. Wagner himself saw the *Roman* as "the actual kernel of present-day poetry."[5] As a self-styled modern poet (and not merely an opera composer), he could hardly escape writing "novels" himself. More recently Peter Conrad has built a whole theory around the idea that operas in general, and Wagner's *Ring* dramas in particular, are closer to the novel than to any other literary form.[6] What I hope to add to the discussion is a renewed sense for exactly *how* the *Ring* tetralogy can be construed as musical novel. In short, I would like to argue that the *Ring* approaches the novel in its recourse to a reflective structure that supplies the backbone without which the work would fly apart at the seams, and that this structure in turn bears directly on the thematic, the meaning of the work.

Paraphrasing Liszt, Baudelaire noted that Wagner's music was saved from the charge of "vague emotionalism" by an intellectual component that forced our minds and memories to reflect.[7] A tendency already present in *Tannhäuser* and *Lohengrin,* the works that Liszt and Baudelaire had in mind, is raised to a far higher power in *The Ring,* where the reflective network counts for practically everything. The narratives first come to mind. Once thought of as necessary evils, as by-products of the work's unusual compositional history that called more for endurance than appreciation, the narrative passages in *The Ring* have come to be recognized by many commentators as crucial to its musico-dramatic action. The question-and-answer game for the Wanderer and Mime in Act I/ii of *Siegfried,* for example, does not just provide an occasion for the composer to review many of the salient points of the drama up to that point. More important for the future course of the proceedings is the fact that the exchange motivates Mime to teach Siegfried what he stubbornly refuses to learn: the nature of fear. In addition, the narratives have been valorized by a critical tradition initiated by Thomas Mann's recognition of their purely musical potential, their engagement in the magical feast of associations (*Beziehungszauber*) that places *The Ring* on a par with the greatest achievements in monumental art that the nineteenth century had to offer.[8]

The dramaturgical problem engendered by the work's incorporation of an epic body of incidents—an affront to the Aristotelian conception of tragedy[9]—thus emerges as a means of providing coherence on the largest scale. What counts for the structural integrity of *The Ring* is not the prehistory that the narratives furnish, but the mutual reflectivity, the web of connections that they establish between and among themselves. This trait was already prefigured in *Siegfrieds Tod,* the single text that would call forth three others to precede its revision as *Götterdämmerung.* The original version of the text for the Norns' scene told of Alberich's theft of the gold, his fashioning of a ring that would give him world power, Wotan's theft of the ring, Siegfried's slaying of Fafner, his passage through the magic fire and awakening of Brünnhilde, the tale of the Wälsung twins, the giants' erection of Valhalla, Alberich's curse on the ring, and Mime's demise. All of these events figure again in the subsequent *Siegfrieds Tod* narratives. Some are told repeatedly: the story of Siegfried's battle with Fafner, for instance, is recounted six times; his approach to the sleeping Brünnhilde five times. The groundwork for the associative network, in other words, was prepared from the start.

Still, the narratives are but one layer in a larger plan. They figure as part of an interrelated series of recapitulatory "centers of attraction" (to borrow Rudolf Stephan's suggestive term)[10] that includes those portions of the music dramas where the motivic work is particularly dense (e.g., the *Todesverkündigung* scene in *Walküre,* Act II) and many of the climactic act finales. Wagner's construction of a practically all-reflective design thus satisfied his "will to large-scale form" and likewise allowed him to confront a major source of anxiety for the composers of the midddle and late nineteenth century: the Beethoven symphonies. (In spite of their differing orientations, Brahms the symphonist and Wagner the music-dramatist faced the same challenge.) The confrontation took shape as a critique of symphonic form, and especially of one component in the form: the recapitulation or reprise.

Recurrence is of course a prerequisite for musical cohesion, yet Wagner troubled over it on two interdependent counts. In the first place, he was averse (in theory and in practice, leitmotifs notwithstanding) to the notion of exact or more or less exact repetition. While discussing the recall of the *Waldweben* in Siegfried's *Götterdämmerung* narrative (Act III/ii) with Cosima, Wagner commented that this music must "only be hinted at in the orchestra, for here it is Siegfried's fate which must make an impact, and a natural phenomenon must not be allowed to obscure it"; Cosima continues: "Anyhow he could never just repeat anything."[11] In the second place, reprise entails a form's turning back on itself, its gesture of retardation markedly at odds with the teleological impulses that drama requires. Wagner confirmed this point in his comments on Beethoven's Third *Leonora* Overture, a work he singled out on several occasions to argue that the conventional, "architectural" forms sacrificed processive growth for symmetry. In "Über die Anwendung der Musik auf das Drama" (1879), Wagner registered his disappointment that Beethoven "still repeated the first section of the tone-poem [exposition], with the customary change of key [recapitulation], exactly as in a symphonic movement—heedless that the dramatic excitement of the middle section [development], reserved for thematic working-out, had already led us to expect the *dénouement.*"[12]

Wagner's way around the contrary demands of musical coherence and dramatic propulsion involved a radical rethinking of each of the categories that we usually associate with the notion of reprise. In Wagner's musico-dramatic world, theme and motive are displaced by motivic complexes; more or less exact recurrence by extremely compressed or apotheotically extended transformation; resolution by dissolution, intensification, or fulfillment. Recurrence of the same (Adorno's "Wiederkehr des Gleichen") becomes transformation *through* the same[13] in Wagner's reflective network of recapitulatory centers.

To be sure, these structural considerations are of no little interest in and of themselves. But as we shall see, the reflective technique is likewise intimately bound up with *The Ring*'s thematic dimension, the layers of meaning unfolded in the work. At the broadest level, self-reflection will afford us a means of situating Wagner's tetralogy within the context of similar tendencies shared by other "monumental" artworks.

Reflection, the Romantic Artwork, and *The Ring*

According to the philosophical idealism of J. G. Fichte's *Wissenschaftslehre* (1794), the self is all-sufficient. It knows two fundamental drives. One is practical, centrifugal; it engages in a continual act of assertion that aims to subject the whole world to the autonomous laws of the self. The other is theoretical, centripetal, reflecting deeper and deeper so that the self may come to know its inner workings. Both activities are capable of infinite extension—and both are potentially dangerous. It would be no exaggeration to say that Romanticism as a philosophical-cultural movement originated as a response to the problematic inherent in the Fichtean worldview. This was the topic so intensely debated by Novalis and Friedrich Schlegel in conversations and letter exchanges of the middle and late 1790s. Their ruminations took shape as critical fragments, Novalis's assembled in the *Fichte-Studien* of 1795–96, Schlegel's scattered throughout collections from the mid-1790s and extending into the next decade. For both thinkers, the sticking point was the same: the notion of reflection, and the attendant threat of paralyzing solipsism. As subjective, inwardly directed thought, reflection stands in opposition to "productive fantasy" or objective thought.[14] It is, as Schlegel asserted, the actual *form* of thought, and as such may initiate an endless chain of thoughts *about* thoughts.[15] Hence reflection "partakes of the Infinite," and this it may do, as Schlegel well realized, "either negatively or positively."[16]

The potential force of reflection is tremendous, but how can its use toward positive ends be ensured? This became the crucial question. And for Schlegel, the answer lay in bringing together two powers that were theoretically opposed: reflection and production. Production, he wrote, "proceeds from within outwards just like reflection proceeds from without inwards."[17] This should strike a familiar chord. In *Athenäum* fragment 116, Schlegel maintained that universal-progressive poetry too was "capable of the highest and most versatile development, not only from within outwards, but also from without inwards." The chief meeting place of reflection and production, in other words, is the work of art.[18] The focal point of the reflective act is thus shifted from the self-absorbed individual to the artistic product, whose creative status is enhanced to the same degree that it reconfigures reflection as internal structure.

Productive reflection is common enough in literature, where it manifests itself most frequently through the self-mirroring technique that André Gide called *mise en abyme*. The play-within-a-play in Shakespeare's *Hamlet* served as a paradigmatic example for the device, which was taken up with great enthusiasm by the first generation of Romantic writers. In chapter 2 we saw how the narrative embeddings in Jean Paul's works (e.g., *Hoppelpoppel* in *Flegeljahre*) functioned not only as diverting asides but, more important, as commentaries on the themes in the main text.[19] The principal *mise en abyme* in Novalis's *Heinrich von Ofterdingen* is supplied by an episode in which the hero discovers a book that recapitulates his life and prefigures what is to come. Gide's statement to the effect that "nothing sheds more light on the work [better than the *mise en abyme*] or displays the proportions of the whole work more accurately"[20] certainly applies here. The episode in Novalis's *Heinrich* allows the hero to see the disparate strands of his life from a uniquely ordered perspective, and reveals for us one of the novel's main themes: the interpenetration of past, present, and future. The author can also turn to the *mise en abyme* in order to place himself or herself, productively, into the text. When the characters in a novel begin to spin their own tales (as Walt and Vult do in *Hoppelpoppel*), they engage in an activity that belongs in the province of the author. Reflective embeddings can also confirm a work's generic status; when Demodokos summarizes the whole of the *Iliad* in his second song in the *Odyssey,* he reminds us that the second of the two works lays claim to the same epic dimensions as the first. And when Cervantes, in Part 2 of *Don Quixote,* retells significant portions of Part 1 so as to "correct" some of the previously narrated details, the *mise en abyme* technique actually enables him to surpass his earlier achievements.[21]

Many of these approaches to the *mise en abyme* intersect in Goethe's *Wilhelm Meister* novels, works whose encyclopedic content is matched by their thoroughgoing dependence on the technique of productive reflection. The first of the two novels, *Wilhelm Meisters Lehrjahre,* was a book that in Schlegel's words "carries its own judgment within it, and spares the critic his labors."[22] In his *Meister* review—a practical demonstration of the poetically framed message of *Athenäum* Fragment 116—Schlegel was able to show just how well "the larger and smaller masses reveal the innate impulse of this work, so organized and organizing down to its finest detail to form a whole."[23] Goethe too was putting theory into practice, even though the theory (his account of "wiederholte Spiegelungen" or "repeated mirrorings"—a rough equivalent of Gide's *mise en abyme*) came almost three decades after he began work on the *Meister* project.[24]

The mirroring technique operates at all levels in the first of the *Meister* novels; objects, characters, situations, and ideas are all drawn into the process. For our present purposes, it is important to note that many of the embeddings cluster around *Hamlet,* that *Bildungsroman* gone wrong that is the subject of much discussion in Books 4 and 5.[25] A work that itself features the *mise en abyme* is here transformed as a *mise en abyme* in another. The contrast between Wilhelm and Hamlet, a reflection of the novel's thematic opposition of bourgeois and aristocratic society, broadens out into a statement about the authors of the texts in which these characters figure as protagonists: by weaving *Hamlet* into the texture of his novel, Goethe makes a claim for his own artistic rank vis-à-vis Shakespeare's. When Schlegel observed that "the fourth volume [Books 7 and 8] is really the work itself,"[26] he must have had in mind scenes like that in the hall of Lothario's castle (Book 7, Chapter 9), where William encounters a string of characters that had appeared earlier in the novel so that Goethe can recapitulate the principal thematic pairs of the work: the conflict between fate and chance, art and life, past and present. The culminating scene from Book 8, where Wilhelm and Natalie visit the Hall of the Past, functions in much the same way. When Wilhelm, awestruck by the architectural orderliness of the hall, asserts, "It speaks to me from the whole, it speaks from every part,"[27] he makes a telling pronouncement on the novel as a whole.

Although thirty-three years separated the final version of *Wilhelm Meisters Wanderjahre* from the completion of the *Lehrjahre,* the two novels are closely related in technique and spirit. In the later work, the mirroring principle emerges in the apparently self-sufficient novellas that continually interrupt the main narrative. And the mirror itself—or its near equivalent, the portrait—figures as a powerful symbol in both linear narrative and embedded tale. The novella "Who is the Betrayer?" for instance, features a hermitage whose walls are covered with historical pictures (comparable to the biblical portrait gallery of the Pedagogic Province, and the historical gallery in the home of Makarie, that bizarre soul who carries the entire solar system within her), while the climax of the tale arrives as Lucidor beholds himself and his beloved in a mirror.

Often the novellas simultaneously reflect both one another and the principal narrative. In both "The Man of Fifty" and "The Foolish Pilgrim," to cite an example, a father and son become rivals for the affection of the same woman, just as Wilhelm and Felix are both drawn to Hersilie in the narrative frame. But the repeated mirrorings are most intensely elaborated here, as in the *Lehrjahre,* in those sections devoted to a recapitulation of the novel's chief thematic pairs—art versus craft, part versus whole, inner world versus outer world. Most impressive is the scene that comes at the novel's center (Book 2, Chapter 7) involving Wilhelm's journey to Lago Maggiore in the company of a painter. The characters indulge in a lengthy excursus on the relationship between art and life, the thematic pair that extends over both *Meister* novels like a great arch, and that is varied here in a most ingenious way: Hilarie and the Widow, two fictional characters from the novella "The Man of Fifty," join two "real" characters (Wilhelm and the painter) from the narrative frame. The episode likewise recalls material from the previous novel, for the painter is fascinated by Mignon, whose songs he has learned from reading the *Lehrjahre.* His rendition of Mignon's "Kennst du das Land" near the end of the chapter, however, is more than a structurally unifying ploy; it motivates Wilhelm to exorcise the spirit of Mignon, a symbol of unfulfilled longing, and inspires him to turn wholeheartedly to an active life as a surgeon.

I have devoted some space to a consideration of reflective literary designs in general and Goethe's "repeated mirrorings" in particular as a means of setting Wagner's musical achievements into relief. Although many of the best-known examples of the *mise en abyme* derive from literature, there is nothing inherently literary about the technique. Gide took the term from heraldry (where it refers to the practice of placing a miniature representation of the original shield within the shield itself), and the device is frequently encountered in painting as well. Gide himself pointed to Quentin Metzys's *Money Changer and His Wife* (1514), where a small mirror reflects the room represented in the painting, as a prime example.[28] This is only to say that painterly reflection provides depth, and literary reflection—certainly as practiced by Goethe—can ensure breadth of design.

Wagnerian monumentality, in turn, partakes of the same spirit as Goethe's. And it was Goethe the novelist, more so than Goethe the dramatist, who furnished Wagner with an immediate and compelling example for the monumental design and dimensions of music drama. In his Beethoven essay of

1870, Wagner wrote that Goethe's poetic creations could be divided into "two main arteries," one represented by *Faust,* the other by the more "tranquillizing treatment" of the same problems in *Meister.*[29] True, he probably held the drama in higher esteem than the *Bildungsromane.* (Cosima reports that Wagner wanted to have *Faust* "splendidly printed for himself on fine vellum paper, as a symbolic, holy book. [It is] the German monument, the German masterpiece.")[30]

Yet the thematic of the *Meister* novels, or more specifically, the inseparability of thematic and form, occupied him no less intensively. When the artist ponders the world around him, Wagner argued in *Opera and Drama,* all that he sees is *"a chaos of unloveliness and formlessness."* Goethe, however, attempted to shroud this disorder "in a cloak of artistic beauty," most obviously in *Meister,* where humankind is actually shown "struggling for an artistically beautiful Form."[31] Almost twenty years later, Wagner and Cosima would spend a month of evenings rereading the *Lehrjahre,* which in spite of their long familiarity with it, still managed to sweep them away "like children."[32] Cosima reports that on the day before they reached the end, Wagner felt once again convinced "of the limited nature of poetry and the unlimited scope of music."[33] At the time, Wagner was testing those limits in the music for the first act of *Götterdämmerung,* the closing music drama in a tetralogy that would match (and was perhaps meant to surpass) Goethe in its rigorous employment of "repeated mirrorings."

The *Ring,* too, is an encyclopedia of reflective devices. Of the many instances of simple duplicative embeddings (those where the internal sequence of events is similar to that of the enclosing work), the Wanderer–Mime dialogue from *Siegfried,* Act I, comes to mind as an especially clear example: the Wanderer's three answers to Mime's questions take us through scenes ii, iii, and iv of *Rheingold* (with the music associated with the Nibelungs, the ring, the giants, and Valhalla), while Mime's responses to the Wanderer hearken back to the closing scenes of *Walküre,* Acts I and III, and the first scene of *Siegfried.* The duplicative potential of Siegfried's *Götterdämmerung* narrative (Act III/ii) is theoretically infinite. If he were allowed to continue recounting his adventures, Siegfried would necessarily reach the same point from which the scene began, with the reassembly of the hunting party, then the hero's offer to tell the tale of his life, and on the sequence might go indefinitely. Autobiographical accounts must by their very nature come to an end through acts of force; Siegfried's murder thus answers to both dramatic and structural requirements. Duplication in the Norns' scene, on the other hand, takes on an aporetic form. The embedding, that is, appears to enclose the work that encloses it, for the Norns at once recall the tetralogy's prehistory (Wotan's desecration of the World Ash Tree) and prophesy its conclusion (the music for the Third Norn's "Gehau'ner Scheite hohe Schicht" will resurface in Brünnhilde's final monologue).

Each of the music dramas, in its own way, plays on the relationships between and among reflective centers such as these. *Rheingold* exhibits an almost symmetrically organized series of mirrored pairings. The material surrounding the gods' entrance into Valhalla at the end of the music drama points back to the exposition of the Valhalla music at the beginning of scene ii (which it developmentally expands), and to several of the Rhinemaidens' *Lieder* from scene i. Overlapping with this frame is another linking Erda's scene iv monologue with the nature music of the *Vorspiel*. And poised within the frame are the two orchestral interludes flanking scene iii, the first depicting Wotan's and Loge's descent into Nibelheim, the second their ascent to Valhalla. Here Wagner accents the symmetry with a simple but striking move. The series of motives and motive families in the "descent" interlude—Loge, Rhinegold, ring, Nibelungs, hammering, Nibelungs, and ring again—are presented in a free retrograde to suggest ascent.

Walküre brings together two narrative strands, the human tragedy of the Wälsung twins and the divine myth, each culminating in the respective finales of Acts I and III, the main musical pillars of the drama. The finales in turn disclose their own recapitulatory networks that intersect in Act II. The love music for Siegmund and Sieglinde from Act I literally "dissolves" in Act II/iii. Surrounding this brief but musically dense episode are two scenes that conversely point toward the music drama's close: Wotan's confessional monologue (to which we will return in the next section) and the *Todes-verkündigung* episode. The dissolution of one story (the human tragedy) is embedded within ominous foretellings of the outcome of its divine complement.

In *Siegfried* the complexity of the recapitulatory web increases, largely due to the presence of the Wanderer. If his exchange with Mime in Act I makes for a simply duplicative *mise en abyme,* then the intermingling of past, present, and future in his encounter with Erda (Act III/i) is suggestive of the aporetic variety. Erda's recreation of the ambience of *Rheingold* (through musical references to her scene iv monologue and the *Rheingold Vorspiel*) balances Wotan's prophetic exposition of the World Inheritance motive, pointing to the *Siegfried* finale and beyond. Likewise, the absolute presentness of the finale, its focus on Siegfried's and Brünnhilde's burgeoning love, is countered by the appearance of music from the *Walküre* Act III finale in all its major sections. The link is also made by means of *The Ring*'s most powerful visual image: the fire with which Wotan encircles Brünnhilde's rock at the close of *Walküre,* and through which Siegfried passes here. (Of course this is the image that Brünnhilde will extinguish at the end of the tetralogy, thereby effecting a return to the primordial image of its opening: water). Hence, the *Siegfried* Act III finale's promise of a new world order resounds with echoes from the past.

Wagner's virtuoso handling of the embedding technique reaches a high point in *Götterdämmerung*, a self-styled "repetition of the whole, an introduction and 3 parts."[34] A network of internal references to all three of the preceding dramas spreads itself out over Acts I–III. The sinister side of the *Rheingold* story is taken up and intensified in the ghostly music for Alberich and Hagen in Act I/i; the divine-myth strand from *Walküre* (Act II/ii and iv; Act III/iii) supplies the basis for Waltraute's Act I/iii narration; and *Siegfried* is retold in the hero's Act III/ii account of his life for Gunther, Hagen, and their vassals. The scheme is further compressed in scene complexes within the acts that again relate summary versions of the earlier dramas. Thus the Norns' scene and Siegfried's orchestrally depicted Rhine journey, from the *Vorspiel,* together recreate the worlds of *Rheingold, Walküre,* and *Siegfried.* In Act III, the first two scenes and the ensuing funeral music articulate a sequence running: *Rheingold* (scene i), *Siegfried* (Acts I, II, III), and *Walküre* (Act I). The reversed order of the second two dramas therefore brings the Wälsung drama to a close by turning it back on itself. And lastly, two scenes in particular—the principal supporting pillars of the final *Ring* drama—seem to enclose the whole of the tetralogy within them. The Norns' scene not only embeds a *Rheingold-Walküre-Götterdämmerung* sequence; by prefiguring and even pointing beyond the drama's outcome, it also functions as aporetic *mise en abyme.* As such, it stands outside the time of the drama that it enfolds. Conversely, Brünnhilde's climactic monologue (where reference is again made to the totality of the cycle's main centers of attraction) is very much a part of the presentness of the dramatic scheme. Indeed, it is Brünnhilde who untangles so many of the earlier dilemmas by demonstrating how the past can and should be employed to influence the course of events in the future.

This brief sketch of the reflective structure of *The Ring* will suffice to drive home the point that what Schlegel said of Goethe's first Meister novel—"Both the larger and smaller masses reveal the innate impulse of this work, so organized and organizing down to its finest detail to form a whole"—applies here with equal force. Yet the structural symmetries and embeddings do not exist for their own sake. They continue to reflect, as we will see in the next two sections, on the thematic of the work.

The Ring
An Epic Portrayal of Interiority

The conjunction of drama and epic that led Thomas Mann to dub *The Ring* a "scenic *epos*" offered Wagner a fruitful opportunity for underpinning the structure of his massive cycle. But there is no denying that drama and novel (the epic's modern counterpart) make strange partners, creating a peculiar tension in the work's thematic dimension, that is, at the level of meaning. Strictly speaking, drama should unfold in the present. (Wagner recognized this as a quality of music too. As he maintained in a conversation with Cosima on Siegfried's funeral music: "Music always expresses the direct present.")[35] In addition, its formal essence is dialogue, which presupposes the ability of the characters to communicate their thoughts and feelings to one another. In short, drama seeks to represent an event in all its presentness through the medium of dialogue.[36] The novel, on the other hand, aims to thematize the passage of time. Its action becomes an inner action, "nothing but a struggle against the power of time," to quote Georg Lukács.[37] The present becomes a mere occasion for calling up the past, which now displaces it as the subject of the work. As Peter Szondi has shown, these novelizing traits came to impinge more and more upon late nineteenth-century drama, eventually leading to a form/content crisis that was left for twentieth-century dramatists to meet. In Ibsen, for instance, the entirety of the present action serves as an excuse for the characters to conjure up their past. Chekhov's characters, too, withdraw from the present into a dreamworld of memories and utopian wishes, their dialogues little more than conversationally framed monologues. In Strindberg's dramas, interpersonal dynamics are renounced in favor of an exploration of an individual psychic life—the author's.[38]

The composer of *The Ring* belongs in this company as well. It was Wagner the dramatist who, in the fall of 1851, wrote to Liszt of his plans to write a tetralogy that would enable him to dispense with the narrative-reflective elements in *Siegfrieds Tod.*[39] Wagner the musician with a passion for grand designs realized that they should be retained, even extended. And Wagner the novelist set out to thematize inwardness through the agency of the all-reflective musical plan. The heroic tragedy of Siegfried evolved into an epic portrayal of interiority.

This is most apparent in the divine myth, in the portions of the cycle that treat Wotan's dilemma. The focus here, as in the "crisis" dramas of the late nineteenth century, is on the portrayal of an inner life and its covert psychic workings. Wotan's pressing concern is lodged not in the future, in his power decisively to influence the course of upcoming events. The real problem lies behind him. How is he to cope with a deeply internalized past? This is the question raised in the great monologue from *Walküre* Act II/ii, which Wagner described as the "most important . . . for the development of the whole of the great four-part drama."[40] Wotan speaks the language of Lukács's "absolutely lonely man."[41] The more he withdraws into the problematic of his own world, the less cognizant he is of his nominal addressee, Brünnhilde. But the motivic fabric, which grows denser as the monologue proceeds, underscores a paradox: with introspection comes the heightened self-awareness signaled by an increase in musical continuity.

The soliloquy is shaped as a series of intensifying waves, though the first is hardly a wave at all. The tenuous textures that support Wotan's account of the follies of his younger days (his *Flegeljahre,* as it were) suggest absence, not presence. The first real "crest" comes with Wotan's troubled references to the free hero who must, though unbidden by the god, carry out his plans (from "Nur Einer könnte, was ich nicht darf"). It falls into two strophes, the first in E minor and the second in A minor, both undergirded by the motive of Wotan's unrest. Together they microcosmically describe the shape of the whole sprawling monologue. The text of the first strophe is directed outward to Brünnhilde; she learns for the first time of Wotan's ingenious but flawed scheme to enlist the unmotivated aid of the freest of heroes. The music, however, arrives at its climactic point (eventually reaching a comfirmatory cadence in A minor) only in the second strophe. And here the text relinquishes its informative role. Wotan's rhetorical questions (initiated by "den freundlichen Feind, wo fände ich ihn?") are not intended for Brünnhilde; they turn back in on the god.

The third wave (from "Ich berührte Alberich") again divides into two strophes, here separated by a statement of the Curse motive (its linearization of an F♯–A–C–E half-diminished chord mediating between the A minor of the previous wave and the C [minor] of this one). With Wotan's passionate cry for the only thing that he now desires—"das Ende"—we approach the wrenching musical climax of the monologue. But Wotan's plea resounds within, not without. The music tells us this through its tortuous chromaticization of C minor, and its juxtaposition of the dominant of A minor *(fortissimo)* with C minor *(pianissimo)* at Wotan's repetition of the crucial words ("das Ende, das Ende").

The thematic point of the monologue, however, is reserved for the fourth and last wave. Far back in the first wave, Wotan had promised to reveal an enigmatic warning that he had received from Erda ("achte es wohl, wes mich die Wala gewarnt"). But the revelation—concerning Alberich's offspring and the impending downfall of the gods—does not come until this closing phase. The monologue thus embeds one narrative (Erda's unheard "Wenn der Liebe finster Feind zürnend zeugt einen Sohn, der Sel'gen Ende säumt dann nicht") within another; the process of interiorization reaches its farthest point of remove. Embedding appears in yet another guise. Wotan's soliloquy moves from absence—in its recitational opening section—to presence—in the intensifying climaxes of the second and third waves—only to dissolve again in its final phase. The same pattern repeats itself in the central waves, their climaxes ultimately broken, muffled. In short, interiority is projected through the form of the whole and the layout of its major parts.[42]

Elements of internalization are just as pronounced in Wotan's dialogue with Erda at the outset of *Siegfried,* Act III. Here too we encounter the "dissolved" climax as a cipher for withdrawal into the self. The exchange presses forward to a single overpowering moment: the luminous statement of the so-called World Inheritance motive in Wotan's final speech. Yet the apparently unbridled optimism of the gesture is considerably darkened by several factors. Its first and grandest statement is truncated after barely four bars. It comes in A♭, at a half-step remove from the prevailing G tonality, so that melodic affirmation is coupled with chromatic alienation. The motive's next appearance (beginning from a quieter dynamic level) proceeds from the tonic G only to deny it with a truncated sequential phrase that dissolves into a diminished-seventh harmony on G♯. And its final statement, though promising resolution onto the tonic, completes itself with G functioning as part of the diminished-seventh chord on C$^\sharp$, the dissonance intensified by an appoggiatura F$^\sharp$ in the bass.

An attenuated climax, though, is more or less what we should expect from a dialogue in name only. Wotan, as the Wanderer, comes to Erda with a question for which he already knows the answer, a question whose pointlessness he has long since recognized. His entreaty for advice on how to "arrest the revolving wheel" of time is posed as a purely rhetorical query. Wotan asks Erda "how a god is to master his care," but winds up *telling her,* in his last speech, what she may not know: the promise for the future held out by Siegfried's and Brünnhilde's imminent union. Neither interlocutor in the dialogue much affects the other: Wotan's peroration comes without any prompting from Erda, who descends into the depths at the end of the scene much as she had risen from them at the beginning. The dialogue form, in other words, is a mere frame for two counterpointed monologues, Erda's characterized by a dreamy and elusive chromaticism, Wotan's by more decisively poised utterances.[43] And of the two monologues, Wotan's clearly dominates. He summons Erda in order to confirm what he knows, and to confirm it for himself.

Memory Preserved

Major segments of the action of *The Ring*—especially those in which the Wotan story plays itself out—develop as inner action. But while Wagner thematizes interiority, largely through the agency of reflective, monologic forms, he does not wholeheartedly endorse it. Schlegel's *Athenäum* fragment 116 tells us that *Universalpoesie* strives to "make poetry lively and sociable," and as odd as the claim may appear, Wagner strives to do just that. More exactly, the obverse of Wagner's epic portrayal of inwardness is his thematicization of its opposite: the ability to communicate directly and openly with others, and through one of the surest and oldest media, the medium of storytelling.

In a beautiful essay entitled "The Storyteller: Reflections on the Works of Nikolai Leskov," Walter Benjamin registered his fears over the gradual but unmistakable waning of the narrative art in the modern world. A receptive "community of listeners" for leisurely told tales was disappearing in an atmosphere where the wisdom of the story, passed on by word of mouth from generation to generation, counted for less than the immediately verifiable (and immediately disposable) information contained in a newspaper report.[44] Wagner had similar fears. The characters in *The Ring* inhabit a world where the power of the tale told for its own sake has been drastically minimized. In the tales told by Thomas Mann's Jacob and Joseph, all is "recollection, confirmation, and edification, a kind of spoken antiphony"; yet there is no "practical exchange of ideas," no "intellectual discussion."[45] Mann's biblical heroes do not engage in narrative retellings for any specific purpose; Wagner's characters often do. Gone too is Benjamin's community of listeners sitting in rapt attention, equally mesmerized by the tale as by the "weaving and spinning" that inevitably accompanies it.[46] To be sure, the Norns weave and spin, but there is no one on hand to hear them. In *Siegfrieds Tod,* Brünnhilde was to be visited by all her sisters. In *Götterdämmerung,* only Waltraute appears, and her doleful tale has little immediate effect. In many of the *Ring* narratives, wisdom is of less moment than information. Loge's account of the Rhinemaidens' plight (*Rheingold,* scene i), for example, is not told for the gods' delectation. There is more than a little mischief at work in his foreknowledge of the dire consequences that the tale will have for Wotan. The purpose of Mime's Starling Song (*Siegfried* I/i) is neither to enlighten nor to entertain, but to perpetuate a falsehood. The Wanderer and Mime may exchange tales, but only as part of what will become a deadly game. The irony embodied in Mime's real need for information at this point speaks further to the devaluation of the storyteller's art; Mime knows all the ancient myths, but realizes too late that they are of no use to him. Hagen too knows many tales, but he tells Gunther of Siegfried and Brünnhilde (*Götterdämmerung* I/i) in order to ensnare his unwitting half brother in a vicious plot. In the end, it is Wagner himself who preserves the art of storytelling by reminding us, through his characters, that it is in danger of becoming extinct.

Why, though, is storytelling such a vital activity? Again according to Benjamin, it is an enclave for the preservation of memory. The value of the story is directly linked to the exercise of the mnemonic faculty, both on the part of the storyteller (whose capacity for remembering a large body of tales is seemingly boundless), and of the listeners (who can place the tale within the context of a commonly shared body of folk wisdom). A highly developed memory is a prime requisite for the bard, the purveyor of the epic art whose ancient Greek Muse (as Benjamin points out) was Mnemosyne, the "Rememberer." It is no less a requisite for the bard's addressees, whose absorption of the tales told will help them to make a coherent "story" out of their own lives.[47] In literature, and especially in the novel, memory provides the hero or heroine with a means of closing the gap between interiority and the outside world. If the protagonist can make sense of his or her individual past, so too will the vagaries of external existence appear in a more comprehensible light.[48]

But memory too is under siege for many of the *Ring* characters—without their even troubling much over the fact. Siegfried does manage to get a taste of fear, but he promptly forgets it: "das Fürchten, mich dünkt, ich Dummer vergaß ich nun ganz" he merrily pipes out over the *Waldvogel* motive just before the final, ecstatic duet passage in *Siegfried* (Act III/iii). Not that Siegfried is without memory. In his *Götterdämmerung* (Act III/ii) narrative, for instance, he demonstrates that much from his past has been retained. At issue is the *quality* of his memory. The magic brew that Hagen prepares for Siegfried in the first act of *Götterdämmerung* causes him to forget any woman that he might have met before Gutrune; but at the same time,

Siegfried's drinking of the potion merely actualizes and intensifies one of his defining character traits: the inability to remember much beyond the present moment. Siegfried's music articulates the same thematic. The transformation of his horn call into the "mature" Siegfried motive that the orchestra triumphantly intones in the *Götterdämmerung Vorspiel* limits itself to this moment (his period of time on the Valkyrie's rock) and the Act III funeral music. While out in the world, Siegfried knows only the perky, "immature" version of the same motive introduced in the previous music drama.[49]

The true epic hero is unable to forget, but Wagner constantly steps in to fill in gaps of which his hero is not even aware. Siegfried's *Götterdämmerung,* Act III, narrative, for instance, begins with the tale of his youthful tutelage under the "ill-tempered dwarf" Mime; but the motivic undergirding in the orchestra, the music that lends a measure of coherence to Siegfried's disjointed utterances, emanates from Wagner, not from the hero. This is made clear from the outset, where the opening lines, "Mime, hieß ein mürrischer Zwerg," are preceded and supported by compact references to Mime's "Sorglose Schmiede" monologue from *Rheingold,* scene iii (and in its associative G-minor tonality)—music that Siegfried has obviously not heard. The first true storyteller, Benjamin tells us, was the teller of fairy tales.[50] The overwhelming irony of Siegfried's last moments in *Götterdämmerung* will become clear if we keep in mind that the fairy-tale hero is called upon to perform this function, a function he is singularly unequipped to fulfill. Siegfried, as neither teacher nor sage, cannot relate his own story properly; the task falls to Wagner, who wrote to Theodor Uhlig that the original *Siegfried* text (*Der junge Siegfried*) had "the enormous advantage of conveying the important myth to an audience by means of actions on stage, just as children are taught fairy tales."[51] Wagner tells the tale; he casts himself, over and above the hapless hero, as teacher and sage.

The devaluation of memory goes hand in hand with another aspect of the thematic of *The Ring*: the reduced ability of many of its characters to know experience in the fullest sense. Here too we may focus the issue by drawing on Walter Benjamin's useful distinction between two fundamentally different modes of experience. On the one hand, Benjamin recognized experience as *Erfahrung,* as the deeply felt continuity that results from the coordination of external events and inner psychic well-being. To partake of *Erfahrung* is to sense a connection with the sustaining traditions that circumscribe and give meaning to one's life. On the other hand, there is experience as *Erlebnis,* the striking event that, inasmuch as it occupies a fixed moment in the individual's existence, disrupts the continuities determining the first mode. Its formal correlative is the shock impulse, the psychic defense mechanism that assigns an incident to a precise point in time at "the cost of the integrity of its contents."[52] For Benjamin, the modern individual's predicament is intimately linked to his or her unrelenting exposure to shocks, to events that simply repeat themselves with mechanical and numbing regularity. The inhabitant of the modern world, in short, is time and again "cheated out of" true experience—experience, that is, as *Erfahrung*.[53] The final enclave of experience in this sense may well be art; hence Benjamin found Baudelaire's poetry so very "true" precisely because, as art, it productively embodied the shock experience as a formal principle; in the *Fleurs du mal,* we encounter *Erlebnis* reconfigured as *Erfahrung*.

Several of the participants in the *Ring* dramas—perhaps Siegfried more than any other—are noticeably deficient on experience as *Erfahrung*. And Wagner no less than Baudelaire celebrates this experiential mode, by inscribing its loss and restitution into the *Ring* music itself. "*Experience* [*Erfahrung*] is everything," Wagner wrote in a long letter to August Röckel detailing the thematic of *The Ring*. "Not even Siegfried alone ... is the complete 'human being': he is merely the half, only with *Brünnhilde* does he become the redeemer; *one* man alone cannot do everything; many are needed, and a suffering, self-immolating woman finally becomes the true, conscious redeemer: for it is love which is really 'the eternal feminine' itself."[54] The letter's references to Siegfried and Brünnhilde suggest a comparison between the two characters as depicted in two of the crucial reflective centers of the *Ring* tetralogy: Siegfried's autobiographical narrative just before his death in the third act of *Götterdämmerung,* and Brünnhilde's subsequent Immolation monologue, each of which complements the other by presenting a radically different outlook on the nature of experience.

Siegfried's narrative presents the whole stuff of the previous music drama in a drastically compressed form, and does so in an entirely straightforward manner: each of the narrative's three main divisions (separated and interrupted by comments from Hagen and the Gibichung vassals) corresponds to each of the three *Siegfried* acts in turn.[55] Hence in the first division (from "Mime hieß ein mürrischer Zwerg"), we hear allusions to the musical highlights of Act I, including Mime's (so-called) Brooding motive, his Starling Song, the Fafner motive, Siegfried's horn call music, and his Forging Song ("Nothung! Nothung! Neidliches Schwert!"). The division's closing line ("dort fällt' ich Fafner, den Wurm") rapidly brings the narrative around to the action of *Siegfried,* Act II, here represented by a reprise of strophes 1–3 of the Woodbird's Song. The final scene of *Siegfried,* Act III, had dramatized the crucial event in Siegfried's life, the encounter with Brünnhilde subsequently dislodged from his memory through the workings of Hagen's potion of forgetfulness. But with his mnemonic faculties restored by a draught of remembrance (administered between the recall of strophes 2 and 3 of the Woodbird's Song), Siegfried proceeds to tell of his ascent of the Valkyries' flaming rock ("Rasch ohne Zögern zog ich nun aus"), his passage through the fire, and (following on the brutal assault in the "real" time of the narrative), his awakening of the sleeping Brünnhilde ("Brünnhilde, heilige Braut! Wach auf!")—all of which are supported by the appropriate musical allusions.

The *mise en abyme,* by compressing what it summarizes, serves to distinguish the essential from the inessential, or as in this case, helps to give us an idea of what is essential and inessential *from the hero's point of view.* Siegfried's account is selective, to say the least, but when he fails to mention his confrontation with the Wanderer, for instance, we should not take it as a deliberate falsification of his story. Wotan, whom he does not even recognize as such, counts for little in the eyes of a hero who lives his life as a series of striking experiences, but who has little sense of the continuity of experience per se.

The narrative, therefore, recounts a colorful series of *Erlebnisse* of striking but essentially isolated events told as musical fragments whose inner connection is tenuous at best. This holds at broad and local levels as well. The tonal course of the whole, for example, is governed by a network of associative tonalities: the G minor and D minor of the first division point back to the G minor and D major of *Siegfried,* Act I; the second division's E major clearly occupies the same tonal locus as the *Waldweben* music from *Siegfried,* Act II; and the C major at the recall of Brünnhilde's Awakening music restates the tonality of the *Siegfried* Act III finale. To be sure, associative tonal dispositions are the rule throughout much of *The Ring;* a fairly sizeable body of literature has been devoted to establishing that the tetralogy's harmonic plan is but one vast system of associative keys.[56] What is at issue here are the necessary connections that would enable us to say that the narrative is *in* this or that key, or that it progresses from one to the other. Obviously, the tonal discourse here revolves not about one key but about the several keys that in turn "stand in" for the respective acts of *Siegfried* (the G-minor tonality of the "Sorglose Schmiede" allusion at the beginning of the narrative traces itself back even further, to *Rheingold,* scene iii). Nor is there any question of an overriding and logically spun-out progression from the G minor of the narrative's opening to the C major (which in any event dissolves into A) at its close. The monologue's various divisions are too often interrupted by tonally wayward asides, and differ so markedly from one another in tone, texture, and motivic substance, that any sense of goal-directed progress from the first moments to the last is noticeably lacking.

Little wonder, then, that Alfred Lorenz had such a difficult time coordinating the narrative with the tonally concentric *Bar, Bogen,* and reprise forms into which he parsed Wagner's music dramas. His division of the narrative into two *Bogen* forms (the second, governed by the "highest freedom," beginning from the third strophe of the Woodbird's Song) does no little violence to what is certainly a three-part scheme.[57] On the other hand, Lorenz's (failed) attempt to bring this music in line with the notion of the neatly structured musical-poetic period touches on an unmistakable quality of Siegfried's narrative: its conception as a sequence of musical fragments that resist the tonal and motivic continuities of internally coherent musical forms.

Take, for example, the narrative's first main division (see Ex. 6.1). On the surface, the form could hardly be more clear. Siegfried's tale of his days with Mime falls into two elided parts (the second beginning with the orchestral preparation for "Er lehrte mich schmieden"), each of which proceeds from G minor to a cadence in D minor, and each initiated by Mime's "Sorglose Schmiede" motive (cf. mm. 654ff. and 667ff.). The passage, in other words, is articulated into two roughly parallel strophes, thus making a structural reference to the *Lied* forms that dominate the first act of *Siegfried.* In that the

EXAMPLE 6.1
Wagner, *Götterdämmerung,* Act III/ii, Siegfried's narrative (opening)

zog er mich auf, dass einst das Kind, wann kühn es er wuchs, einen
granted me care, *to* *count* *on me,* *when man - ful I'd waxed,* *in the*

Wurm ihm fällt' im Wald, der lang' schon hü - tet' ei - nen
wood to slay a Worm, *which* *long* *had hidden* *there a*

Hort. Er lehr - te mich schmieden und Er - ze
hoard. *He trained me to smith's work* *and me - tal*

schmel - zen; doch, was der Künst - ler sel - ber nicht
smelting, *but* *what* *the teacher* *could not at -*

EXAMPLE 6.1 (*continued*)

Lied form well suits the demands of the tetralogy's *Märchenoper,* it is eminently sensible that the *Märchenheld's* retelling of a part of the same should
display the strophic construction that it does.[58] Yet something is amiss. The
overall form may be songlike, but there is nothing in the least songlike about
the melodic course of Siegfried's account. What we have instead are an array
of disjointed utterances and awkward intervallic leaps in the vocal line, whose
most memorable melodic gesture is the recurrent descending skip of an
octave (see mm. 667, 676, 681, 683, and 684–85). This is meant to recall
Siegfried's Forging Song, and it is telling that all he seems to retain is its
ungraceful opening idea at that. The *Lied* form, that is to say, has been imposed from without; far from being a necessary consequence of the verse
melody, it in fact contradicts it.

The cleft between vocal style and framing design corresponds to the many
clefts, both motivic and tonal, that characterize the supporting orchestral fabric. The melodic allusions to *Siegfried* are reduced to the status of fragments
arranged like detachable links in a chain: Mime's Brooding motive occupies
two bars, Fafner's motive another two (in the second strophe this expands to
four), the Starling Song eight bars, Siegfried's horn call music three and a
half, the Sword motive one, and the Forging Song four. Together they do not

make up a "family" with shared melodic characteristics; on the contrary, they are merely subjugated to the propulsive flow of the prevailing $\frac{6}{8}$ meter.

The tonal argument dissolves into fragments as well, especially in the second strophe. While it moves, like the first, from G minor to D minor, what occurs between these tonal end points does not constitute a goal-directed modulation from tonic to minor dominant. The brief excursions to A♭ (mm. 673ff.) and C (for the Sword motive in m. 680) would seem to thwart the arrival of a D minor imposed, as it were, by an act of force. In addition, tonalities are treated as if they were just as detachable from their original contexts as motives were from theirs. The Starling Song fragment begins in G minor (mm. 667–72), the associative tonality of "Sorglose Schmiede." But its subsequent passage into A♭ amounts to a direct quotation from *Siegfried,* Act I/i ("mit klugen Rathe rieth ich dir klug"), where the same A♭ music had appeared within an F-minor context.

The tonal and motivic disjunctions in the narrative point to life's having disclosed itself to Siegfried as a series of shock impulses. The music underscores what a cursory reading of the text might not, namely, that the fairy-tale hero has been overwhelmed by *Erlebnisse,* but has failed to knit them together into a deeply abiding sense for *Erfahrung.* It is even debatable that Siegfried comes to understand the crucial difference between these varying modes of experience by the time he reaches the end of his narrative account. His visionary recall of the music of Brünnhilde's Awakening commences with over thirty measures of exact quotation, just before a thirteen-bar, liquidating close. Even in his final moments, then, Siegfried undergoes little change, development, or transformation. The fairy-tale hero is cheated out of his experience up to the end.

Brünnhilde's music at the very end of the cycle is of a different order. Here, at last, is a statement from an individual who has learned how to piece together isolated events so as to form a coherent picture of the past that will in turn resonate in the future. Here, in other words, is a musical portrayal of experience as *Erfahrung.* Where does Brünnhilde derive the wisdom that elevates her to this new level of understanding? As Christopher Wintle has convincingly argued, it is from the Rhinemaidens. Gutrune, in the brief monologue that opens the final scene of *Götterdämmerung,* voices her suspicions over having seen Brünnhilde walking unaccompanied at night along the shores of the Rhine. And it makes very good sense indeed to assume that the heroine encounters the Rhinemaidens during her nocturnal stroll, and from them gains the insights needed to conclude the cycle.[59] For Carolyn Abbate, the Rhinemaidens' (unheard) narrative is the single most crucial of all the tetralogy's narratives. Through it, Brünnhilde "wird wissend"; and although it is not realized in musico-dramatic form, we will hear echoes of the Rhinemaidens' meeting with Brünnhilde in the Immolation monologue, where the heroine "revoices" what she has learned.[60]

Whether Brünnhilde's closing speech actually recapitulates music that we have not heard (as Abbate suggests) is difficult to ascertain. More to the point, her offstage encounter enables her to understand a stretch of music that we *have* heard before, music that was directed precisely at Brünnhilde, although she attended to it little at the time: Waltraute's admonitory narrative in *Götterdämmerung,* Act I. The Immolation monologue begins with an expanded reference to the earlier scene: the dotted motive that prefaces and undergirds Brünnhilde's command to prepare the funeral pyre had previously supported Waltraute's account of the felling of the World Ash Tree by Wotan's order ("Des Stammes Scheite hieß er sie schichten). It is a motive with a long history in *The Ring,* extending back to the Third Norns' prophetic vision of the conflagration that will mark the end of the gods' reign ("Gehau-'ner Scheite hohe Schicht" and "Des zerschlag'nen Speeres stechende Splitter"), and ultimately to the Wanderer's tale (in response to Mime's third question) of the fashioning of the mighty spear from a branch of the World Ash Tree.

In the Immolation monologue the motive functions much like a refrain: witness its articulation of the scene's midpoint as it recurs in the orchestra just after Brünnhilde's "Ruhe, ruhe, du Gott!" And here it undergoes an important harmonic transformation. Unlike the tonally unstable, chromaticized variants that we hear in the Norns' scene, Waltraute's narrative, and at the beginning of the Immolation monologue, the orchestral refrain restates the motive within a (more or less) clear D^b-major context, bringing it round, in other words, to the tonal realm in which it had first sounded in the Wanderer/Mime dialogue—but then again—*not quite* bringing it round. The quasi-return of the motive to its original tonal sphere, a cipher for Brünnhilde's power to restore *through* transformation, colors the D^b triad with a chromatic neighbor chord (the half-diminished seventh A^b–C^b–E^{bb}–G^b).

What we have, then, is no mere "naïve" return to the D^b world associated with Valhalla since the beginning of *Rheingold,* scene ii, but rather a renewal informed by experience as *Erfahrung.* The music confirms that Brünnhilde's is not an unreflected "first nature" (as Hegel intended the phrase), but a newly won "second nature" informed by wisdom. She gives us a glimpse of that meaning borne of experience that is denied to Siegfried.

The motivic fragments in Siegfried's narrative stare out of the texture like so many snapshots in a photo album. Brünnhilde recalls only to reconfigure, and not just at the level of the motive. Extended stretches of her closing monologue are devoted to summoning up the major reflective centers of the preceding music dramas, which she treats in *reverse* order. First she addresses the murdered hero ("Wie Sonne lauter strahlt mir sein Licht") with a contemplative recreation of the luminous love duet from the *Siegfried* Act III Finale. Her exhortation to the gods ("Ob ihr, der Eide ewige Hüter") points back to the music of *Walküre* (in particular, the Act II *Todesverkündigung* scene, and the Act III finale) and its chief representative in the final *Ring* drama, Waltraute's narrative. Lastly, the speech immediately before she prepares to mount the funeral pyre is directed at the ring, its chief musical material supplied by the Rhinemaidens' *Lieder* first heard in *Rheingold*: "Weia! Waga!"

and "Rheingold! Rheingold! Leuchtende Lust." Step by step, each of the previous dramas is exorcised to clear the way for Brünnhilde's final redemptive act.

The process of tying together the loose threads of the past for the sake of the future's promise of a better order is aptly demonstrated at the conclusion of Brünnhilde's central invocation to the gods. Its entire closing stretch (from "Auch deine Raben hör' ich rauschen") draws liberally on Waltraute's narrative. Indeed, Brünnhilde's final words—"Ruhe, ruhe, du Gott!"—are supported by much the same music that had accompanied Waltraute's "erlös't wär Gott und Welt." But whereas Waltraute merely *asserts* D♭, Brünnhilde *confirms* it by appending the cadential phrase that had articulated the same tonality at the close of Wotan's speech at the beginning of *Rheingold* scene ii. The past, as represented in the Immolation monologue, is thus more than a repository of striking incidents: it is a force that must be reckoned with in the present as a precondition for the meaningful continuation of life in the future.

Each of *The Ring*'s principal characters responds to the claims of the past in a markedly different way. For Wotan, coming to terms with past events leads to withdrawal into the self. Siegfried knows the past only as an array of colorful occurrences. Brünnhilde, on the other hand, shapes the course of things to come by bringing the past in touch with the present. These are all novelistic conceits. Indeed, throughout our discussion I have tried to show how both an all-reflective structure and a temporal thematic interact in a work that is more musical novel (or *Roman*) than anything else. But in fact, *The Ring* is just as much three novels as it is one. The Siegfried story takes shape as a novel of "abstract idealism" (to borrow from Lukács's schema), its hero's soul narrower than the challenges the world has to offer. Wotan, whose soul rises above the petty concerns and intrigues of those around him, stands at the center of a novel of "disillusionment." But Brünnhilde's novel surpasses both of the others. The soul of the heroine comes to be at one with its destiny in a novel of "redemption."

The musical cipher for the Brünnhilde story is none other than the theme that Sieglinde rapturously proclaims to the heroine in the last act of *Walküre* and that figures so prominently in the last stages of the Immolation monologue. More than any other idea, it imparts to the proceedings the all-important sense of presentness needed to balance the monologue's previous fixation on the past. Brünnhilde has made her peace with the events of *Siegfried,* and *Walküre,* and even *Rheingold.* She is now equipped to perform the decisive act of redemption. And what better way to signal this in the music than by calling forth a melodic idea that hasn't had much of a prehistory, an idea steadily sequenced up by half step from D, to E♭, and then to E, before dissolving into the final (or almost final) cadential move toward D♭?

While this theme has only a limited history in the context of the *Ring* music, it lays claim to a considerably more extended past in the Wagner literature. We now know better than to think of it as a musical tag for "Redemption through Love." We also know that Cosima's 1872 diary reference does not identify it as "a hymn to heroes."[61] Both the German and English editions of the diaries are incorrect on this point; apparently Wagner described it to Cosima as "a hymn to the *heroine.*"[62] And in 1875 he authorized her to inform an inquirer that "the motive sung to Brünnhilde by Sieglinde [in *Walküre*] is the glorification of Brünnhilde which at the end of the work is taken up, so to speak, by the entirety [*von der Gesammtheit*]."[63] But the fact that so much spadework has been necessary to disclose the "meaning" of the last bars of *The Ring* (where the "glorification of Brünnhilde" theme sounds in the orchestra for the final time) perhaps indicates that the meaning is not so clear after all.

To what or whom, for instance, does Wagner's reference to "der Gesammtheit" point? Clearly, there is only one voice left at the end of the *Ring* tetralogy, and it is the composer's. We need also recall that Brünnhilde's final cadential gesture is violently undercut by the orchestra; her melodic $D^\flat$—the goal toward which the gesture aspires—is subsumed within the harmonically ambiguous augmented triad ($C^\sharp/D^\flat$–F–A) that sets off the orchestral postlude. It is Wagner who effects the the crucial *musical* act—closure—by contrapuntally combining the Valhalla music, the "Weia, Waga" melody, and the "glorification" theme, all of them now sounding in a $D^\flat$-major context. And Wagner too fulfills the prophecy of Waltraute's narrative. The sequentially rising statements of the Valhalla theme (supported by the dotted motive that we have traced back to the Wanderer/Mime dialogue) come directly out of Waltraute's music, but here the $G^\flat$-major goal of the passage is reinterpreted as a subdominant within the larger progression to $D^\flat$, its arrival articulated by the final appearance of the "glorification" theme.

In November 1880 Cosima reported that Wagner, after glancing through the conclusion of *Götterdämmerung,* swore never again to "write anything as complicated as that."[64] The hero of the fourth *Ring* "novel" turns out to be the artist himself, who by projecting the temporal dilemma that threatens to consume his characters as an all-reflective network, overcomes the subjectivity that threatens to consume him.

7 ❧

Tristan, Parsifal, and the "New" Organicism

Taken as a whole, the
philosophy of classical antiquity
was at once organic and systematic—
with the modern, everything tends
more toward confusion.

– Friedrich Schlegel
Zur Philosophie (1805), fragment 99

The New Mythology and the New Organicism

In the "Rede über die Mythologie," the second section of his *Gespräch über die Poesie* (1800), Friedrich Schlegel sketched out with striking clarity the central problem of modern poetry. "I will get right to the point. Our poetry, I maintain, is lacking in a middle-point like mythology was for the ancients." The literary products of his contemporaries did not match up to those of classical antiquity, and for a simple reason: "We have no mythology. But I might add that we are close to acquiring one, or rather, that we should seriously cooperate in bringing one forth."[1] Since the early years of the nineteenth century, Schlegel's diagnosis of the ills of contemporary art has been restated time and again, if in variable forms. Schiller's "Die Götter Griechenlandes," Hölderlin's "Brot und Wein," Rilke's *Duino Elegies*—all of them are poetic laments on the demise of mythology. Its passing has supplied a leitmotif for criticism as well. Hermann Broch's reminder that every artistic epoch must strive to create a new language out of mythic symbols, for instance, just like his assertion that much of the apparently monumental art of the late nineteenth century collapses into the vacuum of a "nonstyle" (its essential hollowness finding characteristic expression in Wagnerian music drama),[2] both devolve upon Schlegel's claim: "We have no mythology."

Notwithstanding the suspicions vis-à-vis the Wagnerian enterprise that Broch shared with a whole range of ambivalent Wagnerophiles from Friedrich Nietzsche to Thomas Mann, there is at least one sense in which music drama answers to the requirements of the New Mythology. In that Schlegel suggests a return to the *Nibelungenlied* as an inspirational source for the contemporary poet, it is possible to find in *The Ring* a fulfillment of a critical prophecy.[3] The New Mythological fundament of music drama may even lie deeper; it may, that is, reside just as much in form as in content.[4] Schlegel's New Mythology, after all, entailed more than a naïve restoration of the subject matter of national legends. For what ultimately makes mythology mythological, in Schlegel's view, emerges in the shape that it takes as "ordered chaos." Schlegel explains the meaning behind this characteristically paradoxical epithet as follows: "All the poems of antiquity embrace one another, until a whole is formed from ever greater masses and members; everything interpenetrates, and everywhere there is one and the same spirit, only expressed differently. And thus it is no empty assertion that ancient poetry was a single, indivisible, perfect poem. Why shouldn't that which once was come into being again? Of course, in another way. And why not in a more beautiful and greater way?"[5] By way of invoking a familiar catchphrase, we might say that ancient poetry displayed all the unity of a living organism, and that a New Mythology is possible to the extent that the contemporary artist is able to configure a "new" organicism. It will be our aim here to get at the nature of the new organicism, and to analyze its workings in Wagner's later music dramas.

Organicism is a well-worn concept, but it is not yet worn out: witness Murray Krieger's recent defense (based in part on a close reading of Coleridge) of an idea that has come under increasing fire in literary circles since the upsurge of deconstructionist criticism in the 1960s and 1970s.[6] What *is* worn out, though, is the notion of organicism as unruffled unity that still prevails in the popular consciousness, its roots traceable to Friedrich Schlegel's brother, August Wilhelm. The doctrine of the indivisible whole takes on an almost talismanic quality in his writings on art,[7] and with it, so too do a series of corollary precepts: the subordination of the individual parts to a larger entity,[8] the perfect concord between detail and overriding design,[9]

the natural unfolding of a form from within as if from a germinal cell.[10] True
enough, the same points surface in Friedrich Schlegel's poetics, but the
thought complex from which they issue is more richly textured. Although he
took as his starting point the Aristotelian paradigm for the organic artwork—
the notion, that is, that the whole is irreparably disturbed if any of the parts
are disturbed[11]—he soon went beyond it. The apparent contradictions that,
on the one hand, seem to obscure the younger Schlegel's thinking on organicism, can, on the other, be interpreted as tokens of his intensely critical pose.
The theory that questions itself, he must have imagined, holds out the most
promise as an interpretive tool. And as we shall see, Wagner's own outlook
on the "organic" artwork questions itself in similar ways. This fact, taken together with the self-critical stance embodied in Schlegel's assertions, will enable us to employ the new organicism as an evaluative principle capable of
shedding light on the formal constitution of music drama.

Although Schlegel did not speak directly of a new organicism, my trope on
the term will allow for a ready distinction between levels of meaning that are
not always differentiated by Schlegel's use of the terms *Organismus* or
organisch. Simply put, Schlegel held to a dualistic outlook on the nature of
organicism. The "first" organicism is the organicism of perfection that animates the mythology and poetry of the ancient Greeks, all of whose creations
make up "a single poem"; its constituent parts are "coherent, inseparable"—
they "form an organic whole."[12] This is of course the organicism of his brother's account, though here it is specifically located in an irrecoverable epoch.
The perfect fusion of general and particular that was a given in the poetry
and mythology of the ancient Greeks (where all was "singly and uncon-
sciously shaped [*einzeln und bewußtlos*]")[13] can be no more in contemporary poetry. The modern artist, the practitioner of the New Mythology,
engages in a conscious, we could say *self*-conscious, act of shaping materials
that must be created anew.[14] The artistic product may be "organic," but the
organicism embodied therein will be of a different order from that which
animates the poetry of antiquity. The new organicism cannot help but be
"fissured" or "cracked" in some way, but all the same it is no less estimable
than the old.

A. W. Schlegel's doctrine of organicism, like his poetics as a whole, hinges
on a simple opposition. His contrast of the naturally shaped, organic artworks
of the moderns with the "mechanistic" products (their forms imposed from
without) of eighteenth-century neoclassicism likewise implies a higher valuation of the former at the expense of the latter. Friedrich Schlegel's scheme
is considerably subtler, and while he too was no apologist for the turn that
literature (especially French literature) had taken in the early and middle
years of the eighteenth century, the positioning of organicism in his poetics
is largely independent of value judgments. By conjoining the "organic" with
the "chemical" and the "mechanical," Schlegel fashions a flexible triadic
scheme, which he then proceeds to apply either synchronically—to coexis-

tent properties, and to coterminous genres within a literary epoch—or dia-chronically—to historical periods unfolding in time.

Hence, the various mental powers are referable to the triad as follows: "Understanding is mechanical, wit is chemical, genius is organic spirit."[15] The ability to place specific objects or events under a general concept, the busi-ness of the understanding in Kant's philosophy, is mechanical insofar as its end product is an abstraction.[16] Wit (*Witz*), Schlegel tells us, is chemical: as we have seen earlier in this study, the energy required to link together two or more seemingly unrelated ideas is dissipated as if in a lightning flash.[17] Genius, on the other hand, is an evolving process. It culminates in neither an abstraction nor a bon mot, but rather continues to develop unceasingly. The dialectical synthesis of a "mechanical" doing (*Handeln*) and a "physical/ chemical" being (*Sein*) thus yields the "organic" becoming (*Werden*) characteristic of genius.[18] Schlegel orders the classical poetic types under the same pattern—"Epic = chemical. Lyric = mechanical. Drama = organic"[19]—just as the union of the mechanical-chemical-organic triad in the *Roman* is held out as an ideal for the modern poet.[20]

The three members of the scheme likewise function in Schlegel's historical criticism, where combined presence gives way to temporal unfolding. Ac-cording to an early notebook fragment, modern poetry passes through three phases: "The first period . . . [is] abstract-mechanical / the second, chemical / the third, organic."[21] The messianic thrust of the progression, its motion to-ward an organic phase whose outlines are only hinted at in the artistic prod-ucts of the present, is clarified in one of the *Athenäum Fragmente*: the age in which Schlegel lives, colored as it is by the upheavals wrought by the French Revolution, is "a chemical one"; but "an organic age will follow . . . and then the citizens of the next solar revolution will probably think much less of us than we think of ourselves, and look at much of what we now extol as little more than the necessary preliminary exercises of humanity."[22] A cir-cular, or more properly spiraling, motion is complete. The organicism of the age that is to come will renew, though not repeat, the organic workings of an age that is never again to be: the lost Golden Age of Classical antiquity.

Each epoch knows, or will know, its own organicism, and Schlegel has something to say about both. The organic unity of the ancients bound to-gether "Eins u[nd] Eins." In contrast, the new organicism will be energized by a dialectic struggle between "Vielen u[nd] Eins."[23] The peaceful coexist-ence of contrasting tendencies in the old is thus reformulated, in the new, as a dialectical system that contains and embraces unresolved oppositions. The new organicism is just as "systematic" as the old, but it finds room for dis-ruptive elements that the older form would not tolerate: "The criteria for the truth of a system should be organic unity and infinite fullness ([*unendliche Fülle*]) or potency. Every unity might therefore develop in the direction of infinite fullness through the introduction of sharply contrasting elements, and yet, because of its inner conditioning, it still remains a unity."[24] Schlegel's point is not merely to differentiate old and new within the framework of a simple binary opposition, but to locate within modern poetry itself a dialectic that likewise fans out over historical time. The "Schöne Einheit" (beautiful unity) that infuses the poetry of antiquity comes together (and not always harmoniously) with "heilige Fülle" (spiritual fullness) to yield the "vollendete Allheit" (perfected totality) of the poetry of the future.[25] Schlegel thus calls up Kant's three categories of quantity to clarify the relationships in a system that plays on two mythologies, two organicisms, and—paradoxical though it might appear—two brands of unity: the unity of homogeneity ("Einheit der Homogeneität") and the unity of multiplicity ("Einheit des Vielfältigen, Verschiedenartigen, des *organischen Ganzen*").[26] At the same time, Schlegel's dialectical rethinking of concepts that threaten to pale as mere catchwords—mythology, organicism, unity—amounts to no less than a redemptive act for modern criticism.

In *Opera and Drama,* Wagner couches his discussion of organic form in terms of long-familiar categories. The music-dramatist's goal, he argues in the spirit of Lessing, differs fundamentally from the plastic artist's. While the sculptor, for example, takes as his object of imitation a formally finished entity, the poet-musician represents an action and its processive course. Genuine drama therefore unfolds as an "organic Being and Becoming." Furthermore, the form of the organic artwork is a "unitarian" form, its coherence ensured, in the case of musical drama, by a disposition of "melodic moments" determined by the "poetic aim." In this way form becomes a function of content: the design of the whole is organically motivated from within, not mechanically imposed from without. The web of recurrences generated by the association of "melodic moments" with poetic content makes for organic coherence on the largest scale. To carry the metaphor to its logical conclusion: whereas earlier operatic conceptions produced works consisting of a chain of discrete organisms, the musical drama that Wagner envisions will bear comparison with a single metaorganism, all its parts inextricably and causally linked.[27]

If the organicist rhetoric of *Oper und Drama* recalls the ideology of organicism rooted in A. W. Schlegel's "translation" of his brother's refractory romanticism into more readily understandable terms, then there are signs that Wagner, in his later writings, had second thoughts about his confident prescriptions for musico-dramatic coherence. "The science of Aesthetics has at all times laid down Unity as a chief requirement for the artwork," he wrote in "Über die Anwendung der Musik auf das Drama" (1879). "In the abstract this Unity is difficult to define dialectically, and its misapprehension has led to many and grave mistakes."[28] To be sure, Wagner opted not to provide a fully worked-out definition in the context of this essay, although we can piece one together by considering the split in his thinking as regards the linkage of musical ideas over expanses of time both great and small.

One aspect of Wagner's dualistic outlook is represented in an often-quoted letter of 29 October 1859 to Mathilde Wesendonk: "I should now like to call my most delicate and profound art the art of transition, for the whole fabric of my art is made up of such transitions: all that is abrupt and sudden is now repugnant to me; it is often unavoidable and necessary, but even then it may not occur unless the mood has been clearly prepared in advance, so that the suddenness of the transition appears to come as a matter of course."[29] The second, complementary idea comes in "Über die Anwendung der Musik auf das Drama." According to Wagner, the Classical symphonic movement as perfected by Haydn, Mozart, and Beethoven is free from all traces of "rhetorical dialectics." That is to say, it lacks moments in which two themes of "diametrically opposite character" confront each other in a way that will give something of a dramatic quality to the music. In that the contrasting ideas of the symphonic movement are held in check by the syntactic undergirding of an "ideal dance form," they supplement one another: the Classical symphony therefore admits to neither "problem" nor "resolution." The rhetorically dialectic music drama, on the other hand, foregrounds disruptions of all sorts; daring modulations, abrupt affective shifts, and "proselike" phrase construction pose the "problems" that the music dramatist aims to solve.[30] The art of the imperceptibly graduated transition and the "rhetorically dialectic" juxtaposition of motivic ideas are opposite sides of the same coin: a twofold notion of musical unity that makes for a Wagnerian equivalent of Friedrich Schlegel's new organicism.

Wagner criticism has tended to take its bearings from one member of this complementary pair of ideas or the other. Nietzsche's sharp indictment of Wagner, who as "our greatest miniaturist in music" showed a marked "incapacity for giving organic form"[31]—the charge reverberates in Theodor Adorno's critique of Wagner's music-dramatic totality as a "spurious identity"[32]—can be taken as a corrective to the equally one-sided appeal to music drama's undifferentiated ebb and flow that still endures in the popular imagination. Varying opinions on the formative power of Wagner's harmony likewise cluster around one of the two poles that together describe the dialectic of the new organicism. Ernst Kurth's account of the latent energy that drives forward the harmonies of the *Einleitung* to Act I of *Tristan und Isolde* thus proceeds from the (unstated) assumption that the art of transition is paramount. His references to "violently agitated developments," "enlargement and growth," and "willful striving" adopt the rhetoric of "first-order" organicism, the organicism of processively motivated change.[33] Conversely, Carl Dahlhaus's skepticism regarding the long-range formative potential of tonal centers in Wagnerian music drama, like the corollary notion that harmonic progressions take on the character of plastic motives arrayed like links in a chain,[34] will tend to promote rhetorically dialectic hearings.

Neither category—the art of transition on the one hand, rhetorical dialectics on the other—is necessarily better suited to describe Wagner's mature musical language. My point is simply to suggest that the realities of this language will be better served by invoking both categories. To this end, we will look more closely at two sets of examples in the ensuing sections of this chapter—the extended dialogue between the principals in *Tristan,* Act II, and the first- and second-act laments in *Parsifal*—each of which in turn emphasizes one or the other element in the dialectic pair. My intent is also to highlight the degree to which the counterpoles of Wagner's second-order, "new" organicism in fact interpenetrate. Rhetorical dialectics is saved from degenerating into mere disconnectedness through the application of mediating procedures. The art of transition, as Wagner indicates in his letter to Mathilde Wesendonk, not only allows for elements of disruption, it feeds on them; everything depends on the skill with which the "mood" is made to necessitate the "suddenness of the transition." The isolated members of Wagner's second-order organicism count for little in themselves: they derive their meaning from each other.

Tristan and the Art of Transition

"My greatest masterpiece in the art of the most delicate and gradual transition is without doubt the great scene in the second act of Tristan and Isolde. The opening of this scene presents a life overflowing with all the most violent emotions—its ending the most solemn and heartfelt longing for death. These are the pillars: and now you see, child, how I have joined these pillars together, and how the one of them leads over into the other. This, after all, is the secret of my musical form, which in its unity and clarity over an expanse that encompasses every detail, I may be bold enough to claim has never before been dreamt of."[35] This segment of Wagner's description of his art of transition, taken again from the October 1859 letter to Mathilde Wesendonk, is largely free of dialectics. The essence of the musical form-building technique to which Wagner alludes here is an organicism of gradual and imperceptible change, of intimate connection, of an overarching unity where each of the details serves the requirements of the larger whole.

The composer's account moreover contains the germinal cell of an analysis that would give primacy of place to tonality as the actuating force behind the art of transition. The motion in the *Tristan* scene from overflowing vitality to solemn yearning for death is no doubt articulated by a long-range process of motivic transformation (rapturous love music evolves into a prefiguration of Isolde's Act III *Verklärung*) and by an attendant temporal sequence—from acceleration to deceleration and again to acceleration—at once simple and appropriate as a metaphor for the grand emotional surge unleashed in this passage. But the affective "pillars" of the scene serve principally as ciphers for the tonal points of departure and arrival that frame this vast stretch of music. (Ernst Kurth's *Eckpfeiler* or *Gerüstpünkte* come to mind.)[36] In brief, the dialogue turns on the progression from an A/C tonal pair to its "shadow" pair, A♭/B, a semitone lower.[37] The principle of tonal dualism is reflected in the larger form as well: the dialogue divides into two parts separated by an orchestral interlude, the first governed by the C/A pair and the second by its flattened complement. (The symmetry is enhanced by the fact that Part 1 begins, like Part 2 ends, with fragmentary utterances split between two characters speaking as one.) The relationship between the elements in the pairs is by turn hierarchical and directional. In Part 1, A (in major and minor forms) is subordinated to the luminous C major that articulates the principals' affirmative statement of reunion after separation (the duet segment "O Wonne der Seele"), while in Part 2 the members of the pair are progressively disposed to yield a motion upward by minor third from A♭ ("O sink hernieder") to B ("O ew'ge Nacht").

All of this makes eminently good dramatic sense. The harmonic plan of the scene (like that of the entire opera) describes a descent, not just from C to B but from one diatonic tonal pair to its chromatically lowered neighbor, a descent whose scenic enactment takes us from ecstatic reunion to otherworldly and self-annihilating embrace. The tonal descent further represents a kind of distortion. It is a musical consequence of the drastic alteration, under the influence of the love potion, of the lovers' perceptions. Ernst Bloch makes the point that Tristan and Isolde hear Brangäne's warnings as a blissful wash of sound, and that Wagner allows us to hear *what the lovers hear*.[38] When we perceive the A♭/B pair, we likewise experience what Tristan and Isolde experience: a distortion of the "real," C/A world from which the lower pair emanates. The musical flow is warped; it proceeds in and out of phase for the lovers and, through Wagner's medium, for us.

The move from one tonal pair to the other is hardly abrupt. Indeed, Wagner's art of transition plays so subtly on the dual processes of infiltration and dissolution that most traces of sudden change are effectively erased. More specifically, the elements from both tonal complexes are present in both halves of the dialogue, but their respective emphases are reversed from one half to the next. Much as the A♭/B complex insinuates itself into the fabric of Part 1, so the components of the A/C pairing are dissolved in Part 2.

Part 1 takes shape in three stages: first, a duet celebrating the joyous reunion of the lovers; second, a series of strophe-antistrophe exchanges; and lastly, an extended apostrophe to the powers of Night. Inasmuch as the duet is built around the A/C pair, with clear emphasis on (and near closure in) C, it resumes the tonal argument of the scene that concludes Act I. Similarly, Tristan's apostrophe to Night reaffirms the A/C pairing, in spite of a considerable influx of destabilizing chromatic elements. The central exchanges, however, at once weaken the tonal claims of the A/C complex and prefigure the dominating role of A♭ in Part 2. Although the first strophe-antistrophe group (initiated by Tristan's "Das Licht! Das Licht!") promises to close in C, the cadence is undercut by bass motion from G to A♭—a feint that Wagner repeats in proceeding from the A♭-colored second strophe-antistrophe to the no less strongly colored third (at Tristan's "Der Tag!"). The tonal focus on A at the beginning of the fourth rhetorical grouping (Tristan's "Was dich umgliß") dissolves into A♭ music almost immediately (before a lengthy stretch in the "tonic" tonal pair's upper-fifth complement, e/G), thus parallelling the A♭ incursion in Isolde's antistrophe (at "dort zu trinken"). A♭ (together with its enharmonic equivalent, G♯) gains the upper hand in the fifth strophe-antistrophe group (from Tristan's "In deiner Hand"), culminating in a clear prefiguration of the colloquy's central duet, "O sink hernieder.") And although the ensuing exchange (from Tristan's "O Heil dem Tranke!") and Tristan's subsequent monologue ("O nun waren wir Nachtgeweihte!") reassert the primary, A/C pair, A♭ remains as a notable presence in the music's chromatically charged surface.

Only in the orchestral interlude that follows does Wagner effect the decisive move to A♭, the tonality from which Part 2 takes its cue. The antithetical strophe-antistrophe pairs of Part 1 give way here to mutually affirmative statements of union. Hence, the "pillars" of Part 2 are provided by three points of attraction, each a duet for the principals: first an invocation to Night ("O sink hernieder," in A♭),[39] then a mutual dedication to Death ("So stürben wir," moving "centrifugally" from A♭ through B, D, F, and back to A♭ again), and finally a climactic statement of union in Death ("O ew'ge Nacht," in B, colored by both its lower and upper minor thirds). These in turn are separated by passages articulating two textural layers: Brangäne's otherworldly (or so they seem to the lovers) admonitions, followed by a series of dialogic periods. And while the elements of the flattened third pair largely govern the tonal proceedings, after-echoes of the diatonic pair permeate the initial stages of Part 2: witness the references to A in the first duet, Brangäne's interruptive "Einsam wachend," and the dialogue that follows.

The art of transition thus proves to be an art of imperceptibly graduated shifts in emphasis, and this too has its dramatic counterpart. The love potion, to be sure, merely brings to the surface an emotion that was latent in both characters from the start.[40] The musical analogue for this fact comes with the emergent primacy of the A♭/B complex in the course of the Act II colloquy; what was tonally latent in the first part of the scene comes to the surface in the second. A more deftly handled representation of natural growth, of first-order organicism, is hardly imaginable.

Yet there is another side to Wagner's art of transition. The letter to Mathilde Wesendonk alludes to factors that cloud our picture of the unfettered and processive evolution of the musical form from within. Wagner begins by acknowledging the connection between his inner makeup and his outlook on the problematic of artistic creativity:

> I am now becoming increasingly aware of a quality which I have acquired in
> my art, since it also determines me in my life. From the very beginning it
> has been a part of my nature for my moods to change rapidly and abruptly
> from one extreme to another: states of extreme tension, after all, can
> scarcely do otherwise than impinge on each other; indeed, it is because of

this that we are so often able to preserve our own lives. By the same token, true art has basically no other object than to show these heightened moods in their extreme relation to each other: the only thing that can matter here—the important decision—is the result solely of these extreme contrasts.

The course of his own music, Wagner claims to have realized, has been determined as a response to the problem of mediating between mood swings that might easily degenerate into mannerisms:

> I recognize now that the characteristic fabric of my music (always of course in the closest association with the poetic design), . . . owes its construction above all to the extreme sensitivity which guides me in the direction of mediating and providing an intimate bond between all the different moments of transition that separate the extremes of mood.[41]

Whether or not we share Wagner's conviction that his art directly reflects his psychic constitution, it is still obvious that the art of transition in which he takes such pride is unthinkable without reference to those "extremes" (the term recurs with leitmotivic regularity in the letter to Mathilde Wesendonk) that motivate it in the first place. Lurking behind the continuities of the art of transition, in other words, is a rhetorically dialectic stratum that calls it into being. "First-order" organicism is replaced by a new, "second-order" organicism containing the seeds that might potentially destroy it.

Thus, the new organicism is marked by a cleft that, in the *Tristan* colloquy, emerges with particular clarity in those moments where the contrasting A/C and A♭/B tonal spheres (musical ciphers for abrupt mood shifts) come into close contact. To cite an especially telling case: near the end of the fourth strophe-antistrophe pair from Part 1, the move into Isolde's closing quatrain ("dort dir zu trinken ew'ge Minne") is articulated by the so-called Death motive and its merely juxtaposed A♭ and A-major harmonies. Kurth singled out precisely this motive as a prime example of the harmonically "absolute" progression wherein the relationship that either or both of the chords might have to a central tonic is overridden by the startling effect that they make in and of themselves. So far as long-range tonal continuities are concerned, the absolute progression is "destructive, isolating, disintegrative."[42] It literally tears itself out of the surrounding texture, in spite of the logic of the voice leading that binds its members. The Death-motive progression thus encapsulates with incredible terseness the shadow side of the art of transition. The deftness with which Wagner handles the move from the A/C to the A♭/B pair is met by the rhetorically dialectic juxtaposition of A and A♭.

Not surprisingly, rhetorical dialectics come increasingly to the fore in those parts of the scene proximate to the decisive shift in the A♭ direction: the fifth and sixth strophe-antistrophe pairs, and Tristan's ensuing speech. Here the lovers' antithetical positions are sharpened, so that Tristan's dithyrambs to the fantastic powers of the love potion meet with less enthusiastic responses from the still doubtful Isolde. (More exactly, Tristan gives voice to Isolde's ecstasy and she to his circumspection; underneath it all, the characters speak as one in spite of the apparent antitheses of the dialogic form.) In the tonal-harmonic sphere, the A/C realm comes into ever closer touch with the A♭/B realm. Hence Tristan's strophe, beginning "In deiner Hand," occupies an A♭/g♯ world where A, as upper neighbor, appears as a subordinate element. Isolde "takes this back"; a variant of the Death motive brings the music around to A for Tristan's next speech ("O Heil dem Tranke!"). The component parts of the following strophe-antistrophe pair likewise present contrary tonal arguments. Just as the primacy of A in Tristan's segment is threatened by motion in the A♭/C♭(= B) direction ("Durch des Todes Thor, wo er mir floß"), so Isolde's response reverses the foregoing by undercutting an expected cadence in A♭ ("Doch es rächte sich," the first line of her speech) and closing (or nearly closing) with a cadential phrase that promises A minor ("um einsam in öder Pracht schimmernd dort zu leben").

Yet as often as not, the rupture between the A and A♭ worlds is mediated by the *Tristan* chord, which earns its reputation as a preeminent musical figure for the affective ambiguities of yearning and desire insofar as it occupies a place in *both* worlds. Regardless which side we might come down on in the debate over its tonal-harmonic function (as either altered diminished seventh, altered augmented sixth, or—probably the best solution—as self-standing, "absolute" sonority), there is no denying that its first appearance sets off a phrase that ultimately suggests A minor through its dominant seventh. But the *Tristan* chord in its *Urform* is easily respelled to yield an A♭-minor chord with added sixth: A♭-C♭-E♭-F. Likewise, the V^7 of A that so frequently emanates from the *Urform* of the chord is itself the enharmonic equivalent of the German augmented-sixth chord in A♭ minor. Wagner makes these alternatives explicit through his setting of Isolde's "Doch ach, dich täuschte der falsche Trank" (see Ex. 7.1) from the fifth strophe-antistrophe pair. Much the same phrase that we hear at the outset of the Act I *Einleitung* in an A-minor context recurs now in A♭ minor. Nor is this a matter of enharmonic respelling alone. The outlining of the A♭-minor triad in the vocal line assures that what originally sounded in A will now sound—as if by magical forces no less powerful than those of the love potion—in the tonality a half step lower.

The same ploy is considerably expanded at the conclusion of Tristan's monologue immediately preceding the Act II colloquy's central orchestral interlude (see Ex. 7.2). First we have the *Einleitung* progression in its original "A-minor" context (mm. 1076–1100). To this is juxtaposed the A♭ spelling of the *Tristan* chord familiar from Isolde's earlier phrase (m. 1080), and again the triadic pattern in the vocal line affirms the lower key. The orchestral melody too takes a turn aimed at highlighting the shift to A♭. The previous G♯–A–A♯–B is not merely enharmonically respelled, but rather reshaped as

EXAMPLE 7.1

Wagner, *Tristan und Isolde*, Act II, mm. 955–57

A♭–B♭–B–C to initiate a chromatic ascent eventually underpinned by V⁷/A♭ harmony (m. 1083). The expected A♭, however, is withheld. In its place is a diminished-seventh chord (a close relative of the *Tristan* chord; D substitutes for E♭/D♯) that will in turn initiate a tonal shift toward A.

Paradoxically enough, the shift is actuated largely through a series of reinterpretations of the pitches A♭(G♯) and B(C♭), the common tones binding the *Tristan* chord to the V⁷/A that usually proceeds from its *Urform*. First they figure as part of the harmonically ambiguous D–F–A♭–C♭ diminished-seventh chord (m. 1084); next in a V⁴₃ /G♭ (m. 1086; as lower minor third of the diatonic A/C pair, this suggestion of F♯[= G♭] brings us closer to the A realm); then again within a diminished-seventh formation (m. 1088; although the chord is enharmonically equivalent to that at m. 1084, the vocal line and multiple appoggiature in the orchestra imply A minor); and next in the passage's culminating V⁹/a sonority (mm. 1089–90).

But A minor is just as forcefully withheld as A♭ was earlier. Tristan's last phrase is supported by a progression that pits a transposed variant of the *Tristan* chord (G♯–B–D–F♯; note that G♯ and B are still retained) against the chord in its *Urform* (cf. mm. 1091 and 1093 with 1095 and 1097) before giving way to the dominant of A (mm. 1098ff.). The entire passage, therefore, is circumscribed by statements of the *Tristan* chord that tend with equal ease toward A♭ or A.

According to Kurth, the *Tristan* chord is interpretable as a "motive" whose tensions embody the entire music drama *in nuce*.[43] In the light of the thoughts on Wagner's new organicism that we have been developing, this insight takes on a special meaning. The tensions embodied in the *Tristan* chord are at once the microcosmically represented tensions between the art of transition on the one hand and rhetorical dialectics on the other. As an agent of both continuity and disruption, the chord discloses the dialectic interplay of elements that color the newly configured organicism of Wagner's mature style.

EXAMPLE 7.2

Wagner, *Tristan und Isolde,* Act II, mm. 1076–1100

EXAMPLE 7.2 (*continued*)

Parsifal and Rhetorical Dialectics

If the art of transition, as manifest through the graduated shift in emphasis from the A/C tonal pair to its semitonally lowered counterpart, has the upper hand over rhetorical dialectics in the *Tristan* Act II colloquy, then much the reverse is true in large stretches of *Parsifal*. To make the point, we will examine the ties between two widely separated but dialectically related passages: Amfortas's lament during the Act I Grail Ceremony, and Parsifal's significantly altered reprise of this music following on his attainment of "cosmic clear-sightedness" through Kundry's kiss in Act II.

Wagner's recourse to the technique of large-scale reprise came about as the solution to a problem he recognized in the poetic stuff of the *Parsifal* material years before a note of the music was written. Wagner put it thus in a letter of 29/30 May 1859 to Mathilde Wesendonk: "[Parsifal] is indispensably necessary as the longed-for redeemer of Anfortas [*sic*], but if Anfortas is to be placed in the true light due him, then he will acquire such tremendous tragic interest that it will be nearly impossible to set a second principal interest against him; and yet this principal interest must be accorded to Parsifal, if he is not merely to come forward at the end as a contrived Deus ex machina. Consequently, Parsifal's development, his noble purification, even though predestined by his completely thoughtful and deeply compassionate nature, must once again be placed in the foreground."[44]

Wagner settled the two characters' rival claims for center stage by making them one, as it were. Amfortas's troubled soul-state is literally transferred into Parsifal's inner being by means of a surge of Schopenhauerian *Mitleid* (compassion), whose musical consequence is the aforementioned reprise. Although the rough equivalence of the two passages—Amfortas's "Wehvolles Erbe" and Parsifal's corresponding moments of demonic absorption in Act II, "Amfortas! Die Wunde"—has been noted before, the underlying dialectic that supports it has yet to be considered in comprehensive detail.[45] For Wagner to make his dramatic point, he found it necessary not only to restate Amfortas's music but to intensify it radically. This led him to enhance, in Parsifal's monologue, the already highly chromatic surface of Amfortas's Act I speech and, what is even more important for our purposes, to reorder its motivic elements. It led him, in other words, to tip the balance from the art of transition to rhetorical dialectics.

By way of tracing this shift, let us begin by taking note of the most obvious points of contact between the two *Parsifal* laments. Dramatically, both passages function as interruptions. Amfortas's monologue is a disturbance that has become a regular part of the daily ritual enacted in the Grail Temple,[46] while Parsifal's marks a *peripeteia,* or reversal. Musically, both are dominated by the so-called *Liebesmahl* melody (given in its *Urforms,* in A♭ and C minor, in Ex. 7.3). Not only does its C-minor presentation in both laments serve as an associative tonal link between them; its multiple statements also make for

EXAMPLE 7.3
Wagner, *Parsifal, Vorspiel,* mm. 1–6, 20–25: *Liebesmahl* melody

oases of relative tonal stability in passages otherwise characterized by an extreme chromatic flux. But even in the tonally divagatory portions of the laments, the *Liebesmahl* melody is traceable as the source for thematic elements whose ties to it may not be readily apparent. The *Klagemelodie* initiating Amfortas's monologue, for instance, can be heard as one of its tortured derivatives (see Ex. 7.4). The opening gesture of Amfortas's melody inverts the first four pitches (motive A) of the *Liebesmahl* theme, while its cadential measures present interlocking statements of motives B (in inversion) and C.[47] The *Heilandklage* (Ex. 7.5), which figures prominently in both monologues, likewise stems from the same source, for the melodic descent from a¹ (mm. 1316–17), enriched by chromatically descending thirds in the middle voices, elaborates the cadential figure (C) from the *Liebesmahl* melody. And lastly, the phrase that Wagner linked with Amfortas's suffering[48] (Ex. 7.6), sequential statements of which occupy the closing moments in both laments, supplies a chromatic variant of the *Liebesmahl* melody's final two measures.

In addition, the laments share a similar overall design. Each falls into a tripartite scheme that likewise mirrors the rhetorical construction of the respective lament texts: an exordium (exhortatory in Amfortas's case, frenzied in Parsifal's) dominated by the *Heilandklage,* the sonic counterpart of Amfortas's spiritual pain; a central section whose dual statements of the *Liebesmahl* theme aptly represent Amfortas's hallucinatory vision and Parsifal's experience of the same; and a final peroration including climactic pleas for mercy and redemption. These parallels are outlined in Figure 7–1, where diagrammatic summaries of the laments are aligned for comparison.

EXAMPLE 7.4
Wagner, *Parsifal,* Act I, mm. 1297–1300: *Klagemelodie*

EXAMPLE 7.5
Wagner, *Parsifal,* Act I, mm. 1316–18: *Heilandklage*

EXAMPLE 7.6
Wagner, *Parsifal,* Act I, mm. 1393–97: Amfortas's *Schmerzen*

FIGURE 7–1
Parsifal, Acts I and II Laments Compared

Amfortas's Lament, Act I

	Part I Formal Opening	**Part II** preparation for →	Vision	**Part III** preparation for →	Climax 1	Climax 2
motives:	*Klagemel- odie* + *Heiland- klage*	Grail	*Liebesmahl*		*Erbarmen- schrei*	Amfortas's *Schmerzen*
tonality:	e → Mystic Chord on G	C → C	c/E♭	"wander- ing"	Mystic Chord variants	B → D
measures:	1297–1321	1324–45	1346–55	1356–86	1387–92	1394–1404

Parsifal's Lament, Act II

	Part I Frenzied Opening	**Part II** preparation for →	Vision	**Part III** preparation for →	Climax
motives:	*Erbarmen- schrei* + *Heiland- klage*	Grail	*Liebesmahl*		Amfortas's *Schmerzen*
tonality:	"wander- ing" → Mystic Chord on G, B	E → C	c/A♭		E♭ → b
measures:	994–1038, 1043	1046–53	1053–75	1076-80	1081–90

Clearly enough, some of the sharpest divergences between the two passages are located in their respective openings. Parsifal, for instance, makes no reference to Amfortas's *Klagemelodie,* and for the soundest of dramatic reasons. The metrically four-square *Klagemelodie,* like the recitative cadence and orchestral vamp that precede it, is absolutely in line with the formality of the office occupied by the Guardian of the Grail; Parsifal, however, requires no melody for an office that he does not yet hold. Discrepancies of this sort aside, the general congruence of the laments' opening sections is firmed by their culmination in statements of the so-called Mystic chord. If the *Liebesmahl* melody provides much of the laments' thematic substance, then the Mystic chord—the equivalent in interval content to the *Tristan* chord—lends to both monologues a similar harmonic ambience. In addition, both openings are largely given over to elaborations of the *Heilandklage*; Wagner even matches the musical correspondence with an assonant, verbal one: Amfortas's "Oh, Stra*fe*" (I/mm.1315–16) is answered by Parsifal's "Oh, Kl*age*!" (II/1004–6). As indicated in Figure 7–1, the motivic links between the laments from this point on tend toward nearly total conformity.

At the center of both Parts 2 and 3 is a twofold statement of the *Liebesmahl* theme, which in the case of the Act I lament moves on to multiple climaxes on the *Erbarmenschrei* (a variant of the motive linked with Kundry's shriek; see Ex. 7.7) and then the motive of Amfortas's *Schmerzen,* while the Act II monologue proceeds directly to the second of these thematic elements. By the time Parsifal reaches his closing phrase in Part 2 ("Erlöser! Heiland!" mm. 1081ff.) his identification with Amfortas is complete. Not only does the orchestral motive, Amfortas's *Schmerzen,* return to round off the second lament like the first, but Parsifal even takes up Amfortas's vocal melody from the corresponding spot in Act I (mm. 1393ff.); and his text, for the first time, adopts the stylized end rhymes characteristic of Amfortas's speech.

But just as compelling as these points of contact are the numerous transformations that Amfortas's music undergoes in Act II. Given Wagner's desire

EXAMPLE 7.7
Wagner, *Parsifal,* Act I, mm. 1387–89: *Erbarmenschrei*

to transfer the focus from Amfortas to Parsifal without jeopardizing the dramatic integrity of either character, it is hardly surprising that recurrence gives way to an intensification affecting both tonal and motivic dimensions. The harmonic idiom of Parsifal's lament further heightens that of Amfortas's in a number of ways. In the first place, much of the material from Act I recurs a major third higher in Act II. In Parsifal's monologue, the bulk of the music preceding the vision (a chromaticized elaboration of the principal Grail motive), takes E as its tonal point of departure, whereas the corresponding passage in Amfortas's lament proceeds from C. Likewise, the sequential presentations of the motive of Amfortas's *Schmerzen* unfold from an E♭ tonality in Act II (with the "deceptively" reached C♭ in the bass as E♭ substitute; mm.1081ff.) and from B (with added sixth) in Act I (mm. 1394ff.). Sequential extension affords another means of tonal intensification. Hence, the first segment of the *Liebesmahl* melody provides the basis for a whole series of centrifugully projected harmonic excursions (to C minor, E♭, G minor, and D) in Parsifal's lament (mm. 1053–65).

Much of the harmonically attenuated language in both monologues arises from Wagner's treatment of the Mystic chord. In the Act II lament, however, its role is if anything increased. This is particularly evident in Part 1, which drives to two wrenching climaxes, the first (at m. 1014) developed out of the *Heilandklage* and the second (m. 1038) out of the *Zauber* motive. To be sure, the second climax culminates in a statement of the Mystic chord at the same pitch level as in the analogous spot in Amfortas's lament (G–B♭–D♭/C♯–F; cf. I/m.1321), but here it requires a full five measures to dissipate, or rather to dissolve into another statement of the same chord a major third higher. The buildup to the first climax compresses the *Heilandklage* into a series of one-measure rising sigh patterns such that each unit is made up of the Mystic chord and its "resolution" to an augmented triad (see Ex. 7.8), a tortuous progression for which there is no equivalent in Act I. The climax itself, like its after-wave, is marked by chromatically charged variants of the Mystic chord peculiar to Parsifal's lament (labeled Variants 2 and 3 in Ex. 7.9). The spelling and "resolution" pattern of Variant 2 suggest a V⁹ of A minor, with C as grating appoggiatura. And while Variant 3 is equivalent in interval content to Variant 1 (the chord that sets off the *Erbarmenschrei* in both laments), its spelling,

EXAMPLE 7.8
Wagner, *Parsifal,* **Act II, mm. 1011–13, harmonic reduction**

EXAMPLE 7.9

The Mystic chord and its variants

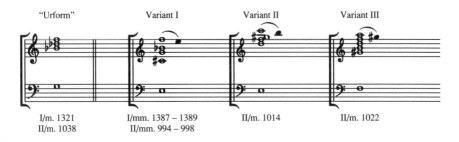

"Urform"	Variant I	Variant II	Variant III
I/m. 1321	I/mm. 1387 – 1389	II/m. 1014	II/m. 1022
II/m. 1038	II/mm. 994 – 998		

spacing, and mode of resolution differ: the dissonant ninth of Variant 3 (reckoning from G♯) moves down by half step, whereas in Variant 1 the dissonant eleventh (from C♯) proceeds by half step. Thus, even the ambiguous signature chord of the music drama is shown capable of harmonic intensification.

An examination of the motivic deviations that separate Parsifal's utterances from Amfortas's can, however, bring us closest to the rhetorically dialectic stratum of the *Parsifal* music. Indeed, a close comparison of the laments' respective motivic courses will reveal a startling fact. Practically every phrase in Parsifal's monologue can be linked with a parallel phrase in Amfortas's, but the quasi-congruence of the two passages is significantly obfuscated by the drastic reordering of the Act I music in Act II.[49] The extent of the reshuffling is demonstrated in Figure 7–2, where the various motivic segments of Parsifal's lament are aligned with their Act I equivalents. We would be hard-pressed to imagine a more effective portrayal of Parsifal's intense psychic disturbance in the wake of Kundry's kiss, for the motivic scrambling tells us, more clearly than any of the words, that the events that Parsifal uncomprehendingly witnessed during the Act I Grail Ceremony are now welling up within him in a confused, helter-skelter fashion. (Wagner himself described the monologue in similar terms as "the vision of Amfortas, abbreviated: everything of course rushes headlong through Parsifal's memory.")[50] As indicated in Figure 7–2, most of the motivic reordering is centered in Part 1 of the Act II lament, wherein the mingling of material from Amfortas's formalized opening (particularly the *Heilandklage*) with flashes of music from his vision produces a convincing representation of Parsifal's distorted recollections.

Furthermore, much of the "distortion" is textually and visually motivated with the utmost precision. It is only logical, for instance, that Parsifal's lament should begin with a statement of the *Erbarmenschrei* (see Ex. 7.10) that appears near the close of Amfortas's lament—and at the same pitch level. Wagner referred to Amfortas's final plea for mercy as the *Hauptmoment* of

FIGURE 7–2

Motivic Reordering in Parsifal's Act II Lament

Parsifal's Lament, Act II	Amfortas's Lament, Act I	Material	Tonality
Part 1			
*mm. 994–1002 =	mm. 1387–92	*Erbarmenschrei*	Mystic chord, Variant 1
*1003–4	1356–59 (also III/mm. 1001–2, 1011, 1017	Amfortas motive	
1004–16	1316–21 (also, I/1369–74)	*Heilandklage*	a
*1016–19	1348–49 (also, I/1365–68)	from the Vision	Mystic chord on D, etc.
1020–25	1316–21	*Heilandklage*	
*1025–36	1381–86, 1360–64	*Zauber* motive; Vision	Mystic chord on E, etc.
1037–43	1316–21	*Heilandklage*	
Part 2			
1043–53	1321–46	Grail; Vision	E → c (Act II) C (Act I)
1053–55	1346–49	*Liebesmahl*	c
*1056–65	1393–98	Amfortas's *Schmerzen*	
1066–75	1351–55	*Liebesmahl*	a$\flat$ (Act III) e$\flat$ (Act I)
Part 3			
1076–78	—		
1079–90	1393–1404	Amfortas's *Schmerzen*	E$\flat$ → b (Act II) B → d (Act I)

* material presented "out of order"

the Act I passage,[51] and it is in all likelihood the musical embodiment of the "stärksten Klagerufe" that causes Parsifal to clutch his breast, both in the 1877 prose sketch and the Act I stage directions.[52] The Act II stage directions also indicate that Parsifal is to "press his hands forcefully to his breast" after the kiss, whereupon he understandably launches into his complaint with the music that was most indelibly impressed upon his mind from Act I—the *Erbarmenschrei*. In short, dramatic motivation, visible action, and musical gesture are in absolute accord at this crucial point in the drama, where with lightning swiftness Parsifal's experience of love as *eros* (suggested by means

EXAMPLE 7.10
Wagner, *Parsifal,* Act II, mm. 994–98: Parsifal's lament, opening

of the tie between the *Erbarmenschrei* and the motive of Kundry's shriek) is transformed into a redeeming love as *agape* or *Mitleid.*

But what functions as a logical component of a musico-dramatic scheme may at the same time be the cause of some consternation when viewed from a purely musical angle. The notion that musical ideas can be reordered practically at will, that they can confront each other in any number of successive combinations, obviously challenges many of the fundamental presuppositions that we harbor in regard to the well-made artwork. It accords ill with an aesthetic rooted in "first-order" organicism, for the interrelated tenets prescribing the subordination of part to whole and the disturbance of the whole upon removal of any of its parts have as their corollary the assertion that the permutation of the constituent parts can only engender the destruction of the whole. More forcefully put: any whole whose parts can be permuted is no whole at all.[53] This line of argument would seem to undergird Nietzsche's critique of Wagner's art as a manifestation of literary decadence: "Life no longer dwells in the whole. The word becomes sovereign and leaps out of the sentence, the sentence reaches out and obscures the meaning of the page, the page gains life at the expense of the whole—the whole is no longer a whole."[54]

Yet in point of fact, it is probably fairer to say that the "second-order" organicism of *Parsifal* (and of *Tristan* as well) itself entails a critique. What Wagner seems to call into question, in an admittedly extreme form, is the very idea that the artwork can ever hope to attain the purposeful and necessary interconnections that determine the workings of a living organism. Hence, *Parsifal* stands poised between two radically different modes of configuring the relationship of part and whole: as an assemblage of epigrammatic fragments whose juxtaposition proceeds from the notion of rhetorical dialectics, or as the tightly knit web of musical ideas joined through the art of transition. Wagner's own sharply contrasting statements on the nature of the *Parsifal* music set the distinction into relief. Commenting to Cosima on the *Vorspiel,* he noted: "Nothing here and nothing there—it was from nothing that God created the world"; Cosima provides the gloss: "What he means is that he has simply placed his themes side by side, like a preacher his Bible passages."[55] (Adorno's latter-day gloss on the gnomic quality of *Parsifal* also comes to mind; its motives, unlike those of *Tristan,* are often "chained together, with an intentional carelessness, as if they were merely tiny pictures.")[56] Yet while actually working on the music for Act I, Wagner maintained with equal conviction: "Sometimes it is just a few bars which hold me up terribly, till one can introduce the key one needs in such a way that it is not noticeable. For more and more I shy away from anything with a startling or blatant effect; then at least four or five possibilities occur to me before I find the one which makes the transition smoothly."[57]

Yet the apparent gulf that separates these conflicting appraisals is hardly unbridgeable. In the *Parsifal* laments, for instance, the mediating element that brings them together as a dialectical unity is supplied by the Mystic chord, for it often marks off the space between motives jostling each other in an order in which they did not originally appear, while at the same time it furnishes the voice-leading logic that allows for a graduated motion from one motivic block to the next. The central allusion to Amfortas's vision in the exordium of Parsifal's monologue (II/1016–19) represents an interruption in the flow of his recollections of the Act I Grail Ceremony. But the harmonic ploy that justifies the disturbance hinges on the properties of the Mystic chord: the preceding phrase (mm. 1004–16) *ends* with the chord, the very sonority with which the motive from the vision *begins* (cf. I/1348, 1365, and II/1016). The same sleight-of-hand permits the intrusion of the *Zauber* motive in mm. 1025–36. Similarly, the move from Amfortas's motive (presented "out of order" in mm. 1003–4) into the *Heilandklage* is mediated by the Mystic chord in m. 1005: in Act I, the signature chord had also issued from Amfortas's motive, but there it supported a series of sequential statements of the *Zauber* motive (I/1360ff.).

The dialectic that informs Wagner's late style precipitates out in the unmistakable distinctions separating the sonic realms of *Parsifal* and *Tristan.* No doubt, many of the prime characteristics of the earlier music drama are echoed in the later work. The conflict between A♭ and A that colors the harmonic surface of the *Tristan* Act II colloquy recurs, in *Parsifal,* in the guise of the tonal-melodic tension embodied in the E/F dyad isolated by Patrick McCreless as a pervasive unifying feature of the score.[58] The *Tristan* chord likewise resurfaces as the Mystic chord in *Parsifal.* But the relative weight of disruptive versus integrative gestures is differently skewed in each case. Our ultimate impression of the harmonic course of the *Tristan* colloquy hinges on the blurring of one tonal pair into its chromatically lowered neighbor. In *Parsifal,* however, E and F are frequently juxtaposed (both sound simultaneously at the opening of Parsifal's lament, for instance) but never assimilated. The dyad represents, to quote McCreless, the "wound" that the work sets out to "heal."[59]

The half-diminished-seventh chord is also made to serve differing ends in the two compositions. As the Tristan chord, it is associated with an erotic longing that can only be fulfilled in the ecstasies of the *Liebesnacht*; as the Mystic chord, it is linked with the sinful *eros* of Klingsohr's realm. And as Alfred Lorenz pointed out, the chord is put to far more varied uses in *Parsifal* than in *Tristan*; his painstakingly thorough account associates the Mystic chord with ninety-two different contexts in *Parsifal,* as opposed to a mere eight in *Tristan.*[60] In composing *Parsifal,* Wagner thus found himself in a situation comparable to that of Thomas Mann's Adrian Leverkühn, who intended his last and greatest composition, the cantata *Dr. Fausti Weheklag,* as a "taking back" (*Zurücknehmen*) of Beethoven's Ninth Symphony.[61] The emphasis on the disjunctions of rhetorical dialectics in *Parsifal* similarly amounts to a "taking back" of the apparently seamless harmonic and melodic continuities of the art of transition as developed in *Tristan.*

The dialectic between the contrasting poles that together define Wagner's "new" organicism is of course but a variant of a larger oppositional pairing embodied in much late nineteenth-century art, the interplay of monumental and miniature that in the works of a composer such as Gustav Mahler turns on the differing claims of symphonic and song forms. The terms of the conflict, in Mahler's case, had evidently changed, but it is interesting to observe the similarities between the consequent compositional and technical results that issued from both Wagner and Mahler. As is well known, the *Immer sehr gemächlich* from the opening movement of Mahler's First Symphony draws liberally on the second of the *Lieder eines fahrenden Gesellen,* "Ging heut' morgen übers Feld." But in the process of transforming a reflective *Lied* form into a dynamic sonata allegro, Mahler was forced to do no little violence to his source material. The song's second strophe by and large furnishes the substance of the sonata-form first group, while the third strophe acts as transition. Only at the end of the exposition—for the second group—does the material of the first strophe come into play. The circular permutation of elements—strophes 1, 2, and 3 reappear in the symphony as 2, 3, 1—may at first strike us as a challenge (quieter than Wagner's, but no less obvious) to the idea that the parts of the well-made artwork can proceed in one and only one order. Yet on reflection, it is clear that the reversal in order of the song's constituent parts was both necessitated and permitted by the distinction between genres. The modulation up by fifth, which occurs in the third song strophe, logically occupies second place in the sonata allegro as transition from tonic to dominant.

According to Leonard Meyer, "One can scarcely imagine a Romantic composer constructing dice games, as Kirnberger, Haydn, and Mozart had done."[62] Yet Wagner and Mahler both indulged in a game of just this sort. Two responses are possible. We can, along with Nietzsche, ascribe the phenomenon to the pernicious effects of artistic decadence. Or we can second Friedrich Schlegel's view that the historical moment for the "organic" artwork remained buried in the past or inaccessible in the future—that it was, in other words, a chimera in the present.

8 ❧

Richard Strauss's *Also sprach Zarathustra* and the "Union" of Poetry and Philosophy

> Whatever can be done while
> poetry and philosophy are
> separated has been done and
> accomplished. So the time has
> come to unite the two.
>
> – Fr. Schlegel
> Ideen, no. 108

Poetry, Philosophy, and Program Music

Of Friedrich Schlegel's many oracular claims, few have more potency for the historian of late nineteenth-century culture than his call for the union of poetry and philosophy. As he put it in the *Kritische Fragmente,* no. 115: "The whole history of modern poetry is a running commentary on the following brief philosophical text: all art should become science and all science art; poetry and philosophy should be made one."[1] Nourished on the conviction that each realm, in isolation, had reached the limits of its effectiveness, Schlegel's imperative points toward a future condition whereby poetry and philosophy will intermingle as components of a utopian system that embraces them both and cannot do without either.

Two of the terms in Schlegel's equation—*philosophy* and *science*—can be read as metaphors. *Philosophy* extends beyond the physical and natural sciences per se to encompass all that is logically or scientifically organized; it is the discipline through which mere data is elevated to the level of knowledge.[2] The remaining terms—*poetry* and *art*—should be subtly differentiated. Hieroglyphic expression only *becomes* art by way of the stringencies of rational planning: "If [the poet] is to be more than a mere contriver or artisan, if he is to be an expert in his field and understand his fellow citizens in the kingdom of art, then he will have to become a philologist as well."[3] If poetry is destined to salvage philosophy from degenerating into a play of dry calculations, then art can aspire to *logos* only through the medium of philosophy.

Schlegel's theorizing registers a loss at the same time that it holds out a promise. To be sure, poetry and philosophy had entered into particularly fruitful symbiotic relationships in the past. Plato's indictment of the creative artist in *The Republic* was, to an extent, a cover for his harboring more than a little of the poetic spirit himself. Dante had poeticized the theological in what, for Schlegel, was the first great *Roman* of Western literature. Why should something similar not occur in modern times? In the lapidary *Ideen* fragments (as well as in the subsequent course of his life), Schlegel sought a mystical synthesis in religion. The *Athenäum Fragmente* pursued a similar end by positing an aesthetic theory that would "waver between the division of philosophy and poetry, between poetry and practice, poetry as such and the genres and kinds of poetry," only to "conclude with their complete union" in a philosophy of the novel.[4] In the realm of artistic practice, Goethe's *Wilhelm Meisters Lehrjahre* prefigures the even greater poetico-philosophical syntheses to come. Indeed, it was Schlegel's express critical aim to find "a system in [Goethe's] presentation of this physics of poetry."[5] The cultural products of modernity, Schlegel seems to say, are inescapably bound to engage poetry and philosophy in a dialogue. Yet the strongest of these, and herein lies the crucial point, will do so with a clear consciousness of the limitations of their medium. The keystone of the aesthetic theory projected in the *Athenäum Fragmente* would be a *philosophy* of the novel. Goethe's *Meister,* for all its philosophising, remains "all *poetry.*"[6]

Both aspects of Schlegel's imperative—the call for a rapprochement between poetry and philosophy, and the insistence on the distance that separates them—can be brought to bear on what still counts as one of the most vexing problems of nineteenth-century music history: the complex of questions surrounding program music. The theory of program music, as articulated in Liszt's review of Berlioz's *Harold* Symphony, centers on the claim that the historical moment has arrived for music's "appropriation of the master-pieces of literature."[7] Proceeding with an unshakable belief in the ability of art forms to evolve along the lines of natural life forms, Liszt arrives at the conclusion that music, in its quest for new modes of expression, can and must absorb those monuments of literary culture that surround it. His con-clusion, however, is easily exploded. Writing well before Liszt published his essay, Schopenhauer had convincingly argued for the insuperable gulf be-tween music and the phenomenal world, which relate as do universal con-cept and arbitrary example.[8] Nietzsche, in his brief essay "Über Musik und Wort" (ca. 1871), drew radical consequences from the negative thesis that a necessary link cannot be established between music and anything lying be-yond it. Like Schopenhauer, he held that music and text in opera or song disclose an allegorical relationship. Moreover, a musical work and any image or idea that may call it forth or accompany it in the manner of a program stand in the very same relationship. In such cases, he concludes, music ac-tually *chooses* the extramusical element as a hieroglyphic representation of itself.[9]

But while the Schopenhauerian line of argument effectively exposes a lead-ing element in the doctrine of program music—the notion that disparate art forms can come together in harmonious union—as ideology, it does not thereby eliminate the programmatic work as aesthetic reality. The doctrine, as Dahlhaus has pointed out, was the product of an age whose culture re-mained largely literary and philosophical.[10] Hence the program allowed for the elevation of music from the dark ambiguity of myth to the intellectual precision of *logos*. Stated in Schlegel's terms, program music serves as a means of imbuing "poetry" with "philosophy." It is then left for criticism to determine the extent to which the mutual interpenetration takes effect. For Adorno, the Straussian tone poem results from the interaction of program and compositional technique. Similarly, Dahlhaus locates the "content" of Liszt's symphonic poems in the play of literary-pictorial subject and "forms moved in sounding."[11] As difficult as it may be to define this interaction with exactitude, it is still possible to distinguish between "biographical," receptive, and productive modes. The stimulus that calls forth the work, in the manner of what Wagner would have called a motivating or "formal" motive, extin-guishes itself in the moment that the work becomes aural reality; it is part of the composition's biography, an aspect of the history that went into its mak-ing, but nothing more. Insofar as a program may stimulate or guide the lis-tener's reflections, it serves as a guide for reception. It approaches the artistic product, but does not necessarily touch it. Only when the program and its musical counterpart share deep structural affinities can we speak of a truly productive, mutually conditioning interaction. In this case, the program acts as a paradoxical reminder that its counterpart is musical through and through (just as Goethe's *Meister,* despite the philosophical disquisitions, remains poetry through and through). And in the gap that separates one art form from the other lies something akin to a tangible meaning.

". . . frei nach Friedrich Nietzsche"

Nietzsche's outlook on texted or program music as instances in which tonal art forms go out in search of metaphorical self-representations, for all its radicality, comes close to describing the aesthetic reality of Richard Strauss's fifth tone poem "für großes Orchester," *Also sprach Zarathustra* (1896). Unbeknownst to the composer, Nietzsche had on more than one occasion assigned his poetic-dramatic philosophical tract to a place "unter die Symphonien."[12] He speculated further in *Ecce Homo* (1888): "Perhaps the whole of *Zarathustra* may be reckoned as music; certainly a rebirth of the art of *hearing* was among its preconditions."[13] How appropriate, then, that a tone *poem* should seek out its subject matter in a prose work that was in some sense *musical*. Nietzsche's text is rich in "formal motives," stimulating images or ideas awaiting the transfiguring touch of the tone poet. Hence the pious religiosity of those who believe in an afterlife—one of the principal objects of Nietzsche's scorn—is represented, in Strauss's work, by a syrupy chorale for strings and organ ("Von den Hinterweltlern"). The scientific preoccupations of the "conscientious man of spirit" (Nietzsche probably alludes to Darwin) find a musical equivalent in a fugue whose subject brings together the twelve pitches of the chromatic scale in a wedge formation ("Von der Wissenschaft"). Zarathustra's dance-song "on the Spirit of Gravity" calls forth an exuberant waltz ("Das Tanzlied"). The midnight tolling of the bell in "The Drunken Song" is faithfully echoed by the twelve bell strokes that initiate "Das Nachtwandlerlied."

But Strauss aimed for more than a mere patching together of colorful images inspired by Nietzsche's text. As if to narrow the gap between tone poem and philosophical disquisition, and thereby give substance to the expectations raised in the composition's title, Strauss allowed for a number of structural parallels between his work and its philosophical-poetic model. Both are framed similarly: Strauss begins with a musical portrayal of the invocation to the sun that heads off "Zarathustra's Prologue" (the pertinent text was printed as a kind of metasuperscription to the 1896 first edition of the full score),[14] and ends with "Das Nachtwandlerlied," the original title of "The Drunken Song," which serves as the penultimate section of Nietzsche's *Zarathustra*. "Von den Freuden und Leidenschaften," the fifth of Zarathustra's discourses, drives home one of the book's central theses: "Man is a thing that must be overcome." Strauss matches Nietzsche's philosophical *Haupt-thema* with a section that functions much like a symphonic *Hauptsatz*.

In all, Strauss "set" eight of the segments from Nietzsche's *Zarathustra* complete (see Fig. 8–1). While retaining the general frame of the literary

FIGURE 8–1
Richard Strauss, *Also Sprach Zarathustra,* Overview

Main Division	Inner Divisions, Titles	Tonality
Introduction	a: [Zarathustra's Prologue, I/1/i]*	C
1. Slow mvt. {Intro. + 1 = sonata-form Intro.}	b^1: Von der Hinterweltlern [I/3] b^2: Von der großen Sehnsucht [III/14]	A♭→V/C B→V/c
2. Fast mvt. {Exposition}	c^1: Von den Freuden und Leidenschaften [I/5] c^2: Das Grablied [II/11]	c/E♭/c→ (b)/C/b→V/f♯
3. Fugue {Development} digression	d^1: Von der Wissenschaft [IV/15] e^1 (m. 239)	C/(B)→V/B B→
fugue, cont.	d^2: Der Genesende [III/13]	(E)→C
sonata form retransition/intro to Finale	e^2 (m. 338)	b→V/C
4. Finale/Apotheosis & Postlude {Recapitulation}	f: Das Tanzlied [II/10]	C/B/C / A♭→ C
{Coda}	g: Das Nachtwandlerlied [= Das Trunkene Lied, IV/19]	C/B/C ?

* Bracketed material gives part, section, and subdivision references from Nietzsche's *Zarathustra*

source, he freely reordered its internal sequence, in part to permit an affective surge toward the climactic "Tanzlied." Taken together with his attraction to the book's frequently ecstatic prose poems ("Von der großen Sehnsucht," "Das Grablied," "Das Tanzlied," "Das Trunkene Lied"), these choices suggest that Strauss approached his literary material much as a *Lieder* composer would a poetic cycle. The "formal motives" that called the tone poem into being may be traceable to Nietzsche, but the metaphorical representation that it "chose" for itself was just as much a product of the composer's imagination.

Strauss insisted that he intended neither to "write philosophical music" nor to "portray Nietzsche's great work musically," though he was often censured for doing just that.[15] According to his notes for the December 1896 Berlin performance, he meant rather "to convey in music an idea of the evolution of the human race from its origin, through various phases of development, religious as well as scientific, up to Nietzsche's idea of the Übermensch."[16] The key words in the composer's statement of intent are "evolution" and "development," for they represent aspects of the philosophical argument, at least in Strauss's reading, that answer to musical techniques readily at hand.

Although opinions have varied widely on what holds together this most rhapsodically conceived of Strauss's tone poems, one thing is certain: a large measure of logical continuity is provided by a developmental linkage technique at once simple but effective. Each of the tone poem's principal sections (the first of course excepted) recalls material from the immediately foregoing. The introductory portion of "Von den Hinterweltlern" (mm. 23–34) presents two thematic fragments (labeled *x* and *y* in Ex. 8.1), the first of which is soon rhythmically reconfigured as the section's *Hauptmotiv,* a lush chorale. (The bass line of the chorale's opening four-bar phrase—Ab–Db–Eb–Ab—further derives from the cadential C–F–G–[A]–G–C of the initial invocation to the sun). The chorale, or segments thereof, resurfaces in the ensuing "Von der großen Sehnsucht," now replete with the rhetorically profiled countermelody that will likewise function as contrapuntal complement to the main idea of "Von den Freuden und Leidenschaften." "Das Grablied" in turn combines this idea with a variant of motive *y,* first introduced in "Von den Hinterweltlern," only to reach its climax with a statement of the work's initiatory C–G–C motive at m. 178. This thematic fragment (in his sketches, Strauss labelled it "Universum")[17] is then extended to create the chromatic fugue subject that dominates the following two sections, "Von der Wissenschaft" and "Der Genesende." The B-major dance episode that figures in both (its scoring and general style owing more than a little to the Venusberg music from Wagner's *Tannhäuser*) comes in for a whirling transformation in the climactic "Tanzlied" (mm. 529ff. and mm. 805ff.), whose statements of the principal motive of "Despair"[18] continue to resound against the bell strokes of the concluding "Nachtwandlerlied." The apparent profusion of musical images is thus held in check by a motivic disposition geared to suggest that each image in fact generates its successor.

Once again though, the "formal motive"—in this case the idea of generative development—would appear to be a product of the composer's own making. Though Nietzsche's *Übermensch* has been interpreted as a symbol

EXAMPLE **8.1**
Strauss, *Also sprach Zarathustra,* motives *x* (mm. 23–24) and *y* (mm. 25–26)

for unfettered progress toward an ideal being, the philosopher meant no such thing. The idea of the *Übermensch* hinges rather on the notion of *self-overcoming*—"the man who has overcome himself has become an overman," Zarathustra proclaims in one of his first speeches—and only the "scholarly oxen" (as Nietzsche derisively called them in *Ecce Homo*) could have mistaken his concept for a Darwinian metaphor.[19] To the "scholarly oxen" we might also add composers in search of hieroglyphic representations for their music. Strauss's *Zarathustra,* "freely adapted from Nietzsche" ("frei nach Nietzsche"), seems more to bear out the polemical argument of the philosopher's little essay on the relationship between word and tone than to reflect the ideas of the work whose name it bears.

Fin de siècle Form

Strauss's tone poem does engage in a dialogue with its philosophical namesake, even if in the process it drowns out the book's message with all the exuberance of Zarathustra himself when he speaks "the language of the dithyramb."[20] The more we attempt to map tone poem onto motivating philosophical tract, the more they proclaim their ultimate separateness. The same paradox results even when proceeding from an area where the two works appear to have much in common: the area of genre.

Nietzsche's reluctance to ascribe his *Zarathustra* to a single genre (was it a poem? a drama? or did it belong "among the symphonies"?)[21] is only fitting, given its wavering between philosophical discourse, poetic reflection, and even music. But we err in reading it as anything other than a philosophical text first and foremost. As Alexander Nehamas has demonstrated, Nietzsche's works often assume the outward trappings of poetic texts, but only to enable their author to argue, albeit obliquely, for philosophical perspectivism (the notion that every view is but one possible interpretation among many) as opposed to relativism (the notion that each of these views is equally correct).[22] Looking at Strauss's work primarily as a vehicle for the presentation of philosophical ideas constitutes no less an error. The tone poem, it can be argued, does disclose ideas, but they are mere by-products of a musically elaborative process that commands attention in and of itself.

Like Nietzsche's *Zarathustra,* Strauss's is a *Mischgedicht* of significant proportions, but a *Mischgedicht* of a peculiarly musical sort. It is easy to trace, in Strauss's various utterances on program music extending from his work on *Don Juan* to *Also sprach Zarathustra,* a marked shift in emphasis from the poetic to the musical idea. Writing to Hans von Bülow in 1888, he complains of the constraints that the "ternary sonata form inherited from the classical composers" places on his desire to convey a specific "musical-poetic content" through the medium of a "new form."[23] Two years later he extols program music as the "true art" (as opposed to the "artificiality" of absolute music), for only by way of the inspirational force of the program can the tone poet fashion the "unique new form" adequate to his newly minted musical ideas.[24] But while he was at work on *Zarathustra,* Strauss's outlook on the poetic dimension had obviously cooled: "I am a musician first and last, for whom all 'programmes' are merely the stimulus to the creation of new forms and nothing more."[25] The leitmotif shared by all of these quotations is the same one that Schumann had sounded earlier in the century: a call for "new forms." Strauss enshrined it in the original subtitle of his Zarathustra tone poem: "Symphonic Optimism in *Fin de siècle* Form, dedicated to the 20th century."[26]

Of what does this *"fin de siècle* form" consist? For one thing, Strauss clearly meant the *fin de siècle* designation in a widely different sense from that of its French popularizers of the decade before. The sordid plot of Francis de Jouvenot and H. Micard's 1888 play *Fin de Siècle,* centers around questionable business deals, murder, and adultery. The wealthy young protagonist of Humbert de Gallier's 1889 novel of the same name finds in suicide a remedy for insuperable boredom.[27] Strauss will have none of this debilitating world-weariness. His *fin de siècle* form was intended to hold out promise for things to come in the new century. Affirmation, for Strauss, is a consequence of combination, specifically the combination of musical forms and genres that seem, at first blush, to be incompatible. It is an old idea (as old as the nineteenth century itself) made new by the scope and breadth of its application, for Strauss attempts the interlacing of no less than six generic types in his *Zarathustra*: musical fragment collection, paired variation set, sonata allegro, symphony, concerto, and music drama.

Debussy's characterization of *Ein Heldenleben* as "a book of pictures, or even a cinematograph" applies with equal validity to *Zarathustra.*[28] Here too we encounter the same penchant for the presentation of musical ideas as a sequence of brilliant images, colorful snapshots, striking excerpts from a larger whole. For Adorno, Strauss's virtuosity resided in his conception of music—an "imageless" art—in imagistic terms.[29] In technical terms, this virtuosity can be analyzed as the dialectic between incompletion and relative self-sufficiency that freezes Strauss's musical fragments as images.

As indicated in Figure 8–1, most of the tone poem's nine principal sections are tonal fragments, links in a chain binding one member to the next. At the same time, each section projects a character whose marked individuality seems aimed at tearing the section out of the contextual flow. According to Arno Forchert, the chief functions associated with the larger tonal forms— introductory, initiatory, transitional, developmental—are consolidated, in Strauss's works, into qualities such as premonition, affirmation, indecision, or conflict. Released from their fixed roles in an architectural design, they may now occur at any point in a composition: an "epilogue," for instance, might figure at the beginning of a piece as a sonic symbol for repose.[30] To this insight can be added the further thought that the rapid-fire shift from one functional character to another has as its consequence the transformation of musical discourse into musical image. The pedal C that underpins the first fourteen measures of *Zarathustra* makes for an apt gesture of introduction. Yet the radical quickening of the harmonic rhythm in the ensuing bars, taken together with the unqualified cadential motion toward C in mm. 18–19, seems to signal a culminating utterance, a conclusion. The grandiose profile of the material is thus at odds with the speed of its progress from preparatory to summarizing gestures. The whole process of beginning, continuing, and concluding takes just a little over twenty bars: the temporal flow is frozen into an image. Section b^2 ('Von der großen Sehnsucht') already begins to develop the musical ideas that have gone before, but with the G pedal of mm. 109–14 (supporting $\flat\substack{6 \\ 4}$ –$\substack{5 \\ 3}$ motion in the upper parts), elaboration gives way to preparation for the turbulent C minor of "Von den Freuden und Leidenschaften." Again, the compression of varying functional characters into a limited space imparts an imagistic quality to the proceedings.

We have already drawn comparisons between Strauss's "setting" of selections from Nietzsche's book and the activity of a *Lieder* composer. The model for Strauss's rethinking of the tone poem as wordless song cycle is most probably to be located in the works of Liszt, each segment of whose *Die Ideale,* for instance, is headed by a portion of Schiller's poem of the same name. Here the older composer provided both an inspirational impetus and a problem to be solved: his symphonic poems too often splinter into a series of striking but not fully integrated details in a manner that Strauss sought to overcome.

The notion of logical evolution—the technique whereby a significant idea from one section in turn informs its successor—offered one means around the dilemma. But *Zarathustra* discloses another, more ingenious method of ensuring the continuity of its musical fragments. Its sections are by and large arranged in pairs (b^1/b^2, c^1/c^2, d^1–e^1/d^2–e^2, f/g), the second member of each presenting a varied restatement of the first. Hence, sections b^1 and b^2 follow an exactly parallel course, with thematic fragments giving way to a series of statements of the four-square chorale melody. Two of its appearances in b^2 even recur at the same pitch level as in the previous section (cf. mm. 99–106 and 51–58). Both c^1 and c^2 share a similar *ABA* shape, its central climax rapidly dissolved in each instance. Sections d^1–e^1 and d^2–e^2 juxtapose a stretch of fugal entries on the chromatically elaborated "Universe" motive with episodes featuring the dance-like "Venusberg" music. Section g evolves out of the terminal appearances of the "Despair" motive in section f. But within each variation pair, the responsive member acts as transformed double to its complement. The lush presentations of the chorale melody b^1 are answered by severely compressed statements in b^2. The c–E$\flat$–c tonal disposition of c^1 is displaced by a highly chromaticized b–C–b plan in c^2. Section d^2–e^2 reverses the last two elements of the preceding section's disposition (fugue–"Venusberg"–fragments) to accommodate a massive upsurge into the ensuing

"Tanzlied." Section *g* responds to its complement's frenzied dance gestures with reflective calm.

The variation technique that Strauss had overtly employed as an organizational framework for the immediately preceding *Don Quixote* thus recurs as a covert means for lending coherence to the *Zarathustra* material. And interestingly enough, the technique itself can be easily traced back to Liszt. The paired variation idea, coupled with the notion of transformational response, is detectable in portions of *Ce qu'on entend sur la montagne* (cf. the opening *poco allegro* and subsequent *poco a poco più di moto*), *Les Préludes* (cf. the *andante, andante maestoso,* and *l'istesso tempo* presentations of the opening material), and *Tasso, Lamento e Trionfo* (cf. its opening *lento* and *allegro strepitoso,* and the following *adagio mesto* and *meno adagio*). Problem and solution derive from the same source.[31]

Given the variation-pair organization in *Zarathustra,* the smaller sections tend to group themselves into larger form-parts or movements. What results, then, is a "multidimensional" form (to borrow Dahlhaus's term)[32] wherein sonata allegro, symphony, and even concerto shade into one another so thoroughly that the boundaries between them are not always easily distinguishable. To be sure, *Zarathustra* is hardly "in" any of these forms, but it draws on all of them. This too was an idea of long standing in the nineteenth century. Schubert had imposed a quasi-sonata-form organization on the continuously linked movements of his *Wanderer* Fantasie, D. 760, thus achieving a balance between structural cogency and improvisatory utterance. Chopin struck a similar balance in the Polonaise-Fantaisie, Opus 61, toward the end of poeticizing its initially unassuming dance topoi. The composition's terminal apotheosis (on the opening polonaise and a portion of the nocturne-like *più lento*) prefigures Liszt, Strauss's immediate model, for whom the multidimensional form answered to the dual exigencies of preserving affective coherence and symphonic breadth. But whereas Liszt often aimed for the latter at the former's expense, Strauss achieved a greater measure of equanimity between them by means of his consistently Janus-faced application of formal categories on the small and large scale.

The inner divisions of *Also sprach Zarathustra,* all but the very first marked off by Nietzsche's chapter headings, readily group themselves into an introductory invocation and four movements (see Fig. 8–1), a division likewise reflected in Strauss's programmatic sketch of the tone poem's expressive sequence: "Worship—Doubt—Despair—Freedom."[33] The character of the movements, however, is oddly askew. Function and affective quality, while at one when sonata allegro and symphony are conceived as independent form and genre types, are unhinged when the genres are commingled. The order reversal of symphonic movements 1 and 2—slow-fast instead of fast-slow—is thus conditioned by the sonata form's traditional slow introduction–*allegro* disposition. Movement 3 begins *sehr langsam,* much as we would expect given its central location in the symphonic plan; but its unfolding as a fugue, each entry a fifth higher than its predecessor, fulfills the developmental demands of the sonata form. Movement 4 takes the affirmative tone appropriate for a finale, but embodies it in a dance type—the waltz—whose placement at the culminating moment of the symphonic design makes for an unusual effect. Yet Strauss writes no ordinary waltz. He raises it from potentially trivializing dance type to grand utterance, first by casting it as a violin concerto movement, and second by assigning it a crucial role in the sonata-allegro scheme.

Clearly enough, the nature of Strauss's Janus-faced, multidimensional forms is such that the compressed symphony will have as its complement a magnification of sonata-form categories not only in terms of length or proportions but also of rhetorical force. The emphatic dominant prolongation at the close of section b^2 figures in the sonata-form scheme by calling forth a gesture massive enough to convert over a hundred bars of music, at one sweep, into an extended preparatory statement. Much of section e^2 is dominated by one of Strauss's most vibrant orchestral textures, the sonorous fabric shot through with pulsating triplets and trills in the upper winds, octave-leap trumpet calls, and sharply profiled interjections from the strings. The upper voice's melodic ascent from G♯, through A and A♯, to B, points toward a single harmonic goal: the establishment of G (supported by B) as dominant of C. The entire segment, in other words, functions as sonata-allegro retransition. And the waltz that ensues is "valorized" as symphonic utterance by the weight placed upon it, the weight of reprise.

Viewed as a quasi-independent movement, the apotheotic waltz (section *f*) exhibits a perfectly sensible pattern of its own: two interlocking *ABA* units centered on C merge into a trio (largely in A♭), followed by a condensed return of the main waltz music. (The return serves in addition as concerto-allegro tutti, its unusual placement—after the soloist's music instead of before it—determined by the symphonic demands for a terminal apotheosis.) That the entire section likewise functions as a reprise is revealed by the fact that the more than four-hundred-measure-long waltz recalls practically all the thematic highlights of the preceding music, but in transfigured form. The main waltz theme is accompanied by a conflation of the "Universe" motive and motive *y*. The theme itself, as well as its A-minor/major continuation, draws on motive *x*. The "Venusberg" music from sections e^1 and e^2 supplies the material both for the opening waltz's B segment and for the second waltz episode as a whole. After presenting transformed variants of the principal theme and chromatic descending motive from sections c^1 and c^2, the trio brings the first of the waltz section's climaxes on motive *y*. A second climax on the opening waltz tune marks the return, which then proceeds to call up a veritable feast of associative references to earlier material. An impressive array of contrapuntal combinations is capped by simultaneous statements of the trio's main theme (a choralelike variant on the c^1 music) and the "Despair" motive, this in turn prefacing a final climax on the main waltz idea.

As Dahlhaus explains in his discussion of multiple-function forms, it is necessary to distinguish among four levels of activity—cycle, movement, principal form part (exposition, development, recapitulation), and subsidiary form part (first group, transition, second group, closing)—all of which may disclose either "superposed" or "subordinate" dimensions. Hence, a subsidiary form part may reflect the pattern of a multimovement cycle in microcosm just as, conversely, a "movement" may function as a form part of the larger cycle.[34] The *Zarathustra* waltz displays just this kind of multidimensionality: at once a condensed summation of the entire cycle, a well-formed ternary movement in its own right, and a quasi-sonata-form reprise, it straddles three levels of structural activity. Symphonic character, *concertante* dance, and sonata-allegro function intermingle with a previously unimagined brilliance.

The picture is further enriched by Strauss's allusions to yet another genre: music drama. Many of *Zarathustra*'s thematic threads exhibit the chiseled cut of Wagnerian leitmotives. They sound and function much like referential tags, yet no name is adequate to them given the absence of any fixed verbal points of reference. The opening C–G–C motive all but demands a leitmotivic designation, but Strauss exegetes have traditionally dubbed it the tone poem's "Nature" motive—whether consciously or not is of little moment—more in deference to the similarities that it shares with the nature motives of *Rheingold* than because of any verifiable connections that it might have with the content of Nietzsche's text. Motives spill over sectional divisions, thereby establishing patterns of premonition, realization, and reminiscence akin to those in a sequence of interrelated operatic scenes. Compare, for instance, the halting presentation of motive y in section b^1, its climactic appearance in the waltz, and its use as a reflective countermelody in the concluding "Nachtwandlerlied." But to hear this motive as an allegory for "Man" (as many commentators have) is to miss the point. It alludes to the *process* of music drama, not to any specific musico-dramatic content.

The same is true of Strauss's employment of associative tonality. To be sure, the tone poem's principal dialectic turns on the conflict between two tonalities a half step apart: the C major of the "Nature" motive, and the B minor/major of motive y and the "Venusberg" music.[35] The "drama" that emanates from their interaction is, however, a purely musical one, involving the gradual assimilation of the B-minor/major music into the C realm (in the "Tanzlied") and its restoration (at least so far as motive y is concerned) to the original B level in the "Nachtwandlerlied." The rapprochement between C and B is negated, as if to confirm Adorno's claim that Strauss had most thoroughly renounced the most important of the arts of his predecessors: the art of transition.[36] Indeed, the subtle play between this technique and its "rhetorically dialectic" counterpart that Wagner unfolded in *Tristan* and *Parsifal* appears to give way here to a wholesale celebration of the shock engendered by tonal juxtaposition. This is the "meaning" behind the supposedly polytonal effects produced by Strauss's presentation of the "Nature" motive in C (or suggesting C) over V/B harmony (see section b^2, mm. 82, 84; section d^1, m. 236; and section e^1, m. 263).

Simultaneous juxtaposition is further answered by successive juxtaposition: Witness the abrupt turn from C to B at the climax of section c^2 (mm. 178–80), the reversal of this move during the second waltz episode (mm. 567–69), and the counterreversal that reestablishes B for the "Nachtwandlerlied" (mm. 945–46). Even when Strauss smoothes the way from C to B (or the reverse) by playing on the enharmonic equivalence of the dominant of C and the German augmented-sixth chord in B (e.g., at the transition into section b^2 mm. 74–75, or during the massive retransition into the "Tanzlied," mm. 392–93), the move is articulated by a marked textural shift. The both simultaneous and successive B/C juxtapositions of the work's celebrated closing bars effectively deny the possibility of a reconciliation between the conflicting realms. All of this is the stuff of music drama, though again, any attempt to link it with a specific content would be futile. The unmediated alternation between upper-register B major and celli-bass pizzicato Cs that makes of the tone poem's conclusion an emphatic question mark would seem as well to articulate the central paradox of program music. The more it strives to speak, the more it simply speaks itself.

The puzzling ending of Strauss's *Zarathustra* reflects back on the tone poem as a whole. It may even lead us to conclude that, in the final analysis, the work invites a reading as critique of the idea that music can "mean" in any kind of straightforward manner. The blending of music and poetry or philosophy, in other words, turns out to be just as refractory an affair as the conjunction of poetry and philosophy. For Adorno, the Straussian tone poem is actually "aware" of its resistance to meaning. The ultratheatrical quality that everywhere underscores this illusion is the intentional work of a supreme artist-trickster—the composer—who sets out to proffer an admittedly paradoxical message.[37]

Whether or not this was Strauss's intended reading is difficult to say. There is, after all, at least one sense in which the *Zarathustra* music actually undermines his programmatic intentions vis-à-vis Nietzsche's work. Strauss set out to depict, in music, the evolution of man toward the *Übermensch*. He opted, in other words, for what we have seen to be a decidedly wrongheaded interpretation of his philosophical source. But the music projects another, more sophisticated reading of Nietzsche as well. If the core of Zarathustra's teachings resides in the imperative "Man is a thing which must be overcome," then Strauss tells us, through his multidimensional metagenre, that musical form also is a thing which must be overcome. *Zarathustra* thus remains "all music," just as Goethe's philosophical *Meister* novels remain, in Schlegel's words, "all poetry."[38]

The "*fin de siècle* form" of Strauss's tone poem, though nourished on Liszt's example, looks forward with optimism toward the twentieth century, and not only as a vehicle for "philosophically" inspired works. As Dahlhaus has demonstrated, multiple-function forms were to become the norm for both program and "absolute" music at the turn of the century.[39] The third-movement scherzo of Mahler's Fifth Symphony (a "giddy dance brimming with life," to quote the composer)[40] provides a case in point. Ostensibly built on the Schumannian "scherzo cum multiple trios" form, the movement discloses the following pattern: scherzo—trio 1 (Ländler)—scherzo fragment—transition—trio 2—development—scherzo reprise—coda. Yet as Adorno argued, this remarkable movement is better viewed as exemplifying an "unprecedented new form," the *Durchführungsscherzo.*[41]

Hyperbole aside, there is no denying that Mahler's scherzo accumulates ever greater developmental weight as it proceeds: the "transition" elaborates on earlier music at the same time that it foreshadows the ensuing trio; references to trio 1 are interwoven with the more lyric material of trio 2; motives from both trios figure in the development proper; the scherzo reprise recalls practically all of the foregoing motivic highlights in some form or other; and the coda ushers in a *Steigerung* culminating in the contrapuntal combination of opening horn call, trio themes, and developmental rhythmic ostinato. Variation technique likewise plays a significant role throughout: as alternative to mere repetition in the bipartite scherzo proper, as catalyst for the processive unfolding of trio 1, and as syntactic frame for the lyricism of trio 2. In a word, Mahler's tendency to blend a variety of formal and generic types is on an order comparable to that already noted in Strauss's *Zarathustra.* Furthermore, the "multidimensionality" of the movement shows itself best in the terminal reprise, where material from the scherzo proper, trio 1, and trio 2 figures in what amounts to a précis of all that has gone before; the scherzo reprise is thus on a par with *Zarathustra*'s climactic "Tanzlied." The hypercharged gestures of Mahler's symphonic movement, like those of Strauss's tone poem, seem poised on the brink of "meaning" ("It is a human being," Mahler said, "in the full light of day, at the pinnacle of his powers");[42] but here too the rhetorical striving turns out to be "all music."

Strauss, charged by many critics as a modernist turned reactionary, might console himself over the fact that Arnold Schoenberg would adapt his *fin de siècle* forms in *Verklärte Nacht,* Opus 4; *Pelleas und Melisande,* Opus 5; the D-Minor String Quartet, Opus 7; and the First Chamber Symphony, Opus 9. But the older composer could not have known that what passed for a token of musical progress in 1896 and throughout the decade thereafter would soon come to be written off as an outmoded and seriously inflated mode of musical utterance. Schoenberg employed a *fin de siècle* form for his D-Minor Quartet "in accommodation to the faith of the time,"[43] but within a few years, the "extravagant abundance of musical themes" and extended structure characteristic of such forms had become problems to be solved by means of a disciplined application of the developing variation technique. The Second String Quartet, the first product of the new outlook, bears all the marks of the composer's struggle to master the difficulties of "condensation and juxtaposition."[44] This shift helps to place Strauss's *Zarathustra* into perspective. Like the work with which we began our inquiry, Schumann's Opus 17 Fantasie, it is a "dialectical sounding image," poised in this case between a century that responded to the call for progress with criticism, and a new age that responded with skepticism.

Epilogue

It is equally fatal for the
mind to have a system or
to have none. One is simply
left to have it both ways.

– Friedrich Schlegel
Athenäum Fragmente, no. 53

The drive that motivated composers to attempt an appropriation of the masterpieces of literature and philosophy has a parallel in the music historian's practice of ordering material under concepts without which isolated facts would remain without meaning, and without which Kant's suspicion, that music was "more enjoyment than culture," would be all too easily confirmed. Roughly speaking, there are two paths open to the historian of art, who can either adopt the categories of the art form in question or draw upon the broader categories of cultural history. In the first case, history becomes a self-referential account of a series of innovations, and specifically musical histories threaten to disintegrate into a sequence of "trade secrets" whose sense is divulged to initiates alone. In the second case, the artwork itself is exposed to a hollowing-out process; the historical object is thereby reduced to a mere index for something that lies beyond it—an idea, a trend, a cultural movement—and to which it stands in a discontinuous relationship. An ideal response to this dilemma would involve a continual mediating between the two extremes, carried out in full consciousness that the gap separating them is as wide as that which Wackenroder proclaimed between *Gefühl* and *Wissenschaft.* A problem, in other words, that might lead to methodological paralysis should instead serve as a stimulus for new approaches. Yet the problem becomes particularly acute for the historian of nineteenth-century music, for in no other period had art turned so decisively inward at the same time that it strove passionately to "speak," to direct its message outward.

Even though several commentators have viewed the year 1850 as a crucial divide in nineteenth-century music history, the categories of Friedrich Schlegel's poetics can be called into service as a useful frame for focusing the dialectic of interiority and exteriority that informed the century as a whole. Schlegel's categories are, on the one hand, categories of art, and as such capable of addressing the individual characteristics that differentiate one work from another. But on the other hand, they disclose the temporal specificity requisite for historical writing. To be sure, Schlegel's thought complex was in large measure the product of a given and unrepeatable circumstance: the crisis of belief following the French Revolution. Yet the justification for adopting his ideas as a conceptual frame is not to be sought in the narrow claims of historicism. It rather resides in one of the afterwaves of the nineteenth century's sociopolitical upheavals that, in our own century, takes the form of an intense skepticism directed at historical knowledge itself. Although the tremors that shook early nineteenth-century Europe have long since dissipated, we too are faced with any number of crises in belief. In short, Schlegel's divinatory criticism affords us with one means of writing history in an age that looks askance at the entire historical enterprise.

The categories of Schlegel's aesthetic—the *Arabeske,* the "witty" chain of fragments, the artwork as critique, the split between symbol and allegory, the romantic imperative, the reflective nature of *Universalpoesie,* the theory of the *Roman,* the New Mythology and the "new" organicism, the interdependence of poetry and philosophy—make it possible for us to bind together the diverse tendencies in nineteenth-century art into a kind of unity. The primary advantage of the system is its lack of closure; any point is theoretically accessible via any other point. Hence it is less a system than a flexible configuration that facilitates varying emphases depending on the artwork under consideration.

The most striking feature of the opening movement of Schumann's Opus 17 Fantasie is the digressive interruption or arabesque, yet the work touches on other categories as well. The *Im Legendenton* section splits the surrounding form into fragments; and as a self-sufficient character piece, it too is a fragment of a larger whole that is not present. Likewise the motivic ties between the *Im Legendenton* and the framing music make it into a reflective center, a productive manifestation of *Universalpoesie.* In that the movement seeks to overcome the generic bounds of the sonata by conjoining sonata allegro and character piece, it also exemplifies the novelizing tendencies of the Romantic imperative. The resultant form can easily be read as a challenge to (or critique of) the idea of the well-made artwork. Yet the movement's formal oddities do make sense if they are viewed in terms of a "new" organicism that has room for displacements and ruptures. And lastly, the figurative titles originally linked with the Fantasie's various movements disclose Schumann's attempt, if not to unite poetry and philosophy, then to bring music in touch with poetry, to imbue it with a self-surpassing dimension. In the vast continuum of artworks that supply the material for a history of nineteenth-century music, Schumann's Fantasie is little more than a grain of sand. But once detached from this continuum and read in tandem with the categories of Schlegel's poetics, it can in fact be shown to encapsulate the entire history of which it ostensibly forms but a part.

The strands connecting Schumann's work to the various points in Schlegel's system crisscross in the other works that we have considered as well. The principle of affective juxtaposition that informs the musical frag- ment collections—Schumann's sets of miniatures for piano—resurfaces in heightened form in the rhetorical dialectics of *Tristan* and *Parsifal.* Strauss's patterning of his *Zarathustra* as a sequence of tone pictures supplies another variant. And *Witz* in turn imparts a measure of unity to the cycle of character pieces, the music drama, and the tone poem alike. Similarly, the interplay of symbolic and allegorical modes in Weber's *Euryanthe,* no less than the attend- ant clefts that this interplay creates in the musical surface, finds a parallel in Wagner's "new" organicism, with its dual embodiment of a finely wrought art of transition and the discontinuities of rhetorical dialectics. Feeding on much the same conflict, Strauss's *Zarathustra* participates in the symbol-versus-al- legory debate by means of its juxtaposition of B and C tonal realms. The transformation of genres into qualities or "tones" that we have noted in Brahms's symphonic and chamber works likewise resurfaces in Strauss's re- configuration of sonata allegro, symphony, and music drama as characters in *Zarathustra.* Its apotheotic celebration of the dance in a grandly conceived recapitulatory center of attraction, moreover, hearkens back to the reflective centers that provide the structural backbone for the *Ring* dramas. Thus each composition, taken as an individual, embodies a number of the system's total categories; but each presents them in a different light, orders them in its own way, gives primacy to one over the other. That they all belong in the same history requires no elaborate proof; Schlegel's categories merely help us to show *how* they belong.

Furthermore, the Schlegelian thought complex opens up possibilities for a musical hermeneutics, for getting at the meanings that lurk behind or be- tween the notes on the page. The meanings that we have uncovered disclose a by and large critical thrust. Each of our compositions serves as a reminder that received ideas and outmoded forms of expression live on (in some form) in artworks, but only to be called into question. Hence, Schumann's Fantasie invites a reading as critique of the synthesizing impulse that runs through the Romantic project (Schumann's writings included) like an ideological thread. His *Novelletten* assert that the aphoristic utterance is capable of the same breadth and depth found by earlier ages in more extended modes of presen- tation that are, to an extent, denied to the modern artist. Weber's *Euryanthe* tells us that the discontinuities of allegory are very much alive in an age that prized the symbolic more highly as a significative mode. Brahms invokes the "Classical" genres as a means of stating the difficult truth that their revival—for a serious artist living and working in the second half of the nineteenth century—is simply not a possibility. Wagner's *Ring* narratives point the way toward a solution of the paradox embedded in the notion of "productive reflection," just as the great colloquy in the second act of *Tristan* and the tortuous laments in *Parsifal* speak to the integrity of an organicism that can sustain the very elements that threaten to destroy it. Strauss's *Zarathustra,* for all its shattering climaxes, states perhaps the most problematic truth of all: the more forcefully music endeavors to communicate, the more it withdraws into itself. None of these meanings is definitive, closed. Nor are they intended to hollow out the artwork, to reduce it to a sign for ideas that stand beyond itself. The application of Schlegel's categories to music merely suggests one method of confirming that in the nineteenth century the art of tone did indeed rise from the level of "enjoyment" to "culture."

At least one important category has not played a part in our discussion. The avoidance of any mention of irony has been quite deliberate, for it has been used so often as a catchword that, like the term *Romanticism,* it can mean everything and hence nothing. For Schlegel, irony is the very "form of paradox" (*Kritische Fragmente,* no. 48). As such, it celebrates the contradictions that emerge in style through the interaction of playfulness and seriousness, or intention and instinct (*Kritische Fragmente,* no. 108). As a structural category, it appears as the "grotesque," the quality that results from incongruities between form and content (*Athenäum Fragmente,* No. 305). In the area of reflective thought it manifests itself as the humorous mediation of being and nonbeing (*Athenäum Fragmente,* No. 305). But why is irony a specifically "*transcendental* buffoonery," to quote the colorful bon mot from *Kritische Fragmente,* no. 42? Why is this feast of contradictions worth celebrating in the first place? Irony, Schlegel tells us, is the very quality that allows the artwork to appear to rise above the limitations of its own medium through the act of objective self-commentary. The same quality allows the individual to transcend his or her limitations by aspiring, as it were, to the internal constitution of the artwork.

The self-commenting artwork will always involve us in a contradiction, and herein may lie its most potent message, a message that does not square well with the demands of positivism, but that is worth articulating nonetheless. If nothing else, the strong artworks of the nineteenth century remind us that there are paradoxes that will not admit to facile syntheses or easy solutions. Late in the eighteenth and early in the nineteenth century Friedrich Schlegel and Novalis placed their hopes in the *Roman* as the genre best equipped to bear this message, although it is arguable that only with the works of Kafka and Hermann Broch did literature evolve the modes of presentation that were up to the task. How ironic then that in the nearly century and a half separating Schlegel's earliest notebook jottings from Broch's last works the task should have fallen to music.

Notes

1. Romantic Ideas and Romantic Music

1. See Terry Eagleton, *Ideology: An Introduction* (London: Verso, 1991), p. 3.
2. For a recent discussion of musical Romanticism emphasizing the artist's estrangement from society and consequent turn inward, see Edward F. Kravitt, "Romanticism Today," *Musical Quarterly* 76 (1992): 93–109. The early Romantics' refractory engagement with social issues is treated sensitively in Jochen Schulte-Sasse, "The Concept of Literary Criticism in German Romanticism," in *A History of German Literary Criticism, 1730–1980,* ed. Peter Uwe Hohendahl (Lincoln: University of Nebraska Press, 1988), pp. 99–109, 113–14.
3. Quoted in Hans Eichner, "Germany/Romantisch–Romantik–Romantiker," in *"Romantic" and Its Cognates: The European History of a Word,* ed. H. Eichner (Toronto: University of Toronto Press, 1972), p. 135.
4. Robert Schumann, *Gesammelte Schriften über Musik und Musiker* [*GS*] (Leipzig: Breitkopf & Härtel, 1914), vol. 1, p. 249; from "Drei Impromptus für das Pianoforte von Stephan Heller, Werk 7."
5. Arthur O. Lovejoy, "On the Discriminations of Romanticism," *Papers of the Modern Language Association* 39(1924): 229–53. F. L. Lucas (*The Decline and Fall of the Romantic Ideal,* 1948), claimed to have counted some 11, 396 definitions of *Romanticism*; see Alex Preminger, ed., *Princeton Encyclopedia of Poetry and Poetics,* enlarged ed. (Princeton, NJ: Princeton University Press, 1974), p. 717.
6. See the commentary on Lovejoy's and Wellek's contrary positions as a sign of the contradictions inherent in Romanticism itself in Jerome J. McGann, *The Romantic Ideology: A Critical Investigation* (Chicago: Chicago University Press, 1983), pp. 17–20.
7. Carl Dahlhaus, *Nineteenth-Century Music,* trans. J. Bradford Robinson (Berkeley and Los Angeles: University of California Press, 1989; orig. publ. *Die Musik des 19. Jahrhunderts, Neues Handbuch der Musikwissenschaft,* vol. 6 [Wiesbaden: Akademische Verlagsgesellschaft Athenaion, 1980]), pp. 16–25.
8. Maurice Blanchot, "The *Athenaeum,"* *Studies in Romanticism* 22 (1983): 168.
9. *Athenäum Fragmente* (1797–98), no. 146, in *Kritische Friedrich Schlegel Ausgabe* [*KA*], vol. 2, *Charakteristiken und Kritiken I* (1796–1801), ed. Hans Eichner (Munich, Paderborn, Vienna: Schöningh, 1967), p. 188; cf. *Fragmente zur Litteratur und Poesie* (1797), no. 32: "Three predominant poetic types. 1) Tragedy, for the Greeks 2) Satire, for the Romans 3) The novel, for the moderns," *KA* 16, *Fragmente zur Poesie und Literatur I,* ed. Hans Eichner (Paderborn: Schöningh, 1981), p. 88.

229

On Schlegel's use of *Romantic* as a genre designator, see Eichner, "Germany: Roman-tisch. Romantik, Romantiker," pp. 102–3, 109–10; idem, *Friedrich Schlegel* (New York: Twayne, 1970), pp. 51–54; "Friedrich Schlegel's Theory of Romantic Poetry," *Publications of the Modern Language Association of America* 71 (1956): 1018–41; and Peter Szondi, "Friedrich Schlegel's Theory of Poetical Genres: A Reconstruction from the Posthumous Fragments," in *On Textual Understanding and Other Essays,* trans. Harvey Mendelsohn, Theory and History of Literature, vol. 15 (Minneapolis: University of Minnesota Press, 1986), pp. 90–94.

10. *Fragmente zur Litteratur und Poesie* (1797), no. 590, *KA* 16: 134. Similarly, Fragment 606 from the same collection reads: "Alle Geisteswerke sollen romantisiren, dem Roman sich möglichst approximiren" [All products of the imagination should novelize, should ap-proximate the novel as closely as possible] (*KA* 16: 136).

11. See Eichner, "Germany/Romantisch–Romantik–Romantiker," pp. 102–3, 142–43. Novalis's usage is particularly telling; just as *Dramatik* refers to the theory of the drama, so, in the fragments of *Das allgemeine Brouillon* (1797/98), does *Romantik* refer to the theory of the novel. See Novalis, *Schriften,* vol. 3, ed. Richard Samuel (Stuttgart: Kohlhammer, 1968), pp. 75, 88.

12. See *Brief über den Roman, KA* 2: 335–37; *Athenäum* Fragment no. 116, *KA* 2: 182–83; and "Die Spanisch-Portugiesische Literatur" (1803–4), *KA* 11, *Wissenschaft der Europäischen Literatur* (1795–1804), ed. Ernst Behler (Munich: Schöningh, 1958), pp. 159–62. For sum-mary accounts of Schlegel's theory of the novel, see Eichner, *Friedrich Schlegel,* pp. 44–83; idem, "Friedrich Schlegel's Theory of Romantic Poetry," pp. 1039–41; and Klaus Peter, *Friedrich Schlegel* (Stuttgart: Metzler, 1978), pp. 38–42.

13. *KA* 2, p. 336.

14. On Schlegel as "divinatory" critic, see Erich Heller's commentary on Thomas Mann's *The Magic Mountain* in *Thomas Mann: The Ironic German* (1958; South Bend, Ind.: Regnery/Gateway, 1979), pp. 169–214.

15. Friedrich Blume, *Classic and Romantic Music,* trans. M. D. Herter Norton (New York: Norton, 1970; orig. publ. in *Die Musik in Geschichte und Gegenwart,* 1958, 1963), pp. 124–171, passim.

16. Dahlhaus, *Nineteenth-Century Music,* pp. 391–92. See also Leon Plantinga, *Romantic Mu-sic: A History of Musical Style in Nineteenth-Century Europe* (New York: Norton, 1984), p. 22.

17. Cf. Blume, *Classic and Romantic Music,* pp. 147–48, and Dahlhaus, *Nineteenth-Century Music,* pp. 170, 391.

18. Dahlhaus, *Nineteenth-Century Music,* p. 391.

19. Arno Forchert, "'Klassisch' und 'romantisch' in der Musikliteratur des frühen 19. Jahr-hunderts," *Musikforschung* 31 (1978): 424–25.

20. Wilhelm Heinrich Wackenroder, "Das eigentümliche innere Wesen der Tonkunst, und die Seelenlehre der heutigen Instrumentalmusik" (1799), *Werke und Briefe* (Heidelberg: Schneider, 1967), pp. 220–27.

21. *KA* 2, p. 312. On the role of the aesthetic of production in Schlegel's critical and philo-sophical writings, see Marcus Bullock, "The Coming of the Messiah or the Stoic Burning: Aspects of the Negated Text in Walter Benjamin and Friedrich Schlegel," *Germanic Re-view* 60 (1985): 9–13, and Schulte-Sasse, "The Concept of Literary Criticism," p. 156.

22. See Schlegel, *Fragmente zur Litteratur und Poesie,* no. 851: "For romantic art forms, the determining categories are manner, tendency, and tone; for classical poetic types, on the other hand, they are form, content, and style" (*KA* 16, p. 157), and the commentary on this fragment in Szondi, *On Textual Understanding,* p. 90.

23. *Fragmente zur Litteratur und Poesie,* no. 4, *KA* 16, p. 85.

24. McGann, *Romantic Ideology,* pp. 1–56, passim. As Herbert Lindenberger puts it, we must "learn to resist the rhetorical seduction of theories of romanticism"; see *The History in Literature: On Value, Genre, Institutions* (New York: Columbia University Press, 1990), p. 80.

25. Leonard B. Meyer, *Style and Music: Theory, History, and Ideology* (Philadelphia: University of Pennsylvania Press, 1989). See especially Part 3, "Music and Ideology: A Sketch-History of Nineteenth-Century Music," pp. 163–336.

26. Ibid., p. 308.

27. McGann, *Romantic Ideology,* p. 134.

28. T. W. Adorno, *Aesthetic Theory,* trans. C. Lenhardt, ed. Gretel Adorno and Rolf Tiedemann (London and New York: Routledge & Kegan Paul, 1972; orig. publ. *Aesthetische Theorie,* Frankfurt, 1970), p. 50.

29. *Fragmente zur Litteratur und Poesie,* no. 845, *KA* 16, p. 157.

30. Georg Wilhelm Friedrich Hegel, *Einleitung in die Aesthetik* (1842), ed. Wolfhart Henckmann (Munich: Wilhelm Fink Verlag, 1985), p. 112.

31. Meyer, *Style and Music,* pp. 208–9. For an alternative view of the musical literacy of nineteenth-century audiences, see Leon Botstein, "Time and Memory: Concert Life, Science, and Music in Brahms's Vienna," in *Brahms and His World,* ed. Walter Frisch (Princeton, N.J.: Princeton University Press, 1990), pp. 4–9.

32. Dahlhaus, *Nineteenth-Century Music,* pp. 34–35.

33. Walter Benjamin, *Der Begriff der Kunstkritik in der deutschen Romantik* (1920; Frankfurt: Suhrkamp, 1973), p. 67.

34. Carl Dahlhaus, *Die Idee der absoluten Musik* (Kassel: Bärenreiter, 1978), p. 143.

35. See, for example, Schlegel's comments in his review of Goethe's *Wilhelm Meisters Lehrjahre* (1798): "But only he who reads it [*Wilhelm Meister*] aloud and understands it thoroughly can make palpable, to listeners with a sense for such things, the irony that hovers over the entire work" (*KA* 2, pp. 137–38).

36. Lawrence Kramer, in "Dangerous Liaisons: The Literary Text in Musical Criticism," *19th-Century Music* 12 (1989): 161, speaks of the sharing of "deep structures."

37. See Hayden White's compelling attempts to defuse the negativity surrounding the narrativity issue in *The Content of the Form: Narrative Discourse and Historical Representation* (Baltimore: Johns Hopkins University Press, 1987), esp. "The Value of Narrativity in the Representation of Reality" (pp. 1–25), and "The Question of Narrative in Contemporary Historical Theory" (pp. 26–57).

38. Quoted from a letter to Christian Rang of 9 December 1923, in Rainer Nägele, "Introduction: Reading Benjamin," in R. Nägele, ed., *Benjamin's Ground: New Readings in Walter Benjamin* (Detroit: Wayne State University Press, 1988), pp. 14–15.

39. See Dahlhaus, *Nineteenth-Century Music,* pp. 1–3, 390, 393–94.

40. *Fragmente zur Litteratur und Poesie,* no. 1130, *KA* 16, p. 178; cf. *Zur Poesie und Litteratur II* (1800), no. 527: "[Elegies should be] musical to the highest degree, as if aspiring to pure instrumental music" (*KA* 16, p. 297).

41. *Athenäum Fragmente,* no. 444, *KA* 2, p. 254.

42. Novalis, *Schriften,* vol. 3, p. 309.

43. See *Philosophische Fragmente: Zweite Epoche II* (1799), nos. 180, 494, *KA* 18, *Philosophische Lehrjahre, 1796–1806, Erster Teil,* ed. Ernst Behler (Zurich: Thomas-Verlag, 1963), pp. 337, 361; *Athenäum Fragmente,* nos. 253, 365, *KA* 2, pp. 208, 232; *Ideen* (1800), no. 70, *KA* 2, p. 263.

44. See *Fragmente zur Litteratur und Poesie,* nos. 48, 402, 705, 760, 1130; *KA* 16, pp. 89, 118, 145, 150, 178.

45. For references to "symphilosophizing" in the Novalis-Schlegel correspondence, see Novalis, *Schriften,* vol. 4, ed. R. Samuel (Stuttgart: Kohlhammer, 1975), pp. 241, 263, 488, 490, 614–15.

46. See René Wellek, *A History of Modern Criticism, 1750–1950,* vol. 2, *The Romantic Age* (Cambridge: Cambridge University Press, 1981), pp. 36ff.; and Eichner, "Germany/Romantisch–Romantik–Romantiker," pp. 136–37.

47. See August Wilhelm Schlegel, *Sämmtliche Werke,* ed. E Böcking (Leipzig: Weidmann'sche Buchhandlung, 1846), vol. 5, p. 68, where opera is described as an "anarchy of the arts in which music, dancing, and decoration seek to outdo one another through the lavish-

ness of their most luxuriant charms." August Wilhelm, like Friedrich, also recommends the "marvelous" as the appropriate content for an operatic text.

48. Hoffmann's diary entry for 12 January 1811 reads: "Read much in Schlegel's *Lectures on Dramatic Art*; I will copy out the most important definitions *ad usum*" (quoted in Harvey W. Hewett-Thayer, *Hoffmann: Author of the Tales* [New York: Octagon, 1971], pp. 352–53).

49. *Cosima Wagner's Diaries,* trans. Geoffrey Skelton (New York: Harcourt Brace Jovanovich, 1978), vol. 1, p. 523; cf. also the entry for 28 August 1872, p. 529. Wagner read Friedrich Schlegel, too; see Cosima's diary entry for 1 February 1874: "In the evening Fr. Schlegel's book on Greeks and Romans [*Die Griechen und Römer,* 1797]" (vol. 1, p. 730).

50. For further commentary on this scheme, see Peter Szondi, "Friedrich Schlegel and Romantic Irony, with Some Remarks on Tieck's Comedies," in *On Textual Understanding,* pp. 57–58.

51. *Neue Zeitschrift für Musik* [*NZfM*] 2 (1835): 3; see also the discussions in Dahlhaus, *Nineteenth-Century Music,* pp. 247–48; *Klassische und Romantische Musikästhetik* (Laaber: Laaber Verlag, 1988), pp. 258–61; and Rudolf Pečman, "Schumanns Schaffensästhetik im Lichte seiner Zeit," in *Robert-Schumann-Tage 1985,* pp. 82–84.

52. *KA* 2, p. 184.

53. Schulte-Sasse, "The Concept of Literary Criticism," p. 170.

54. See Rose R. Subotnik, "The Historical Structure: Adorno's 'French' Model for the Criticism of Nineteenth-Century Music," in *Developing Variations: Style and Ideology in Western Music* (Minneapolis: University of Minnesota Press, 1991), pp. 206–7.

55. *KA* 1, *Studien des Klassischen Altertums,* ed. Ernst Behler (Paderborn: Schöningh, 1979), p. 219.

56. On the redemptive aspect of Schlegel's critique of modernity, see Bernd Bräutigam, *Leben wie im Roman: Untersuchungen zum ästhetischen Imperativ im Frühwerk Friedrich Schlegels, 1794–1800* (Paderborn: Schöningh, 1986), pp. 49–51; Szondi, *On Textual Understanding,* pp. 63–65; and Bullock, "Coming of the Messiah," p. 14.

57. "Über die Grenzen des Schönen," *KA* 1, p. 35.

58. *KA* 2, p. 198.

2. Schumann's Opus 17 Fantasie and the *Arabeske*

1. Charles Rosen, *The Classical Style: Haydn, Mozart, Beethoven* (New York: Norton, 1972), p. 451.

2. Hermann Erler, *Robert Schumann's Leben aus seinen Briefen geschildert* (Berlin: Ries & Erler, 1887), vol. 1, p. 101. The collection of funds for the monument, unveiled in Bonn by 1845 for the seventy-fifth anniversary of Beethoven's birth, was coordinated by a committee set up in the early 1830s and presided over by August Wilhelm Schlegel.

3. Erler, *Schumann's Leben,* vol. 1, p. 102.

4. *Neue Zeitschrift für Musik* [*NZfM*] 4 (1836): 212.

5. See his letter to Clara of 19 March 1838: "Moreover I have completed a Phantasie in three movements, which I sketched out in all but its details during June 1836" in *Clara und Robert Schumann, Briefwechsel: Kritische Gesamtausgabe* [*BrKG*], ed. Eva Weissweiler (Frankfurt: Stroemfeld, Roter Stern, 1984), vol. 1, p. 126.

6. Quoted from *Konvolut* "N" (fragments on theories of knowledge and progress, 1927–37) of Benjamin's *Arcades Project* (*Passagen-Werk*); see the translation by Leigh Hafrey and Richard Sieburth in Gary Smith, ed., *Benjamin: Philosophy, Aesthetics, History* (Chicago: University of Chicago Press, 1989), pp. 50, 60.

7. Diary entry for late October 1837, in Robert Schumann, *Tagebücher,* vol. 2, 1836–1854 [hereafter *TB* II], ed. Gerd Nauhaus (Leipzig: VEB Deutscher Verlag für Musik, 1987), p. 42.

8. Anthony Newcomb has recently questioned whether Schumann actually intended the spot as a quotation from Beethoven's cycle. See "Schumann and the Marketplace: From

Butterflies to *Hausmusik*," in *Nineteenth-Century Piano Music,* ed. R. Larry Todd (New York: Schirmer Books, 1990), pp. 295–96. Newcomb also provides a useful account of the critical tradition (initiated in the second edition of Hermann Abert's *Robert Schumann* [1910], p. 64) that posited the link in the first place. Nicholas Marston likewise questions the notion of the song cycle reference as "quotation" in "Schumann's Monument to Beethoven," *19th-Century Music* 14, no. 3 (1991): 248. To be sure, Schumann's *adagio* theme (and its close relative in mm. 394ff. of the finale of the Second Symphony, Opus 61) is not an exact citation of Beethoven's *Lied* melody. But whether acknowledged by Schumann and his circle or not, the similarities between the themes are unmistakable. Did Schumann perhaps affirm his fascination with Beethoven's song cycle by employing a variant of the *adagio* theme (and in its, at least for Schumann, referential key of C major) in one of his own cycles: the sixth song of *Frauenliebe und Leben,* Op. 42, at "Bleib' an meinem Herzen" and the preceding piano interlude?

9. As Schumann related in his 19 December 1836 letter to Kistner: "In the 'Palmen' the Adagio [*sic*] of the A major Symphony [of Beethoven] puts in an appearance." See Erler, *Schumann's Leben,* vol. 1, pp. 102–3. All that remains of the original allusion in the present finale is a reference to the rhythm of Beethoven's theme in the bass, mm. 30–33, 87–90. Cf. Arnfried Edler, *Robert Schumann und seine Zeit* (Laaber: Laaber-Verlag, 1982), pp. 140–41.

10. "Theory" is an unavoidably invoked misnomer. Like all Schlegel's theories, that of the *Arabeske* must be pieced together from fragmentary and sometimes contradictory utterances.

11. See Eric A. Blackall, *The Novels of the German Romantics* (Ithaca, N.Y.: Cornell University Press, 1983), pp. 30–39, and Karl K. Polheim, *Die Arabeske: Ansichten und Ideen aus Friedrich Schlegels Poetik* (Paderborn, Munich: Schöningh, 1966), pp. 12–13.

12. "Sonaten für das Clavier," in Robert Schumann, *Gesammelte Schriften über Musik und Musiker* [hereafter *GS*], ed. Martin Kreisig (Leipzig: Breitkopf & Härtel, 1914), vol. 1, p. 395; and *NZfM* 10 (1839): 134. Cf. the similar comments in a review of the piano sonatas of Lacombe, Heller, and Grund, where Schumann claimed that the sonata was "smiled upon with pity" in France and "barely tolerated" in Germany; *NZfM* 11 (1839): 185.

13. "Konzerte für Pianoforte," *GS* 1, pp. 385–86; *NZfM* 10 (1839): 6.

14. "Neue Sinfonien für Orchester," *GS* 1, p. 424; *NZfM* XI (1839): 1. "Preisquartette von Julius Schapler," *GS* 2, p. 71; *NZfM* 16 (1842): 142. "Variationen für Pianoforte," *GS* 1, p. 219; *NZfM* 5 (1836): 63.

15. "Etüden für Pianoforte," *GS* 1, pp. 389–90; *NZfM* 10 (1839): 74. "Pianoforte Concerte," *GS* 1, p. 163; *NZfM* 4 (1836): 123.

16. Cf. *GS* 1, p. 424; *NZfM* 11(1839): 1; and *NZfM* 6 (1837): 207, a review of L. Schuberth's *Große Phantasie in Form einer Sonate (Souvenir à Beethoven),* Opus 30, where Schumann refers to the composer disparagingly as a "Beethovenverewiger."

17 Erler, *Schumann's Leben,* vol. 1, p. 177.

18. Cf. Linda Correll Roesner, "Schumann's Revisions in the First Movement of the Piano Sonata in G Minor, Op. 22," *19th-Century Music* 1 (1977–78): 97–109; and Newcomb, "Schumann and the Marketplace," pp. 285–94. Newcomb takes issue with Roesner's interpretation of a marginal note in the autograph regarding the *appassionato* section and a portion of the transition that follows. While Roesner takes Schumann's note "Dieses B gilt erst Seite 5" to call for the complete excision of the G-minor *appassionato* and the first twelve measures of the *vivo* transition, so that this music would appear first in its major-key form (*alla fantasia*) at the corresponding spot in the recapitulation, Newcomb argues that Schumann rather intended for the *appassionato* to *replace* the recapitulation's *alla fantasia* while at the same time maintaining its position within the exposition. Although Newcomb's reading makes more philological and musical sense, he does not necessarily succeed in countering Roesner's assertion that Schumann's early compositional procedures involved "extracting, moving about, omitting, and substituting large blocks of finished material, while at the same time leaving intact the surround-

ing musical text," thus revealing a "piecemeal approach to composition ... antithetical to the nineteenth-century ideal of the essential unity of a sonata movement" ("Schumann's Revisions," pp. 108–9). Whichever interpretation of the passage we opt for, the element of wholesale excision and substitution remains. Likewise, Newcomb's attempt motivically to relate the *appassionato* and the opening theme (a bow in the direction of "essential unity") is questionable. It is difficult to hear just how the later motive is to be interpreted as a "development of the headmotif" of the earlier one. ("Schumann and the Marketplace," p. 286).

19. For a somewhat different interpretation of this passage, see Linda Correll Roesner, "Schumann's 'Parallel' Forms," *19th-Century Music* 14, no. 3 (1991): 268–69. Roesner places the transposed (and temporally compressed) variant of the second group within an ostensible development section beginning at m. 54, thus creating an artificial division between clearly complementary events. She also downplays the disruptive effect of the *animato* at mm. 62ff., which is described as a "lyric transformation of the principal theme."

20. Charles Rosen, *Sonata Forms* (New York: Norton, 1980), p. 315.

21. Franz Brendel, "Robert Schumann mit Rücksicht auf Mendelssohn-Bartholdy, und die Entwicklung der modernen Tonkunst überhaupt," *NZfM* 22 (1845): 145: "The basis for Schumann's artistic creations is his subjectivity, so that at times he lacks in unity of style and character when he ventures into the epic sphere."

22. C. Koßmaly, "Ueber Robert Schumann's Claviercompositionen," *Allgemeine musikalische Zeitung [AmZ]* 46 (1844): col. 35.

23. Markus Waldura, *Monomotivik, Sequenz und Sonatenform im Werk Robert Schumanns* (Saarbrücken: Saarbrücker Druckerei & Verlag, 1990), p. 15.

24. There is some precedent for this line of argument as well in the Schumann critical tradition. As Ignaz Moscheles put it in his review of Schumann's Opus 11, "Clara zugeeignet von Florestan und Eusebius," *NZfM* 5 (1836): 137: "Perhaps it is just that unity-destroying element that provides the essential character of Schumann's intended portrayal."

25. Letter to Clara of 19 March 1838: "Moreover, I have completed a Phantasie in three movements that I sketched out in all but its details in June 1836. The first movement is no doubt the most refined that I've yet composed—a deep lament for you—the others are weaker, though nothing exactly to be ashamed about" (*BrKG* 1, p. 126). Recently there has been some controversy over whether Schumann wrote "Raffiniertestes" ("most refined") or "Passioniertestes" ("most passionate"); see Nicholas Marston's remarks in "Comment and Chronicle," *19th-Century Music* 15, no. 2 (1991): 166. It seems to me that a contrast between refinement and (compositional) weakness makes more sense than one between passion and (affective) weakness.

26. See Thomas Alan Brown, *The Aesthetics of Robert Schumann* (New York: Philosophical Library, 1968), p. 157; Joan Chissell, *Schumann Piano Music* (Seattle: University of Washington Press, 1972), p. 37; Kathleen Dale, "The Piano Music," in *Schumann: A Symposium,* ed. G. Abraham (London: Oxford University Press, 1952), p. 47; A. Edler, *Robert Schumann und seine Zeit,* p. 142; Gernot Gruber, "Robert Schumann: Fantasie Op. 17, 1. Satz: Versuch einer Interpretation," *Musicologica Austriaca* 4 (1984): 105–6 (Gruber's discussion tends to downplay sonata-form elements, so that he leans more strongly in the direction of taking the *Im Legendenton* as the central section of a three-part song form); Rosen, *Classical Style,* p. 453 (for Rosen, the *Im Legendenton* lends to the first movement the ternary shape of a da capo aria); and Frank Schneider, " 'Im Legendenton': Fragwürdiges zu einem musikalischen Topos," *Gattungen der Musik und ihre Klassiker,* ed. Hermann Danuser (Laaber: Laaber-Verlag, 1988), p. 559.

27. See Anthony Newcomb, "Schumann and Late Eighteenth-Century Narrative Strategies," *19th-Century Music* 11, no. 2 (1987): 170; and Roesner, "Schumann's 'Parallel' Forms," pp. 274–75.

28. Roesner, in her discussion of the first movement of the Fantasie ("Schumann's 'Parallel' Forms," pp. 274–75), acknowledges the recurrence at m. 97, but minimizes its structural import by describing it as "a renewed *postponement* of the tonic, not a return to it." Yet if Schumann really wanted to postpone the tonic, why did he replay the opening music at its original pitch level? Also, why the thumping bass Cs in mm. 120ff.? Roesner places the passage from mm. 97–128 within a development beginning at m. 82 to preserve (at least on paper) the symmetry of Schumann's supposedly parallel form. For the same reason, she locates the beginning of the recapitulation at m. 225—in E♭—and then must place the exposition proper at m. 29, also in E♭. This leaves the otherwise unaccounted-for mm. 1–28 as a "pre-exposition." It would seem, however, that Schumann's design actually fights against the kind of balance that this analysis goes to such pains to impose. My own thinking is more in line with David Montgomery, who likewise recognizes m. 97 as the point of reprise; see "The Myth of Organicism: From Bad Science to Great Art," *Musical Quarterly* 76 (1992): 66.

29. This is the trap into which Gruber falls ("Robert Schumann: Fantasie Op. 17," pp. 121–22) in proposing a far-fetched chain of associations that runs from Schlegel's "Gebüsche," to the cycle that it is drawn from (*Die Abendröte*), to the cycle's place in Schlegel's plans for a continuation of his *Roman, Lucinde,* to Schumann's possible reading of the same, and finally to the poetic content of the Fantasie.

30. *Philosophische Fragmente: Erste Epoche II* (1796–98), no. 380, *KA* 18, p. 57.

31. Ibid., no. 884, *KA* 18, p. 103.

32. "Rede über die Mythologie," from *Gespräch über die Poesie* (1800), *KA* 2, pp. 318–19.

33. *Fragmente zur Poesie und Litteratur II* (1800–1801), no. 15, *KA* 16, p. 342.

34. For a comprehensive discussion of this debate, see Günther Oesterle, "Vorbegriffe zu einer Theorie der Ornamente: Kontroverse Formprobleme zwischen Aufklärung, Klassizismus und Romantik am Beispiel der Arabeske," in *Ideal und Wirklichkeit der bildenden Kunst im späten 18. Jahrhundert,* ed. Herbert Beck (Berlin: Mann, 1984), pp. 119–39.

35. See Wolfgang Kayser, *The Grotesque in Art and Literature,* trans. Ulrich Weisstein (New York: Columbia University Press, 1981; orig. publ. *Das Groteske,* Oldenburg, 1957), pp. 19–21.

36. See Oesterle, "Vorbegriffe," pp. 120–22, 133–34. Eduard Hanslick's allusions to the painterly arabesque as an analogue for the autonomous play of pure instrumental music are in line with the mode of thought initiated by Moritz. See *On the Musically Beautiful,* trans. and ed. Geoffrey Payzant from the 8th edition (1891) of *Vom Musikalisch-Schönen* (Indianapolis: Hackett, 1986), pp. 30–32; and Lothar Schmidt, "Arabeske: Zu einigen Voraussetzungen und Konsequenzen von Eduard Hanslicks musikalischen Formbegriff," *Archiv für Musikwissenschaft* 46 (1989): 91–120. Similar musical/painterly analogies had been made before Hanslick by Johann Triest and Georg Nägeli.

37. Johann Wolfgang Goethe, "Von Arabesken," in *Gedenkausgabe der Werke, Briefe und Gespräche,* vol. 13, *Schriften zur Kunst* (Zurich: Artemis Verlag, 1954), pp. 62–66.

38. For descriptions, see Philipp Otto Runge, *Hinterlassene Schriften,* hrsg. von dessem ältestem Bruder (Hamburg: Perthes, 1840), pp. 226ff.

39. Schlegel, *Fragmente zur Litteratur und Poesie* (1797), no. 986, *KA* 16, p. 167; and *Fragmente zur Poesie und Litteratur II* (1800), no. 860, *KA 16,* p. 326.

40. *KA* 2, p. 238. In the *Charakteristiken und Kritiken von A. W. Schlegel,* published in Königsberg in 1801, the term *grotesques (Grotesken)* was replaced by *arabesques (Arabesken).* Both were employed more or less interchangeably not only by Schlegel but by art critics writing before him; J. D. Fiorillo devoted an essay, "Ueber die Groteske" (1791), to an attempt at differentiating them; see Oesterle, "Vorbegriffe," p. 124.

41. Cf. *Fragmente zur Litteratur und Poesie,* no. 1075, *KA* 16, p. 174: "The opposite of the naïve . . . is the grotesque or the infinitely arbitrary and contingent (as in the fairy tale and the arabesque);" and *Athenäum* fragment 305, *KA* 2, p. 217: "Just as the naïve deals

with the contradictions between theory and practice, so the grotesque plays with the wonderful permutations of form and matter, loves the illusion of the random and the strange, and as it were, coquettes with infinite arbitrariness."

42. The dualistic elements in the Fantasie have counterparts in the earlier sonatas. In the finale of Opus 11, the first group couples E♭ and C minor (C and A minor in the recapitulation), while the second group brings together A and F♯ minor (E♭ and C minor in the recapitulation). The most thoroughgoing employment of pairing, however, comes in the first movement of Opus 14, its second group laid out as follows:

Measure	Thematic Element	Tonality
26	a1-*cantabile*	Cm/E♭
38	b1-March	E♭
54	b2-March	→
62	*animato* interlude	A♭
	(on first group, mm. 8ff.)	
70	a2	A♭
76	b3	A♭
84	b4	→V/Cm

Not only do we have two varied presentations of the same thematic complex (first in Cm/E♭, then in A♭), but the complex itself is comprised of two thematic ideas, *cantabile* and march, the second of which is varied within each complex. The entire pattern is then repeated at the lower fifth in the recapitulation.

43. *KA* 11, p. 89.
44. *Fragmente zur Litteratur und Poesie,* no. 429; *KA* 16, p. 121.
45. See Polheim, *Die Arabeske,* pp. 221–22.
46. *Fragmente zur Litteratur und Poesie,* nos. 137, 463; *KA* 16, pp. 96, 123.
47. *Fragmente zur Poesie und Litteratur II,* no. 182; *KA* 16, p. 269. On the interdependence of *Parekbase* and *Arabeske,* see Polheim, *Die Arabeske,* pp. 219–22.
48. Carolyn Abbate, *Unsung Voices: Opera and Musical Narrative in the Nineteenth Century* (Princeton, N.J.: Princeton University Press, 1991), pp. 14–19, 21–29.
49. For further details on the motivic interrelationships between and among the *Im Legendenton,* the Beethoven allusion, and the surrounding music, see Gruber, "Robert Schumann: Fantasie op. 17," pp. 107–15; Montgomery, "Myth of Organicism," pp. 48–53; and my "Schumann's 'Im Legendenton' and Friedrich Schlegel's *Arabeske,*" *19th-Century Music* 11, no. 2 (1987): 157.
50. See Schneider, "'Im Legendenton,'" pp. 556–57. Schlegel himself supplies an interesting connection between *Legende* and *Arabeske* in *Fragmente zur Poesie und Litteratur II,* no. 376: "Sagas, fairy tales, and novellas deal with real life; arabesques, pastoral poetry, and legends are all poetic poetry—representations of art, of poetry, of artistic people and the poetic life" (*KA* 16, p. 284).
51. "Sonaten für das Clavier," *NZfM* 10 (1839): 138; *GS* 1, p. 399.
52. *KA* 2, p. 337.
53. *KA* 2, p. 331.
54. *KA* 2, p. 331.
55. See "Etüden für das Pianoforte," *NZfM* 10 (1839): 74; *GS* 1, p. 389.
56. *KA* 2, pp. 318–19.
57. *TB* 1, pp. 82–83.
58. On Schumann's fascination with the works of Jean Paul, see, among other studies, Robert L. Jacobs, "Schumann and Jean Paul," *Music and Letters* 30 (1949): 250–58; Leon Plantinga, *Schumann as Critic* (New Haven, Conn.: Yale University Press, 1967), pp. 63ff.; and Frauke Otto, *Schumann als Jean Paul Leser* (Frankfurt: Haag & Herchen, 1984).

59. See Newcomb, "Schumann and Late Eighteenth-Century Narrative Strategies," p. 169.

60. "In all of his works, Jean Paul mirrors himself, but always in two people; he is Albano and Schoppe, Siebenkäs and Leibgeber, Vult and Walt. . . . Only the single Jean Paul could bind together, within himself alone, such differing pairs; it is superhuman, yet such is Jean Paul: he always yokes together sharp contrasts, if not extremes, in his work and in himself" (diary entry of May 1828, *TB* 1, p. 82).

61. "Die C-dur Sinfonie von Schubert," *NZfM* 12 (1840): 82, *GS* 1, p. 463.

62. "Neue Sonaten für das Pianoforte," *NZfM* 14 (1841): 39; *GS* 2, p. 13.

63. *Athenäum* fragment 421, *KA* 2, pp. 246–47; according to Schlegel's tongue-in-cheek account, Jean Paul was an author "who hasn't control of the basic principles of art, cannot express a bon mot purely, cannot tell a story well, at least not according to what is accepted as good storytelling," and in spite of it all is still a great poet. He noted similarly in the *Gespräch über die Poesie*: "The negligible story is told too poorly to serve as a story; one must merely guess at it. But if one wanted to put it together, and simply relate it, it would at best come out as a confession" (*KA* 2, p. 329). In his 1812 manuscript notebook "Zur Poesie und Literatur," Schlegel simply stated that Jean Paul was one of the main practitioners of the modern "arabesque- and humor-*Roman*" (see Polheim, *Die Arabeske,* p. 205).

64. *BrKG* 1, p. 100.

65. The following draws on the useful account in Blackall, *Novels of the German Romantics,* pp. 71–94.

66. Letter to Clara of 17 March 1838, in Robert Schumann and Clara Schumann, *Briefe einer Liebe,* ed. Hanns-Josef Ortheil (Königstein: Athenäum Verlag, 1982), p. 85.

67. The *mise en abyme* figured in the works of other early nineteenth-century writers (who probably learned it from Cervantes) as well. For an account of its role in Novalis's *Heinrich von Ofterdingen,* see Tzvetan Todorov, "A Poetic Novel," in *Genres in Discourse,* trans. Catherine Porter (Cambridge: Cambridge University Press, 1990), pp. 56–58, and Lucien Dällenbach, *The Mirror in the Text,* trans. Jeremy Whiteley and Emma Hughes (Chicago: University of Chicago Press, 1989), pp. 67–70.

68. See also the commentary in Dällenbach, *Mirror in the Text,* pp. 36–37.

69. "Clara zugeeignet von Florestan und Eusebius," *NZfM* 5 (1836): 135.

70. F. Gustav Jansen, ed., *Robert Schumanns Briefe: Neue Folge,* 2d ed. (Leipzig: Breitkopf & Härtel, 1904), p. 157.

71. "Leipziger Musikleben 1837/38," *NZfM* 8 (1838): 116; *GS* 1, p. 380. Though Schumann was referring specifically to the String Quartets, Op. 127 and Op. 131, these remarks might well be extended to the entire corpus of late music.

72. See Schumann's review of a 28 March 1834 performance of *Christus am Ölberg* and the *Missa solemnis* in *NZfM* 1 (1834): 8; *GS* 1, pp. 16–17.

73. Schumann sensed a "spiritual relatedness" between Mendelssohn's Opus 6 and Beethoven's A-Major Piano Sonata, Opus 101; see "Sonaten für Pianoforte," *NZfM* 3 (1835): 207 8; *GS* 1, p. 124. He likewise compared the character of Julius Schapler's "Preisquartett" to the affective sequence of movements in Beethoven's A-Minor String Quartet, Opus 132. See *NZfM* 16 (1842); *GS* 2, p. 71.

74. Review of piano sonatas by Lacombe, Heller, and Grund, *NZfM* 11 (1839): 185.

75. Concert report for the Brockhausschen *Allgemeine Zeitung,* 3 January 1840; *GS* 1, p. 420. For an excellent account of Schumann's enthusiasm for the late quartets, an enthusiasm he shared with composer-critic Hermann Hirschbach, see Marston, "Schumann's Monument to Beethoven," pp. 249–51.

76. "Preisquartett von Julius Schapler," *NZfM* 16 (1842): 142; *GS* 2, p. 71.

77. *NZfM* 12 (1840); *GS* 1, p. 463.

78. True, most of Schumann's comments on the late quartets date from the late 1830s and early 1840s. Among the first references are a diary entry of 11 November 1837, "heard Beethoven's C$^\sharp$-Minor Quartet [Op. 131] for the first time" (*TB* 2, p. 45), and a brief account of this performance along with that of the Quartet in E$^\flat$, Op. 127, in a review

of 10 April 1838 ("Rückblick auf das Musikleben 1837/38," *NZfM* 8 [1838]: 116; *GS* 1, p. 380). Both references thus date from a time when the Fantasie was complete in some form. But Schumann's first having heard the Opp.127/131 Quartets performed in 1837 does not preclude earlier study. His dithyrambic praise for the works in the "Leipziger Musikleben" review of 1838 (see note 71) sounds like that of an individual already familiar with them. Also, it is impossible to say what shape the Fantasie had taken by the fall of 1837. The version that Schumann offered to Kistner in December 1836 (see Erler, *Schumann's Leben,* vol. 1, pp. 101–3) is presumably lost; most probably this was the same version that Tobias Haslinger received the following month (see Schumann's letter of 31 January 1837 to Haslinger, in *Briefe und Gedichte aus dem Album Robert und Clara Schumann,* ed. Wolfgang Boetticher [Leipzig: VEB Deutscher Verlag für Musik, 1979], p. 262), and that he listed as a "Sonate f. Beethoven" in an October 1837 diary entry (*TB* 2, p. 42). The subsequent history of the Fantasie is equally obscure. Although Schumann indicated in a letter to Raimund Härtel of 4 February 1838 (Erler, *Schumann's Leben,* vol. 1, p. 139) and a diary entry of 31 March 1838 (*TB* 2, p. 53) that he was at work on revisions, we do not know what exactly he was revising or what the revisions amounted to (the 31 March diary entry is preceded by another of 20 March that the describes the Fantasie as complete; see *TB* 2, p. 52). Nor can the earlier version of the Fantasie (with the subsequently deleted reference to the *An die ferne Geliebte* music at the end of the third movement) transmitted in Budapest, National Széchényi Library, Ms. Mus. 37, the *Stichvorlage* for the 1839 printing, be dated with any certainty. All that can be said is that the Fantasie as we know it was complete by 19 December 1838, the date of the *Stichvorlage*.

79. The literature on Beethoven's late-period instrumental music is vast; but on the specific question of its status as a kind of musical "critique" of classical forms, see Dahlhaus, *Nineteenth-Century Music,* pp. 84–87; and Rudolf Stephan, "Zu Beethovens letzten Quartetten," *Musikforschung* 23 (1970): 249–56.

80. "Leipziger Musikleben 1837/38," *NZfM* 8 (1838): 116; *GS* 1, p. 380.

81. The inelegant move from A♭ to E♭ is matched by the abrupt leap from tonic to dominant that makes do as a transition in the exposition (mm. 37ff.).

82. "Sonaten für das Clavier," *NZfM* 10 (1839): 135; *GS* 1, p. 396.

83. Entry for early September [1–7?] 1836; *TB* 2, p. 25.

84. In a letter to Clara of 19 March 1838, however, Schumann wrote that he had drafted the Fantasie in June 1836 (*BrKG* 1, p. 126); and in another letter of 22 April 1839, he linked the Fantasie to "the unhappy summer of 1836" (*BrKG* 1, p. 495). There is a good chance that Schumann's predating of his first ideas for the work was off by several months. In an 1838 chronicle of his compositional activities (see *TB* 1, p. 422), he placed the Opus 14 *Concert sans Orchestre* in the summer of 1836, while the Fantasie was not mentioned at all. Letters to Simonin de Sire (15 March 1839) and Carl Koßmaly (5 May 1843) put the Fantasie in 1836 plain and simple, and thus are not much help (Erler, *Schumann's Leben,* vol. 1, pp. 193–94, 297); neither is Schumann's comment to Clara in a letter of 26 January 1839 that the Fantasie was composed when they were unhappily separated (i.e., from February 1836 to August 1837; see *BrKG* 2, p. 369). As all these references come some time after the completion of the earliest version of the Fantasie in December 1836, priority should probably be given to the September 1836 diary entry cited in the text above (see also Roesner, "Schumann's 'Parallel' Forms," pp. 272–73). Further support for localizing the principal work on the first version of the Fantasie in the fall, as opposed to the summer of 1836, is provided by a sketch for a "Trio zur Polonaise" dated 30 November 1836; this material, in altered form, eventually found its way into the third movement of the Fantasie, mm. 34ff. (see Edler, *Robert Schumann,* p. 141). For an alternate account of the dating of the Fantasie, see Marston, "Comment and Chronicle," p. 166.

85. Although Schumann did not send off the review until 13 October 1831, significant

portions had been sketched by mid-July; see his diary entry for 17 July 1831, *TB* 1, p. 351.
86. *TB* 2, p. 26.
87. Erler, *Schumann's Leben,* vol. 1, pp. 94–95.
88. "F. Chopin," *NZfM* 15 (1841), p. 141; *GS* 2, p. 31.
89. For discussions of Chopin's continued cultivation of interruptive episodes in the F$^\sharp$-Minor Polonaise, Opus 44, the Fantasie, Opus 49, and the A$^\flat$-Major Polonaise-fantasie, Opus 61, see Jeffrey Kallberg, "Chopin's Last Style," *JAMS* 38 (1985): 269–70, 273–74, 294–96, and Jim Samson, *The Music of Chopin* (London: Routledge & Kegan Paul, 1985), pp. 108, 199, 206, 210.
90. See also Samson's description, *Music of Chopin,* pp. 178–79.
91. Schumann might have been thinking of places like this when he wrote, in his review of the B$^\flat$-Minor Sonata, Opus 35, that Chopin, like Jean Paul, had his "knotty clauses and parentheses over which one shouldn't tarry too long on a first reading" (*NZfM* 14 [1841]: 39; *GS* 2, p. 13).
92. The A-Minor goal of the Ballade is already hinted at in the opening A1 section (see mm. 18ff. and 35ff.). For a detailed description of the tipping of the tonal balance from F to A minor, see Harald Krebs's quasi-Schenkerian account, "Alternatives to Monotonality in Early Nineteenth-Century Music," *Journal of Music Theory* 25 (1981): 11–13.
93. In this regard, the two compositions stand in inverse relationship to one another. The emerging *Hauptwerk* in the Fantasie is a dreamy aside, in the Ballade, a vehement *presto con fuoco.*
94. Chopin's rhapsodic engagement with the "higher forms" would come later, in the Fantasie, Opus 49, and the Polonaise-fantasie, Opus 61 (the latter in essence a tone poem for piano).
95. "Sinfonie von Hector Berlioz," *NZfM* 3 (1835): 33; *GS* 1, p. 70.
96. "Sonaten für das Klavier," *NZfM* 10 (1839): 134; *GS* 1, p. 395.
97. *GS* 2, p. 207.
98. See "Etüden für das Pianoforte," *NZfM* 10 (1839): 74 (*GS* 1, p. 389); "Für Pianoforte," *NZfM* 21 (1844): 58 (*GS* 2, p. 348); and "Sonaten für das Clavier," *NZfM* 10 (1839): 134 (*GS* 1, p. 395).
99. *NZfM* 2 (1835): 127; *GS* 1, p. 59.
100. See Roesner, "Schumann's 'Parallel' Forms," pp. 276–78.
101. Linda Roesner has pointed out connections between mm. 5–6 of the Fantasie's last movement and several spots in the first: the right hand alludes to the closing theme of the *Im Legendenton* (mm. 216–19), the left hand to the rhythmic-melodic shape of the first movement's main theme ("Schumann's 'Parallel' Forms," p. 276). Still, the subtlety of the references borders on the oblique. Opus 11 features a more apparent web of thematic ties: melodic elements from the first-movement *Introduzione* (mm. 22ff) recur as the main theme of the second movement. Likewise, the *Andantino* of Opus 14, a set of variations on a theme by Clara Wieck, serves as a motivic repository for the other movements: its opening gesture parallels the head motive of the first movement, while the beginning of variation 4 hearkens to the principal scherzo theme.
102. The earlier ending is reproduced in Robert Schumann, *Fantasie Opus 17,* ed. Wolfgang Boetticher (Munich: Henle, 1987), p. 39.
103. Several years later, Schumann would criticize just this feature of Mendelssohn's *Midsummer Night's Dream* music: "I was struck by the fact that fragments of the overture often appeared in later movements, and would take issue only with the almost literal recurrence of the close of the overture in the finale. The composer's intention to round off the whole is clear, but it seems to me to have been too rationally realized" (*NZfM* 20 [1844]: 7; *GS* 2, p. 156).
104. See Schumann's comments on Ch. G. Müller's Third Symphony, *NZfM* 2 (1835): 48; *GS* 1, pp. 67–68.

105. "Neue Sonaten für das Pianoforte," *NZfM* 14 (1841): 39; *GS* 2, p. 13: "That [Chopin] called [his Op. 35] a sonata is certainly a caprice, if not a downright presumption, for he has simply harnessed together four of his wildest children, hoping with this name to smuggle them into a place where they wouldn't otherwise be admitted."

3. Schumann's Systems of Musical Fragments and *Witz*

1. Carl Koßmaly, "Ueber Robert Schumann's Claviercompositionen," *AmZ* 44 (1844): col. 17.
2. Franz Brendel, "Robert Schumann mit Rücksicht auf Mendelssohn-Bartholdy," *NZfM* 22 (1845): 92.
3. Letter to Robert of 3 March 1838, *BrKG* 1, p. 108. Cf. her plea in a letter of 4 April 1839: "Listen Robert, can't you just once compose something brilliant, and easily understandable" (*BrKG* 2, p. 469).
4. Letter to Clara of 15 April 1838, *BrKG* 1, p. 146.
5. *TB* 1, p. 397.
6. Letter to Henriette Voigt of 22 April 1838, quoted in Wolfgang Boetticher, *Robert Schumanns Klavierwerke: Neue biographische und textkritische Untersuchungen*, vol. 1, *Opus 1–6* (Wilhelmshaven: Heinrichshofen's Verlag, 1976), p. 165.
7. See his letter to J. W. von Wasielewski of 1 January 1857; in *Franz Liszt's Briefe*, ed. La Mara (Leipzig: Breitkopf & Härtel, 1893), vol. 1, p. 257.
8. Letter to Schumann of 5 June 1839, *Franz Liszt's Briefe*, vol. 1, p. 27.
9. *AmZ* 46 (1844): col. 36.
10. *AmZ* 35 (1833): col. 616.
11. *NZfM* 22 (1845): 82. For a recent echoing of this point of view, see Andreas Traub, "Die 'Kinderszenen' als zyklisches Werk," *Musica* 35 (1981): 425.
12. *AmZ* 46 (1844): 20.
13. Quoted from a June 1832 review (*Caecilia*), in Boetticher, *Robert Schumanns Klavierwerke*, vol. 1, p. 54.
14. Letter to Robert of 4 April 1839, *BrKG* 2, p. 469.
15. See also the discussion in Peter Kaminsky, "Principles of Formal Structure in Schumann's Early Piano Cycles," *Music Theory Spectrum* 11, no. 2 (1989): 213–16.
16. *NZfM* 16 (1842): 174.
17. See *NZfM* 1 (1834): 113–14; 14 (1841): 181; 17 (1837): 200; and 19 (1843): 35. Similarly, Coleridge tried to convince Wordsworth on more than one occasion to write more than "little poems." See Thomas McFarland, *Romanticism and the Forms of Ruin: Wordsworth, Coleridge, and Modalities of Fragmentation* (Princeton, N.J.: Princeton University Press, 1981), p. 20.
18. See the discussion of Rellstab's 1834 review (in *Iris*) of the Opus 4 Intermezzi, and the upset it caused Schumann, in Boetticher, *Robert Schumanns Klavierwerke*, vol. 1, p. 113.
19. See the outline of Adorno's unremittingly bleak account of fragmentation in nineteenth-century music in Subotnik, *Developing Variations*, pp. 122, 209–11, 219.
20. *Fragmente zur Litteratur und Poesie* nos. 960 and 1068, *KA* 16, pp. 166, 173.
21. *Fragmente zur Litteratur und Poesie* no. 524, *KA* 16, p. 128.
22. *Philosophische Fragmente, Erste Epoche II,* no. 301, *KA* 18, p. 48.
23. *Philosophische Fragmente, Zweite Epoche II,* no. 118, *KA* 18, p. 333.
24. *Athenäum Fragmente* no. 225, *KA* 2, p. 201.
25. *Fragmente zur Litteratur und Poesie* no. 536, *KA* 16, p. 129.
26. *Athenäum Fragmente* no. 216, *KA* 2, p. 198.
27. *Athenäum Fragmente* no. 26, *KA* 2, p. 169.
28. *Fragmente zur Litteratur und Poesie* no. 1001, *KA* 16, p. 168.
29. Cf. the suggestive appraisal in Harald Eggebrecht, "Töne sind höhere Worte," *Musik-*

Konzepte 1 (1981): 115; Schumann's piano music is characterized, according to the author, by its "manifold fractures, dissociation, and incongruities."

30. Patrick McCreless, "Song Order in the Song Cycle: Schumann's *Liederkreis*, Op. 39," *Music Analysis* 5 (1986):. 5–10; Jonathan Dunsby, "The multi-piece in Brahms: *Fantasien* Op. 116," in *Brahms: Biographical, Documentary, and Analytical Studies* (Cambridge: Cambridge University Press, 1983), pp. 167–74; P. Kaminsky, "Principles of Formal Structure," passim; and idem, "Aspects of Harmony, Rhythm, and Form in Schumann's 'Papillons,' 'Carnaval,' and 'Davidsbündlertänze'" (PhD diss., University of Rochester, 1990).

31. *Athenäum Fragmente* no. 77, *KA* 2, p. 176.

32. *Philosophische Fragmente, Zweite Epoche I,* no. 462, *KA* 18, p. 232.

33. I will take up Schumann's response to Jean Paul's aesthetics at a later point; for references to his youthful appreciation of Novalis and Hoffmann, see *TB* 1, pp. 96, 336–37, 354.

34. Letter to Clara, 13 July 1833, *BrKG* 1, p. 7.

35. To what might he have been referring in a tantalizing diary entry of 5 June 1831: "ueber Beethoven'sche u. Schubert'sche Fragmente"? See *TB* 1, p. 337.

36. *NZfM* 1 (1834): 151.

37. *TB* 1, pp. 336–37.

38. Eggebrecht, "Töne sind höhere Worte," p. 109.

39. It is worth mentioning here that a year after the *Papillons* were published Schumann wrote to Breitkopf (letter of 22 November 1832) of his having completed "XII Burlesken [Burle] nach Art der Papillons"); Erler, *Schumann's Leben,* vol. 1, p. 34. Although the collection never appeared in print, the letter reference attests to the strength of the *Papillons* idea.

40. *TB* 1, p. 407.

41. See Schumann's diary entry for 9 June 1832, *TB* 1, p. 407; and his comments in a letter to Clara of 24 January 1839: "In *Carnaval* one piece continually annuls the other: something that not all listeners can endure. But in the *Phantasiestücke,* you can spread yourself out quite comfortably" (*Jugendbriefe,* p. 298).

42. "At present there is no genre fragmentary in both content and form, at once completely subjective and individual, completely objective and like a necessary part in a system of all sciences" (*Athenäum Fragmente* no. 77, *KA* 2, p. 176).

43. See his letters to Simonin de Sire and Carl Koßmaly of 8 February 1838, 15 March 1839, 5 May 1843, and post-January 1844; Erler, *Schumann's Leben,* vol. 1, pp. 142, 192, 296, 304.

44. *BrKG* 2, p. 435.

45. In a letter of 11 August 1839 to Henriette Voigt, Schumann described the *Blumenstück* as a less "melancholy" but also less "significant" work than the Humoreske.

46. Letter to Th. Töpken of 5 April 1833; Erler, *Schumann's Leben,* vol. 1, p. 37.

47. For a discussion of the quotations in Schumann's music as manifestations of romantic irony, see Heinz J. Dill, "Romantic Irony in the Works of Robert Schumann," *Musical Quarterly* 73 (1989): 176.

48. Letter to Clara, 24 January 1839, *BrKG* 2, p. 367.

49. The conjecture is even embedded in the compositional history of some works. To take an example: what eventually became the eleventh of the *Papillons* drew liberally on drafts of two independently conceived polonaises, works that are in a sense "quoted" in Opus 2. See Gerhard Dietel, *"Eine neue poetische Zeit": Musikanschauung und stilistischen Tendenzen im Klavierwerk Robert Schumanns* (Kassel: Bärenreiter, 1989), p. 56.

50. See Schumann's diary entries for 5 June 1831, *TB* 1, pp. 336–37.

51. The terminal fragmentation in No. 7 of the *Davidsbündlertänze* may be viewed in the same light.

52. Entry of 28 May 1832, *TB* 1, p. 399.
53. Diary entry for 9 June 1832, *TB* 1, p. 407.
54. The sequence of tonalities in Schumann's *Entwurf* for an earlier, ten-movement version of the *Papillons* (given in Boetticher, *Robert Schumanns Klavierwerke,* vol. 1, pp. 75–77) includes only one unusual cleft: between No. 7 in E$^\flat$ (a dance with no equivalent in the final version) and No. 8 in D minor (transposed to C$^\sharp$ minor as No. 8 of the final version). The resultant scheme is perhaps less disruptive than that of the final version, but not, for this reason, any better.
55. Roland Barthes, "Rasch," in *The Responsibility of Forms,* trans. Richard Howard (New York: Hill & Wang, 1985), p. 300.
56. "Loving Schumann," *Responsibility of Forms,* p. 295.
57. For a sensitive account of the subtle harmonic connection of Nos. 17 and 18, see Kaminsky, "Principles of Formal Structure," pp. 222–24.
58. Letter of 15 March 1839; Erler, *Schumann's Leben,* vol. 1, p. 192.
59. See Moscheles's review of the F$^\sharp$-Minor Sonata, Opus 11, in *NZfM* 5 (1836): 136, and Brendel, "Robert Schumann," *NZfM* 22 (1845): 90. Brendel suggests that the "Entgegensetzung" of musical moods in the *Davidsbündlertänze* is no less than the guiding principle for all of Schumann's early music.
60. Jean Paul, *Vorschule der Ästhetik,* in *Werke,* vol. 5, pp. 131–32.
61. Ibid., p. 129.
62. On this point, see Walter Gieseler,"Schumanns frühe Klavierwerke im Spiegel der literarischen Romantik," in Julius Alf and Joseph A. Kruse, eds., *Robert Schumann: Universalgeist der Romantik* (Düsseldorf: Droste, 1981), pp. 73–74.
63. *Beyond Good and Evil* (1886), trans. Walter Kaufman (New York: Vintage Books, 1966), p. 181.
64. Letter to Clara of 15 April 1838, *BrKG* 1, p. 146.
65. *GS* 1, p. 107.
66. *GS* 1, p. 389.
67. *GS* 1, p. 252.
68. Letter of 17 March 1838, *Jugendbriefe,* p. 280.
69. Schumann justified what was in the 1830s still deemed an unusual practice in a review of Karl Mayer's Opus 31 (a set of variations on a theme by Auber). Mayer's D$^\flat$ introduction and F-major variations demonstrated that "one can begin and end in different keys and still compose quite nicely. To be sure, this should remain an exception, though it needn't be prohibited" (*NZfM* 5 [1836]: 80).
70. For a more extended discussion of this point, see Kaminsky, "Aspects of Harmony, Rhythm, and Form," pp. 89–92. A comparable case is provided by No. 15 of the *Davidsbündlertänze,* whose framing B$^\flat$-major vamps enclose a central binary structure in E$^\flat$.
71. Letter of 7 August 1839 to Ernst Becker, *Briefe, Neue Folge,* p. 166.
72. Entry for 13 August 1828, *TB* 1, p. 105.
73. See *TB* 1, pp. 133, 142.
74. Letter to G. A. Keferstein of 31 January 1840; Erler, *Schumann's Leben,* vol. 1, p. 222.
75. See *KA* 2 (frag. 220), p. 200; *KA* 3, p. 84; *KA* 16 (frag. 882), p. 160; *KA* 18 (frag. 729), p. 381.
76. Cf. Schlegel, *Philosophische Fragmente 1796,* no. 14, *KA* 18, p. 507; Jean Paul, *Vorschule,* in *Werke,* vol. 5, p. 172: *Witz* allows the discovery of "relationships between incommensurable magnitudes, similarities between the physical and spiritual worlds"; and Novalis, *Das Allgemeine Brouillon,* frag. 732: "*Witz* is creative—it creates similarities" (*Schriften* 3, p. 410).
77. *Philosophische Fragmente, Erste Epoche III,* frag. 149, *KA* 18, p. 134.
78. *Ideen,* frag. 26; *KA* 2, p. 258. Cf. also *Kritische Fragmente,* no. 90: "*Witz* is an explosion of constrained spirit" (*KA* 2, p. 158); Jean Paul's comments on the "lightning flash" and

"electric charge" of *Witz* in the *Vorschule,* in *Werke* 5, pp. 197, 199; and Novalis's *Logologische Fragmente,* no. 441: "*Witz* is spiritual electricity" (*Schriften* 2, p. 621).

79. See *Athenäum Fragmente,* no. 366: "Understanding is mechanical, wit is chemical, genius is organic spirit" (*KA* 2, p. 232), and *Philosophische Fragmente, Zweite Epoche I,* no. 813: "*Witz* merely consists of the synthesis of dichotomies" (*KA* 18, p. 262).
80. Manfred Frank makes this point in *Einführung in die frühromantische Ästhetik* (Frankfurt: Suhrkamp, 1989), p. 295.
81. *Fragmente zur Litteratur und Poesie,* no. 542, *KA* 16, p. 129.
82. See *Athenäum Fragmente,* no. 220, *KA* 2, p. 200; *Zur Poesie und Litteratur II,* frag. 165, *KA* 16, pp. 267–68; *Philosophische Fragmente, Zweite Epoche I,* no. 379, *KA* 18, p. 226; *Zur Poesie und Litteratur,* frag. 287, *KA* 16, p. 277; and *Athenäum Fragmente,* no. 426, *KA* 2, pp. 248–49.
83. *Philosophische Fragmente, Zweite Epoche I,* no. 462: "The system of chemical fragments must culminate in an apotheosis of *Witz*" (*KA* 18, p. 232). Cf. also the remarks in *Die Entwicklung der Philosophie in Zwölf Büchern* (1804–5), *KA* 12, p. 392: "The activity . . . through which consciousness most clearly manifests itself as a fragment is *Witz,* whose essence consists precisely in the quality of rupture, and emerges from the ruptured, derivative nature of consciousness itself."
84. *Philosophische Fragmente, Zweite Epoche II,* no. 177, *KA* 18, p. 337.
85. *Philosophische Fragmente, Zweite Epoche II,* no. 729, *KA* 18, p. 381.
86. "Lessings Gedanken und Meinungen" (1804), *KA* 3, p. 84.
87. Ibid., p. 84.
88. According to *Kritische Fragmente,* no. 96, "enigmatic" ideas are the "wittiest" of all, for they demand "unriddling" (*KA* 2, p. 158).
89. Cf. Karl Solger's commentary on *Witz* in his *Erwin* (1816) as emerging through "relationships and opposites, and not by means of unfolding and development," quoted in Kathleen Wheeler, *German Aesthetic and Literary Criticism: The Romantic Ironists and Goethe* (Cambridge: Cambridge University Press, 1984), p. 145.
90. "Aspects of Harmony, Rhythm, and Form," p. 4; cf. McCreless, "Song Order," p. 6.
91. "Variationen für Pianoforte," *NZfM* 5 (1836): 67.
92. "Schumanns Kinderszenen: quasi Thema mit Variationen," *Musik-Konzepte, Sonderband: Robert Schumann II* (December 1982): 275–98.
93. See his letter to Clara of 24 January 1839: "Also, I've finished some variations, but *not* on a theme: I'll call the work Guirlande [a reference to the Opus 18 Arabeske?]," (*BrKG* 2, p. 367). Schumann also drew attention to Heinrich Elkamp's Opus 15, a "riddle without a solution," for its singular conception as a series of "themeless" variations (*NZfM* 5 [1836], p. 68).
94. *KA* 2, p. 197.
95. Letter to H. Hirschbach, 30 June 1839, Erler, *Schumann's Leben,* vol. 1, pp. 206–7.
96. Letter of 30 June 1839, *BrKG* 2, p. 608.
97. Letter to Clara, 6 February 1838, *BrKG* 1, p. 91.
98. See his letters of 5 May 1843 and post-January 1844[?] to Carl Koßmaly, Erler, *Schumann's Leben,* vol. 1, pp. 296, 304.
99. Letter to Clara, 6 February 1838, *BrKG* 1, p. 90.
100. See also Newcomb, "Schumann and the Marketplace," in *Nineteenth-Century Piano Music,* pp. 298–99.
101. *BrKG* 1, p. 100.
102. As noted above, the principal work on the *Novelletten* occurred during the first four months of 1838; see Schumann's diary entries for 19–24 January (*TB* 2, p. 50), 2 February ("Macbeth-Novellette gemacht," a reference to the Intermezzo of no. 3; *TB* 2, p. 50), 12 March, 20 March, 1–10 April, 22 April (including references to nos. 2 and 5, and to ordering the pieces already composed; *TB* 2, pp. 52–54), and 30 August ("die Novellet-

ten ganz in Ordnung gebracht," *TB* 2, p. 64). On 13 April Schumann reported to Clara that since his last letter (4 April) he had finished "ein ganzes Heft neuer Dinge" (*BrKG* 1, p. 138), although what is now the last piece of the set was not completed until 3 May (*TB* 2, p. 55). Five days later, he offered the work to Joseph Fischof for publication (Erler, *Schumann's Leben,* vol. 1, p. 154). The *Novelletten,* therefore, were conceived before but finished after the *Kreisleriana,* and did not appear in print until June 1839; see Schumann's letters, both of 30 June 1839, to H. Hirschbach and Clara (ibid., vol. 1, pp. 206–7; *BrKG* 2, p. 608).

103. The B-Minor *Novellette* that eventually found its way into the *Bunte Blätter,* Opus 99, likewise features a middle section in D.
104. Barthes, "Loving Schumann," in *Responsibility of Forms,* p. 296.
105. See his letters to H. Hirschbach and Clara, both of 30 June 1839; Erler, *Schumann's Leben,* vol. 1, pp. 206–7; *BrKG* 2, p. 608.
106. See Schumann's letters of 3 April 1838 and 30 June 1839; Erler, *Schumann's Leben,* vol. 1, pp. 151, 206–7.
107. Letter to Clara of 1 December 1839, *BrKG* 2, p. 809.
108. See Schumann's diary entry for 30 August 1838: "die Novelletten ganz in Ordnung gebracht" (*TB* 2, p. 64).
109. Barthes, "Rasch," in *Responsibility of Forms,* p. 300.
110. On the "Ganzheit" issue and Schumann's sometimes patchwork compositional method, see Gerhard Dietel, *"Eine neue poetische Zeit": Musikanschauung und stilistische Tendenzen im Klavierwerk Robert Schumanns* (Kassel: Bärenreiter, 1989), pp. 55–56. Schumann's adoption of "classical" developmental techniques is treated in Waldura, *Monomotivik, Sequenz und Sonatenform,* passim; and the teleology of his miniature collections in Kaminsky, "Aspects of Harmony, Rhythm, and Form," pp. 145, 178–79, and idem, "Principles of Formal Structure," p. 213.
111. Cf. Franz Brendel on the contemporary musical scene: "The comprehensive whole, previously continuous and closed, disintegrated into its various parts; isolated moods, which in earlier times had comprised only moments of a larger whole, now became independent entities" (in "Robert Schumann mit Rücksicht auf Mendelssohn-Bartholdy," *NZfM* 22 [1845], p. 82).
112. On the question of reordering, see Boetticher, "Weitere Forschungen an Dokumenten zum Leben und Schaffen Robert Schumanns," in *Robert Schumann: Ein romantisches Erbe in neuer Forschung* (Düsseldorf: Robert-Schumann-Gesellschaft, 1984), p. 46. For studies of individual works, see Boetticher, *Robert Schumanns Klavierwerke,* vol. 1, pp. 75–77 (*Papillons*), and Linda Correll Roesner, "The Sources for Schumann's *Davidsbündlertänze,* Op. 6: Composition, Textual Problems, and the Role of the Composer as Editor," in *Mendelssohn and Schumann: Essays on Their Music and Its Context,* ed. Jon W. Finson and R. Larry Todd (Durham: Duke University Press, 1984), pp. 54–58.
113. Walter Benjamin, *The Origin of German Tragic Drama* (1928), trans. John Osborne (London: New Left Books, 1977), pp. 176, 186.
114. Ibid., p. 188.
115. For a detailed analysis, see Newcomb, "Once More between Absolute and Program Music."
116. *KA* 2, p. 159.

4. *Euryanthe* and the Artwork as Critique

1. Walter Benjamin, *Das Passagen-Werk* (Frankfurt: Suhrkamp, 1982), vol. 1, p. 574.
2. Notice of 23 September 1847, *GS* 2, p. 161.
3. Franz Liszt, "Weber's *Euryanthe*" (1854), *Gesammelte Schriften,* vol. 3/i (Leipzig: Breitkopf & Härtel, 1881), pp. 16–17.
4. See Eduard Hanslick, "Aus Deutschlands romantischer Schule (Beethoven. Weber.

Marschner)," in *Die moderne Oper: Kritiken und Studien* (Berlin: Hofmann, 1875), p. 69; and Hugo Wolf, "Euryanthe," in *The Music Criticism of Hugo Wolf,* trans. Henry Pleasants (New York: Holmes & Meier, 1978), p. 245. According to Tovey, *Euryanthe,* with its dozen or so fully developed leitmotives, is a more developed Wagnerian music drama than *Lohengrin* ("Weber. Overture, *Euryanthe,*" in *Essays in Musical Analysis,* vol. 4, *Illustrative Music* [London: Oxford University Press, 1937], pp. 54–55). And Anna Amalie Abert, in "Webers 'Euryanthe' und Spohrs 'Jessonda' also große Opern," in *Festschrift Walter Wiora* (Kassel: Bärenreiter, 1967), p. 439, states flatly that *Euryanthe* is a "music drama that points directly to the young Wagner."

5. Richard Wagner, *Opera and Drama,* in *Prose Works* [hereafter *PW*] vol. 2, trans. William Ashton Ellis (London: Routledge & Kegan Paul, 1893), pp. 83–85. Wagner's critique is discussed in detail in Michael C. Tusa, "Richard Wagner and Weber's *Euryanthe,*" *19th-Century Music* 9 (1986): 206–21.

6. Bernhard Adamy, ". . . eine der genialsten Opernmusikern: unbekannte Anmerkungen zur *Euryanthe,*" *Hans Pfitzner-Gesellschaft Mitteilungen* 49 (1988): 57–58.

7. Micheal C. Tusa, *Euryanthe and Carl Maria von Weber's Dramaturgy of German Opera* (Oxford: Clarendon Press, 1991), pp. 61–68.

8. "Euryanthe, Oper von K. M. Weber" (1823), in *Grillparzers Sämtliche Werke,* ed. August Sauer (Stuttgart: Cotta, 1893), vol. 15, p. 130.

9. "Fragen an die, welche zu antworten wissen," *AmZ* 49 (1826): col. 800; Adolph Bernhard Marx, *Die Kunst des Gesanges* (Berlin: Schlesinger, 1826), p. 232; Amadeus Wendt, "Ueber Weber's Euryanthe: Ein Nachtrag," *Berliner Allgemeine Musikalische Zeitung* 3 (1826): 55–56.

10. *PW* 2, p. 85.

11. Dahlhaus, *Nineteenth-Century Music,* pp. 72–73; cf. also "Wagner's Place in the History of Music," in Ulrich Müller and Peter Wapnewski, eds., *Wagner Handbook,* trans. and ed. by John Deathridge (Cambridge, Mass.: Harvard University Press, 1992; orig. publ. *Richard-Wagner-Handbuch,* Stuttgart, 1986), p. 108.

12. Tusa, *Euryanthe,* p. 275.

13. Carl Maria von Weber, *Writings on Music,* trans. Martin Cooper, ed. John Warrack (Cambridge: Cambridge University Press, 1981), pp. 200–201.

14. See, however, Hermann Danuser's account of "proselike" and musically regulative syntax in Lysiart's Act II Scena ed Aria (no. 10), in *Musikalische Prosa* (Regensburg: Gustav Bosse Verlag, 1975), pp. 41–43; and Tusa'a analyses of the Scene und Chor (no. 4), Euryanthe's Cavatina (no. 5), and her Scena "Schirmende Engelschaar" (no. 16), in *Euryanthe,* pp. 222–29.

15. *KA* 2, pp. 133–34.

16. Quoted in Hanslick, *Die moderne Oper,* p. 71.

17. Tusa, *Euryanthe,* pp. 49–56.

18. Weber, *Writings on Music,* p. 201.

19. See Charles Batteux, *Les beaux arts reduits à un même principe,* rev. ed. (Paris: Durand, 1747), pp. 299ff., and Jean-Jacques Rousseau, *Dictionnaire de musique* (Paris, 1767), p. x: "Opera—a dramatic and lyrical spectacle in which one endeavors to combine all the graces of the fine arts in the representations of a passionate action, with the intention of arousing interest and creating illusion by means of pleasant sensations." Rousseau's account is obviously modeled on Aristotle's famous definition of tragedy in the *Poetics.* For a thorough account of the philosophical background for the *Gesamtkunstwerk* idea, see Stefan Kunze, "Richard Wagners Idee des 'Gesamtkunstwerks,'" in *Beiträge zur Theorie der Künste im 19. Jahrhundert,* vol. 2 (Frankfurt: Klostermann, 1972), pp. 196–229.

20. Max Maria von Weber, *Carl Maria von Weber: Ein Lebensbild* (Leipzig, 1866), vol. 2, pp. 585–86. Cf. also Constantin Floros, "Carl Maria von Weber: Grundsätzliches über sein Schaffen," *Musik-Konkepte* 52 (November 1986), special issue, *Carl Maria von Weber,* p. 9.

21. Friedrich Wilhelm Joseph Schelling, *The Philosophy of Art,* trans. Douglas W. Stott (Minneapolis: University of Minnesota Press, 1989), p. 280. On the point of contact between Weber's aesthetics and Schelling's transcendental idealism, see Mathias S. Viertel, "Carl Maria Weber: Der 'künftige Schreiber einer Ästhetik'," in *Weber: Jenseits des Freischütz,* ed. Friedhelm Krummacher and Heinrich W. Schwab (Kassel: Bärenreiter, 1989), pp. 167–75.

22. See August Wilhelm Schlegel, *Sämmtliche Werke,* vol. 5, p. 64: "The best prescription for the composition of an opera is, take a rapid poetical sketch and then fill up and color the outlines by the other arts. This anarchy of the arts, in which music, dancing, and decoration seek to outdo each other through the lavishness of their most luxuriant charms, constitutes the very essence of opera."

23. Grillparzer, *Werke,* vol. 15, p. 130.

24. Cf. Adolf Müllner, "Ueber Karl Maria von Webers Melodie zu dem Liede der Brunhild im Yngard, Act 5, Sc. 3" (1817), and C. M. v. Weber, "Antwort auf Müllners Bermerkungen" (1817), in *Hinterlassene Schriften von Carl Maria von Weber* (Dresden and Leipzig: Arnoldische Buchhandlung, 1827–28), vol. 3, pp. 25–32.

25. Grillparzer, "Der Freischütz, Oper von Maria Weber" (1821), in *Werke,* vol. 15, pp. 126–29. For a detailed discussion of Grillparzer's thoughts on the text-tone issue, and his notion of "musical prose," see Danuser, *Musikalische Prosa,* pp. 33–50.

26. Ibid., p. 126.

27. For an excellent summary, see Tzvetan Todorov, *Theories of the Symbol,* trans. Catherine Porter (Ithaca, N.Y.: Cornell University Press, 1982; orig. publ. *Théories du symbole,* 1977), pp. 198–218.

28. *Zur Poesie und Litteratur II,* frag. 287, *KA* 16, p. 277.

29. *Ideen zu Gedichten,* frag. 59, *KA* 16, p. 209.

30. See *Philosophische Fragmente, Zweite Epoche I,* frag. 663: "Allegorie ist das Zentrum von poetischen Spiel und Schein" (*KA* 18, p. 249).

31. See *Fragmente zur Litteratur und Poesie,* frag. 957, *KA* 16, p. 165, and *Zur Poesie und Litteratur II,* frag. 148, *KA* 16, p. 266.

32. *Zur Poesie und Litteratur,* frag. 358, *KA* 16, p. 283; *Fragmente zur Poesie und Litteratur II,* frag. 29, *KA* 16, p. 344.

33. *Philosophische Fragmente, Erste Epoche II* (1799), frag. 621, *KA* 18, p. 81.

34. See *Ideen zu Gedichten,* frag. 78, *KA* 16, p. 238, and *Philosophische Fragmente, Zweyte Epoche II,* frag. 315, *KA* 18, p. 347.

35. Manfred Frank, *Das Problem "Zeit" in der deutschen Romantik* (Munich: Winkler, 1972), pp. 28–32. See also *Einführung in die frühromantische Ästhetik,* pp. 291–94.

36. See Weber's comment on his attempts at through-composition in this work in *Writings on Musik,* p. 160.

37. Ibid., p. 160.

38. See also Tusa, *Euryanthe,* pp. 160–80.

39. Ibid., p. 166.

40. "Bemerkungen zur Komp. der Musik des Schauspiels: Preciosa. Von Wolf" (1820), in *Hinterlassene Schriften,* vol. 3, p. 64.

41. "Ueber Weber's Euryanthe," pp. 44–45.

42. Tusa, *Euryanthe,* p. 225.

43. "Ueber Weber's Euryanthe," p. 45.

44. *Writings on Music,* pp. 201–2.

45. *Kritische Fragmente,* no. 14; *KA* 2, p. 148.

46. "Ueber Weber's Euryanthe," p. 44.

47. Ibid.

48. Tusa, *Euryanthe,* p. 225.

49. *Writings on Music,* p. 200.

50. See *Writings on Music,* pp. 302–6, for Weber's tempo indications and general perform-ance suggestions. The metronome markings were subsequently taken up by Ernst Rudorff in his 1866 edition of the full score for Schlesinger.
51. See Tusa, *Euryanthe,* pp. 93–95.
52. Ibid., p. 115. Although Chézy attributed the idea to Weber, it is almost impossible to know exactly who was responsible.
53. Ibid., pp. 116–17.
54. Cf. Tusa, *Euryanthe,* pp. 247–48.

5. Brahms and the Romantic Imperative

1. "Der romantische Imperativ fodert [*sic*] die Mischung aller Dichtarten" (*Fragmente zur Litteratur und Poesie,* no. 586, *KA* 16, p. 134).
2. *Fragmente zur Litteratur und Poesie,* no. 341, *KA* 16, p. 113. See also fragment 420 from the same collection: "Absolute *Roman* = psychological *Roman* + philosophical *Roman* + fantastic *Roman* + absolute mimicry + absolute sentimental-fantastic + absolute poetic drama + rhetorical drama + prophecy" (*KA* 16, p. 120). Schlegel provides a more complete description of the *Roman* in "Die Spanisch-Portugiesische Literatur," from the Paris lectures of 1803–4: "The concept of the *Roman,* as established by Boccaccio and Cervantes, is that of a *Romantic book,* a Romantic composition, in which all forms and genres are blended and inextricably intertwined. . . . It contains historical and rhetorical portions, and dialogues; all of these styles are bound together and interwoven in the most ingenious and artful fashion. Poetic types of every kind—lyric, epic, Romantic [i.e., romancelike], didactic—permeate the whole, and adorn it with luxuriant abundance and diversity in the richest and most brilliant manner. The *Roman* is a Poem of Poems, a whole web of poems" (*KA* 11, pp. 159–60).
3. See, for instance, *Fragmente zur Litteratur und Poesie,* no. 613: "Critical prose must partake of all styles just like Romantic [i.e., novel-like] prose, but in antithetical combi-nation" (*KA* 16, p. 136). Cf. also the discussion in Chapter 1.
4. *Kritische Fragmente,* no. 78, *KA* 2, p. 156.
5. For a detailed account of the encyclopedic character of Beethoven's finale, see also Leo Treitler, "History, Criticism, and Beethoven's Ninth Symphony," *19th-Century Music* 3 (1980): 193–210, reprinted in idem, *Music and the Historical Imagination* (Cambridge, Mass.: Harvard University Press, 1989), pp. 19–45.
6. On the peculiar status of the symphonic cantata as genre, see Carl Dahlhaus, "Zur Prob-lematik der musikalischen Gattungen im 19. Jahrhundert," in *Gattungen der Musik in Einzeldarstellungen, Gedenkschrift Leo Schrade* (Bern and Munich: Francke, 1973), p. 878.
7. Translation quoted from D. Kern Holoman, *Berlioz* (Cambridge: Harvard University Press, 1989), p. 261. Berlioz's foreword is printed in full in *Hector Berlioz: New Edition of the Complete Works,* vol. 18, ed. Kern Holoman, *Roméo et Juliette* (Kassel: Bärenreiter, 1990), p. 2.
8. Related to this phenomenon is the violin-concerto-as-*Gesangsszene,* a genre cultivated by Louis Spohr (Concerto No. 8, *In modo di scena cantante*) and thereafter by Max Bruch (Concerto No. 1, Opus 26), and Antonin Dvořák (Concerto, Opus 53).
9. *Athenäum Fragmente,* no. 324, *KA* 2, p. 221.
10. See *NZfM* 20 (26 February 1844): 66.
11. Holoman, *Berlioz,* p. 261.
12. *Fragmente zur Litteratur und Poesie,* no. 692, *KA* 16, p. 136. Cf. also fragment 589 from the same collection: "In genuine romantic prose all the component parts must be fused [*verschmolzen*] until they neutralize one another" (*KA* 16, p. 134).
13. *Fragmente zur Poesie und Litteratur II,* no. 4, *KA* 16, p. 341. Schlegel apparently contra-

dicts himself in *Zur Poesie und Litteratur II,* no. 4, where idyll and arabesque are said to yield the novella (*KA* 16, p. 294). What counts, though, is the form and not the specific content of the formulas.

14. Brahms provides little help here. He was present at an 1891 performance of all the *Romanzen* by Ludwig Wüllner (see Max Kalbeck, *Johannes Brahms* [Berlin: Deutsche Brahms-Gesellschaft, 1912–21], vol. 4, p. 224); and the songs' dedicatee, Julius Stockhausen, is known to have done them as a group (Kalbeck, *Brahms,* vol. 1, p. 429). But in a letter of March 1870 to Adolf Schubring, the composer flatly stated: "One should not think of the *Magelone Romanzen* as a totality; furthermore, they have nothing to do with [Tieck's] story. It's only because of a certain German thoroughness that I set them from first to last" (Johannes Brahms, *Briefwechsel* [*BW*], vol. 14 [Berlin: Deutsche Brahms-Gesellschaft, 1920], p. 219). According to Kalbeck, Brahms "was totally against performing all the songs as a cycle" (*Brahms,* vol. 1, p. 428). The *Entstehungsgeschichte* of the *Romanzen,* on the one hand, and their publication history (two volumes of three songs appeared in September 1865, the three remaining books in December 1869), on the other, have been employed to shore up conflicting points of view on the cycle-versus-collection issue. George Bozarth has assembled strong evidence in favor of the idea that several of the supposedly later songs (nos. 7, 8, 12, and 13) were composed before the first six were published; see "Brahms's 'Liederjahr' of 1868," *Music Review* 44 (1983): 215–17. While this might indicate that, his assertions to the contrary aside, Brahms was indeed thinking in cyclic terms, Peter Jost points to the four-year hiatus between the publication of the first series of *Romanzen* and the second as support for his hypothesis that the original idea to write a closed cycle was abandoned after the composition of the first six songs; see "Brahms und die romantische Ironie: Zu den 'Romanzen aus L. Tieck's Magelone' Op. 33," *Archiv für Musikwissenschaft* 47 (1990): 45–47.
15. See Kalbeck, *Brahms,* vol. 1, pp. 439–40.
16. See Malcolm MacDonald, *Brahms* (New York: Schirmer Books, 1990), p. 186; Michael Musgrave, *The Music of Brahms* (London: Routledge & Kegan Paul, 1985), p. 38; and Leon Plantinga, *Romantic Music* (New York: Norton, 1984), p. 431.
17. Cf. Kalbeck, *Brahms,* vol. 1, pp. 429–39; Eric Sams, *Brahms Songs* (Seattle: University of Washington Press, 1972), pp. 25–26; and Thomas Boyer, "Brahms as Count Peter of Provence: A Psychosexual Interpretation of the *Magelone* Poetry," *Musical Quarterly* 66 (1980): 262–86.
18. See, e.g., Jost, "Brahms und die romantische Ironie," pp. 48–49.
19. See *Brahms Songs,* p. 26.
20. See Kalbeck, *Brahms,* vol. 1, p. 424.
21. Eduard Hanslick, *Aus dem Concertsaal: Kritiken und Schilderung aus den letzten 20 Jahren des Wiener Musiklebens* (Vienna, 1870), pp. 100–101. See also the commentary in Edward F. Kravitt, "The Lied in 19th-Century Concert Life," *Journal of the American Musicological Society* 18 (1965): 207–18.
22. See Brahms's comments to Schubring in note 14, above.
23. *Fragmente zur Litteratur und Poesie,* nos. 960 and 1241, *KA* 16, pp. 165–66, 188.
24. A number of *Kunstmärchen* from the period likewise featured interpolated lyrics, e.g., Goethe's *Märchen,* Novalis's *Klingsohrs Märchen,* Eichendorff's *Das Marmorbild,* Brentano's *Das Märchen von dem Myrtenfräulein,* and Tieck's *Der Runenberg.*
25. Peter Jost, however, probably goes too far in suggesting that Brahms intentionally set out to distance himself from Tieck's lyrics. Brahms's affirmative ending for no. 3 ("Sind es Schmerzen"), for instance, is less an out-and-out denial of the sense of the lyric (which Tieck titled "Zweifel" [Doubt] in the *Gesamtausgabe* of his poems) than a simplification. See "Brahms und die romantische Ironie," pp. 50–51.
26. Cf. Frank, *Einführung in die frühromantische Ästhetik,* p. 399.
27. Ludwig Tieck, *Phantasus,* 2d ed. (Berlin: Reimer, 1844–45), vol. 1, p. 131.

28. Cf. his 1870 letter to Schubring, quoted in note 14 above.

29. Kalbeck, *Brahms,* vol. 1, p. 429.

30. Tieck, *Phantasus,* vol. 2, p. 4.

31. Friedrich Schiller, *On Naïve and Sentimental Poetry,* trans. Julius A. Elias (New York: Ungar, 1966), p. 129

32. Ibid., p. 153.

33. See also the discussion in Maynard Solomon, "The Ninth Symphony: A Search for Order," in *Beethoven Essays* (Cambridge: Harvard University Press, 1988), pp. 11–14.

34. *Fragmente zur Litteratur und Poesie,* no. 845, *KA* 16, p. 157.

35. See *Fragmente zur Litteratur und Poesie,* no. 32, *KA* 16, p. 88.

36. *Athenäum Fragmente,* no. 146; *KA* 2, p. 87. Cf. also Peter Szondi's explication of this seminal fragment in "Friedrich Schlegel's Theory of Poetical Genres," in *On Textual Understanding,* p. 87.

37. For a general discussion of several of these, see Robert Pascall, "Some Special Uses of Sonata Form by Brahms," *Soundings* 4 (1974): 58–63.

38. See James Webster's discussion of the first movement of the C-Minor Piano Trio, Opus 101, in "The General and the Particular in Brahms's Later Sonata Forms," in *Brahms Studies: Analytical and Historical Perspectives,* ed. George Bozarth (Oxford: Clarendon Press, 1990), p. 72; Robert Bailey's account of the Third Symphony finale, "Musical Language and Structure in the Third Symphony," *Brahms Studies,* pp. 412–13; and Siegfried Kross's comments on the first movement of the G-Minor Piano Quartet, Opus 25, in "Thematic Structure and Formal Processes in Brahms's Sonata Movements," *Brahms Studies,* pp. 432–33.

39. See Pascall, "Special Uses," pp. 58–63, and Arnold Whittall, "Two of a kind? Brahms's Op. 51 finales," in *Brahms 2: Biographical, Documentary and Analytical studies* (Cambridge: Cambridge University Press, 1987), p. 152.

40. See Donald Francis Tovey, "Brahms's Chamber Music," in *The Mainstream of Music and Other Essays* (New York: Oxford University Press, 1949 [reprinted from the 1929 article in *Cobbett's Cyclopedic Survey of Chamber Music*]), p. 244, on the finale of the F-Minor Piano Quintet, Opus 34.

41. *Fragmente zur Litteratur und Poesie,* no. 4, *KA* 16, p. 85.

42. There are some notable examples in Beethoven (e.g., the finales of the Fourth Piano Concerto, Opus 58, the E-Minor "Rasoumovsky" Quartet, Opus 59, No. 2, and the F-Minor "Serioso" Quartet, Opus 95) and Schubert (e.g., the finales of the G-Major String Quartet, D. 887, and the C-Major String Quintet, D. 956) as well.

43. For examples from Mozart's concerti, see the finales of K. 299, 314, 364, 413–15, 456, 459, 466, 488, 537, 595, and 622. Concertante chamber work finales adhering to the design include K. 306, 452, 478, 493, 515, 516, 526, 542, 548, 563, and 617.

44. *Fragmente zur Litteratur und Poesie,* no. 851, *KA* 16, p. 157.

45. According to Hölderlin's poetological theory of the "Wechsel der Töne" (alternation of tones), the description of events or feelings corresponds with the "naïve" tone, the delineation of passions or aspirations with the "heroic" tone, and the shaping of fantasies or intellectual perceptions with the "ideal" tone. See "Über den Unterschied der Dichtarten," in *Hölderlin Sämtliche Werke,* ed. Friedrich Beissner, vol. 4 (Stuttgart: Kohlhammer, 1961), pp. 266–67.

46. Adolph Bernhard Marx, *Die Lehre von der musikalischen Komposition,* vol. 3 (Leipzig: Breitkopf & Härtel, 1845), p. 193

47. Cf. Adorno's assertion: "The fiber and the form of Brahms's music already point in different directions" (*Introduction to the Sociology of Music,* trans. E. B. Ashton [New York: Continuum, 1976; orig. publ. *Einleitung in die Musiksoziologie,* Frankfurt, 1962]), p. 65. Whereas Adorno reads the disparity between "fiber and form" as a sign of the arbitrariness with which Brahms imposes classical structural types on his ultra-expressive mate-

rials, we might just as well interpret the contradiction as a consequence of the composer's individualization of the classical genres. See also Subotnik, *Developing Variations*, pp. 216–17.

48. Cf. Robert Pascall, "Genre and the Finale of Brahms's Fourth Symphony," *Music Analysis* 8 (1989): 236–43.

49. See in particular David Osmond-Smith, "The Retreat from Dynamism: A Study of Brahms's Fourth Symphony," in *Brahms: Biographical, Documentary and Analytical studies*, ed. Robert Pascall (Cambridge: Cambridge University Press, 1983), pp. 151–56.

50. Gustav Jenner, *Johannes Brahms als Mensch, Lehrer und Künstler: Studien und Erlebnisse*, 2d ed., (Marburg, 1930; 1st ed., 1905), p. 75.

51. *KA* 2, p. 154.

52. *Athenäum Fragmente*, no. 434, *KA* 2, p. 252.

53. *Fragmente zur Litteratur und Poesie*, no. 1103, *KA* 16, p. 176.

54. *Fragmente zur Litteratur und Poesie*, nos. 322 and 1073, *KA* 16, pp. 111, 174. See also the commentary in Szondi, "Friedrich Schlegel's Theory of Poetical Genres," pp. 91–93.

55. Quoted in Christian Martin Schmidt, *Johannes Brahms und seine Zeit* (Laaber: Laaber-Verlag, 1983), p. 100.

56. Although the autograph of the Quintet is undated, it was probably completed by the end of the summer of 1890. Brahms made reference to it, as if to a finished work, in a letter to Clara Schumann dated August of that year; see Berthold Litzmann, ed., *Letters of Clara Schumann and Johannes Brahms, 1853–1896*, vol. 2 (New York and London, 1927), p. 176; and Margit L. McCorkle, *Johannes Brahms: Thematisch-Bibliographisches Werkverzeichnis* (Munich: Henle, 1984), p. 445. While Brahms indicated in a letter to Simrock of 11 December 1890 that he had decided to halt his compositional activities (*BW* 12 [Berlin: Deutsche Brahms-Gesellschaft, 1919], p. 35) Mühlfeld's artistry inspired him to continue, as the composer himself expressly stated in a letter of 25 July 1891 to Baronin von Heldburg, wife of the duke of Meiningen; the letter appears in Herta Müller,"Brahms Briefwechsel mit Meiningen," *Beiträge zur Musikwissenschaft*, 20 (1978): 117–18.

57. Letter to Brahms of 22 March [1893], *BW* 6 (Berlin: Deutsche Brahms-Gesellschaft, 1912), p. 286.

58. *BW* 6, pp. 258–59. Elisabeth von Herzogenberg likewise expressed her fondness for the two middle movements of the Quintet, praising the slow movement for its "wonderful unity and consistency of mood" (*BW* 2 [Berlin: Deutsche Brahms-Gesellschaft, 1907], pp. 239–40; letter to Brahms of 9 October 1890).

59. For a recent account of the Opus 111 *adagio* as a series of freely elaborated variations, see Elaine R. Sisman, "Brahms and the Variation Canon," *19th-Century Music* 14, no. 2 (1990): 132–53, and also her comments in "Brahms's Slow Movements: Reinventing the 'Closed' Forms," in *Brahms Studies*, pp. 81–82. Tovey similarly viewed the movement as a cavatina, that is, "a single melody achieving the spaciousness of an entire movement by expanding without allowing a middle section to partition itself off" ("Brahms's Chamber Music," in *The Mainstream of Music*, p. 264). By way of contrast, Michael Musgrave hears a "broad ABA structure" with an "impassioned central section" (*Music of Brahms*, p. 208). Robert Pascall opts for an anomalous strophic design, but allows that a sonata-form analysis is also a possibility; see "Formal Principles in the Music of Johannes Brahms" (D. Phil. thesis, Oxford, 1972), pp. 31–33.

60. Letter to Schubring of 16 February 1869, *BW* 8 (Berlin: Deutsche Brahms-Gesellschaft, 1915), pp. 217–18; and to E. von Herzogenberg of 20 August 1876, *BW* 1, pp. 7–8.

61. See Sisman, "Brahms and the Variation Canon," p. 136.

62. See, for instance, the discussion in Pascall, "Formal Principles," pp. 32–33.

63. *BW* 12, p. 35.

64. The dynamic marking in the accompanying voices was the cause of some controversy in Brahms's circle. He at first gave tacit approval to Joachim's suggested *diminuendo* to *mezzo-forte* in mm. 2–3, but then, with typical stubbornness, retained the original dy-

namic in the first published edition. (In doing so, he also ensured that the element of struggle implicit in the concerto idea was retained as well). See Kalbeck, *Brahms,* vol. 4, pp. 208–9, and *BW* 6, p. 259.

65. Letter of 9 October 1890, *BW* 2, p. 241.

66. Cf. Clara Schumann's colorful description of the first movement as "just the sort of magnificent confusion one hears in a dream after a *Zigeuner* evening in Pest" (Litzmann, *Letters of Clara Schumann,* p. 188; letter to Brahms of 4 March 1891).

67. The third movement, *adagio,* of Schumann's A-minor String Quartet, Opus 41, No. 1, is also cast in three bipartite strophes, the second including a terminal development, and the third answering the half-close of the first with a full cadence in F. But the simplicity of phrase structure and the limitation of tonal elaboration to the second strophe make for a less adventuresome conception here than in the Opus 41, No. 3, slow movement.

68. Other possible models for the form of the *adagio* include the slow movement Fantasia of Haydn's Opus 76, No. 6, String Quartet, the quasi-variations of Schubert's "Wanderer" Fantasy, D. 760 (see Sisman, "Brahms and the Variation Canon," p. 152), and the slow movement of Schumann's Fourth Symphony, Opus 120 (see Hans Kohlhase, "Brahms und Mendelssohn: Strukturelle Parallelen der Kammermusik für Streicher," in *Brahms und seine Zeit: Symposion Hamburg 1983,* ed. Friedhelm Krummacher and Wolfram Steinbeck [Kassel: Bärenreiter, 1984], pp. 67, 82). In these works, however, the strophic element is considerably less pronounced than in Brahms's movement. Haydn's Fantasia subjects its opening eight-bar theme to considerably more far-flung transformations than Brahms does his opening A–B–A′ unit. Schubert's tonally open-ended variations are concerned with the gradual dismantling of a theme, not (as in Brahms's *adagio*) its regularization. And Schumann's movement presents a derivative of the traditional *ABA* form that has relatively little to do with the variation idea.

69. See Carl Dahlhaus, "Sonata Form in Schubert: The First Movement of the G-major String Quartet, Op. 161 (D. 887)," in *Schubert: Critical and Analytical Studies,* ed. Walter Frisch (Lincoln: University of Nebraska Press, 1986), pp. 1–4.

70. Arnold Schoenberg, *Fundamentals of Musical Composition,* ed. Gerald Strang and Leonard Stein (London: Faber, 1967), p. 142.

71. *Fragmente zur Litteratur und Poesie,* no. 1197, *KA* 16, p. 183.

6. Wagner's *Ring* and *Universalpoesie*

1. *KA* 2, pp. 182–83.

2. Cf. Walter Benjamin's reading in *Der Begriff der Kunstkritik,* pp. 85–86.

3. *Gespräch über die Poesie, KA* 2, p. 313.

4. It is still interesting to point out that Wagner was well versed in the writings of both Schlegel brothers. As Anette Ingenhoff has shown, Wagner's thoughts on drama owed much to the Schlegels' theories as presented in Adolf Wagner's *Theater und Publicum* (Leipzig, 1826); see *Drama oder Epos? Richard Wagner's Gattungstheorie des musikalischen Dramas* (Tübingen: Max Niemeyer Verlag, 1987), p. 85. From Cosima's diaries we learn that Wagner took pleasure in reading A. W. Schlegel's critical essays; see the entries for 14 and 28 August 1872 in *Cosima Wagner's Diaries* [*CWD*], trans. Geoffrey Skelton (New York: Harcourt Brace Jovanovich, 1978), vol. 1, pp. 523, 529. Several of Friedrich Schlegel's works were also the subject of evening discussions at Wahnfried: the *Vorlesungen über die neuere Geschichte* (entry for 17 December 1871, *CWD* 1, p. 440); *Die Sprache und Weisheit der Inder* (entry for 5 March 1872; *CWD* 1, p. 601); the lectures on classical comedy (presumably the "Charakteristik der griechischen Komödie," from which Wagner would have read about the doctrine of *Witz* firsthand) (entry of 18 December 1872, *CWD* 1, p. 572); and *Die Griechen und Römer* (which contains Schlegel's important early essay setting out the distinction between the beautiful and the characteristic) (entry for 1 February 1874, *CWD* 1, p. 730).

5. *Opera and Drama,* in *Richard Wagner's Prose Works* [PW], trans. William Ashton Ellis, vol. 2 (London: Routledge & Kegan Paul, 1893), p. 124. See also the commentary in Dieter Borchmeyer, *Das Drama Richard Wagners: Idee, Dichtung, Wirkung* (Stuttgart: Reclam, 1982), pp. 125–51.

6. Peter Conrad, *Romantic Opera and Literary Form* (Berkeley and Los Angeles: University of California Press, 1977), pp. 1, 35–36.

7. "Richard Wagner and Tannhäuser in Paris" (1861), in *The Painter of Modern Life and Other Essays,* trans. and ed. Jonathan Mayne (London: Phaidon Press, 1964), p. 133.

8. See in particular Thomas Mann, "Richard Wagner and *The Ring*" (1937), in *Thomas Mann Pro and Contra Wagner,* trans. Allan Blunden (Chicago: University of Chicago Press, 1985), pp. 186–89. For more recent accounts of the narratives' role in enriching the symphonic weave and dramatic texture of the *Ring* dramas, see Carl Dahlhaus, *Richard Wagner's Music Dramas,* trans. Mary Whittall (Cambridge: Cambridge University Press, 1979), pp. 86–87, 135; idem, "Entfremdung und Erinnerung: Zu Wagners *Götterdämmerung,*" in *Vom Musikdrama zur Literaturoper* (Munich: Katzbichler, 1983), pp. 126–31; Reinhold Brinkmann, "Richard Wagner der Erzähler," *Österreichische Musikzeitschrift* 37 (1982): 297, 303; idem; "Szenische Epik: Marginalien zu Wagners Dramenkonzeption im *Ring des Nibelungen,*" in *Richard Wagner: Weg und Wirkung,* ed. Carl Dahlhaus (Regensburg: Bosse, 1971), pp. 85–96; and Ingenhoff, *Drama oder Epos?,* pp. 120–23.

9. See Aristotle's *Poetics,* trans. Richard Janko (Indianapolis: Hackett, 1987), p. 24: "The poet ought to remember what we have often said, and not compose a tragedy with an epic structure (by an 'epic' structure I mean one with more than one plot), e.g. if someone were to compose [a tragedy with] the whole plot of the *Iliad.* For there, the parts receive suitable magnitude because of the length [of the epic]; but in dramas the result is far from one's expectations." Aristotle does not object to episodic—that is, epic—elements per se in a dramatic work; what he questions is whether they will be given the proper magnitude within which to unfold. Wagner, to be sure, had little difficulty in providing a design whose breadth was sufficient for the incorporation of epic elements.

10. Rudolf Stephan, "Gibt es ein Geheimnis der Form bei Richard Wagner," in *Das Drama Richard Wagners als musikalische Kunstwerk,* ed. Carl Dahlhaus (Regensburg: Bosse, 1970), pp. 13–14.

11. Entry of 22 September 1874, *CWD* 1, p. 788.

12. *PW* 6, *Religion and Art* (London, 1897), p. 179. Cf. the similar charge in the 1857 essay, "On Franz Liszt's Symphonic Poems," *PW* 3, *The Theatre* (London, 1894), p. 245. For a comprehensive discussion of Wagner's view of the reprise as the most problematic aspect of the sonata form, see Klaus Kropfinger, *Wagner and Beethoven: Richard Wagner's Reception of Beethoven,* trans. Peter Palmer (Cambridge: Cambridge University Press, 1991; orig. publ. *Wagner und Beethoven,* Regensburg, 1975), pp. 78–80, 88–89; and also Thomas S. Grey, "Wagner, the Overture, and the Aesthetics of Musical Form," *19th-Century Music* 12, no. 1 (1988): 9–10.

13. Cf. Kropfinger, *Wagner and Beethoven,* p. 204.

14. Schlegel, *Philosophische Fragmente, Erste Epoche III,* no. 643, *KA* 18, p. 179.

15. Cf. also Benjamin, *Der Begriff der Kunstkritik,* pp. 21ff.

16. *Philosophische Fragmente, Zweite Epoche I,* no. 1060, *KA* 18, p. 285.

17. *Philosophische Fragmente, Zweite Epoche II,* no. 1004, *KA* 18, p. 404.

18. For explicit statements to this effect from Schlegel's output, see *Zur Philosophie nro. iii* (1804), no. 227: "The impossibility of reaching the highest through reflection alone leads to allegory, that is, to mythology and the plastic arts" (*KA* 19, p. 25); and *Zur Philosophie,* no. 84: "Only poetic thought (productive reflection) is transcendental" (*KA* 19, p. 164). As Schlegel saw it, poetry was not alone in its attempts to synthesize production and reflection. The same dialectic played itself out in modern philosophy, which "contains within its system of transcendental thoughts a critique of transcendental thinking" (*Athenäum Fragmente,* no. 238, *KA* 2, p. 204), and in art criticism, itself a form of "objective

reflection" (*Zur Philosophie. 1806. I,* no. 112, *KA* 19, p. 167). For an account of Novalis's similar point of view, see Benjamin, *Der Begriff der Kunstkritik,* pp. 35, 57–59.

19. See Chapter 2, pp. 00–00.
20. Dällenbach, *The Mirror in the Text,* p. 69.
21. Ibid., pp. 87–88.
22. "Über Goethes Meister" (1798), *KA* 2, pp. 133–34. Cf. Novalis's similar appraisal in *Das Allgemeine Brouillon,* fragment 445, *Schriften* 3, p. 326.
23. *KA* 2, p. 131.
24. "Wiederholte Spiegelungen" (29 January 1823), in *Goethes Werke,* Hamburger Ausgabe, ed. Erich Trunz, vol. 12 (Munich: Beck, 1981), pp. 322–23.
25. For a discussion of the "Confessions of a Beautiful Soul" (Book 6) and the notion of productive reflection, see Franz Norbert Mennemeier, *Friedrich Schlegels Poesiebegriff: Dargestellt anhand der literaturkritischen Schriften: Die romantische Konzeption einer objectiven Poesie* (Munich, 1971), pp. 251–54. The "beautiful soul's" self-absorption exemplifies the negative side of the reflective idea that is valorized as the constructive force behind the *Roman* as a whole.
26. *KA* 2, p. 146.
27. Goethe, *Gedenkausgabe der Werke, Briefe und Gespräche,* ed. Ernst Beutler, (Zürich: Artemis Verlag, 1948–54), vol. 7, p. 581.
28. See Dällenbach, *Mirror in the Text,* pp. 7–8.
29. "Beethoven," *PW* 5, *Actors and Singers* (London, 1896), p. 124.
30. *CWD* 1, p. 393. For commentaries on Wagner's preoccupation with *Faust,* see Borchmeyer, *Das Theater Richard Wagners,* pp. 48–55; and also Ingenhoff, *Drama oder Epos?,* pp. 63–66.
31. *PW* 2, p. 176.
32. *CWD* 2, p. 238, entry of 25 June 1870.
33. Ibid., p. 239, entry of 27 June 1870.
34. "Eine Wiederholung des Ganzen, ein Vorspiel und drei Stücke" (*CWD* 1, p. 921, entry of 9 September 1876).
35. *CWD* 1, p. 418, entry of 29 September 1871.
36. See also Peter Szondi, *Theory of Modern Drama,* trans. Michael Hays (Cambridge: Polity Press, 1987; orig. publ. *Theorie des modernen Dramas,* 1965), pp. 7–9, 45.
37. *The Theory of the Novel,* trans. Anna Botstock (Cambridge: MIT Press, 1971; orig. publ. *Die Theorie des Romans,*1920), p. 122.
38. Szondi, *Theory of the Modern Drama,* pp. 16–31.
39. Letter of 20 November 1851, in *Selected Letters of Richard Wagner,* trans. and ed. Stewart Spencer and Barry Millington (London: Dent, 1987), pp. 236–38.
40. Letter to Liszt of 3 October 1855, *Selected Letters,* p. 352.
41. *Theory of the Novel,* p. 45.
42. For Carolyn Abbate, the cyclic, quasi-strophic form of the monologue is an emblem of Wotan's tragic situation. By continually playing out the same pattern in his *Walküre* narrative (which Abbate configures as abandonment-force-payment/death), Wotan comes to realize that the sequence will hold in the future, eventually leading to his own destruction. He therefore projects a view of history "not as progress but as a recurrent wrenching-back, as error replayed," an outlook confirmed by his music's virtual lack of clearly goal-directed modulations (see *Unsung Voices,* pp. 170–94). This interpretation strikes me as overly bleak. Wotan's monologue enfolds narration within narration, forms within forms, but the resultant design is hardly static. Wotan does "progress" (as does his music: only in the first wave are the harmonic cadences "reified as objects"); through introspection, he comes to a better understanding of his own ethical makeup. William E. McDonald ("What Does Wotan Know? Autobiography and Moral Vision in Wagner's *Ring,*" *19th-Century Music* 15, no. 1 [1991]: 36–51) comes to a similar conclusion, and calls attention to an additional positive effect of Wotan's narrative account; through it, the god calls into

being the "Other" who will act independently of his power: Brünnhilde. Cf. also the discussion of the monologue in Arnold Whittall's review of Abbate's book, *Music Analysis* 11, no. 1 (1992), esp. pp. 97–106.

43. On this point, see Anthony Newcomb, "The Birth of Music out of the Spirit of Drama," *19th-Century Music* 5, no. 1 (1981): 58–64.

44. The essay appears in Walter Benjamin, *Illuminations: Essays and Reflections,* ed. Hannah Arendt, trans. Harry Zohn (New York: Schocken, 1969); see especially pp. 83–89.

45. Thomas Mann, *Joseph and His Brothers,* trans. H. T. Lowe-Porter (New York: Knopf, 1956), p. 73.

46. Benjamin, "Storyteller," p. 91.

47. Ibid., pp. 97–98.

48. See Lukács, *The Theory of the Novel,* p. 127.

49. See Egon Voss, "Siegfrieds Musik," in *Das Musikalische Kunstwerk,* p. 266.

50. Benjamin, "Storyteller," p. 102.

51. Letter of 10 May 1851, *Selected Letters,* p. 223.

52. Benjamin, "On Some Motifs in Baudelaire," in *Illuminations,* p. 163.

53. Ibid., pp. 179–80.

54. Letter of 25/26 January 1854, *Selected Letters,* p. 307; italics in original.

55. Cf. William Kinderman, "Dramatic Recapitulation in Wagner's *Götterdämmerung,*" *19th-Century Music* 4 (1980): 101–12. Kinderman's otherwise insightful account of the recapitulatory dimension of the monologue curiously begins from "Jetzt aber merkt wohl auf die Mär," that is, from the music corresponding to *Siegfried,* Act II. The soliloquy's central structural feature, its summation of the earlier drama in toto, is therefore missed.

56. See in particular Robert Bailey, "The Structure of the *Ring* and its Evolution," *19th-Century Music* 1 (1977–78): 48–61; Patrick McCreless, *Wagner's Siegfried: Its Drama, History, and Music* (Ann Arbor: UMI Research Press, 1982), pp. 85–100; and idem, "Schenker and the Norns," in *Analyzing Opera: Verdi and Wagner,* ed. Carolyn Abbate and Roger Parker (Berkeley and Los Angeles: University of California Press, 1989), pp. 277–84.

57. Alfred Lorenz, *Das Geheimnis der Form bei Richard Wagner: Der musikalische Aufbau des Bühnenfestspiels Der Ring des Nibelungen* (Berlin: Hesse, 1924), pp. 45, 202, 219.

58. Cf. Dahlhaus, *Richard Wagner's Music Dramas,* pp. 128–29.

59. See Christopher Wintle, "The Numinous in *Götterdämmerung,*" in *Reading Opera,* ed. Arthur Groos and Roger Parker (Princeton: Princeton University Press, 1988), p. 215.

60. Abbate, *Unsung Voices,* p. 216.

61. Entry of 23 July 1872, *CWD* 1, p. 515.

62. See Barry Millington, review of *Wagner in Retrospect: A Centennial Reappraisal* (Amsterdam: Rodopi, 1987), in *Musical Times* 129 (1988): 88.

63. Quoted from John Deathridge, review of monographs by Curt von Westernhagen (*Wagner: A Biography,* trans. Mary Whittall, Cambridge, 1978) et al., in *19th-Century Music* 5, no. 1 (1981): 81–89.

64. Diary entry of 25 November 1880, *CWD* 32, p. 562.

7. *Tristan, Parsifal,* and the "New" Organicism

1. *KA* 2, p. 312.

2. Hermann Broch, *Hugo von Hofmannsthal and His Time: The European Imagination, 1860–1920,* trans. M. P. Steinberg (Chicago: Chicago University Press, 1984), pp. 46–56.

3. *KA* 2, p. 303. Anette Ingenhoff puts it succinctly: Schlegel "practically wrote the programme for the Wagnerian Nibelungen drama" (*Drama oder Epos?,* p. 112).

4. Cf. Claude Lévi-Strauss's argument in favor of accepting Wagner as the "undeniable originator of the structural analysis of myths" (*The Raw and the Cooked,* trans. John and Doreen Weightman [New York: Harper & Row, 1969], pp. 15, 30).

5. *KA* 2, p. 313.
6. Murray Krieger, *A Reopening of Closure: Organicism against Itself* (New York: Columbia University Press, 1989); see especially pp. 35–53.
7. See, in particular *Sämliche Werke*, ed. Böcking, vol. 8, p. 122.
8. *Vorlesungen über schöne Litteratur und Kunst*, ed. J. Minor (Stuttgart, 1884), vol. 2, p. 358.
9. *Sämliche Werke*, vol. 9, p. 187.
10. *Über dramatische Kunst und Litteratur* (Heidelberg, 1817), vol. 3, p. 8. (In a recent article, David Montgomery traces the notion of organicism as emanation from a germ cell to Robinet's *De la nature* [1761–68]; see "The Myth of Oranicism," pp. 18–20, 27–39). For a summary account of the place of organicism in A. W. Schlegel's critical theory, see René Wellek, *A History of Modern Criticism, 1750–1950*, vol. 2, *The Romantic Age* (Cambridge: Cambridge University Press, 1981), pp. 48–49.
11. On the Aristotelian overtones in Schlegel's theory of organicism, see Margaret R. Higonnet, "Organic Unity and Interpretative Boundaries: Friedrich Schlegel's Theories and their Application in His Critique of Lessing," *Studies in Romanticism* 19 (1980): 167.
12. *Ideen*, no. 95, *KA* 2, p. 265.
13. *Zur Poesie und Litteratur II*, no. 798, *KA* 16, p. 320. Cf. Schelling's concept of the symbolic as an absolute synthesis of the general and the particular, and its realization in ancient mythology and mythologically inspired poetry (*The Philosophy of Art*, pp. 45–46).
14. See "Rede über die Mythologie," p. 312.
15. *Athenäum Fragmente*, no. 366, *KA* 2, p. 232. Cf. also frag. 412 from the same collection (*KA* 2, p. 243), and the variation in *Philosophische Fragmente, Erste Epoche III*, frag. 213 (*KA* 18, p. 139): "*Imagination* is an organic philosophical power, *reason* is chemical, and *understanding* is mechanical."
16. Cf. *Philosophische Fragmente, Erste Epoche III*, no. 6, which equates "mechanical" and "abstract" (*KA* 18, p. 123).
17. Cf. Chapter 3.
18. See *Philosophische Fragmente, Erste Epoche III*, no. 117, *KA* 18, pp. 131–32. Other fragments that equate organicism with progress or genetic growth include *Fragmente zur Litteratur und Poesie*, no. 953, *KA* 16, p. 165 and *Philosophische Fragmente, Erste Epoche III*, no. 6, *KA* 18, p. 123.
19. *Philosophische Fragmente, Zweite Epoche I*, no. 439, *KA* 18, p. 230. Hölderlin likewise designated the drama as a primarily organic genre; see "Über den Unterschied der Dichtarten," *Hölderlin Sämtliche Werke* 4, p. 269. His call for a fusion of organic or organizing and "aorgic" (*aorgisch*) or chaotic qualities in modern poetry (*Werke* 4, pp. 152–54) is likewise comparable to what I am calling Schlegel's "new" organicism.
20. *Philosophische Fragmente, Zweite Epoche I*, no. 429, *KA* 18, p. 229.
21. *Fragmente zur Litteratur und Poesie*, no. 1199, *KA* 16, p. 183.
22. *Athenäum Fragmente*, no. 426, *KA* 2, pp. 248–49.
23. *Von der Schönheit in der Dichtkunst*, *KA* 16, p. 29.
24. *Zur Philosophie*, frag. 106, *KA* 19, p. 52.
25. *Philosophische Fragmente, Zweyte Epoche II* (1798), no. 104, *KA* 18, p. 332.
26. *Geschichte der Europäischen Literatur* (1803–4), *KA* 11, p. 63. Not surprisingly, Schlegel held up Goethe's *Meister*, a work whose "cultivated randomness" precludes subsumption under the ideology of the beautifully rounded whole, as a prime example of "Einheit des Vielfältigen" (see "Über Goethes Meister," *KA* 2, pp. 134–46).
27. *PW* 2, pp. 337–50. See also Tibor Kneif, "Die Idee der Organischen bei Richard Wagner," in *Das Drama Richard Wagners als Musikalische Kunstwerk*, ed. C Dahlhaus, pp. 73–74.
28. *PW* 6, *Religion and Art* (London: Routledge & Kegan Paul, 1897), p. 182.
29. *Selected Letters of Richard Wagner*, p. 475.
30. *PW* 6, p. 176–77.

31. *The Case of Wagner,* pp. 170–71.

32. Theodor Adorno, *In Search of Wagner,* trans. Rodney Livingstone (Trowbridge and Esher: NLB, 1981; orig. publ. *Versuch über Wagner,* Suhrkamp Verlag, 1952), p. 102.

33. Ernst Kurth, "[The *Tristan* Prelude]," from *Romantische Harmonie und ihre Krise in Wagners "Tristan,"* excerpt trans. Robert Bailey, in *Wagner: Prelude and Transfiguration from Tristan and Isolde,* ed. R. Bailey, Norton Critical Score (New York: Norton: 1985), pp. 201–4.

34. See in particular, Carl Dahlhaus, *Between Romanticism and Modernism,* pp. 68–69, 73; and "Tonalität und Form in Wagners 'Ring des Nibelingen,'" *Archiv für Musikwissenschaft* 40 (1983): 167–70. Patrick McCreless's view of the closing pages of *Götterdämmerung,* Act I, as a web of associative tonalities likewise exemplifies a rhetorically dialectic reading: "The pitch-related associations and cross-references tell virtually the whole story: lines and voice leading are present, as they must be; but surely . . . they are subordinate to the associative references, and not vice versa" (see "Syntagmatics and Paradigmatics: Some Implications for the Analysis of Chromaticism in Tonal Music," *Music Theory Spectrum* 13, no. 2 [1991]: 178).

35. *Richard Wagner: Selected Letters,* p. 475.

36. See "Paths of Tonal Development; Paths of Harmonic Expansion" [*Romantische Harmonik,* Part 5, Chapter 1], in *Ernst Kurth: Selected Writings,* ed. and trans. Lee A. Rothfarb (Cambridge: Cambridge University Press, 1991, pp. 143–46).

37. Cf. Lawrence Kramer, *Music as Cultural Practice, 1800–1900* (Berkeley and Los Angeles: University of California Press, 1990), pp. 155–57; and Raymond Knapp, "The Tonal Structure of *Tristan und Isolde*: A Sketch," *Music Review* 45 (1984): 19–22. Knapp's location of the tonal underpinning of the music drama in a shift from an A–C–E♭ axis to an A♭–B–D–F axis somewhat obsures the simplicity of Wagner's plan. William Kinderman's account of the art of transition in *Tristan* likewise differs from my own. His tracing of the large-scale progression whereby the dissonant *Tristan* chord is transformed into the relatively consonant B–D♯–F♯–G♯ at the climax of the *Liebestod* gives insufficient attention to the tonal descent by half step that informs the music of the Act II colloquy. See "Das Geheimnis der Form in Wagners *Tristan und Isolde,*" *Archiv für Musikwissenschaft* 40 (1983): 183–86.

38. *Essays on the Philosophy of Music,* p. 164.

39. For a discussion of the relationship between the harmonic language of this segment and the second of the *Fünf Gedichte für eine Frauenstimme* ("Träume" from the "Wesendonk" Lieder), see Robert Gauldin, "Wagner's Parody Technique: 'Träume' and the *Tristan* Love Duet," *Music Theory Spectrum* 1 (1979): 37–42.

40. See Dahlhaus, *Richard Wagner's Music Dramas,* p. 51.

41. *Richard Wagner: Selected Letters,* pp. 474–75.

42. Kurth, *Romantische Harmonik,* pp. 263–67.

43. Bailey, *Wagner: Prelude and Transformation,* pp. 195–96.

44. Richard Wagner, *Sämtliche Werke,* vol. 30, *Dokumente zur Enstehung und ersten Aufführung des Bühnenweihfestspiels Parsifal,* ed. Martin Geck and Egon Voss (Mainz: Schott, 1979), p. 16.

45. See Hans-Joachim Bauer, *Wagners Parsifal: Kriterien der Kompositionstechnik* (Munich: Katzbichler, 1977), pp. 178–79; William Kinderman, "Wagner's *Parsifal*: Musical Form and the Drama of Redemption," *Journal of Musicology* 4 (1985–86): 438–42; David R. Murray, "Major Analytical Approaches to Wagner's Style: A Critique," *Music Review* 39 (1978): 220; Rudolf Stephan, "Gibt es ein Geheimnis der Form bei Richard Wagner," in *Das Drama Richard Wagners als musikalische Kunstwerk,* ed. C. Dahlhaus, pp. 13–14; and Arnold Whittall, "The Music," in Lucy Beckett, *Parsifal* (Cambridge: Cambridge University Press, 1981), p. 77. Accounts of the extent of the parallelism between the two laments likewise tend to be incomplete. Kinderman, for instance, links the last fifty bars or so of Parsifal's passage to several spots in Amfortas's lament; and Murray, who notes that the two laments

share approximately thirty-five measures of music, recognizes a reprise of even smaller dimensions. Yet in fact there are a mere three measures (II/1076–78, to be exact) from Parsifal's nearly hundred-bar monologue that are not directly referable to Amfortas's only slightly longer complaint.

46. Alfred Lorenz makes this point. See *Das Geheimnis der Form bei Richard Wagner,* vol. 4, *Der Musikalische Aufbau von Richard Wagners "Parsifal"* (Tutzing: Schneider, 1966; reprint of Munich, 1933 ed.), p. 78.
47. Ibid., p. 79.
48. *CWD* 2, p. 977, entry for 11 August 1877.
49. Although he did not elaborate the point in much detail, Lorenz similarly noted that much of the material from the Act I *Vorspiel* recurred in the Transformation music and subsequent Grail scene, but in a different order and intermingled with freshly conceived developmental passages. See *Parsifal,* pp. 96–97.
50. *CWD* 2, p. 85, entry of 5 June 1878.
51. Wagner, *PW,* p. 185: "This [I/1392] is the principal moment of all that Parsifal experiences here but will only later come to understand."
52. Ibid., p. 81.
53. Cf. Grillparzer's pejorative comments on the methods of the musical "prose writer," who can "begin anywhere and end anywhere, because the individual fragments and sections [of his work] can easily be rearranged and put in another sequence; but he who has a sense of a whole can give it only in one piece or not at all" (*Grillparzers Werke,* ed. Rudolf Franz, vol. 5 [Leipzig: Bibliographisches Institut, (1903)], p. 374).
54. *The Case of Wagner,* p. 170.
55. *CWD* 2, p. 542, entry of 22 September 1880.
56. "Zur Partitur des Parsifal," in *Richard Wagner und das neue Bayreuth,* ed. Wieland Wagner (Munich: Paul List, 1962), p. 176.
57. *CWD* 2, p. 214, entry of 29 November 1878.
58. "Motive and Magic: A Referential Dyad in *Parsifal,*" *Music Analysis* 11, no. 1 (1990): 227–65.
59. Ibid., p. 254.
60. Lorenz, *Parsifal,* pp. 32–44.
61. Thomas Mann, *Doktor Faustus* (1947), Chapters 45–46.
62. *Style and Music,* p. 193.

8. Richard Strauss's *Also sprach Zarathustra* and the "Union" of Poetry and Philosophy

1. *KA* 2, p. 161. See also *Anthenäum Fragmente,* no. 302, *KA* 2, 216.
2. See *Athenäum Fragmente,* no. 98: "Everything is philosophical that contributes to the realization of the logical ideal and possesses scientific organization" (*KA* 2, p. 179); and no. 252: to those who know a subject "philosophy of course brings nothing new; but only through it does it become knowledge and thereby assume a new form" (*KA* 2, p. 208).
3. *Athenäum Fragmente,* no. 255; *KA* 2, pp. 208–9.
4. *Athenäum Fragmente,* no. 252; *KA* 2, pp. 207–8.
5. "Über Goethes Meister," *KA* 2, p. 132.
6. Ibid.
7. Liszt, *Gesammelte Schriften,* vol. 4, p. 58.
8. Arthur Schopenhauer, *Die Welt als Wille und Vorstellung,* in *Sämtliche Werke,* ed. Paul Deussen (Munich, 1911), vol. 1, pp. 307–14.
9. See Walter Kaufmann's translation of Nietzsche's essay in Dahlhaus, *Between Romanticism and Modernism,* pp. 109–12.
10. Dahlhaus, *Esthetics of Music,* pp. 59–60.
11. Cf. Theodor Adorno, "Richard Strauss: Zum 60. Geburtstage: 11. Juni 1924," in *Gesam-*

melte Schriften, vol. 18, *Musikalische Schriften V,* ed. Rolf Tiedemann and Klaus Schultz (Frankfurt am Main: Suhrkamp, 1984), p. 258; Dahlhaus, *Esthetics of Music,* p. 59; and idem, *Idea of Absolute Music,* p. 132.

12. See Nietzsche's letters to Peter Gast and Ernst Schmeitzner of 2 April 1883, 18 January 1884, and 30 March 1884, *Nietzsche Briefwechsel: Kritische Gesamtausgabe,* ed. G. Colli and M. Montinari (Berlin and New York: de Gruyter, 1981), Part 3, vol. 1, pp. 353, 466, 491.

13. Quoted from Walter Kaufman's translation (New York: Vintage Books, 1967), p. 295; Nietzsche's italics.

14. Strauss's sketch for *Zarathustra* includes the following inscription over the opening bars: "Die Sonne geht auf. Das Individuum tritt in die Welt oder die Welt ins Individuum" (quoted in Willi Schuh, *Richard Strauss: Jugend und Frühe Meisterjahre: Lebenschronik, 1864–1898* [Zürich: Atlantis, 1976], p. 430).

15. See, for example, Eduard Hanslick, "Richard Strauss' 'Also sprach Zarathustra,'" in *Am Ende des Jahrhunderts* [1895–99] (Berlin: Allgemeiner Verein für Deutsche Litteratur, 1899), pp. 265–66.

16. Quote from Norman Del Mar's preface to the Eulenberg score (London, 1974), p. v.

17. See Schuh, *Richard Strauss,* p. 430.

18. Ibid.

19. *Ecce Homo,* trans. Kaufmann, p. 261 ["Why I Write Such Good Books," section 1]; see also Walter Kaufmann, *Nietzsche: Philosopher, Psychologist, Antichrist,* 4th ed. (Princeton, N. J.: Princeton University Press, 1974), pp. 309–11.

20. *Ecce Homo,* trans. Kaufmann, p. 306 ["Also Sprach Zarathustra," section 7].

21. In addition to the letters cited in note 12, see also Nietzsche's letters to Franz Overbeck (10 February 1883) and Erwin Rohde (22 February 1884), in *Nietzsche Briefwechsel,* vol. 1, pp. 326, 479.

22. Alexander Nehamas, *Nietzsche: Life as Literature* (Cambridge, Mass.: Harvard University Press, 1985), pp. 3–5.

23. Quoted from Ernst Krause, *Richard Strauss: The Man and His Work* (Boston: Crescendo, 1969), p. 217.

24. Ibid., letter to Johann Bella.

25. Ibid., p. 216. Strauss commented in his sketches for *Zarathustra* that the unprepared listener will require "something to latch on to" in order to follow the musical argument of a densely developmental work. This "something," however, should be limited to the "briefest hints—an apt desription of the superscriptions (Nietzsche's chapter headings) that punctuate the *Zarathustra* score. See Schuh, *Richard Strauss,* p. 430. Interestingly enough, Strauss directed that the superscriptions be withheld from the printed programs for the Frankfurt premiere (27 November 1896) and a subsequent performance in Cologne. See *Richard Strauss und Franz Wüllner in Briefwechsel,* ed. Dietrich Kämper (Cologne: Arno Volk-Verlag, 1963), p. 34.

26. Ibid., p. 190.

27. See Eugen Weber, *France: Fin de Siècle* (Cambridge: Belknap Press, 1986), p. 10.

28. Claude Debussy, "Richard Strauss," in *Three Classics in the Aesthetic of Music* (New York: Dover, 1962), p. 45.

29. Adorno, "Richard Strauss: Zum hundertsten Geburtstag: 11. Juni 1964," in *Gesammelte Schriften,* vol. 16, *Musikalische Schriften I–III,* ed. Rolf Tiedemann. (Frankfurt am Main: Suhrkamp, 1978), p. 572.

30. Arno Forchert, "Zur Auflösung traditioneller Formkategorien in der Musik um 1900: Probleme formaler Organisation bei Mahler und Strauss," *Archiv für Musikwissenschaft* 32 (1975), pp. 93–98.

31. Strauss himself noted that Wagner had taken Liszt to task (and not without some justification) for the "inordinate length of his development [sections]" (see Schuh, *Richard Strauss,* p. 430). Through his consistent employment of the paired variation technique,

Strauss discovered a means of holding his potentially diffuse flights of developmental fancy in check.

32. See Dahlhaus, *Nineteenth-Century Music,* p. 239; and idem, "Liszt, Schönberg und die große Form: Das Prinzip der Mehrsätzigkeit in der Einsätzigkeit," *Musikforschung* 41 (1988): 202–12.

33. Quoted in Schuh, *Richard Strauss*, p. 430.

34. Dahlhaus, "Liszt, Schönberg," pp. 204–5.

35. In Strauss's words: "From a musical point of view, *Zarathustra* is laid out as an alteration between the two most remote keys (the second)" (quoted in Schuh, *Richard Strauss,* p. 429).

36. Adorno, "Richard Strauss: Zum hundertsten Geburtstag," p. 591.

37. Ibid., p. 572; cf. also Hans-Ulrich Fuss, "Richard Strauss in der Interpretation Adornos," *Archiv für Musikwissenschaft* 45 (1988): 69–70.

38. See note 6.

39. Dahlhaus, *Nineteenth-Century Music*, pp. 360–66.

40. Herbert Killian, ed., *Gustav Mahler in den Erinnerungen von Natalie Bauer-Lechner* (Hamburg: Wagner, 1984), p. 193.

41. Theodor W, Adorno, *Mahler: Eine musikalische Physiognomik* (Frankfurt: Suhrkamp, 1960), p. 139.

42. Killian, *Mahler*, p. 193.

43. Schoenberg, "Analysis of the First Quartet," in Ursula von Rauchhaupt, ed., *Schoenberg, Berg, Webern: The String Quartets* (Hamburg: Deutsche Grammophon Gesellschaft, 1971), p. 36.

44. See Schoenberg, "A Self-Analysis" (!948), in *Style and Idea,* pp. 77–78.

Bibliography

ABBATE, CAROLYN. "Opera as Symphony: A Wagnerian Myth." In *Analyzing Opera: Verdi and Wagner,* edited by C. Abbate and Roger Parker, 92–124. Berkeley and Los Angeles: University of California Press, 1989.

———. *Unsung Voices: Opera and Musical Narrative in the Nineteenth Century.* Princeton: Princeton University Press, 1991.

ABERT, ANNA AMALIE. "Carl Maria von Webers 'Arbeit' an 'Euryanthe.'" In *Weber: Jenseits des "Freischütz,"* edited by Friedhelm Krummacher and Heinrich W. Schwab, 6–13. Kassel: Bärenreiter, 1989.

———. "Webers 'Euryanthe' und Spohrs 'Jessonda' als große Opern." In *Festschrift Walter Wiora,* 435–40. Kassel: Bärenreiter, 1967.

ADORNO, THEODOR W. *Aesthetic Theory.* Translated by C. Lenhardt and edited by Gretel Adorno and Rolf Tiedemann. London and New York: Routledge and Kegan Paul, 1986. (Orig. publ. *Aesthetische Theorie.* Frankfurt, 1970.)

———. *In Search of Wagner.* Translated by Rodney Livingstone. Trowbridge and Esher: New Left Books, 1981. (Orig. publ. *Versuch über Wagner.* Frankfurt, 1952.)

———. "Richard Strauss: Zum hundertsten Geburtstag: 11. Juni 1964." In *Gesammelte Schriften,* vol. 16, *Musikalische Schriften I–III,* edited by Rolf Tiedemann, 565–606. Frankfurt: Suhrkamp, 1978.

———. "Richard Strauss: Zum 60. Geburtstage: 11. Juni 1924." In *Gesammelte Schriften,* vol. 18, *Musikalische Schriften V,* edited by Rolf Tiedemann and Klaus Schultz, 254–62. Frankfurt: Suhrkamp, 1984.

ALF, JULIUS, and JOSEPH A KRUSE, eds. *Robert Schumann: Universalgeist der Romantik.* Düsseldorf: Droste, 1981.

BAILEY, ROBERT, ed. *Wagner: Prelude and Transformation from "Tristan and Isolde."* Norton Critical Score. New York: Norton, 1985.

BARTHES, ROLAND. *The Responsibility of Forms.* Translated by Richard Howard. New York: Hill & Wang, 1985.

BENJAMIN, WALTER. *Der Begriff der Kunstkritik in der deutschen Romantik.* 1919–20. Frankfurt: Suhrkamp, 1973.

———. *Illuminations: Essays and Reflections.* Edited by Hannah Arendt and translated by Harry Zohn. New York: Schocken, 1968.

———. *The Origin of German Tragic Drama.* 1924–25. Translated by John Osborne. London: New Left Books, 1977.

BLACKALL, ERIC A. *The Novels of the German Romantics*. Ithaca, N.Y.: Cornell University Press, 1983.

BLANCHOT, MAURICE. "The *Athenaeum*." *Studies in Romanticism* 22 (1983): 163–72.

BLOCH, ERNST. *Essays on the Philosophy of Music*. Translated by Peter Palmer. Cambridge: Cambridge University Press, 1985. (Orig. publ. *Zur Philosophie der Musik*. Frankfurt, 1974.)

BLUME, FRIEDRICH. *Classic and Romantic Music*. Translated by M. D. Herter Norton. New York: Norton, 1970. (Orig. publ. in *Die Musik in Geschichte und Gegenwart,* 1958, 1963.)

BOETTICHER, WOLFGANG. *Robert Schumann in seinen Schriften und Briefen*. Berlin: Hahnefeld, 1942.

———. *Robert Schumanns Klavierwerke: Neue biographische und textkritische Untersuchungen*. Vol. 1, *Opus 1–6*. Wilhelmshaven: Heinrichshofens Verlag, 1976. Vol. 2, *Opus 7–13*. Wilhelmshaven: Heinrichshofens Verlag, 1984.

———, ed. *Briefe und Gedichte aus dem Album Robert und Clara Schumanns*. Leipzig: VEB Deutscher Verlag für Musik, 1979.

BORCHMEYER, DIETER. *Das Drama Richard Wagners: Idee, Dichtung, Wirkung*. Stuttgart: Reclam, 1982.

BOZARTH, GEORGE, ed. *Brahms Studies: Analytical and Historical Perspectives*. Oxford: Clarendon Press, 1990.

BRAHMS, JOHANNES. *Briefwechsel*. 16 vols. Berlin: Deutsche Brahms-Gesellschaft, 1907–22.

BRÄUTIGAM, BERND. *Leben wie im Roman: Untersuchungen zum ästhetischen Imperativ im Frühwerk Friedrich Schlegels (1794–1800)*. Paderborn: Schöningh, 1986.

BRENDEL, FRANZ. "Robert Schumann mit Rücksicht auf Mendelssohn-Bartholdy, und die Entwicklung der modernen Tonkunst überhaupt," *Neue Zeitschrift für Musik,* 22 (1845): 63–67, 81–83, 89–92, 113–15, 121–23, 145–47, 149–50.

BROCH, HERMANN. *Hugo von Hofmannsthal and His Time: The European Imagination, 1860–1920*. Translated by M. P. Steinberg. Chicago: University of Chicago Press, 1984. (Orig. publ. *Hofmannsthal und seine Zeit*. Frankfurt, 1975.)

BROWN, MARSHALL. *The Shape of German Romanticism*. Ithaca, N.Y.: Cornell University Press, 1979.

BULLOCK, MARCUS. "The Coming of the Messiah or the Stoic Burning: Aspects of the Negated Text in Walter Benjamin and Friedrich Schlegel." *Germanic Review* 40 (1985): 2–15.

DAHLHAUS, CARL. *Between Romanticism and Modernism: Four Studies in the Music of the Later Nineteenth Century*. Translated by Mary Whittall. Berkeley and Los Angeles: University of California Press, 1982. (Orig. publ. *Zwischen Romantik und Moderne: Vier Studien zur Musikgeschichte des späteren 19. Jahrhunderts*. Munich, 1974.)

———. *Esthetics of Music*. Translated by William Austin. Cambridge: Cambridge University Press, 1982. (Orig. publ. *Musikästhetik*, Köln, 1967.)

———. *Foundations of Music History*. Translated by J. Bradford Robinson. Cambridge: Cambridge University Press, 1983. (Orig. publ. *Grundlagen der Musikgeschichte*. Köln, 1967.)

———. *The Idea of Absolute Music*. Translated by Roger Lustig. Chicago: University of Chicago Press, 1989. (Orig. publ. *Die Idee der absoluten Musik*. Kassel, 1978.)

———. *Klassische und romantische Musikästhetik*. Laaber: Laaber Verlag, 1988.

———. "Liszt, Schönberg und die große Form: Das Prinzip der Mehrsätzigkeit in der Einsätzigkeit." *Musikforschung* 41 (1988): 202–12.

———. *Ludwig van Beethoven und seine Zeit*. Laaber: Laaber-Verlag, 1988.

———. *Nineteenth-Century Music*. Translated by J. Bradford Robinson. Berkeley and Los Angeles: University of California Press, 1989. (Orig. publ. *Die Musik des 19. Jahrhunderts*. Vol. 6 of *Neues Handbuch der Musikwissenschaft*. Wiesbaden, 1980.)

———. *Richard Wagner's Music Dramas*. Translated by Mary Whittall. Cambridge: Cambridge University Press, 1979. (Orig. publ. *Richard Wagners Musikdramen*. Velber, 1979.)

———. *Schoenberg and the New Music*. Translated by Derrick Puffett and Alfred Clayton. Cambridge: Cambridge University Press, 1987.

———. "Sonata Form in Schubert: The First Movement of the G-Major String Quartet, Op. 161 (D. 887)." Translated by T. Reinhard. In *Schubert: Critical and Analytical Studies,* edited by Walter Frisch, 1–12. Lincoln: University of Nebraska Press, 1986.

———. "Tonalität und Form in Wagners 'Ring des Nibelungen.'" *Archiv für Musikwissenschaft* 40 (1983): 165–73.

———. *Vom Musikdrama zur Literaturoper.* Munich: Katzbichler, 1983.

———. *Wagners Konzeption des musikalischen Dramas.* Regensburg: Bosse, 1971.

———. "Zur Problematik der musikalischen Gattungen im. 19. Jahrhundert." In *Gattungen der Musik in Einzeldarstellungen: Gedenkschrift Leo Schrade,* 840–95. Bern and Munich: Francke, 1973.

DÄLLENBACH, LUCIEN. *The Mirror in the Text.* Translated by Jeremy Whiteley with Emma Hughes. Chicago: University of Chicago Press, 1989.

DANUSER, HERMANN. "Gustav Mahlers Symphonie 'Das Lied von der Erde' als Problem der Gattungsgeschichte." *Archiv für Musikwissenschaft* 40 (1983): 276–86.

———. *Die Musik des 20. Jahrhunderts.* Vol. 7 of *Neues Handbuch der Musikwissenschaft,* edited by Carl Dahlhaus. Laaber: Laaber-Verlag, 1984.

———. *Musikalische Prosa.* Regensburg: Bosse, 1975.

DAVERIO, JOHN. "Brahms's *Magelone Romanzen* and the Romantic Imperative." *Journal of Musicology* 7 (1989): 343–65.

———. "Brünnhilde's 'Immolation Scene' and Wagner's 'Conquest of the Reprise,'" *Journal of Musicological Research* 11 (1991): 33–66.

———. "Schumann's 'Im Legendenton' and Friedrich Schlegel's *Arabeske.*" *19th-Century Music.* 11 (1987): 150–63.

DIETEL, GERHARD. *"Eine neue poetische Zeit": Musikanschauung und stilistische Tendenzen im Klavierwerk Robert Schumanns.* Kassel: Bärenreiter, 1989.

DILL, HEINZ J. "Romantic Irony in the Works of Robert Schumann," *Musical Quarterly* 73 (1989): 172–95.

EAGLETON, TERRY. *Ideology: An Introduction.* London: Verso, 1991.

EDLER, ARNFRIED. *Robert Schumann und seine Zeit.* Laaber: Laaber-Verlag, 1982.

EGGEBRECHT, HARALD. "Töne sind höhere Worte." *Musik-Konzepte, Sonderband, Robert Schumann* 1 (November 1981): 105–15.

EICHNER, HANS. "Friedrich Schlegel's Theory of Romantic Poetry." *Publications of the Modern Language Association* 71 (1956): 1018–41.

———. "Germany/Romantisch–Romantik–Romantiker." In *"Romantic" and Its Cognates: The European History of a Word,* ed. H. Eichner, 98–156. Toronto: University of Toronto Press, 1972.

ERLER, HERMANN. *Robert Schumann's Leben aus seinen Briefen geschildert.* 2 vols. Berlin: Ries & Erler, 1887.

FLOROS, CONSTANTIN. "Carl Maria von Weber: Grundsätzliches über sein Schaffen." *Musik-Konzepte* 52 (November 1986), *Sonderband,Carl Maria von Weber,* 5–21. Munich: Edition Text & Kritik, 1986.

———. *Gustav Mahler,* 3 vols. Wiesbaden: Breitkopf & Härtel, 1977–85.

FORCHERT, ARNO. "'Klassisch' und 'romantisch' in der Musikliteratur des frühen 19. Jahrhunderts." *Musikforschung* 31 (1978): 405–25.

———. "Zur Auflösung traditioneller Formkategorien in der Musik um 1900: Probleme formaler Organisation bei Mahler und Strauss." *Archiv für Musikwissenschaft* 32 (1975): 85–98.

FRANK, MANFRED. *Einführung in die frühromantische Ästhetik.* Frankfurt: Suhrkamp, 1989.

———. *Das Problem "Zeit" in der deutschen Romantik.* Munich: Winkler, 1972.

FUSS, HANS-ULRICH. "Richard Strauss in Interpretation Adornos." *Archiv für Musikwissenschaft* 45 (1988): 67–85.

GERBER, GERNOT. "Robert Schumann: Fantasie op. 17, 1. Satz: Versuch einer Interpretation." *Musicologica Austriaca* 4 (1984): 101–30.

GOETHE, JOHANN WOLFGANG. *Gedenkausgabe der Werke, Briefe und Gespräche.* 24 vols. Edited by Ernest Beutler. Zürich: Artemis Verlag, 1948–54.

————. *Goethes Werke: Hamburger Ausgabe in 14 Bänden.* Edited by Erich Trunz. Munich: Beck, 1981.

————. *Wilhelm Meister's Apprenticeship.* Edited and translated by Eric A. Blackall with Victor Lange. New York: Suhrkamp, 1989.

Grillparzers Sämtliche Werke. Edited by August Sauer. 5th ed. Stuttgart: Cotta, 1893.

HANSLICK, EDUARD. *On the Musically Beautiful.* Translated and edited by Geoffrey Payzant, from the 8th edition (1891) of *Vom Musikalisch-Schönen.* Indianapolis: Hackett, 1986.

HEGEL, GEORG WILHELM FRIEDRICH. *Einleitung in die Ästhetik.* 1842. Edited by Wolfhart Henckmann. Munich: Wilhelm Fink Verlag, 1985.

HIGONNET, MARGARET R. "Organic Unity and Interpretative Boundaries: Friedrich Schlegel's Theories and Their Application in His Critique of Lessing." *Studies in Romanticism* 19 (1980): 163–92.

HOFFMANN, E. T. A. *Die Serapionsbrüder.* Munich: Winkler, 1963.

————. *E. T. A. Hoffmann's Musical Writings: Kreisleriana, The Poet and the Composer, Music Criticism.* Edited by David Charlton and translated by Martyn Clarke. Cambridge: Cambridge University Press, 1989.

INGENHOFF, ANETTE. *Drama oder Epos: Richard Wagners Gattungstheorie des musikalischen Dramas.* Tübingen: Max Niemeyer Verlag, 1987.

JANSEN, F. GUSTAV, ed. *Robert Schumanns Briefe.* 2d ed. Leipzig: Breitkopf & Härtel, 1904.

JEAN PAUL [JOHANN RICHTER]. *Werke.* 5 vols. Munich: Hanser, 1959–63.

JOST, PETER. "Brahms und die romantische Ironie: Zu den 'Romanzen aus L. Tieck's Magelone' Op. 33." *Archiv für Musikwissenschaft* 47 (1990): 27–61.

KALBECK, MAX. *Johannes Brahms.* 4 vols. Berlin: Deutsche Brahms-Gesellschaft, 1912–21.

KALLBERG, JEFFREY. "Chopin's Last Style." *Journal of the American Musicological Society* 38 (1985): 264–315.

KAMINSKY, PETER M. "Aspects of harmony, rhythm and form in Schumann's 'Papillons,' 'Carnaval' and 'Davidsbündlertänze,'" 2 vols. Ph.D. diss., University of Rochester, 1990.

————. "Principles of Formal Structure in Schumann's Early Piano Cycles." *Music Theory Spectrum* 11, no. 2 (1989): 207–25.

KAPP, REINHARD. *Studien zum Spätwerk Robert Schumanns.* Tutzing: Schneider, 1984.

KAUFMANN, WALTER. *Nietzsche: Philosopher, Psychologist, Antichrist.* 4th ed. Princeton: Princeton University Press, 1974.

KILLIAN, HERBERT, ed. *Gustav Mahler in den Erinnerungen von Natalie Bauer-Lechner.* Hamburg: Wagner, 1984.

KINDERMAN, WILLIAM. "Das Geheimnis der Form in Wagner's *Tristan und Isolde.*" *Archiv für Musikwissenschaft* 40 (1983): 174–88.

————. "Wagner's *Parsifal*: Musical Form and the Drama of Redemption." *Journal of Musicology* 4 (1985–86): 431–46.

KNEIF, TIBOR. "Die Idee des Organischen bei Richard Wagner." In *Das Drama Richard Wagners als musikalische Kunstwerk,* edited by Carl Dahlhaus, 63–80. Regensburg: Bosse, 1970.

KOHLHASE, HANS. "Brahms und Mendelssohn: Strukturelle Parallelen in der Kammermusik für Streicher." In *Brahms und seine Zeit: Symposion Hamburg 1983,* 59–85. Laaber: Laaber-Verlag, 1984.

KRAMER, LAWRENCE. *Music as Cultural Practice, 1800–1900.* Berkeley and Los Angeles: University of California Press, 1990.

KRAUSE, ERNST. *Richard Strauss: Gestalt und Werk.* Leipzig: Breitkopf & Härtel, 1975.

KRAVITT, EDWARD F. "Romanticism Today." *Musical Quarterly* 76 (1992): 93–109.

KRIEGER, MURRAY. *A Reopening of Closure: Organicism against Itself.* New York: Columbia University Press, 1989.

KROPFINGER, KLAUS. *Wagner and Beethoven: Richard Wagner's Reception of Beethoven.* Translated by Peter Palmer. Cambridge: Cambridge University Press, 1991. (Orig. publ. *Wagner und Beethoven.* Regensburg, 1975.)

KRUMMACHER, FRIEDHELM and HEINRICH W. SCHWAB, eds. *Weber: Jenseits des "Freischütz."* Proceedings of the Eutiner Symposium Commemorating the 20th birthday of Carl Maria von Weber. Kassel: Bärenreiter, 1989.

KUNZE, STEFAN. *Der Kunstbegriff Richard Wagners.* Regensburg: Bosse, 1983.

KUNZE, STEFAN. "Richard Wagners Idee des 'Gesamtkunstwerks,'" in *Beiträge zur Theorie der Künste im 19. Jahrhundert* 2:196–229. Frankfurt: Klostermann, 1972.

KURTH, ERNST. *Romantische Harmonie und ihre Krise in Wagners 'Tristan.'* 2d ed. Berlin: Hesse, 1923.

———. *Selected Writings.* Edited and translated by Lee A. Rothfarb. Cambridge: Cambridge University Press, 1991.

LIPPMAN, EDWARD A. "Theory and Practice in Schumann's Aesthetics." *Journal of the American Musicological Society* 17 (1964): 310–45.

FRANZ LISZT. *Briefe.* Edited by La Mara [Marie Lipsius]. Leipzig: Breitkopf & Härtel, 1893.

———. *Gesammelte Schriften.* 6 vols. Leipzig: Breitkopf & Härtel, 1880–83.

———. "Robert Schumann's Klavierkompositionen: Opus 5, 11, 14." in *Gesammelte Schriften,* vol. 2, edited by L. Ramann, 99–107. Leipzig: Breitkopf & Härtel, 1881.

LORENZ, ALFRED. *Das Geheimnis der Form bei Richard Wagner.* 4 vols. Berlin: Hesse, 1924–33.

LUKÁCS, GEORG. *The Theory of the Novel.* Translated by Anna Bostock. Cambridge: MIT Press, 1971. (Orig. publ. *Die Theorie des Romans.* Berlin, 1920.)

MAHLING, CHRISTOPH-HELLMUT. "Nähe und Distanz: Bemerkungen zum Verhältnis von Robert Schumann zu Frédéric Chopin und Franz Liszt." In *Gattungen der Musik und ihre Klassiker,* edited by Hermann Danuser, 517–25. Laaber: Laaber-Verlag, 1988.

MANN, THOMAS. *Pro and Contra Wagner.* Translated by Allan Blunden. Chicago: University of Chicago Press, 1985. (Orig. publ. *Wagner und unsere Zeit.* Frankfurt, 1963.)

MARSTON, NICHOLAS. "Schumann's Monument to Beethoven." *19th-Century Music* 14, no. 3 (1991): 247–64.

MARX, ADOLPH BERNHARD. *Die Kunst des Gesanges.* Berlin: Schlesinger, 1826.

MCCRELESS, PATRICK. "Motive and Magic: A Referential Dyad in *Parsifal.*" *Music Analysis* 11, no. 1 (1990): 227-65.

———. *Wagner's Siegfried: Its Drama, History, and Music.* Ann Arbor: UMI Research Press, 1982.

MCFARLAND, THOMAS. *Romanticism and the Forms of Ruin: Wordsworth, Coleridge, and Modalities of Fragmentation.* Princeton: Princeton University Press, 1981.

MCGANN, JEROME. *The Romantic Ideology: A Critical Investigation.* Chicago: University of Chicago Press, 1983.

MENNEMEIER, FRANZ NORBERT. "Fragment und Ironie beim jungen Friedrich Schlegel: Versuch der Konstruktion einer nicht geschriebenen Theorie." In *Romantikforschung seit 1945,* edited by Klaus Peter, 229–50. Verlagsgruppe Athenäum-Hain-Scriptor-Hanstein, 1980.

———. *Friedrich Schlegels Poesiebegriff: Dargestellt anhand der literaturkritischen Schriften: Die romantische Konzeption einer objectiven Poesie.* Munich: Fink, 1971.

MEYER, LEONARD B. *Style and Music: Theory, History, and Ideology.* Philadelphia: University of Pennsylvania Press, 1989.

MITCHELL, DONALD. *Gustav Mahler: The Wunderhorn Years.* London: Faber & Faber, 1975.

MONTGOMERY, DAVID. "The Myth of Organicism: From Bad Science to Great Art." *Musical Quarterly* 76 (1992): pp. 17–66.

MUSGRAVE, MICHAEL. *The Music of Brahms.* London: Routledge & Kegan Paul, 1985.

———, ed. *Brahms 2: Biographical, Documentary and Analytical Studies.* Cambridge: Cambridge University Press, 1987.

NATTIEZ, JEAN-JACQUES. *Music and Discourse: Toward a Semiology of Music.* Translated by Carolyn Abbate. Princeton: Princeton University Press, 1990.

NEHAMAS, ALEXANDER. *Nietzsche: Life as Literature.* Cambridge, Mass.: Harvard University Press, 1985.

NEWCOMB, ANTHONY. "The Birth of Music out of the Spirit of Drama." *19th-Century Music* 5 (1981): 38–66.

———. "Once More between Absolute and Program Music: Schumann's Second Symphony." *19th-Century Music* 7 (1984): 233–50.

———. "Schumann and Late Eighteenth-Century Narrative Strategies." *19th-Century Music* 11, no. 2 (1987): 164–74.

———. "Schumann and the Marketplace: From Butterflies to *Hausmusik.*" In *Nineteenth-Century Piano Music,* edited by R. Larry Todd, 258–315. New York: Schirmer Books 1990.

NIETZSCHE, FRIEDRICH. *The Birth of Tragedy* and *The Case of Wagner.* Translated by Walter Kaufman. New York: Vintage Books, 1967.

———. *On the Genealogy of Morals* and *Ecce Homo.* Translated by Walter Kaufmann. New York: Vintage Books, 1969.

NOVALIS [FRIEDRICH VON HARDENBERG]. *Schriften.* Edited by Paul Kluckhohn and Richard Samuel. 4 vols. Stuttgart: Kohlhammer, 1960–75.

OESTERLE, GÜNTER. "'Vorbegriffe zu einer Theorie der Ornamente': Kontroverse Formprobleme zwischen Aufklärung, Klassizismus und Romantik am Beispiel der Arabeske." In *Ideal und Wirklichkeit der bildenden Kunst im späten 18. Jahrhundert,* edited by Herbert Beck, 119–39. Berlin: Mann, 1984.

OSTWALD, PETER. *Schumann: The Inner Voices of a Musical Genius.* Boston: Northeastern University Press, 1985.

PASCALL, ROBERT. "Genre and the Finale of Brahms's Fourth Symphony." *Music Analysis* 8 (1989): 233-45.

———. "Some Special Uses of Sonata Form in Brahms." *Soundings* 4 (1974): 58–63.

———, ed. *Brahms: Biographical, Documentary and Analytical Studies.* Cambridge: Cambridge University Press, 1983.

PLANTINGA, LEON. *Romantic Music: A History of Musical Style in Nineteenth-Century Europe.* New York: Norton, 1984.

———. *Schumann as Critic.* New Haven, Conn.: Yale University Press, 1967.

POLHEIM, KARL K. *Die Arabeske: Ansichten und Ideen aus Friedrich Schlegels Poetik.* Paderborn and Munich: Schöningh, 1966.

———. "Studien zu Friedrich Schlegels poetischen Begriffen." *Deutsche Vierteljahrsschrift für Literaturwissenschaft und Geistesgeschichte* 35 (1961): 363–98.

POOS, HEINRICH. "Die *Tristan*-Hieroglyphe: Ein allegoretischer Versuch." *Musik-Konzepte* 57/58 (1987), *Sonderband, Richard Wagner: Tristan und Isolde,* 46–103.

RAUCHHAUPT, URSULA VON, ed. *Schoenberg, Berg, Webern: The String Quartets.* Hamburg: Deutsche Grammophon Gesellschaft, 1971.

ROESNER, LINDA CORRELL. "The Autograph of Schumann's Piano Sonata in F Minor, Opus 14." *Musical Quarterly* 61 (1975): 98–130.

———. "Schumann's 'Parallel' Forms." *19th-Century Music* 14, no. 3 (1991): 265–78.

———. "Schumann's Revisions in the First Movement of the Piano Sonata in G Minor, Op. 22." *19th-Century Music* 1 (1977–78): 97–109.

———. "The Sources for Schumann's *Davidsbündlertänze*, Op. 6: Composition, Textual Problems, and the Role of the Composer as Editor." In *Mendelssohn and Schumann: Essays on Their Music and Its Context,* edited by Jon W. Finson and R. Larry Todd, 53–70. Durham: Duke University Press, 1984.

ROSEN, CHARLES. *The Classical Style: Haydn, Mozart, Beethoven.* New York: Norton, 1972.

———. *Sonata Forms.* New York: Norton, 1980.

ROTHFARB, LEE A. *Ernst Kurth as Theorist and Analyst.* Philadelphia: University of Pennsylvania Press, 1988.

SCHELLING, FRIEDRICH WILHELM JOSEPH. *The Philosophy of Art.* Edited and translated by Douglas W. Stott. Minneapolis: University of Minnesota Press, 1989. (Orig. publ. *Die Philosophie der Kunst* [1801–4], 1859.)

SCHER, STEVEN PAUL, ed. *Music and Text: Critical Inquiries.* Cambridge: Cambridge University Press, 1992.

SCHLEGEL, AUGUST WILHELM VON. *Sämtliche Werke.* Edited by E. von Böcking. 12 vols. Leipzig: Weidmann'sche Buchhandlung, 1846.

SCHLEGEL, FRIEDRICH. *Kritische Friedrich Schlegel Ausgabe.* Edited by Ernst Behler, Jean-Jacques Anstett, and Hans Eichner. 35 vols. Munich, Paderborn, Vienna: Schöningh, 1958–.

SCHMIDT, CHRISTIAN MARTIN. *Johannes Brahms und seine Zeit.* Laaber: Laaber-Verlag, 1983.

SCHNEIDER, FRANK. "'Im Legendenton': Fragwürdiges zu einem musikalischen Topos." In *Gattungen der Musik und ihre Klassiker,* edited by Hermann Danuser, 555–63. Laaber: Laaber Verlag, 1988.

SCHOENBERG, ARNOLD. *Style and Idea.* Edited by Leonard Stein. Berkeley and Los Angeles: University of California Press, 1984.

SCHOPENHAUER, ARTHUR. *Sämtliche Werke.* Edited by Wolfgang Frhr. von Löhenseyn. Stuttgart: Cotta, 1960–65.

SCHUH, WILLI. *Richard Strauss: Jugend und Frühe Meisterjahre: Lebenschronik 1864–1898.* Zurich: Atlantis, 1976.

SCHULTE-SASSE, JOCHEN. "The Concept of Literary Criticism in German Romanticism." In *A History of German Literary Criticism, 1730–1980,* edited by Peter Uwe Hohendahl, 99–178. Lincoln: University of Nebraska Press, 1988.

SCHUMANN, CLARA, ed. *Jugendbriefe von Robert Schumann.* 4th ed. Leipzig: Breitkopf & Härtel, 1910.

SCHUMANN, ROBERT. *Gesammelte Schriften über Musik und Musiker.* Edited by Martin Kreisig. 2 vols. Leipzig: Breitkopf & Härtel, 1914.

———. *Tagebücher.* Vol. 1, 1827–1838. Edited by Georg Eismann. Leipzig: VEB Deutscher Verlag für Musik, 1971.

———. *Tagebücher.* Vol. 2, 1836–1854. Edited by Gerd Nauhaus. Leipzig: VEB Deutscher Verlag für Musik, 1987.

SCHUMANN, ROBERT and CLARA SCHUMANN. *Briefe: Kritische Gesamtausgabe.* Edited by Eva Weissweiler. 3 vols. Frankfurt: Stroemfeld/Roter Stern, 1984–87.

SISMAN, ELAINE. "Brahms and the Variation Canon." *19th-Century Music* 14, no. 2 (1990): 132–53.

SMITH, GARY, ed. *Benjamin: Philosophy, Aesthetics, History.* Chicago: University of Chicago Press, 1989.

STEPHAN, RUDOLF. "Gibt es ein Geheimnis der Form bei Richard Wagner." In *Das Drama Richard Wagners als musikalischer Kunstwerk,* edited by Carl Dahlhaus, 9–16. Regensburg: Bosse, 1970.

STRAUSS, RICHARD. *Recollections and Reflections.* Edited by Willi Schuh and translated by L. J. Lawrence. London: Boosey & Hawkes, 1953.

SUBOTNIK, ROSE ROSENGARD. "Adorno's Diagnosis of Beethoven's Late Style: Early Symptom of a Fatal Condition." *Journal of the American Musicological Society* 29 (1976): 242–75.

———. *Developing Variations: Style and Ideology in Western Music.* Minneapolis: University of Minnesota Press, 1991.

Swift, Richard. "1–XII–99: Tonal Relations in Schoenberg's *Verklärte Nacht.*" *19th-Century Music* 1, no. 1 (1977): 3–14.

Szondi, Peter. *On Textual Understanding and Other Essays.* Translated by Harvey Mendelsohn. Minneapolis: University of Minnesota Press, 1986.

———. *Theory of the Modern Drama.* Translated by Michael Hays. Cambridge: Polity Press, 1987. (Orig. publ. *Theorie des modernen Dramas.* Frankfurt, 1965.)

Tibbe, Monika. *Lieder und Liedelemente in instrumentalen Symphoniesätzen Gustav Mahlers.* Munich: Katzbichler, 1971.

Tieck, Ludwig. *Phantasus.* 2d ed. Berlin: Reimer, 1844–45.

Todorov, Tzvetan. *Genres in Discourse.* Translated by Catherine Porter. Cambridge: Cambridge University Press, 1990. (Orig. publ. *Les genres du discours,* 1978.)

———. *Theories of the Symbol.* Translated by Catherine Porter. Ithaca, N.Y.: Cornell University Press, 1982. (Orig. publ. *Théories du symbole,* 1977.)

Tusa, Michael C. *"Euryanthe" and Carl Maria von Weber's dramaturgy of German Opera.* Oxford: Clarendon Press, 1991.

———. "Richard Wagner and Weber's *Euryanthe.*" *19th-Century Music* 9 (1986): 206–21.

Viertel, Matthias S. "Carl Maria von Weber: Der 'künftige Schreiber einer Ästhetik,'" In *Weber: Jenseits des Freischütz,* edited by Friedhelm Krummacher and Heinrich W. Schwab, 167–75. Kassel: Bärenreiter, 1989.

Voss, Egon. "Siegfrieds Musik." In *Das Musikalische Kunstwerk: Festschrift Carl Dahlhaus,* edited by Hermann Danuser et al., 259–68. Laaber: Laaber-Verlag, 1988.

Wackenroder, Wilhelm Heinrich. *Werke und Briefe.* Heidelberg: Schneider, 1967.

Wagner, Cosima. *Diaries.* Translated by Geoffrey Skelton. 2 vols. New York: Harcourt Brace Jovanovich, 1978.

Wagner, Richard. *Gesammelte Schriften.* 4th ed. 10 vols. Leipzig: Siegel, 1907.

———. *Prose Works.* Translated and edited by William Ashton Ellis. 8 vols. London: Routledge & Kegan Paul, 1892–99.

———. *Sämtliche Werke.* Vol. 30, *Dokumente zur Entstehung und ersten Aufführung des Bühenenweihfestspiels Parsifal.* Edited by Martin Geck and Egon Voss. Mainz: Schott, 1970.

———. *Selected Letters.* Translated and edited by Stewart Spencer and Barry Millington. London: Dent, 1987.

Waldura, Markus. *Monomotivik, Sequenz und Sonatenform im Werk Robert Schumanns.* Saarbrücken: Saarbrücker Druckerei & Verlag, 1990.

Walker, Alan. "Schumann, Liszt, and the C Major Fantasie, Op. 17: A Declining Relationship." *Music and Letters* 60 (1979): 156–65.

Weber, Carl Maria von. *Hinterlassene Schriften.* 3 vols. Dresden and Leipzig: Arnoldische Buchhandlung, 1827–28.

———. *Writings on Music.* Translated by Martin Cooper and edited John Warrack. Cambridge: Cambridge University Press, 1981.

Weinland, Helmuth. *Richard Wagner: Zwischen Beethoven und Schönberg.* Musik-Konzepte 59. Munich: Edition Text & Kritick, 1988.

Wellek, René. *A History of Modern Criticism, 1750–1950.* Volume 2, *The Romantic Age.* Cambridge: Cambridge University Press, 1981.

Wendt, Amadeus. "Ueber Weber's *Euryanthe*: Ein Nachtrag." *Berliner Allgemeine Musikalische Zeitung* 3 (1826): 11–12, 21–23, 26–29, 37–39, 43–45.

White, Hayden. *The Content of the Form: Narrative Discourse and Historical Representation.* Baltimore: Johns Hopkins University Press, 1987.

Index

269